INDIE MARKETING POWER

The Resource Guide for Maximizing Your Music Marketing

By Peter Spellman

Turning music business data into useful knowledge
ISBN # 0-9742684-3-7
Cover design by Mike Roberts

www.mbsolutions.com

Music Business Solutions

Training Resources for 21st Century Music Entrepreneurs

Peter Spellman, Director

www.mbsolutions.com

TABLE OF CONTENTS – *Quick View*

TABLE OF CONTENTS – *Full View*

Introduction

"Music is the timeless experience of constant change." - Jerry Garcia

This book is written as a companion volume to my 2004 book, *Indie Power: A Business-Building Guide for Record Labels, Music Production Houses, and Merchant Musicians*. That book is a handbook for the indie revolution. It supplies guidance on planning out a music-related business, and its primary audience is those starting record labels or music production houses in a rapidly changing entertainment market.

While this book also has that audience in mind, it is broader in scope and is designed to give any musician or music business owner crucial guidance on creating effective marketing programs for any music-related product and service today.

These are certainly interesting times we are living in. I've been saying for many years that every business is becoming a music business and, indeed, it's a computer company (Apple) and a coffee company (Starbucks) that are teaching the music industry how to sell music in the new economy. Simultaneously, the traditional music business itself is contracting as a vast web spins around it and it pays the price for its own excesses.

But though the core record industry may be in decline, there has been no decline in musical appetite or in music activities of all kinds. In fact, the demand for music in all its forms is multiplying with every iPod and cell phone sold, every new cable TV show that debuts, every corporate video conceived, and every new web site that's developed.

I could easily have written 1000 pages on the subject of music marketing because the area is so rich and broad in content. Instead I opted to make this more a practical handbook that can provide quick reads on the numerous topics covered, and essential guidance through the various phases of setting up a marketing strategy within different music markets.

"Marketing" is defined by the American Marketing Association as *"the performance of business activities directed toward, and incident to, the flow of goods and services from producer to consumer or user."* Ok; that's a start.

But let's get to the ***essence of marketing***. When you boil all the definitions down to their essence, you find that marketing is, quite simply, *communication.* All the possible expressions of marketing: advertising, publicity, email, promotion, phone calls, buttons, blimps, stickers, street teams, billboards, radio, brochures, networking, logos, displays, web sites, trade shows, packaging, sampling, public relations, performances, press kits, bios, photos - what do they all have in common?

Communication. ***The effectiveness of your marketing will be a direct result of how well, how effective, how targeted, and how prepared your communication is.***

A key assumption in this book is that humans are now standing at the edge of an unprecedented opportunity. Available tools and resources are now in our corner that are providing individuals with a reach and efficiency only large, deep-pocket companies traditionally enjoyed.

In a neat reversal of Marxist ideology, we now find ourselves living in a capitalist economy in which we as workers own the primary means of production. Those means of production - our ideas, our thoughts, and our very brains - are lodged in our heads and get into the elevator with us when we leave for home each night. This gives us a level of power we may not have recognized or accepted.

Indie Marketing Power is written to both inform and enable this for you - to help you effectively use the powerful tools at your disposal.

How This Book is Organized

Chapter 1 sets the table, providing a sweeping look at the days of music past. It's always helpful to look at a topic in its broader historical context so that you get a more detailed understanding of its dynamics and expressions, and how it compares to today's practices. The more you see the roots of things, the deeper your understanding of their offshoots.

After this, **chapter 2** addresses the most primary question: *What are you selling?* All the marketing in the world will be only surface dressing if it doesn't result in sales. And the first step here is clarifying exactly what your product or service is, and then staking out your market niche. *Niche* will be an important concept throughout this book because it is the segmentation of the marketplace into niches that affords indie music marketers such great opportunities today.

That leads to **chapter 3** where we explore how the music market is changing, and what trends you should be aware of as you form your own plans and strategies for moving your music out into the world. There have been more changes in the marketplace over the last ten years than in the previous fifty, and the more you grasp these "straws blowing in the wind" the better prepared you'll be to respond to the opportunities when they appear.

Once you have a clear idea of what you're marketing and also what the environmental conditions are you'll be marketing in, **Chapter 4** launches into all the marketing basics you should understand in order to market effectively and efficiently. We'll address everything from key terminology to sourcing the best market information, from the essentials of product development to creating strategy and budgets. We'll also look at the importance of design and branding in your overall marketing approach.

Since the Internet is the most powerful tool available for music entrepreneurs to market their products and services, **Chapter 5** will focus exclusively on this medium. You'll learn all the essentials for designing and promoting your own ecommerce web site, preparing your music for digital distribution, and finding online affiliates and partners to help you maximize your online presence. We'll also examine some advanced online marketing techniques to help you amplify your online sales.

Then we turn to the "markets" themselves.

Chapters 6-15 explore all the various music markets available to you and how to *work* each one. Every chapter begins with a section called "Context" which sets a framework and then moves into "Approach" – practical, success-proven strategies and guidelines for how to work each market most effectively:

Chapter 6 – Marketing Direct to **Fans & Customers**

Chapter 7 – Marketing thru **Live Performances**

Chapter 8 – Marketing to **Producers & Record Labels**

Chapter 9 – Marketing to **Distributors & Retailers**

Chapter 10 – Marketing to **Radio**

Chapter 11 – Marketing thru **B-2-B (Business-to-Business) Licensing**

Chapter 12 – Marketing to **Music Publishers**

Chapter 13 – Marketing to **Media through Publicity**

Chapter 14 – Marketing to **Foreign Music Markets**

Chapter 15 – Marketing thru **Sponsorships**

Chapter 16 walks you step-by-step through the creation of a marketing plan, helping you to knit together all the different strands of this book.

Information is crucial for effective marketing, so **Chapter 17** offers 33 pages of the best resources to help inform your music marketing programs and campaigns.

Three different **Glossaries** follow and an **Index** tops it off.

Throughout, you'll find worksheets, charts, questionnaires, and samples to help you work through and absorb all the material.

You're going to learn a lot of tools & techniques to apply to your own marketing program in these pages, but don't ever forget the primacy of tapping your own creativity: all the market research in the world should never replace hunch and intuition. Afterall, we're dealing with music (the extensions of spirit), not lawn chairs and toasters.

Dig in, enjoy and grow!

Thanks & Kudos!!!

Thanks first to those who have helped me see the light: The Almighty, Linda Sullivan, John Donne, Thomas Carlyle, George Herbert, C.S. Lewis, Herbert Marcuse, Thomas Howard, Rudolph Steiner, Alvin Toffler, J.R.R. Tolkien, and Lyall Watson.

For their contributions to independent music (and to this book) the author wishes to thank Bob Baker, John Braheny, Dave Cool, Wendy Day, Eric de Fontenay, Suzanne Glass, Jeri Goldstein, Bruce Haring, Dave Herlihy, Keith Holzman, George Howard, Dan Kimpel, Maggie Lange, Steve Lurie, Kevin McCluskey, Daylle Deanna Schwartz, Jodi Krangle, Moses Avalon, Gerd Leonard, Mark Northam, Panos Panay, Diane Sward Rapaport, Derek Sivers, Tim Sweeney, and Jenny Toomey.

For inspiration: thanks to Gilli Moon, Scooter Scudieri, Amanda Hunt-Taylor, Aimee Mann, Steve Kercher, Brooke Fox, Matt Jenson, Robin Avery, Grey Larsen, Kate Michaels, Joe Giardella, Lauren Passarelli and all other indie musicians who are working the trade. Thanks also to Berklee College of Music for continuing to provide a lab in which contemporary music can thrive.

For their support at different stages of the project, I wish to thank: Robert Bloodworth, Chris Farrell, Meg McArdle, Jay Andreozzi, Logan Albright, Dan Bennett, Natalia Bernal, Scott Canney, Jeff Dickson, Phil Ruokis, Joy Daniels, Moana Dherlin, Brendan Garland, Gabe Berthe-Suarez, Lisa Testa, and Natalie Weaver.

When all is said and done...

"Music is just a means of creating a magical state." – Robert Fripp

May the magic **grow**.

CH 1
CONTEXT: THE MANY WAYS MUSIC GETS FROM ARTISTS TO OUR EARS

"... I don't know anything about music. In my line you don't have to."
- Elvis Presley

Been There, Done That:
How the Record Industry Developed & Thrived (for a time)

Imagine it's Boston, around 1890, and you want to hear some music. What are your options?

Well, you have three. You either:

- ...play the family piano (*if* your family could afford one);
- ...pay to see a concert performance (*if* one is available in your area);
- ...hear 'folk' musicians play in pubs and on the street;

These were the only music enjoyment options for all of recorded history up to 1890. This was the sum total of music *activity.* Of course, in some places (though not in 1890's Boston), you also had the option of jamming down with the community on drums and gourds.

Sometime around 1770, however, western Europeans began *paying* for live music performances and a nascent music *industry* was born. It began among musicians themselves, who pioneered a kind of "do-it-yourself" approach familiar to many artists today.

Beethoven is a good example of an early DIY musician: He traveled across Germany, contacted and contracted with agents, who rented halls, sold concert tickets, and advertised his arrival. He marketed himself as a composer, conductor and performer, and did quite well until Austria's economic depression in the mid-1820s. There was little in the way of *industry* to support musicians at the time, so the DIY approach was essential.

And, of course, there was always "folk" music from the streets as opposed to patron-supported "courtly music" commissioned by the wealthy. This music grew from the oral traditions of collective memory. Songs like "Ring Around the Rosie," for example, are believed to extend back to the Black Plague era one thousand years ago.

But there were no recordings; no record *stores*; no cassette or CD players; no downloads or iPods; few accessible concerts; no radios, TV shows or films; no music charts, blogs or 'zines; no music publishers; certainly no record companies or other music services; and only rarely, *very* expensive, handwritten sheet music or folios.

What there was still, however, was that ancient, pristine relationship between musician and audience. Musicians played *directly* to their audience without mediator. This was the music *trade.* What you produced went from your mind and hands directly to the ears of listeners. Eventually, as the modern world evolved and populations increased, greater organizational structures became necessary to manage the needs and wants of modern society.

More and more entities rose to *mediate* (that is, 'judge' and 'distribute') things to us. In music this meant the rise of the great music publishing empires, powerful impresarios (concert presenters), and soon enough, recording companies, promoters, personal managers, booking and other kinds of agents. These became the "gatekeepers", the ones who determined which music eventually got to our ears. And so it was for almost a hundred years.

Ironically, what we're seeing today is a return to the artist-to-audience relationship, but this time as the result of globaly linked computers. In a strange sort of way, the computer sets the music industry back 300 years to the time when a musician could go direct to his audience and that audience, in turn, could directly support the artist.

A networked computer gives music workers a reach and speed only very rich companies enjoyed until recently. Digital tools not only take the power of *production* from the industry monopoly, they are now also taking the power of *distribution* from it as well.

This essentially is the indie marketing power the title of this book speaks of. There is a power in the corner of musicians today that is truly unprecedented.

In addition to musician empowerment, we're also seeing an immense wave of consumer empowerment. Technology and consumer preferences are facilitating a restructuring of the music industry that is leading to an unprecedented shift of power.

But let's not get ahead of ourselves. How did we get here?

The Way it Became: The Music Industry's Baby Steps

One of the most obvious things about the history of the music industry is how technology has driven its development from the very beginning.

The following chart illustrates how these technological developments effected how music was made and consumed:

TECHNOLOGY DRIVING MUSIC

YEAR	CONFIGURATION
1878	Thomas Edison invents the phonograph, Emile Berliner develops audio platter (shellac disc) to replace Edison's wax cylinder.
1915	78-RPM records introduced.
1928	33-1/2 RPM records introduced.
1947	Magnetic tape recorders enter the US market.
1948	45-RPM records enter the US market.
1958	Stereo records are produced.
1965	Audio cassette tape introduced.
1966	In-dash eight track tape players appear in automobiles after use in Lear-jet business planes.
1969	Klass Company conceives idea for compact disc.
1983	CDs are introduced to the US market.
1991	Sony announces creation of MiniDisc players and discs.
1993	MP3 audio file format is developed.

Consider how it must have felt to be standing on the verge of a technological explosion. By the end of the 19th century huge industrial enterprises were being created on the basis of new inventions. The Singer sewing machine, the Kodak camera, the telephone, wireless telegraph, the electric light and moving pictures wowed the public and encouraged industrialists to invest their funds in inventions whose future was still uncertain. Just like in the mid-90s when the 'New Digital Economy' magnetized investment capital everywhere.

Thomas Edison's wax cylinder phonograph brought recorded music to the masses for the very first time. It was initially marketed exclusively as a "business machine" and its primary use was dictation. Then someone thought of recording *music* on the wax cylinder and placing phonographs in coin-operated machines. Surprisingly, these early jukeboxes, installed in amusement parlors, produced more profit than the equipment hired to offices. Sound quality was crude (to say the *most*) but the public was responding positively to this new way of enjoying music.

From 1889 onwards, both Edison and the Columbia Phonograph Co. began regularly producing recorded music cylinders and the recording industry was born. Each phonograph cost about $40 at the time ($1500 in today's dollars). But they soon became available everywhere, and by 1899 over 150,000 of them had been manufactured and sold.

It's an interesting fact that all the earliest recordings were *unique* performances. If you wanted 1000 recordings of, say, "Alexander's Ragtime Band", it had to be performed 1000 times by the musicians. *Duplication* of recordings didn't begin until around 1915. So every early recording was truly unique.

Emile Berliner's competing *Gramophone* took the playing of music recordings in a different direction. The basic principle of the gramophone was the same as Edison's phonograph: recording sound mechanically by means of a needle. Berliner's invention, however, differed fundamentally in two respects. First, the sound vibrations were recorded not on a cylinder but on a flat disc, in the grooves of which the needle vibrated laterally (not vertically as on the phonograph). And secondly, Berliner's *intention* from the start was to reproduce records *industrially*, and not be limited to single copies ("one-offs"), as was the case with Edison's phonograph.

Coming up with the right material for the gramophone recordings was the biggest challenge. After dozens of attempts, Berliner finally tried a material used in making telephone parts – *shellac.* When an associate designed a reliable motor operated by a spring (it had formerly been operated by turning a handle and winding it up), Berliner's gramophone became a viable product. The first flat-disc shellac records were made and released in 1889 and that format, improved with vinyl, dominated well into the 1980s.

SOME HIDDEN HISTORY

Other strange, short-lived 'record player' attempts: Many others tried their hand at sound reproduction. For example, the "Auxetophone" used compressed air to amplify sound; the "Flamephone" used a column of air heated by a gas flame to enhance sound (the record player had to be connected to the gas mains when in use); and the German Stollwerk factory manufactured miniature record players intended for children's rooms. They played records pressed out of chocolate!

One of the biggest breakthroughs in recording sound came with *electric recording*. The first known instance of making recordings using microphones was in England in 1919. This was a very significant invention because it allowed the singer/soloist to come forward in the recording session, allowing both more volume and greater nuance to the human voice. It's not a stretch to say that the basic form of the modern pop song was born with this invention.

Early "Record Companies"

The first "record companies" grew out of toy, furniture and utility companies. The earliest ones included RCA, Columbia and Brunswick, all backed by deep corporate dollars. Among the medium-sized American labels there were Gennett, Paramount, Banner, Cameo, Perfect and Grey Gull. Many "micro-lables" were also coming on the scene as demand for recorded music mounted across the world.

Though the early recording companies grew rapidly, the majority of music-related profits were still in the *music publishing* arena, particularly in sheet music sales. In fact, recordings didn't overtake publishing profits until well into the 1940s.

But for record companies worldwide, recorded music sales increased throughout the 1920s, and 1929 was the best year since the invention of the gramophone. In that year about 150 million records were sold in the U.S. alone, and by all accounts it seemed that the sky was the limit. But the crash of '29 changed all that and, by 1933, sales had slumped to only 10 million units owing to the dire effects of the Great Depression.

In the 1920s and early 30s it was actually rare to hear records played on the radio. Radio stations mainly produced dramatic shows which were enjoyed in homes coast-to-coast. Big radio stations had their *own* musicians, and famous dance bands would play *live* every week on the air. Records, in fact, were regarded as a form of *poverty* by these stations.

When the "talking picture" (film with sound) was invented, radio gradually began to change. The audio-visual nature of movies now allowed dramatic performances a bigger and better format for public enjoyment. This stole into radio's purpose, resulting in the medium shifting to playing more music and less dramatic shows. In time, radio and recordings would alter the appreciation of music profoundly by increasing the quantity and diversity of peoples' musical education, and expanding market demand.

Though the Great Depression lasted into the early 40s, by the mid-30s conditions began to improve for the record business. One of the key contributors to this recovery was the rapid deployment of second-generation *jukeboxes*. Over half a million of these music-playing machines were installed in almost every bar and restaurant in the U.S., exposing people to new artists and creating a greater demand for records. New popular music forms like jazz and swing also helped feed the rapidly expanding music business.

This period is also significant because it saw the rise of *the record producer* as a key player in music recordings (perhaps ideally personified in John Hammond – best known for his discoveries of Bessie Smith, Billie Holiday, Bennie Goodman, and later, Aretha Franklin, Bob Dylan and Bruce Springsteen).

With Europe and Asia devastated after WWII, the United States was in a fortunate position economically. American corporations, increasingly multinational in nature, scampered to fill the marketing vacuums left by the slowly recovering British, French, Dutch, German and Japanese economies.

Armed Forces Radio, broadcast during the war, had spread the sounds of American pop music around the globe. By the end of the 1940s, more than half the records in the world were made and sold in the United States.

By the end of WWII, the major record companies had lost interest in blues/r&b (then called, "race records") and folk/country music ("hillbilly records"), and dropped or deemphasized these "fringe" businesses when a wartme shortage of shellac cut into production. The so-called *independent record labels* stepped in to fill this vacuum. Here's an interesting fact: Of the 50 best-selling R&B records between 1949-1953, only four were from major labels. The rest were put out by small concerns like Modern, Atlantic, Specialty, Imperial, Savoy, Vee-Jay, Peacock – and later, Sun, Stax, Chess and Motown. This heralded the rise of the indies, small companies driven by passionate devotion to 'niche musics'.

))) ILLUMINATING TRIVIA (((

Did you know?...
The total cost to Disney Studios for using Stravinsky's "Rite of Spring" in the film "Fantasia" was $2500, of which $500 went to Stravinsky, and $2000 went to his agent?

The Ascension & Dominance of Rock

Prior to the rise of Rock 'n' Roll, popular music was dominated by Tin Pan Alley and show tunes. Mitch Miller, Frank Sinatra, Doris Day and Bing Crosby were the industry rainmakers. Sheet music publishers still played a major role in making hits and focused their efforts on 'crooner pop'.

The major players of the day, like old-line music publisher representative, ASCAP, ignored small radio stations and indie labels and their music. At one point they even boycotted radio, refusing to let stations play its members' music (Gershwin, Cole Porter, Irving Berlin) and would not allow blues, R&B, Country & Western, and other representatives of newer musics to join the organization.

Radio stations responded by founding their own organization, BMI (Broadcast Music Inc.), and in the first half of 1941, two-thirds of all the hit records sold in the U.S. were BMI-represented compositions, without a single ASCAP tune in the Top 20. The times were a-changin' and the public let the industry know it. Tastes too were changing and a new generation of music appreciators was on the rise.

Between 1948 and 1950 two new inventions hit the scene signifying great things for the record industry. The first was magnetic tape recording (a technology pilfered from the Germans after WWII). The use of tape had two immense advantages: performances could be recorded in a more manageable fashion than cutting a groove on a disc and, very significantly, the recording could be *edited*. Tapes could be cut at certain locations and pasted together with adhesive tape, a technique called 'splicing'.

Tape could also have multiple tracks. Multiple track recording allows individual "tracks" of sound (such as drums, guitar, voice, etc.) on one tape. These tracks are later "mixed," adjusting the levels of individual tracks to make a master tape. Adding effects like delay, echo, flanging, and phasing was also found to be possible with taped recordings.

The second great invention was the vinyl LP (long-playing record). Vinyl was quieter than the shellac gramophone records, significantly improving the signal-to-noise ratio. Vinyl also had smaller grooves and revolved at 33 1/3 times a minute, much slower than the gramophone, allowing 25 minutes of playing time per side for the 12" LP record. The 7" record, or the 'single,' revolved at 45 RPM (revolutions per minute) and allowed 8 minutes of playing time. Larger-scale works were issued on the 12" LP , and the single at 45 rpms established itself as the format for popular hits.

With these new formats in place, the music industry was poised to experience its greatest growth ever. New major record companies began to emerge as well. Alongside Columbia, RCA and Decca, now rose three new giants: Capitol (1942, Los Angeles),

Mercury (1945, Chicago), and MGM (1946, Los Angeles).

Around 1953 certain radio stations in northern cities, whose listeners were mostly young and white, began playing R&B records regularly. More and more white audiences began turning up at concerts by black musicians. White artists began imitating these records (for example, Pat Boone borrowed Fats Domino's "Ain't That a Shame", and Bill Haley copied Joe Turner's "Shake, Rattle & Roll"). Radio DJ Alan Freed invented a term for the phenomenon – *Rock 'n' Roll* – and thus a musical wave was started whose influence would soon be felt around the globe.

ILLUMINATING TRIVIA

Early in his career, when asked about the origins of his rock 'n' roll music, Elvis stated, *"The colored folks been singing and playing it just like I'm doing now, man, for more years than I know. They played it like that in the shanties and in their juke joints and nobody paid it no mind until I goosed it up. I got it from them."*

The combination during the 1960s of high demand, massive profits and distribution challenges forced a much greater degree of organization and hierarchy onto the record industry that for the most part had been nothing more than a back-room affair for years. This is the time the industry went from being a *music-driven* industry to a *business-driven* industry. Industry bureuaracracy grew rapidly and lawyers and accountants ascended to key positions of leadership, becoming moguls of taste and determiners of "hits". What *artist* development there had been was now being replaced by *Product* Development departments at labels, as bottom-line profits and pressures began dominating label staff meetings.

Marketing Artists Through the Corporate Machine

When trying to grasp how music gets to our ears, it's helpful to understand that music industry staff who are involved in acquiring, developing and marketing artists are not simply working for record companies. As Tony Powell, then-managing director of MCA Records remarked in 1992: "Record companies don't see themselves as record companies anymore. They see themselves as *entertainment* companies." Since the late 80s these companies have been explicitly defining themselves as "global entertainment organizations".

Record companies are primarily concerned with developing global personalities exploitable across multiple media: through recordings, videos, films, television, magazines, books and via advertising, product endorsement and sponsorship over a range of consumer merchandise. The quest is for entertainment icons whose sound and image can be inserted into the media and communication networks which are enveloping the globe.

A look at the inner dynamics of record companies reveals some all-to-common human frailties often resulting in artists feeling constrained in their contracts (and their careers).

In the past, executive staff have often signed artists without reference to the opinions of other personnel within their company. However, as the costs of producing and marketing popular music have increased, and as record companies have been reorienting themselves towards entertainment rather than just music, other divisions within the corporations began exerting a greater influence over the type of artists which are acquired.

In addition to working with artists, all divisions of the record company are attempting to represent themselves as an indispensable component of the recording industry to each other. The day-to-day work of dealing predominantly with one specific medium, whether the music, the image in the video, the radio media, or the press, tends to result in different staff assessing the potential of artists in different ways and developing their own agendas and goals rather than working towards a shared overall vision.

Tensions and turf battles (especially between A&R and Marketing) have, thus, become a "normal" part of the record company work climate. A major label president once confided to me that when he assumed his post he was astonished to discover how little company departments actually communicated with each other on projects necessitating joint-action. One of his first acts was to call all staff members out of their offices into the hallway for an ad-hoc pow-wow just to dramatize his concern. He didn't last long as president.

Such an incident highlights an ongoing problem for artists signed to major labels. With ten to twenty monthly releases, major labels and their respective departments cannot possibly get behind every single record. Each album may have a formal marketing plan but that plan can be cut short if another record scores a hit. Company resources are suddenly tipped in favor of the hit and other releases will often get left in the lurch. There simply are not enough staffers to work every record.

Further, inter-departmental rivalries and power plays commonly lead to high job turnover. An artist's lead champion (often the one who initiated the signing) leaves the company for another and the artist is stuck, no longer a priority yet tied to the record company for several more years. And it doesn't have to be someone *leaving* that changes the artist's destiny. It may also be the *arrival* of a new executive with a different agenda.

The following chart shows how music product moves through the music production system. It starts with the songwriter and recording artist, and works its way through a labyrinth of mediators until finally reaching the consumer's ears (adapted from *Inside the Music Industry* by Michael Fink):

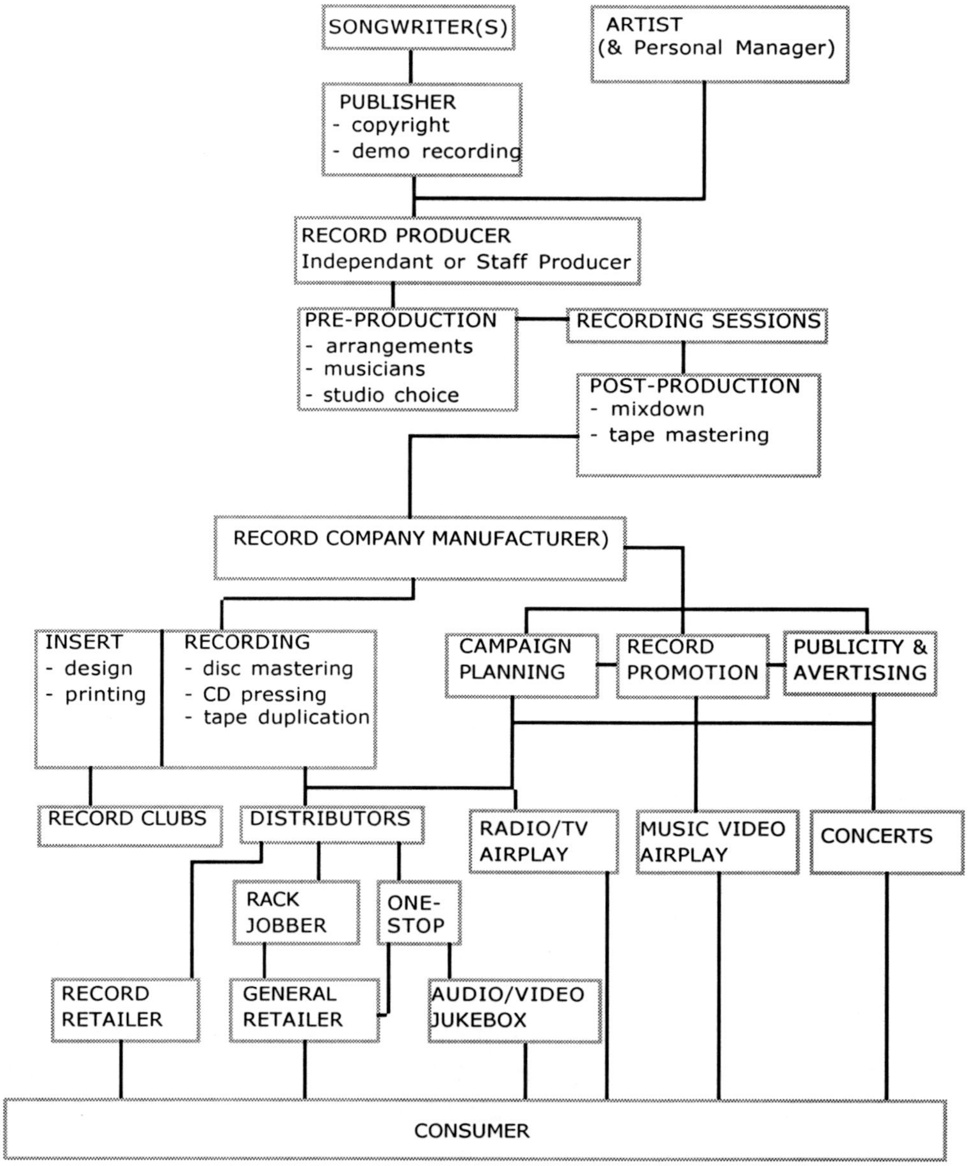

FLOW OF MUSIC PRODUCT

A lot of records are released in the hope and belief that they will succeed. However, there are occasions when staff know that a particular record is *not* going to make it, but are obliged to go through the motions anyway. This is done to maintain a relationship with an artist, lawyer or manager, and is variously referred to as a "political signing", "grace and favor deal", "courtesy signing", or "public relations exercise". If a manager represents a successful act, for example, then that manager can often use the incentive of future access to that act to persuade companies to sign other artists.

Alternatively, major artists themselves may be able to get deals for their friends, with senior record company staff issuing contracts merely to keep an artist happy and maintain a working relationship, rather than for any creative or commercial reasons. A marketing director at one of the labels confided that it was often easier to put out a record, rather than fight with a manger who was important to the company.

A lot of the above goes far in explaining why 9 out of 10 newly signed "major label" releases never recoup their production cost, nevermind turn a profit. This kind of mortality rate would sink almost any other industry but it's acceptable in music. Sort of gives a whole new meaning to the industry phrase "breaking an act", doesn't it?.

Though the big labels are putting out less music today and are also beginning to revive phrases like "long-term artist development," don't be duped. As divisions within major corporations, they are beholden to corporate imperatives that inevitably handcuff any altruism they may personally want to show to artists and their music.

Core Music Marketing Systems or, How the Majors Try to Do It

Four recording and distribution companies dominate the global music industry. Together, they manufacture and distribute over two hundred record labels, supplying music wholesalers and retailers with about 80% of the U.S. market. They are: Universal-Def Jam, Warner Bros., Sony-BMG Distribution, and EMD Distribution.

Major record labels are optimized for promoting and marketing *pop artists*. Their entire machine has been designed and developed to generate *hits*. They seek to appeal to the mass market by adhering to a formulaic sound that doesn't stray too far afield into the unusual or creative. Their very nature requires them to be risk-*averse*.

To repeat, record companies are concerned with developing global personalities exploitable across multiple media: through recordings, videos, films, television, magazines, books and via advertising, product endorsement and sponsorship over a range of consumer merchandise. The quest is for entertainment icons whose sound and image can be inserted into the media and communication networks which are enveloping the globe. In other words, to fit the "pop star" mold. This is their specialty and they do it pretty well when all the stars line up just right.

But the incessant quest to repeat and clone "hits" is ruining record companies. It's what I call the "all or nothing" investment strategy. "All or nothing" because unless the act comes screaming out of the starting blocks with a "hit" album, it will not survive past its first or second album. Running multinational record companies like MacDonalds franchises may be less stressful for the business affairs departments of these labels, however unlike hamburgers, homogenized music that looks and sounds the same is ultimately doomed to failure.

These companies ceased being "record companies" in the traditional sense of the word when they were bought out by multinational corporations. They lost their "ear-to-the-ground" instincts and instead became mere distribution companies. They also relinquished their artist development practices and, instead, looked to smaller companies to do the "research & development" (read, true A&R) necessary to bring artists to market.

HOW MUCH CAN AN INDIE SELL FOR?

Seller	Yr. founded	Buyer	Year	Amount
Asylum	1970	Warner	1972	$7m
Motown	1959	MCA	1988	$61m
Island	1973	Polygram	1989	$272m
Chrysalis (50%)	1972	EMI	1989	$75m
A&M	1962	Polygram	1989	$460m
Virgin	1973	EMI	1991	$872m
Windham Hill	1976	BMG	1991/96	$40m
SubPop(45%)	1986	Elektra	1994	$20m
Rykodisc	1983	Palm Pict.	1998	$125m

For over forty years now, the music industry has practiced a strategy of "growth through acquisition". The strategy now has been to let the indies do the artist development work, and then sign the artist to the major or buy the indie (along with the artist contracts) outright. Today, many artists and their managers, see record companies less as creative and business partners than as firms out to profit from them.

Fortunately, with or without the bureaucratic corporate empires, music will flourish simply because it doesn't need a mega structure. A number of trends are encouraging this, which we will examine in Chapter 3.

Paving New Roads to Stardom

The music biz stands at an historical crossroads - almost every aspect of the way people create, consume and listen to popular music is changing, dwarfing even the seismic shift in the 1890s when music lovers turned from sheet music and player pianos to wax cylinders and later, in 1915, newfangled 78 rpm phonograph records.

Radio used to be the primary channel for music promotion. Today, in lieu of constrictive radio play lists, touring, blogs, ringtones, podcasts, downloads, Internet and satellite radio, videogame tie-ins, alliances with brand marketers, film and TV exposure, sponsorships and placements in commercials are all growing in value.

The marketing strategies for a number of big-name artists this past year show that labels are reaching out to consumers through a variety of new channels:

• In a nod to the growing importance of Web communities, Geffen Records' Weezer has become the latest rock act to debut a new album on social networking site myspace.com. The band's "Make Believe," became available on the site as a free on-demand stream through release date. Since launching in 2003, myspace.com has gained more than 14 million users, and in February 2005 it was the No. 7 Internet site in page views, according to Media Metrix. More than 200,000 bands have their own pages on the site, including major-label acts like Queens of the Stone Age and Oasis. Though purchased by News Corp. in late '05, it continues to symbolize new, more direct, ways of exposing music today.

• Capitol Records debuted the Coldplay single "Speed of Sound" as a ringtone through Cingular Wireless.

• V2 Records rushed "Blue Orchid," the first single from the White Stripes' "Get Behind Me Satan," to iTunes just two weeks after the duo completed the album.

• Many artists, of course, have recognized the remarkable power digital tools and multimedia provide. Boston-based Freezepop not only recorded a demo but also animated a digital video, designed logo gear, and booked an international solo tour. For their effort, the computer-pop artists got the kind of exposure that usually requires a cigar-chomping manager and a record label's budget: The band opened for the Sneaker Pimps and got songs on PS2 games, including the hit Karaoke Revolution. Freezepop's 2004 release, *Fancy Ultra*Fresh*, was sold on iTunes and Napster even before the CD was picked up for distribution in brick-and-mortar stores. This goes to show, a big break can be more than luck today – it can be *engineered*.

• Another Myspace.com success story: The popular online hangout often features unknown bands, like the L.A.-based rock band the 88, on its front page, where 25 million members sign in. The 88's songs were streamed to users' computers nearly 70,000 times in June '05, and 17,000 people added the band to their list of friends. As word spread around the web site, hundreds of messages a day began pouring in from places as distant as Malaysia.

• Rockers R.E.M. became the first band from a major record label to stream a whole album on MySpace before its release. Several bands followed suit, including the hip-hop group Black Eyed Peas, whose members had been using MySpace to meet people and find parties while on tour.

Even as record labels struggle against file-sharing services that allow users to trade pirated music, their willingness to stream songs and sometimes whole albums on MySpace for free suggests that there's more than one way to satisfy the market's hunger for free tunes without destroying the industry.

• The Libertines have helped build a reputation as a band of the people by bypassing the traditional promotional route and using the Internet to break down the barriers between themselves and their fans. Trawlers of Internet message boards might find themselves at an impromptu gig at a band member's flat, and the group once sold 5,500 tickets for a secret gig after posting a single message on the Web.

The Internet has done a world of good for music. It's making the industry examine its own operations, it's driving creativity, it's building emotional connections with bands, and it's opening new areas of revenue. More on this in chapter 5.

As the industry passes through this maturation we can only hope it will adapt and change instead of continuing to respond with fear and subpoenas. We'll look at the current landscape in more detail in chapter 3, but at this juncture a more fundamental question needs to be answered: *what* are *you* selling?

Read on.

The Sia of India say, "My friend, without songs you cannot do anything." According to Hindu scripture, the inaccurate singing of a raga could be fatal to the singer. According to the Australian aboriginees, it it was a song that brought the world into existence and music that sustains it.

CH 2
WHAT ARE YOU SELLING?

"Most of you out there are better than us, but you're too fucking lazy!"
- Johnny Lydon (Rotten)

This chapter will give you a clearer sense of what constitutes a marketing program, help clarify and assess your current marketing efforts, and then focus the lens on what your own unique niche can be in the music marketplace.

Getting a Read on Your Current Marketing Program

Most readers have already been doing some marketing before they picked up this book. It helps every now and then to pause and put your current marketing and promotion program through an objective review. So let's perform an inventory on your current marketing practices. The following questions are designed to help you review and assess your current work and clarify your essential core mission as a provider of music products and services today.

Answer the questions as honestly as you can. Those you can answer will both help illuminate efforts that you want to continue *and* underscore those efforts that have *not* been very effective. Those you can't answer right now, put aside until a later time when you can. Some will overlap and some may not apply to your project at all. Don't worry if you don't understand some of the terms. You will shortly. You can consult the General Marketing Glossary after chapter 17 for additional help.

Get your highlighter out. OK, here we go:

1. What initially got me started in my business or career (what motivation, occurrence, etc.)?

2. When I first started, where did my clients or promotions progress come from (what process, method, or action did I use)?

3. Why did clients originally buy from me?

4. Why do clients buy from me now?

5. What primary method of generating clients was used to build my business/career?

6. Which of my marketing or sales efforts brought in the bulk of my sales or clients? What percentage of my business comes from this particular effort?

7. Do I test the various aspects of my marketing and selling activities to make sure they're producing the best and most profitable results?

8. How well connected or how involved am I with my clients at the sales/networking or transaction level (do I still sometimes take orders or sell or follow up)?

9. What ongoing sales/networking efforts do I personally perform today? How do these functions differ from those I performed when I started my business/career?

10. Where do my clients come from specifically (demographics)?

11. Would I rather attract more new clients or garner more money from my existing clients, and why?

12. Who else benefits from my success, excluding my clients, my employees, and my family members?

13. How many of my suppliers/business colleagues would be motivated to help me grow my business more because it will directly benefit them at a very high level? Who are they?

14. When I create a new client for my business or profession, whom else have I directly created a new client for?

15. Describe completely what my business/career does (*what* I sell, *how* I sell it, and *whom* I sell to by industry, commercial category, or specific niche).

16. What is my business philosophy as it relates to my clients?

17. How have my method of doing business, or the product or service line(s) I market, changed since the inception of my business?

18. What are my sales per employee or personal/departmental performance levels? Is that above, below, or equal to my industry average?

19. What is the lifetime value of my typical client (or my contribution to explore) (i.e., how much revenue will he or she generate for me over the entire period he or she does business with my company)?

20. What is the biggest client complaint about my company, and how does my company successfully address this problem?

21. What is my unique selling proposition or USP? (Why do my clients buy from me—what is it about my product and/or service that distinguishes me from my competition? Do I have more than one USP for different product/service lines or segments of my business?)

22. Is my USP a consistent theme in all of my marketing and sales efforts? If yes, how, and if no, why not?

23. Briefly describe my marketing program or marketing mix (all the different types of marketing I use and how they interrelate—i.e., sales letters, direct mail, direct sales, personal networking inside, outside my company, industry, marketplace, Yellow Pages, spot advertisements, etc.).

24. Who are my biggest competitors and what do they offer that I do not?

25. What steps do I take to offset their advantage? Are they working?

26. What is my competition's biggest failing, and how do I specifically fill that void?

27. What do my clients *really* want (be specific, don't just answer "a quality product or service")? How do I know?

28. Do clients buy from me exclusively or do they also patronize my competitors? What steps cab I take to get the main portion of their business (preempt and dominate)?

29. What's my market potential (universe) and my current share of that market?

30. What does it cost me to get a new client? (If I ran an advertisement that cost $1,000 and I obtained two new clients, my cost would be $500.) Translate this to whatever your acquisition cost is.

31. What is my biggest and best source of new business, and am I doing everything possible to secure this business?

32. What has been my biggest marketing success to date (defined as a specific promotion, advertising campaign, sales letter, etc.)?

33. What is my biggest marketing problem or challenge today? Describe in its entirety as candidly and directly as possible, including personal, financial, and transactional implications it may impose.

34. How many better ways could I reduce the risk of transaction, lower the barrier of entry, or reduce the hurdle for my client to make it easier for that person to do business with me?

35. After the initial sales, are there systematic, formal methods I use to communicate and resell to my clients—strengthening the relationship and bonding them to me?

36. Do I have an adequate supply of client testimonials, and is there a system in place for their capture? Are they written, on audiotape, or on videotape, and how are they used in my marketing? Also, can I measure, compare, or quantify the tangible impact I make on my clients?

37. Do I actively solicit referral business?

38. Have I ever tried to reactivate my former clients and unconverted prospects? Do I maintain systematic contact?

39. Have I ever tried selling a list of my unconverted prospects to my competitors, or turning enemies into allies?

40. Do I make consistent efforts to communicate with my clients about what my company is doing to help them?

41. In what ways do I try to up-sell my clients?

42. Do I need to make money on first-time buyers, or am I satisfied with only making it on the back end (recorders), short- or long-term strategy.

43. Do I ever barter my products, services, or assets with other companies in exchange for their products, services, or assets?

44. What kind of guarantee or warranty do I give my clients, to take away the risk of the transaction, and how does it compare with my competitors' or what the industry at large offers?

45. What is my client attrition rate?

46. How do I capture the names, addresses, and phone numbers of all my clients and prospects? Do I use them in my marketing programs?

47. What are my average order, transaction size, amount, and what are the steps I can take to increase them?

48. How much is the initial sale to a new client worth?

49. Do I use a list broker or data experts? If not, where do I get my prime prospect names?

50. Do I joint-venture my client names with other companies? If so, what are the results?

Is your head spinning? Don't get scared. I listed these questions at the front end so that you can get that "bird's eye view" of where we are going in this book.

Again, the questions you can currently answer should give you some helpful insight to what has been most and least effective in your marketing up to now. I hope it provides some clarity as you more clearly define your market niche and your marketing program.

You don't need to be a marketing guru in all of these matters. No one is. But you will inevitably have to wear several marketing hats, at least until your budget allows you to hire out some of the heavy lifting to experts.

At the very least, though, you WILL be involved in the following:

- ***setting marketing goals***
- ***discerning your target market***
- ***researching & conversing with your target market***
- ***building contact databases***
- ***deciding on an image***
- ***analyzing your competition***
- ***developing your product or service***
- ***choosing your branding language***
- ***figuring out your media mix***
- ***monitoring your budget,***

and...

- ***managing every detail of the whole process.***

Preparing to Become an Effective Marketer

Last year I decided to survey a few do-it-yourself marketers I know in order to get a sense of what skills and traits they feel are required to be effective in their work.

I divided them into "skills" and "personality traits." *Skills* are abilities you acquire through practice; while *traits* are the more innate qualities that identify you as *you*.

Here are the results of the survey:

❒ **Essential Marketing Skills:**

- *Creative thinking* = original, critical, and analytical thinking.

- *Search & Retrieval skills* = ability to locate and process information quickly.

- *Competence in relationships* = emotional stability, sociability, good personal relations, consideration, cheerfulness, cooperation, and tactfulness.

- *Communications skills* = verbal comprehension, and oral and written communication abilities.

- *Technical knowledge* = basic comprehension of the digital tools and process of producing goods or services, and the ability to locate and use information purposefully.

❐ **Personality Traits helpful to market effectively:**

- *Drive* = vigor, initiative, persistence and physical health.
- *Decisiveness* = ability to "think on one's feet" and come to a decision even under pressure.
- *Sociability* = enjoining presence, charisma.
- *Self-discipline* = effective and efficient management of one's time and energy.
- *Adaptability* = willingness to change and morph as required by circumstances.
- *Thick-skinned* = able to take criticsim and rejection, and hang tough.

Notice I wrote "needed" when lisiting skills and "helpful" when listing traits. Skills can be acquired through practice; traits often cannot.

It's important that you have the skills listed but you may not feel you have the personality necessary to "market" and "sell" things. That's OK. There are plenty of music markets out there that don't require you to do heavy selling, make presentations, or engage in "up-close-and-personal" marketing.

You should also consider this story about guitarist, Stevan Pasero. Pasero didn't feel like he was the kind of artist who could perform incessantly, push his recordings to radio and retail, and essentially do all the things he'd heard he would need to do to make a living as a musician.

Fortunately, an old college friend of his came to the rescue. This friend (who had majored in business marketing in college) offered an idea. He introduced Pasero to premiums and incentives (see chapter 11), a market segment he hadn't heard of before. He and his friend formed a record label, calling it Sugo Music (*Sugo* is an Italian word that refers to a family's sauce recipe). They decided to target large businesses with his recording of classical guitar pieces, called *Heartsongs.*

Calling their plan an "executive gift program", they began contacting large companies. Corporate executives were invited to purchase discounted CDs to give as gifts and incentives to employees and customers. One of Pasero's first clients was a rather new company at the time, Apple Computer, which was seeking a special musical gift for their executives and partners. Their initial order? Nine-thousand please! Since inking similar deals with other companies, the feisty Sugo label was eventually picked up by Allegro for national retail distribution in 1993, and continues to have a strong, "under-the-radar" presence in today's music marketplace.

So don't worry if you're not "salesman material." Neither was Stevan. The music marketplace is enormous. In fact, it is bigger and more varied today than at any other time in history, and there is a segment out there that's right for you and your music. Like Stevan, you may also want to find an appropriate marketing partner who can complement your own unique skills.

Defining Your Market Niche

"I often notice, when I'm talking with people involved in the arts, that their concept of what they want to do is to aim for the biggest, most obvious target, and hit it smack in the bull's eye. That's success, whatever the particular field is. Of course with everybody else aiming there as well, that makes it very hard to hit.... As Jon Hassell always says, I prefer to shoot the arrow, then paint the target around it. You make the niches in which you finally reside."

—Brian Eno

As mentioned earlier, I define marketing as, essentially, *communication*. But it's a particular kind of communication***. Marketing is communicating with your market so well that it wants to know more about you.*** Let's repeat that:

Marketing is communicating with your market so well that it wants to know more about you.

Every word you choose, the font that expresses it, the tone of your phone message, the colors on your liner notes, and the way you shake hands at a networking event are *communicating*, marketing, always, incessantly.

Types Of Markets: Where Does Your Project Fit?

A "market" is simply any group of actual or potential buyers of a product or service. There are three major types of markets. Which one will you be primarily targeting?:

1. *The Consumer Market.* Individuals and households who buy goods for their own use or benefit are part of the consumer market. An example would be selling a CD to a buyer at a performance.

2. *The Industrial /Business Market.* Represents individuals, groups or organizations that purchase your specific product or service for direct use in producing other products or for use in their day-to-day operations. This could be licensing a track to an advertising agency for the production of a TV commercial.

3. *The Reseller Market.* Represents middlemen or intermediaries, such as wholesalers and retailers who buy finished goods and resell them for the purpose of making a profit. An example would be selling a music video DVD to a distributor who then manufactures them and eventually ships them to music retail chains.

Some music companies engage all three markets; others focus on just one. You will need to determnine which of the three are appropriate for what you are selling and how you'd like to sell it. Part of figuring this out is coming to understand what your own particular market niche is.

The Challenge of Finding Your Market Niche

In study after study of successful individuals, one trait found to be common among them is this: they were all highly focused. At some point along the way, they had each realized that they had to make a committment to *one* business idea. And, in fact, many of them had to make difficult choices and let go of some possibilities that seemed appealing.

People don't focus for a number of reasons: Perhaps they fear that by focusing on one thing they risk not having enough business; or, maybe they don't want to miss an opportunity; or perhaps they just plain have multiple interests.

Whatever the reason, you need to become attuned to the fact that the times call for focus. Mass customization and a segmenting marketplace allow for the development of products and services of a "niche" nature. Since few of us have the time, money or energy to mount national marketing campaigns, it is in your best interest to discover and concentrate on a niche that you can develop towards successful enterprise.

What is a "niche"? *Niche* is an architectural term referring to a special place that's designed to display or show off an object of some kind, like an ornament, that's placed in a recess of a wall or an arched area of a room. And that's just what a niche can be for you. Finding your niche will set you off from others who offer something similar and draw the best possible attention to you and what you can offer.

Examples of niche marketing abound in the world of music:

• Chris Silvers, a Dallas trumpeter, used to take out every Latin music recording from the Dallas Public Library and play along with them, until he mastered the horn lines. As a result, he became a first-call musician and horn arranger for all latin bands passing through the Dallas-Fort Worth area and beyond.

• Austin native Joycie Mennihan was always drawn to music's power to heal. She took this interest and turned it into "Sound Health", a company providing workshops, seminars and books about music therapy and its health benefits.

• Lee Jason Kibler (aka DJ Logic) turned an interest in sampling and a love of multiple music styles, into a unique production sound so that his chops are some of the most in-demand from top recording artists.

• Boston's Rosie Cohen, took a love of singer songwriters, a passion for adult literacy, and tireless devotion, and turned it into Big Girl Records' first release, "Can You Read This Boston?," a compilation album of singer-songwriters, with a portion of the proceeds going to the Boston Adult Literacy Fund.

• Nashville's Eric Stone took a love of music and boating and in 1999 turned it into boatsongs.com, music CDs and performances with a nautical theme. So far he's played in four continents and sold over 250,000 CDs, and his audience continues to grow.

Exercise - The niche you decide to focus on will be a reflection of your interests, values, personality and skills, as well as the times your living in. Your goal should be to define what you do by depth, not by breadth.

To help you decide on the one niche you want to become known for in music, or to just bring clearer focus to the music niche you already identify with, weigh your options by asking yourself:

- Which things do I do best in music?
- Which activities do I enjoy most in music?
- What do I do that people need and appreciate most?
- In what areas do I have the greatest expertise and experience?
- What am I already best known for?
- What do I have the best contacts to do?
- What will people most readily pay me for?
- What involves the least risk?
- What fits best with my lifestyle and personal goals?
- What comes most naurally to me?
- What am I most eager to promote?

If you notice the same activity showing up as an answer over and over again, you're getting close to understanding what your niche is.

INDIE LABEL NICHES/MISSION STATEMENTS

AcousticDisc "dedicated to the preservation and integrity of acoustic music, musicians, and instruments."
Alula Records "a contemporary world music and Americana label featuring Celtic, Flamenco, Cuban, and other global sounds!"
Appleseed Recordings "sowing the seeds of social justice through music."
Arhoolie Records "The best in authentic Blues, Cajun, Tejano, Zydeco, Country, Jazz, Regional, & World Music"
Bloodshot Records "Think of our releases as finely crafted manifestos, each uniquely capable of moving our cause forward."
Borealis Recording Company "a Canadian record company dedicated to seeking out and presenting the very best in contemporary and traditional folk music."
Culburnie Records "quality music steeped in the Celtic tradition"
Dead Reckoning "Artist-owned label of Americana & country roots music"
Flying Fish "Traditional folk, country, bluegrass, blues, and ethnic music."
Folk-Legacy Records "Traditional and contemporary folk music since 1961: Gordon Bok, Bill Staines, The Boarding Party, Archie Fisher, many more."
Foot Stompin' Celtic Music "For the bright young stars of Scottish Traditional Music"
Gourd Music "Part folk, part classical, all acoustic music."

(con't.)

HighTone Records "one of this country's leading independent labels specializing in American roots music, from country to rockabilly, western swing, blues, and gospel."
Indiegrrl Records "Began as a forum for information, networking, and conversation about independent music from a female perspective.
Jazart Records "an independent record label located in San Francisco for the discerning jazz listener and artists everywhere."
Maggies Music "From The Deep Well of Our Ancient Folk Traditions"
Putumayo World Music "Guaranteed to make you feel good!"
Razor & Tie "your source for cool new music, classic reissues and the best hit collections!"
Red House Records "where roots meet the here & now"
Rounder Records "The Mother-ship label of roots music and its contemporary offshoots."
Rykodisc Records US "a family of affiliated labels sharing a commitment to present the finest in contemporary and traditional music across a highly diverse landscape of style and genre."
Smithsonian Folkways "helps support the continuity and integrity of traditional artists and cultures."
Sugar Hill Records "contemporary music with traditional roots."
Tangible Music "Your folk, roots and Americana music alternative."
Tayberry Music "Celtic music recordings from Scotland, Ireland, Wales, Nova Scotia,
Triloka Records "World Music That Speaks To The Spirit"
Vanguard Records "the Independent Leader of Distinctive Recordings"
Windham Hill "devoted to offering innovative music, selected for its artistic quality"

Strategies for Finding Your Niche

"Fashion can be bought. Style one must possess."
- Edna Chase, American fashion journalist

Finding a niche means clearly identifying a group of people who need a particular product or service you're distinctly able to provide. Your niche needs to be small enough that you don't have much competition and can still reach most of your potential customers within the limits of your time and budget, yet large enough to include ample customers you can support yourself by serving.

Here is a samping of strategies for scoping out a niche that is right for you:

1) Select a growth area. When a market is growing, there is more room for everbody. Therefore, your chances of winning are highest when you pick a market that is on the upswing. This can apply to musical styles as well as to entire industries. For example, the technology explosion in media and entertainment is creating and will continue to create new jobs for musicians and all other digital content providers.

2) Don't automatically follow the crowd, and don't necessarily pick the obvious. It's always a good idea to select a market with as few competitors as possible. Do you want to be one of 400 bands trying out for the same gig? Me neither. Always look for opportunities that everyone else is overlooking.

3) Attempt to put a lock on a specific market niche. This is one of the most important competitive strategies. A market niche is a specialization witin a market. For example, a studio musician in the L.A area who primarily plays piano on country sessions has created a personal niche as did the previously-mentioned Chris Silvers of Dallas. Select a market niche that is large enough to pay you well, one that you believe you can dominate. Then take charge of it. Meet all the important people, develop an excellent reputation, and maintain the highest standards.

4) Be memorable. This is a stylistic version of items 2 and 3. If you want to go far in the music industry, you need to give others a reason to remember you. Whether you have a unique appearance, sound, stage presence, packaging or whatever, you must stand out from the crowd.

5) Excel at what you do. While technical skill and polish don't guarantee you success, there is *never* a penalty for being too good at what you do. And there are plenty of situations where the better player or the more confident performer wins.

Your ideal niche will lie at the crossroads where your interests and assets intersect with opportunities you have to meet real-life needs around you.

We will re-visit this statement a little later.

Once you commit to focusing all your available time, money and effort on one endeavor, you'll be in a position to become known for that activity; and as your reputation grows, word of mouth will start bringing business to you.

If you're already doing or considering a multiplicity of things, you need to decide what you want your focus to be, what one thing you want to become known for. Making such a choice may not be easy. You may feel torn between pursuing what you enjoy doing and what people seem to be most willing to pay you to do. You may have to let go of some of your pet projects in order to pursue only one of them.

Choosing a focus will open certain doors for you while closing others. But just as you'll never get to see the world if you can't decide which destination to head for first, so it is with committing to one focus for your business marketing. The doors that will open to you once you fully commit to one endeavor will present new opportunities you may have never imagined.

Here are three additional ways to help define your focus:

1. Just pick one. In some cases the best decision is simply to pick one of the things you've been considering or pursuing and let the others fall by the wayside. That's essentially what I did when I started Music Business Solutions.

In order to commit to this focus I had to give up a lucrative performing schedule and booking agency gig. For me, time and family became extremely important when my first child was born. I could have kept on gigging four times a week but it would have meant little time with my growing family. Too, I could have kept the booking agency but it would have meant having less time to develop my consulting and writing pursuits.

Tip - Your customers, friends, relatives and colleagues are constantly providing you with clues to where you truly shine. Following these clues can help you to focus on how you can use your unique assets. Listen to their compliments, what they spontaneously praise you for, what they say when they brag about you. Don't slough these comments off. Note them and recognize that these things are the very things you want to become known for, the very things that will draw business to you.

2. Create an Umbrella Concept. Sometimes it's not possible to earn a full-time living doing a particular business. There may not be enough demand for what you want to offer, or you may live in an area where there aren't enough people to support such a business full-time. In this case, you can avoid the problems of being unfocused by providing a variety of closely related services under a unifying umbrella concept.

Singer/songwriter Ellen Bernfield and her composer/conductor friend Anne Bryant began singing lullabies to soothe and calm their new English springer spaniel puppies. Then their creative juices started flowing, and they decided to produce an entire album of music for dogs and the people who love them. Working out of Anne's home where Ellen has a recording studio, they produced a CD and fully illustrated book called *Songs for Dogs.* In order to expand their business, however, they've needed to add other CDs to their line, so now the are creating CDs under the umbrella concept music for pet owners. Their next album is *Songs for Cats and the People Who Love Them.*

As you can see, the secret to creating a successful umbrella concept is providing a cluster of products or services that are clearly related in the minds of those who need the service.

3. Develop a Hybrid. Some people don't want to chose among the various things they're doing, so instead of doing multiple things, they combine the activities they love most into one hybrid business.

Marcy Hamm, for example, has three great loves: mathematics, music, and computers. But instead of trying to offer three different services like tutoring, composing, and computer programming, Hamm left her prestigious job as a software engineer to produce computer-generated music that reduces stress and speeds healing.

Matrixing: The Crossroads Where Niches Lie

There is a tool that is used in many businesses called "matrixing". It's a process developed by marketing analysts that provides a formula for finding your niche. It can be graphically illustrated as follows:

(NOTE: I suggest you make copies of this matrix and try different combinations until you find your own unique niche)

MATRIXING

Your ideal niche will lie at the crossroads where your INTERESTS and RESOURCES intersect with OPPORTUNITIES you have to meet REAL-LIFE NEEDS around you.

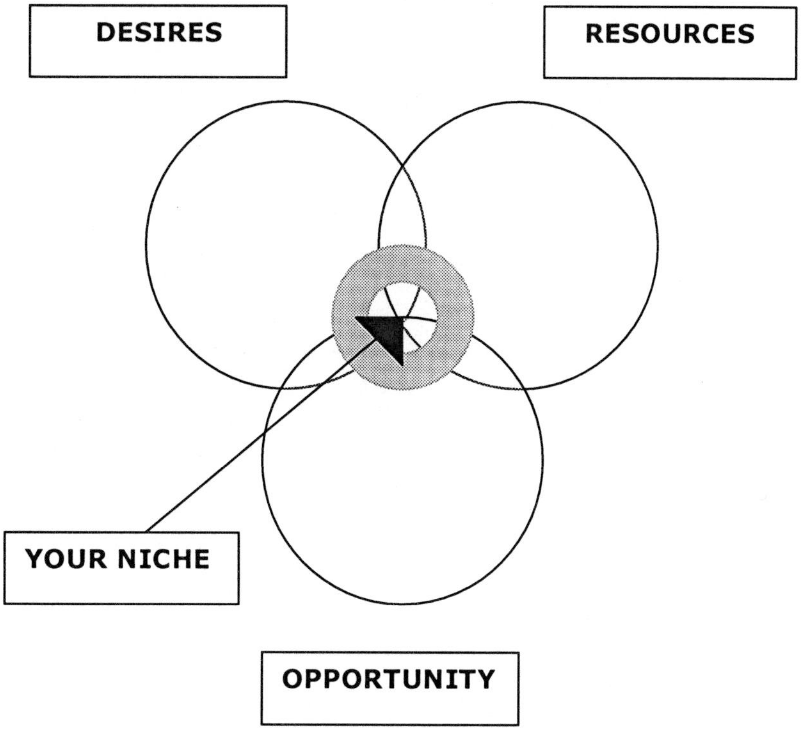

• *Compelling Desires:* the things in life you feel most passionate about, interested in, or concerned for.

• *Personal Resources:* your background, education, experiences, contacts, and other assets.

• *Opportunities:* problems, needs, and desires people are willing to pay you to address.

For me, it was a compelling combination of a love of music, a desire to help people realize their potential, and a love for research and writing that led me to my present work. My background included twenty years of music performing and recording experience, Sunday school teaching, a Masters degree in cultural history, management of a community center, and a co-authored book. The opportunity presented itself one night as I pondered all the information I had gathered over the years to help promote the bands I played with and the music I wrote. I knew there were many other musicians, like me, who needed practical guidance about how to create success for themselves in the unforgiving world of modern business. Thus, in 1991,Music Business Solutions was born.

The key is to find overlaps between your interests and passions, your background and experience, and the opportunities you see. Take one interest at a time and try different possibilities. You can do this by filling in the following statements:

"I could combine my interest in

____

with my experience, background, and/or contacts in

____

to meet the needs ___________(type of people, companies, industries)__________________________________ have for

____.

Exercise: Interview
Locate someone in music (preferably someone you know) who seems to have discovered a unique market niche and interview them. Try to discover how their niche expresses (or doesn't express) this dynamic formula of Compelling Desires + Resources + Opportunity. Here are some sample questions you may want to consider when formulating your interview Qs:

- What kind of business are you in and when did you start in it?
- What products and/or services do you sell?
- What opportunity did you see that motivated you to start this business?
- What kind of preparation did you receive for this kind of work?
- How would you describe the niche market(s) you cater to?
- What kinds of trends do you see unfolding in your business niche?
- If you could start over, what, if anything,would you do differently?

Tip: If you don't know anyone personally, then try contacting someone via the Internet. Go to Yahoo >> choose a musical topic that encompasses your niche and start surfing.

Conclusion

To identify a niche, you must find good answers to the following:

- What can you offer they (your nearest competition) do not?
- Why will people come to you rather than going to them?
- What will you be able to say about yourself and your product or service that sets you apart from them?

Obviously there needs to be a market for what you settle on. But assuming there is one, can you see how much easier it is to answer the questions above about the need for a narrower focus?

In a narrow niche, it is much easier to set yourself apart from your competitors. Much easier to let your web site, for example, speak for itself and demonstrate your expertise.

And it answers the question of why people should come to you, for you are now a specialist, soon to become an expert.

You will get more qualified customers coming to your business if you consciously develop a specific niche market. This doesn't mean you can't "do it all." ***The point is to lead with what you do best.*** Once you attract customers to your business because of your specialty, you can introduce them to the other products or services you offer.

In the matrixing exercise, it's relatively easy to list your compelling desires and your resources. The tough part is discerning the opportunities. The following chapter explores how the marketplace is changing and will hopefully suggest some special opportunities for your own unique music products and services.

CH 3
HOW THE MUSIC MARKETPLACE IS CHANGING

"For the first time in history the artist is realizing financial success in his lifetime."
– Joe Walsh, rock musician

"Within the next two years, videogames will become the new radio, the new MTV and the new record store all in one."
-Steve Schnur, Electronic Arts, Executive of Music Worldwide

It's time now to do an environmental scan. In this chapter we'll explore the current "lay of the land" in the marketplace. An important part of this includes exploring trends that are impacting the way people view and use entertainment products and services.

First, some noise from the trenches:

• There is now a music chart for "Game Music" in the UK;

• Music sales were *up* 9% in the U.S. in 2004;

• More people own mobile phones than CD players in Europe;

• The best-selling CD today is *blank*;

• Last year the Los Angeles Philharmonic performed the music from "Final Fantasy," a popular series of action-adventure video games;

• Crunk artist Lil' John teamed up with BlingTones in 2005 to create the world's first wireless record label;

• Computer makers and coffee companies are teaching the music industry how to sell music in the early 21st century.

All of the above are straws blowing in the wind, indicators of development, barometers registering the sea change in music industry dynamics.

Let's delve a little deeper into this "creative destruction".

When I talk about "trends" I don't mean the common definition of "trendy, faddish or fashionable". These are usually short-lived, "flavor-of-the-week" happenings that grip the market's attention for a time and then quickly fade into oblivion. Beanie Babies, Pokemon and 8-track tapes fall into this category.

What I'm referring to when I say "trends" are emerging meta-currents in our social and cultural lives that herald new ways of living and thinking. These unfoldings have been gradual and sometimes difficult to arrest and analyze.

Nevertheless, they are very real and they are changing the world, especially the world of the independent music provider. It wouldn't be extreme to say that for the past 50 years the world has been experiencing a comprehensive global restructuring of economic and social life.

The 50,000-Foot View: Meta Trends in Entertainment Marketing

Entertainment marketing left second-class status in its rear-view mirror decades ago, and as a result, created a heavily trafficked marketplace, constantly faced with the collision of time, money, and changing trends.

There are enormous trends unfolding in entertainment marketing. Consider these factors:

- Entertainment marketing is consumed with speed – there is little or no time to test-market before release, before one source or another gets word of the buzz on a project and broadcast is to the world at large.

- Every film and CD is a new product, and each one is different: different content, different audiences, different deal structures. These may be two or three – or a thousand - of these products released every week, yet every campaign must hit the target on the money, on time.

- With film, any misfire – any hint of bad box office- must be counteracted immediately, since the window of first-run distribution is only three to four weeks.

- Budgets for entertainment marketing can be huge - the average marketing budget for a film that costs between $50 and $100 million to produce is between $25 and $40 million - but the burn rate is extremely high, with much of the budget being spent during the six to eight-week period just before and during the film's theatrical release dates.

- The product of entertainment content is based totally on creativity; therefore, it is fraught with the possibilities of human frailties. Production and release dates can change with the sneeze of a star. Bringing a product to the market often combines a fine balance of crossed fingers and creative finagling.

- Entertainment marketing first focuses on selling an experience rather than an object. The audiences must first buy into the event, before the sale of objects associated with that encounter – a high desirable outcome, not to mention revenues streams – can occur.

- Entertainment is subject to the same whim and vagaries as fashion. Trends and styles change; with the pre-production planning and strategizing stretching out years before actual release, entertainment producers must strive to catch the wave before it crashes into the cliffs of consumer apathy.

- Award shows - not within the control of the marketer - can make or break entertainment products. Very few consumers may care what seal of approval a chair, a car, or a carton of eggs may carry, but the profitability – or failure- of a film, or an album, can rest on the opening of an envelope one evening each spring.

- The changing face of technology carries with it ever-expanding channels of distribution for entertainment products, many of which have their own particular following. Each of these channels must be addressed, and marketers must be constantly aware of the demographics involved in every new format.

- The marketing of entertainment focuses not only on the initial product itself- the movie, the CD, the program, the sports spectacle – but also on all the associated products spun off through licensing and merchandizing. Each product can launch billions of dollars in revenue, if carefully handled and strategized across all channels.

- The global desire for entertainment requires a universal understanding of the language needed to promote the product, both locally and internationally.

Keep in mind that every single one of these factors impacts every single entertainment product - above and beyond all of this is the single biggest challenge facing every release and every promotion: competition from all other forms of entertainment.

That's the 50,000 foot view. Now let's get a little closer to the music entertainment landscape and explore some of the "megatrends" within *it*.

SAD BUT TRUE. "Bob Marley probably wouldn't have been signed because of his strong dialect, Pink Floyd would have been too weird to take a risk on, the Beatles probably had too strong a regional accent - all of them could have been ignored by record companies in today's environment".

From a discussion titled, *"Label Mergers: Bigger 'n' Better 'n' Rougher 'n' Tougher?* At musictank.co.uk (great resource!)

MEGATREND #1:
Every Business is Becoming An Entertainment Business

Toyota has started a record label. So have Artois Brewery and Song Airline (how appropriate!). Apple Computer and Starbucks, two companies outside the orbit of the traditional music business, are spearheading successful initiatives in the music space that record companies themselves seem constitutionally incapable of carrying out.

Pharmaceutical giant Lilly has chosen music as the primary platform to convey marketing and educational messages to middle-aged men concerning its sexual dysfunction treatment Cialis. Now operational in six countries, the first-of-its-kind global music initiative "Music for 2" features live concert events, original music and health-themed websites, and custom CD giveaways.

The Hollywood organizational model is quickly being adopted by a number of the cutting-edge industries of the twenty-first century. Andy Grove, former chairman of Intel, compares the software industry to the theater, where directors, actors, musicians, writers, technicians, and financial backers are brought together for a brief moment of time to create a new production. Even though the number of successes are few and far between, says Grove, the process also creates smash hits.

In his book *Jamming: The Art and Discipline of Business Creativity,* John Kao of the Harvard Business School urges CEOs to integrate the Hollywood network model into their long-term strategic plans. "You need to act like today's version of a Hollywood studio," says Kao, and practice business like an "improvisational jazz band".

It's no mere coincidence that other industries try to model the way the entertainment industry is organized. The cultural industries - including the recording industry, the arts, television, and radio - commodify, package, and market *experiences* as opposed to physical products or services. Their stock and trade is selling short-term access to simulated worlds and altered states of consciousness. The fact is, they are an ideal organizational model for a global economy that is metamorphosing from commodifying goods and services to commodifying cultural experience itself.

MUSICAL COCOONS ON WHEELS. In the wake of its startup record label, Toyota continues to explore the music market landscape.

The Japanese automaker recently unveiled an automobile that it coyly calls a "car-shaped music player." The Toyota dB, a compact hatchback, is geared for customers who want to completely immerse themselves in sound. A subwoofer is located in the center console and eight additional speakers surround the interior of the car. The car, introduced in Japan on Tuesday, also includes 11 flashing lights located on the speakers, cup holders and door trim.

Source: News.com (12/05)

Companies way outside the orbit of the traditional music business are waking up to this all around the planet. Every business is becoming an entertainment business. As a result, you are no longer beholden to traditional "music industry companies" to achieve music success.

We'd mostly agree that the major record companies served their purpose well: They made recorded music available to us on a fairly vast scale for seventy-plus years, instilling an insatiable appetite for music in the process.

As a result music "sells". Music has accompanied just about every product that's come to market since the 1930s. In fact, today some of the most interesting music is heard more readily on TV commercials than on the radio. Wherever we go we hear music. Why? Because we love it and we want it. We want it when we drive, eat breakfast, shower, work, make love, shop for stuff – It's the aural landscape of our lives.

We hear music on recordings, on our computers, at concerts, on commercials and at the airport; we listen to music over the phone and in our video games, Walkmen, iPods, Rios and cell phones. The global demand for music is chronic and ever-expanding.

We're purchasing music just about everywhere too. 25 years ago you bought records at record stores; today you can get them at record stores, grocery stores, drug stores, book stores, consumer electronic stores, department stores, plant stores, tattoo parlors, bars, gyms, museum shops, thru the mail, over the Internet, at kiosks, at the airport, at MacDonald's, at Starbucks, at Victoria's Secret, thru 800#s, and hundreds of other places – MUSIC IS EVERYWHERE!

Why?

Because music is a universally loved value and activity, and companies across the board are looking to associate themselves with music and its fans.

The lesson: These trends require a new way of thinking about the "music business" and "industry careers." It's time to stretch our minds and get outside the box of traditional music business models. The "digital common" brings all kinds of non-music businesses into a space where creative partnerships can develop. Non-music partners are fresh and unjaded, and excited about associating with musical and entertainment arts as a way of adding value to what they're offering.

We should reflect on where musical products and services are *used* rather than on where they have traditionally been *sold*. For example, think of companies you personally resonate with and then focus on those that may have an affinity with the kind of music product you offer. Make an alliance and use that alliance to market your music. Consider Craig Dory and Brian Levine of Dorian Recordings who got their recordings played on all the new hardware at consumer electronics shows. Smart alliances.

Remember, the economic structures of the last century are being torn apart. The rules are being rewritten. Anything goes in the business world today. Therein lie many opportunities *for you*.

MEGATREND #2: Rise of the Customer-Creator

Consumers can now get more information about products and companies from Internet sources than previously available through traditional marketing communications. The most productive response to this is to bring customers into the value chain through collaboration and dialogue that make them part of a brand's story – and vice versa. Evidence of this should permeate marketing communications and be apparent at all customer contact points.

It's nothing short of reinvention of the business of market communications, a fundamental transformation from an intrusion-based marketing economy to an invitation-based model. This switch from the push model to the pull, from intrusion to invitation is a fundamental transformation for everyone involved in the business of content, whether the content is a 2-hour film, a half-hour sitcom, a radio program, recorded music, an Internet site, or a 30-scond advertising message. The end users rather than the creators and distributors of content are in control. And that changes all the rules.

Not only is the customer king: now he is market-research head, R&D chief and product development manager, too. More and more innovation is being driven by customer feedback. For example, the fan community has had a tremendous influence on game design and the games are better as a result. When Peter Jackson set out to film *The Lord of the Rings* trilogy, he tapped into the rich community of Tolkien enthusiasts around the world via Internet portal sites like theonering.net and listened to fans' concerns and expectations.

Researchers call such customers "lead users" and their importance to product and service development continues to grow.

Today may be the very best time to be a music fan, especially one looking for a connection to a favorite artist or guidance and access to the exotic or rare.

Be it the iPod, alluring satellite radio services such as XM, the fan-beloved minutiae posted on Web sites, the availability of live music performances on AOL, the esoteric music videos streaming off Launch.com or the self-tailored satisfaction of burning a homemade mix on CD at home, there is singular zest to the modern fan experience today.

The public is now driving the market. The challenge to the industry is to respond positively in such a way as to secure the future of music while satisfying customer demand and providing choice.

And so it has gone with the creative arts. From musicians to Hollywood studios, and from network executives to owners of newspapers, the creators and purveyors of arts are realizing that Americans increasingly are unwilling to sit down, shut up and consume their culture in the time-honored fashion of grateful passivity.

In other words, this is the age of arts consumer as an empowered co-generator. And it's revolutionary.

The 10 Demandments of Customer Service

Mooney's Ten Demandments for turning the most demanding customers into the most delighted customers are:

1. *Earn my trust* through respect, integrity, advocacy and quality.
2. *Inspire me* through immersive experiences, motivating messages and related philanthropy.
3. *Make it easy* with simplicity, speed and usefulness.
4. *Put me in charge* of making choices and give me control.
5. *Guide me* with expert advice, education and information.
6. *Give me 24/7 access*, from anywhere, at anytime.
7. *Get to know me* - listen, learn and study me, the real consumer, not just data.
8. *Exceed my expectations* with uncommon courtesies and surprising services.
9. *Reward me* with points programs, privileges of access or other worthwhile extras.
10. *Stay with me* with follow through and meaningful follow-up.

Adapted from, ***The Ten Demandments: Rules to Live By in the Age of the Demanding Customer*** by Kelley Mooney, with Laura Bergheim

Revolutions are nothing new in culture. In the 1950s, the rebellion was in the sound of rock 'n' roll, in its swagger and raunchy swivel, and in the 1960s the lyrics reflected and shaped youth culture, fashion and politics. The 1970s had punk and disco skirmishing with big-money rock, while the 1980s saw the rise of hip-hop, music that waged (and won) a street fight against the music industry status quo.

But by the end of the 1990s the new revolution, for the first time, wasn't in the music itself but in the *medium* - and for the first time the consumer called the tune. They are increasingly in the driver's seat of all economic transactions.

Music consumer reward systems are also emerging. Have you heard of Weedfiles (http://www.weedfiles.com)? They have a very unique approach – sort of a combination of P2P and property sales. And it's legal. The idea is that they *encourage* P2P file sharing, realizing that it is the most effective and cheapest form of advertising and distribution available, and the most credible. Nothing beats word of mouth. However, when you share a song with a friend, they can play it back only a limited number of times (three). Then they have to buy if they want to keep listening to it. This follows the assumption that you are basically auditioning the song, and you will know whether or not you like it after a few listens.

Entertainment Media Industry Overview

	Amount	Date	Source
Total Consumer Spending on Media*, U.S.	$199 bil.	2005	Veronis Suhler Stevenson
Radio			
FM Radio Stations (Including Educational FM Stations), U.S.	8,841	Sep-05	FCC
AM Radio Stations, U.S.	4,758	Sep-05	FCC
Number of Radio Stations Broadcasting Digitally, U.S.	600	2005	Plunkett Research Estimate
Print Media			
U.S. Magazine Revenues	$22.4 bil.	2005*	Publishers Information Bureau
Total Number of Daily and Sunday Newspapers, U.S.	2,250	2005	Plunkett Research Estimate
Total Book Publishing Net Sales, U.S.	$24 bil.	2005	Plunkett Research Estimate
Television			
U.S. Households With Televisions	109.6 mil.	2005	Nielsen Media Research
Number of Broadcast TV Stations, U.S.	1,749	Sep-05	FCC
Cable TV Subscribers, U.S.	69 mil.	2005	In-Stat
Worldwide Digital Cable Subscribers	44 mil.	2005	In-Stat
Worldwide Cable Modem Subscribers	50 mil.	2005	In-Stat
Number of Mobile Phone TV Subscribers	1 mil.	2005	Plunkett Research Estimate
Mobile Phone TV Revenues	$50 mil.	2005	Plunkett Research Estimate
Number of TiVo Subscribers, U.S.	4.3 mil.	2005	Plunkett Research Estimate
Total Digital Televisions (DTVs) Sold	10.8 mil.	2005	CEA
Music			
Album Sales, U.S.	600 mil.**	2005	Nielsen Media Research
Global Downloaded Music Sales incl. Internet & Cell Phone	$1.1 bil.	2005	IFPI
Satellite Radio Subscribers	8.2 mil.	2005	Plunkett Research Estimate
Number of iPods Sold	22.4 mil.	2005	Apple Computer, Inc.
Other			
Cell Phone Subscribers, U.S.	190 mil.	2005	Plunkett Research Estimate
Gambling Revenues, U.S.	$50 bil.	2005	Plunkett Research Estimate
Internet Users, Worldwide	1.1 bil.	2006	Int'l Telecon Union
Film			
U.S. Box Office Revenues	$8.95 bil.	2005	Exhibitor Relations/Adams Media
Number of Movie Tickets Sold, U.S.	1.43 bil.	2005	Plunkett Research Estimate
DVD Rentals and Sales at Retail, U.S.	$23.4 bil.	2005	Exhibitor Relations/Adams Media
Number of Movie Screens, U.S.	37,000	2005	Plunkett Research Estimate
Electronic Games			
Total Video Game Industry Revenues, Worldwide	$27.0 bil.	2005	Plunkett Research Estimate

IFPI = International Federation of the Phonographic Industry

**Estimate. Includes consumer spending on cable and satellite TV access and services; consumer books; consumer internet access and content; consumer magazine subscriptions entertainment (box office. Home video, interactive television, recorded*

music and video games); newspaper subscriptions; satellite radio subscriptions.

***Estimate. Includes downloaded music with 10 downloaded song tracks counted as one album. Source: Plunkett Research Ltd., Plunkett's Entertainment & Media Industry Almanac 2006*

Here's the interesting part of Weed: if you buy it, the money is divided up three ways: to the provider, to the artist, and to the person who recommended it. The model is so perfectly capitalist! It rewards people monetarily for turning their friends on to music. In a way, it is similar to the practice of getting a discount or a month off health club membership when you get a friend to join. Only this rewards you in cash. It works off the idea that networks of friends know each other's listening/buying habits and influence each other quite a bit when it comes to music. Brilliant!

It's becoming increasingly more difficult for companies to treat us like "mass market" ciphers. The trend is towards "mass customization" where consumers' unique needs are front and center. Some marketing gurus call this trend "The 1-to-1 Future".

The online environment also allows fans to try before they buy and enables them to experiment with new artists and genres. For example, a middle-aged Kinks fan might discover Blur and then listen to Damon Albarn's Mall Music to discover indigenous Malian artists such as Salif Keita.

Previewability is probably the most important revolution in recent music. Despite what the RIAA would have you believe, the shifts the industry has witnessed haven't been a matter of *quantity* so much as they've been a matter of *quality*. People are making their purchasing decisions less on the basis of hype and blind faith, and more on the basis of what they actually enjoy listening to.

The positive benefit of all this to consumers and the industry alike is that consumers' musical horizons are expanding and there will be more sales of more formats from a wider selection of 'retailers'. To flip Paul Simon's words, "the *music business* suffers, while the *music* thrives."

And the market is responding. This can be seen in the many new "customize your own CD" web sites and, on the darker side, in the blatant disregard for copyright laws in P2P music file sharing. The thought is: "We want it our way and if the major labels won't give us the music the way we want it, we will find a way to get it!"

How File-Sharing Informs the Industry

The classic case for how **BigChampagne** (bigchamgagne.com) supports a client – who can range from struggling new artists to the entire roster of a major – is by analyzing whether listeners have found a hit before radio. Let's say that in a given market, a single hasn't broken onto radio, but BigChampagne discovers that listeners in that city are swapping it in huge volume; the label can take that information to radio programmers and urge them to spin the song to death, turning it into an official hit.

MEGATREND #3: Music as Service

"Music can be made anywhere, is invisible...and does not smell."
- W.H. Auden

In 1973, sixty-five out of every hundred workers were already engaged in services. In the European community, 47.6 percent of workers were in the service sector in the early 1970s. Today, the service industries employ more than 77 percent of the U.S. economy and more than half of the value added in the global economy. Percy Barnevik, the former CEO of Asea Brown Boveri Ltd., predicts that by the year 2010, services will make up more than 90 percents of the U.S. economy, and manufacturing activities less than 10 percent.

In a service economy, it is human time that is being commodified, not places or things. Services always invoke a relationship between human beings as opposed to a relationship between a human being and a thing.

The old broadcast model is being replaced by total customer access to, and interaction with, the marketplace. Marketing becomes a network of relationships and responsibilities throughout the value and information chain. "Old" marketing, operating as it does on the venerable model of trying to sell through a vague notion of brand, promotion, entertainment and consumer manipulation, is unprepared for this change.

In marketing circles, using technologies to commodify long-term commercial relationships is called "controlling the customer." Continuous cybernetic feedback allows firms to anticipate and service customer' needs on an ongoing open-ended basis.

By turning goods into services and advising clients on upgrades, innovations, and new applications, suppliers become an all-pervasive and indispensable part of the experiential routines of customers. To borrow a Hollywood term, companies serve as "agents," performing a range of services. The goal is to become so embedded in the life of the customer as to become a ubiquitous presence, an appendage of the customer's very being, operating on his behalf in the commercial sphere.

Consumers have spoken, and they demand access to content by any means necessary. Digital distribution of music to consumers, via the Internet, allows recording companies to do away with suppliers, warehouses, inventories, distributors, and shippers, saving on the costs of handling a physical version of the recording. The electronic transmission of music products is still another example of the new weightless capitalism that is emerging in the cyberspace economy.

The future isn't about a change in distribution, it's about the *atrophy* of distribution itself. Instead of distributing things, we'll get *access*. It's a critical difference. The future isn't about downloading songs and burning CDs. It's about just-in-time customized delivery. *Music as service, not product.*

Presenting music as a service, like radio or TV, would seem on the surface to be less profitable than selling millions of CDs, but actually, this change will be positive for the music industry. It will be able to sell more things associated with music. But the actual sale of music as a product will make less sense. It will be a move from transaction-based *push* to flat-fee *pull*. Just as AOL has gone from selling you five minutes of access to a take-whatever-you-want model, music too will move to a flat-fee model.

The reason the future is so bright is that soon we'll all plug into around-the-clock streaming Internet audio, happily paying a few extra dollars a month to our Internet service provider (ISP) for the privilege.

We're not there just yet. But in the next few years, the requisite technology will fall into place. Then most of us will carry a wireless Internet uber-gadget wherever we go – a unified cellphone/personal digital assistant/Blackberry/camera/GPS locater/video recorder/co-pilot for life. This device will receive wireless Internet audio, a loose term I use to describe the various forms of streaming audio starting to appear on the Internet. With streaming audio, you can hear the music you love any time, anywhere.

"I don't know that it's wise to generalize from the few young people I've encountered, but what the hey. I definitely think they don't fetishize physical objects the way my generation does (hell, I still mourn the loss of 12" lp covers, cuz the art was so much better). I know young folks who download more than they could ever listen to, which seems like some weird kind of hoarding behavior to me.

But the thing you can always count on about young people is that they turn into old people. Eventually, they have more money than time, and that's when you can sell them music as a service rather than music as a product. The biggest effect I think they'll have isn't so much their demand that music be free, but their demand that you offer them access to EVERYTHING. And as a guy who grew up lamenting the fact that radio always played the same damn groups over and over again, I love them for that."

– Tim Quick, formerly of Too Music Joy (now of Wonderlick)

So how will musicians make a living in the new world? We'll simply expand existing compensation systems. The owners of restaurants, bars, health clubs and other music-playing public venues already pay fees to central clearing houses (the peforming rights organizations, or PROs) that forward the money to composers and performers based on how often their music is played. One simple option is to put a flat surcharge on Internet service providers of only $7 a month – about what the average household in Canada pays per month on CDs. This creates a pool of money that can be distributed fairly to composers (and their publishers), artists (and their agents or labels), ISPs and the music providers (perhaps like Kazaa or son of Kazaa) – *all based on actual use*.

Rather than shoe-horning an old revenue model into a new technological environment, as "digital rights management" (copy-prevention systems) or other digital audio security schemes attempt, open licensing takes advantage of the properties of digital technology, like ease of copying and distributing. Artists' fans become their top promoters, by passing on the music that they like to friends along with means to connect with the artists, such as Web or e-mail addresses. This kind of "viral marketing" or super-distribution of artists' music provides an unprecedented opportunity for independent artists around the world to pursue their passions. The challenge is now to the electronic pioneers to use these new tools to build new business models or new twists on the old ones that sustain and enhance artists' livelihood in a digital world.

We are already seeing a pronounced shift of record company income from primary sources (selling records) to secondary sources (collection of publishing and performing rights). The old music business of selling packages of music to relatively passive consumers will remain a large business for quite some time. The point is that a very different sort of music business is growing up along side it, one where music is becoming a *service* rather than a *product*. The digital downloading revolution is going to transform the music business into a service business. No longer will we see the music industry as the selling of goods, but rather, as the provision of a distribution service, not unlike TV. This is why it is important to ask, not so much, where music is *sold*, but where music is being *used*.

In general, labels are not looking to change the media. They're going from today's media to digital wireless delivery. Eventually, it will come down to the point where you don't need the hard medium. But the emphasis online today and for the next several years (to 2007-ish) is to drive consumer awareness and to drive album sales.

All the products out there are just derivative of the CD. The next revolution in prerecorded medium will be on a chip with no moving parts. The popularity of devices like Apple's IPod are indicative of this.

MEGATREND #4:
New Music Company Models

Organizations used to have stable industries, predictable customers, and five and ten year strategic plans. Today whole industries are being turned completely upside down within two years.

And now the musical industrial complex is losing control. They can sue file-traders all they want, but they will not be able to prevent individuals from making their own music and distributing it via new technologies.

The EMI/Robbie Williams' deal represented a major cultural shift on the part of a major record company. What made it different was that the deal recognized that everything to do with the artist counts. Traditionally, record companies would spend money developing an artist's income stream through sales of T-shirts, screen savers, ring tones and so-on, only to see none of the revenue. Now they do. The EMI deal includes a percentage cut of everything to do with the sales of Robbie Williams's related products, for the label. The Sanctuary Group in the UK follows a similar practice with its artists.

> ***"The majors will embrace any formula that sells records until it stops working. As a result, the corporate machine cannot deliver an adequate diversity of sounds, only a homogenized, prepackaged product."***
>
> – Michael Roberts, in *Rhythm & Business* (2005, Akashic Books)

Artists are increasingly looking outside of album sales for revenue and looking to exploit all rights as a brand.

Perhaps the term record company is becoming outdated- "Music Company" is more relevant, dealing as it does with a bundle of rights. But the knowledge to exploit these is of paramount importance.

"I think we'll mutate into a new type of company – a mixture of artist management, publisher, marketing consultant, agent and promoter." *Steve Becket – Warp Records.*

"We're a communications company and that's what we're becoming more everyday. I don't think the model foe a traditional record label will exist in this environment anymore." *Marc Jones – Wall of Sound.*

While mega-media has consolidated, *micro*-media has exploded. A "mainstream artist" seeking CHR (contemporary hit radio) fame *has* to align with the conglomerates who own record labels, magazines, TV networks, film studios, and toy companies because these media giants control what hits the mainstream. In that system the artist will be one of a few of several who may get a chance to shine before a hunger for quarterly profits, marketing mis-haps or personnel changes derail the project.

On the other hand, micro-media targets the tributaries off the mainstream and if the artist occupies one of these "niche streams", they have an open and ready channel for exposure to their target audience. Each niche stream has its own burgeoning media culture and the smart combination of high-quality music, good stories, creative event-making and strategic alliances gets the tastemakers interested.

Remember, every business is becoming a music business – actually an entertainment business. Entertainment is a much-coveted value businesses are seeking to add to their image all over the world.

This was highlighted in 2001 when Sting announced that Compaq Computers would now serve as his marketing arm for his release, *Brand New Day*. Sting was an A&M recording artist and A&M was one of those labels folded into Interscope during the Polygram-Universal merger. Well, Sting and his manager Miles Copeland began to see that they could not count on A&M to provide the marketing push they need for Sting's upcoming release. Soooo...Compaq was looking for a high-level artist to work with, Sting needed a new marketing partner, and voila!

We're also seeing new models emerging that are redefining the artist/label relationship. Equity Records out of Nashville, TN does just what its name suggests: rather than going on a royalty-bearing model, it opts for an equity-sharing model. Taking a que from EMI's multi-revenue deal it made with artist Robbie Williams in 2003, other labels and artist are creating similar agreements where labels get more access to income streams previously off-limits, and artists receive higher advances and larger marketing commitments from the company.

All of this, if properly executed, could lead to a more efficient method of marketing acts by putting power in a largely singular and unified marketing vision. The Sanctuary Group, Wind-Up Records, Vector/Combustion, and ATO/Redlight are some of the companies who have made considerable ventures into these new models of operation.

The traditional music industry is transforming. Companies are morphing into new hybrid service businesses. We need to think outside the box of the musical industrial complex and explore fresh possibilities.

What can your company look like and who can you partner with?

MEGATREND #5: Rapidly Segmenting Music Markets

> *"There are myriad ways to distribute music, so the key question is how to acquire customers?"* - Mark Cuban

I often hear musicians and industry critics alike moaning about how the monopolization of radio by companies like Clear Channel threatens musical diversity, yet I can hear and obtain more interesting music today than I could ever have obtained in the 1980s.

It's myopic and selfish to think that some music "deserves" to be heard and some doesn't, as the old music industry preached. The listening public is conditioned to being told what they like. But the wall has come down, and music fans are becoming overwhelmed with new choices. The old-school gatekeepers have been too slow to realize this.

The new plurality of music requires the listener to actively LISTEN for what they like instead of just HEARING what they are told to like. This means there is an increasing need for people willing to guide others through the expanded choices, without dictating choice.

To put it simply, the *patterns* that used to govern sales no longer work. The industry's biggest successes are now small ones.

Industry insiders are just as confused by the good news as they are by the bad. Here are the kinds of questions they've been asking themselves: Why doesn't Eminem break out on the order of the Beatles and sell 10 million copies of every release? Why can't Britney, Whitney, Madonna and Mariah make hits like they used to? Why can't the Strokes break through to the mainstream, stymied at 500,000 units shifted? Conversely, they wonder how a one-off Sub Pop release like the Postal Service's *Give Up* — a mash-up of the niche genres of bedroom electronica and emo-punk — has sold well over 250,000 copies. How could Matador sell a half-million copies of the debut by an unheralded New York band like Interpol? Why are bands like Modest Mouse, the Shins, the Yeah Yeah Yeahs and Wilco selling hundreds of thousands of records, where a few years ago they would have — optimistically — sold 50 thousand?

It's a strange landscape.

When the Grammys started in 1958 there were 28 categories of awards; in 2006 there were 105! Check out the "Music Styles" chart below and then look at the sub-genres of "Dance" on the following page.

Even the pop charts, which have made room in recent years for PJ Harvey, Modest

Mouse, Diana Krall and Franz Ferdinand, suggests there's an audience starving for something other than musical junk food.

The music market continues to segment and each segment is a "world", a portal, through which small companies can create value and success.

While good news for niche companies, this is bad news for the musical industrial complex. The major labels cannot justify going after these smaller markets because they are optimized instead for the larger, pop mainstream. These niche music cultures can't generate the sales needed to float the major label boat. While 20,000 unit sales are a cause to celebrate at a micro-label, they hardly register a blip on big company radar screens.

COMMON MUSIC STYLES

A Cappella	EarlyMusic	Pop
Alternative	Electronica	Punk
Ambient	Emo	Rap/Hip Hop
Asian	Experimental	Reggae
Bluegrass	Film	R & B
Blues	Folk	Rock
Celtic	Funk	Ska
Childrens'	Fusion	Soul
Classical (pre-20th c.)	Gospel	Women's
Classical (contemporary)	Heavy Metal	
Christian	Industrial World	
Country	Jazz (instrumental) Zydeco	
Crunk	Jazz (vocal)	
>> Dance <<	Latin	
DJs	Mashup/Mixup	
Dub	New Age	

The times call for focus. Mass customization and a segmenting market encourage the development of products and services of a "niche" nature. Since few of us have the time, money or energy to mount national marketing campaigns, it is in our best interest to discover and concentrate on a niche, a segment, we can explore towards successful enterprise. Whether your specialty is house, trance, bluegrass or neo-soul, learn to work that niche and scope out relationships and opportunities within it.

The "cost-of-entry" bar has been lowered, and the average skill level of recording engineers with it. This is bittersweet.

My son never took a music lesson in his life, but with Apple's Garageband software, he's whipping up tunes like I've never heard before. As musicians we have to resist the urge to complain that the masses are now munching our caviar.

DANCE *SUB*-STYLES

Though some of these sub-styles overlap with others, each one has been singled out in the marketplace as distinct in its own way.

- abstract beat
- abstract drum-n-bass
- acid house
- acid jazz
- acid rave
- acid-beats
- acid-funk
- acid-techno
- alchemic house
- ambient dance
- ambient drum-n--bass
- amyl house
- analogue electro-funk
- aquatic techno-funk
- aquatic-house
- atomic breaks
- avant-techno
- bass global
- big beat
- bleep-n-bass
- blunted beats
- breakbeat
- chemical beats
- Chicago garage
- Chicago house
- coldwave
- cosmic dance
- cyber hardcore
- cybertech
- dark ambient
- dark core
- downtempo funk
- downtempo future jazz
- drill-n-bass
- dronecore
- drum-n-bass
- dub
- dub-funk
- dub-hop
- dub-n-bass
- electro
- electro-acoustic
- electro-breaks
- electro-dub
- freestyle
- future jazz
- futuristic breakbeat
- futuristic hardbeats
- futuristic hardstep
- gabber
- garage
- house
- global trance
- goa-trance
- happy hardcore
- hardcore techno
- hard chill ambient
- intelligent drum-n-bass
- intelligent jungle
- intelligent techno
- lounge-downtempo
- miami bass
- minimal-abstract
- minimal techno
- minimal trance
- morphing
- mutant techno
- mutated minimal techno
- mystic-step
- neurofunk
- noir-house
- nu-dark jungle
- old school
- organic chill out
- organic electro
- organic electronica
- progressive house
- progressive jungle
- progressive trance
- ragga
- rave
- techno jungle
- trance
- tribal
- trip-hop
- two-step
- underground
- world-dance

But just because you *can* record and release a CD doesn't mean you *should* record and release a CD. Musical clutter is increasing (John Doe has a great song called "Too Many Goddamn Bands"), and only promises to get worse, and it will always take serious bucks and muscle to rise above the noise. Or creativity.

This is part of what Clay Shirky calls "The Big Flip" – where the old notion of "filter then publish" is giving way to the new practice of "publish then filter." Thus, the growing need for *context*.

MEGATREND #6:
The Growing Need for Context

Every spare moment of our time is being filled with some form of commercial connection, making time itself the scarcest of all resources. Our fax machines, e-mail, voice mail, and cell phones, our twenty-four hour trading markets, instant around the clock ATM and online banking services, all night e-commerce and research services, twenty-four hour television news and entertainment, twenty-four hour food services, pharmaceutical services, and maintenance services, all holler out for our attention. They worm their way into our consciousness, take up much of our waking time, and occupy much of our thoughts, leaving little respite.

They also *overfill* us with information. This has come to be known as *infoglut*.

> ***"Too much information running through my brain;***
> ***Too much information driving me insane."***
>
> - The Police, 1982

Futurist Paul Saffo talks about the different "scarcities" the world has experienced over the past hundred and fifty years. First there was a scarcity of "conduit" (that is, pipeline). Then electric wires were strung coast to cost and conduit was hyperabundant. We then had a scarcity of "content", that is, information and programming to fill the conduit. Then content became hyperabundant too until today we're drowning in information.

The new scarcity, according to Saffo, is "context", that is, giving meaning to all this information. This increasing flood of information has now created an urgent need for "filters", "editors" and "portals". The need for context is so strong that Saffo sees a time when people like Oprah Winfrey and Peter Jennings will be licensing their "worldviews" to software companies to create products that screen vast amounts of information and present digestible info-bites in an acceptable framework for users!

A good example of providing context in the hyperabundant field of music is the compilation. Once a mere afterthought of the recording industry, these "variety packs of music" have emerged as a vital force in the market.

Have you noticed all those compilations on the counters of lifestyle retailers Pottery Barn, Structure, Williams-Sonoma and others? One man - Rock River Communications' Jeffrey Daniel - usually chooses the music. If mixing tapes is an art, then Daniel is the most popular artist you've never heard of: his branded compilations have sold nearly 5 million copies. Rock River's annual wholesale revenue is about $8 million, on par with a midsize record label.

How might you, in your area of expertise, be a meaning-giver in the world of music? Are you an expert in the use of ProTools or on 70s soul? Is bluegrass your passion or is it music education for kids? Are you highly informed about microphones, roots reggae, or lyric writing? How can you put that to use using channels like the Internet and other digital tools?

Provide significant meaning in your niche and people will shove money in your pockets.

MEGATREND #7: Resurgent Indie Culture

Historically, "indie" has been shorthand for second shelf quality, but it can't be looked at that way any longer. The gulf between indie and major artists has narrowed greatly. Major label philosophy used to be "spend the money" because at the end of the day it will be recoupable to the artist anyway, but today's world is all about what makes good business sense.

For several decades now *financial* people have been making all the decisions at the majors, so they can't invest long term in an artist's career. One or two shots and it's time to move on the next flavor. That opens an opportunity for indies. Profit margins and staffing have shrunk, so the human resources issues that were an advantage for major labels no longer exist. They are outsourcing almost as much as indies now.

Indie market share has grown from 9% in 1990 to about 20% today. That's based on *Billboard* magazine and Soundscan metrics that see indie market share as comprising all releases with indie distribution. But if you use the measurements of AAIM (American Association of Independent Music), which also counts indie product that goes through major-label owned distributors, then indie market share climbs to over 28% - a significant difference.

In the past major labels kept their foot on the throat of indies just by using their financial resources to horde all the opportunities. They can't do that anymore. The majors themselves are in a state of flux. There are cutbacks, mergers and proposed mergers everywhere. All those gulfs have tightened. We are looking at a historical crossroad. It's an exciting time to be an indie. The state of affairs we now find ourselves in isn't so much an end of the music industry as it is a new beginning. Today's indie labels can realistically expect to have the same financial roll if not the cultural impact that Sun, Chess, Atlantic and Specialty did in the 1950s. In short, 2006 is beginning to look like 1959 all over again.

Indies like Ubiquity, Nuclear Blast, Or, Ultra/Sequence, Definitive Jux, Enjoy, Stone Throw, Domino, Octone, Beach Street, Century Media, and MapleCore are all making themselves felt in this shaky marketplace for recorded music.

Also, as major label dynamics change, and as management and artists get dropped by these labels, indie label upstarts are able to recruit new executive talent and sign acts looking for more nimble handlers. Witness Sanctuary Records' niche with formerly-signed artists.

As the world of retail and consumer preferences become more digital, the indies will be at less of a disadvantage as compared to the majors. It will be artist and music direct to consumer and the role of middlemen will be diminished. We used to talk about the CD being the hardcover and the cassette being the paperback. Now we say the digital single is the paperback and the CD is the hardcover edition. Down the road it will be even *less* important whether you are indie or major, because no is going to care.

The next Big Thing is *small*.

The analogy is television. 30 years ago, the three broadcast networks (CBS, NBC and ABC) had a ninety plus share of the viewing audience. Today it's less than forty. Where's the other 60%? Watching cable. Though cable channels have miniscule ratings, they're profitable. Why? Because they've discovered and developed their niche.

And this is what indie labels do – the Americana sounds of New West Records, Red House Records' focus on singer/songwriters, the creative acid jazz of Instinct, and the deep reggae catalog of Trojan insures listeners they can expect quality discs from each company within their respective niche.

Read about how this relates to the "Long-Tail Market" in chapter 5, "Understanding Your Online Marketing Tools."

Other Music Market Micro-Trends

1. Sizeable Music Spending Continues. While most consumers aren't banging down the doors of traditional retailers, many continue to spend modest amounts on recorded music. According a recent report released by research firm IDC, 70 percent of US households report spending some amount of money on music every month. And 23 percent of US households spend between $10 and $24.99 a month on music, whether in the form of CDs, paid download services, or satellite radio subscriptions. While FM radio and CDs still dominate the landscape for many of these buyers, new technologies are also starting to gain a bigger share.

"Our survey shows that incumbent technologies, such as CD and FM radio, are still favored, while ownership of, awareness of, and intention to purchase MP3 players, satellite radio, music via legitimate online music services, among other devices and technologies, is on the rise," explained report author Susan Kevorkian. 7/7/05

2. The Resurrection of the Single. One of the most interesting trends of the legal music downloading craze is the resurrection of the single. In the '50s and the '60s, the industry was driven by the A-side, B-side format (many of The Beatles' best songs were B-sides), but by the late 1990s, people basically only bought albums, and record companies didn't see singles as a viable option for profits.

Thanks to iTunes, however, anyone can just download a song for 99 cents, changing the entire strategy of record companies marketing bands. In the 1990s, lame one-hit wonders could sell platinum albums because there was no other alternative. Now, users can download the song, hear 30-second samples of the rest of the album, realize it sucks and go about their daily lives free of the weight of the twelve other tracks. This sort of forces the creation of better music if you ask me.

Downloading makes the *track* paramount. Some artists have slowed the process by insisting that their albums not be broken up into singles available for individual sale.

Meanwhile, some of the hottest artists have limited the amount of time their record companies can sell digital downloads, waiting to see how the royalties will flow from online sales. Punk band The Offspring, for example, agreed to sell their music on iTunes for only six months.

The conflicts are likely to be amplified as the labels seek to expand online services beyond the U.S. to foreign markets, where the industry earns two-thirds of its revenue. Outside the U.S., the services will confront a web of different licensing procedures and copyright rules.

In Europe, for example, the services may have to secure rights from music publishers and set up payment systems in each nation individually. And while the major labels are happily licensing U.S. online services, iTunes and other services will have to start from scratch in Japan, where artist management firms—not the labels—control many artists' master recordings.

How fast will the sun set on the compact disc?

Quarter-size cds that can float among compatible music players, computers, game devices, digital cameras and personal digital assistants are already developed. But a massive installed base of CD players means that the traditional recording industry markets are not going to disappear or even be impacted by digital distribution any time soon.

3. A Yearning for the Authentic. We're seeing a strong return to basics throughout American life as we seek to bring our complicated and suddenly more dangerous world under control. In an "overcommunicated" society, it's harder to develop a message that penetrates and sticks. The new customer majority loathes artifice and is turned off by manipulative advertising. Powerful brands are simple messages that get through and provide comfort—an assurance of a company that has been and will be around. An increasingly high *tech* society will increasingly value high *touch*.

Putting It All Into Perspective

In 2004 *Billboard* magazine's, Ed Christman tracked a total of 90,347 albums (CD's/Cassettes/Vinyl LP's) using the point-of-purchase SoundScan system between 1999 and the end of 2003. The lesson learned from this was that only 554 albums sold more than 500,000 units, and that these accounted for 43% of all album purchases during that time. Of the remaining releases, 52,078 albums sold less than 1,000 copies each.

You can look at this 2 different ways, either as:

There is no way to compete in this overcrowded market, so why bother.?,

Or,

There is a huge opportunity for low volume sales.

I prefer to view this as an opportunity. What if you have something to offer that is different and unique? If you measure your success in terms of blockbuster releases, then you've forgotten that it sometimes takes a while to build an audience. You also need to realize that large record companies are not willing to take many risks because they (and the distributors) don't want to end up with a warehouse full of your music. They deal in terms of large releases - you don't have to.

This is one of the reasons that independent record companies exist. They are more willing to take a risk and often do so in terms of smaller release quantities; but even then, they need to make money too. If you look in the classified sections of the most musicians magazines (ie. *Guitar Player, Keyboard, Electronic Musician*, etc.) you'll see that its not that difficult or expensive anymore to do a run of 300 to 1000 CDs or even audio cassettes. Its even possible to do a run of 5 or 10 CDs (using a CD burner and some PC or Macintosh based software). You can easily create a low volume run of audio cassettes using your own home gear. And many people are doing just that – like lemonade stands popping up on a hot summer day, indie labels are rising everywhere.

New Beginnings

The only way to lead in the new world of music is to deconstruct the ruling dogmas of our industry (like, for instance, that records are the best vehicles to convey music and they should remain the chief support pillar of the industry), to generate heretical ideas to challenge that dogma, and then to build strategies around them.

There's a new dynamic in the biz today, one that flies in the face of all received wisdom. It can be said the first phase of the music industry (c. 1935-70) was *music*-driven, new sounds came up from the streets and clubs, and entrepreneurs responded.

The second phase (c. 1970-1995) was *business*-driven, lawyers and accountants ascending to decision-making posts and corporate imperatives dictating "hits".

The third phase (1995-now...) seems to be *market*-driven, consumers themselves are taking control of their music consumption.

There, of course, are elements of all three approaches at all times, but one has dominated each era.

Moving forward to individual audience empowerment brings music back into a more purely aesthetic relationship again, which is good for the art itself, and better for artists too. Artists may never recapture the kind of control of their relationship with their audience that they had in the past (except live, in concert), but a genuine aesthetic interplay with their audience is much better than being beholden to the least common denominator of the average of a mass audience's taste.

The current difficult climate serves as a form of reckoning. The tougher the times, the more clarity you gain about the difference between what really matters and what you only pretend to care about.

No one knows where all the cards will fall in this industry-wide shake up, but the good thing about radical change is that, during those times, the little person has a chance to make a big difference. It is the time when big ideas are brought to life, big names are made, and, yes, even big money is made.

The power's in your corner.

Let's get to work.

STAYING AHEAD OF THE CURVE

- Wired Magazine (http://www.wired.com)
- Digital Music News (http://www.digitalmusicnews.com)
- Iconocast (http://www.iconocast.com)
- Trendcentral (http://www.trendcentral.com)
- Trendwatching (http://www.trendwatching.com)

CH 4
MUSIC MARKETING BASICS

"I am only a public entertainer who has understood his time." - Pablo Picasso

How many times have you thought this: "I'm just not cut out to be a salesman"; "I don't like promoting myself;" and "I'm too busy to spend my time marketing"?

At one time or another we've all shared these concerns. They are real. Fortunately, to get the business you need, you don't have to have a sales personality, or try to become someone you're not, or grit your teeth to do things that you find offensive.

But, until you become known and sought after, you *will* need to find ways to "toot your own horn" that are you're comfortable with, ways that will produce the results you want.

The way you *think* about the fact that you'll only have as much business as you can generate will have a great deal to do with how much business you get and how easy, or difficult, it is for you to get it. If marketing feels like a burden or toil you'd rather not do, it will be difficult, if not impossible, for you to communicate the kind of enthusiam and excitement that will draw clients and customers to you.

Or, if marketing is something you only think about when you're desperately in need of business, and you must force yourself to do it begrudgingly, you'll have a hard time developing a creative and effective plan for getting the business you want and need.

Developing a Marketing Mindset

I've found that people who have plenty of business don't think about marketing as a drag. Whether they're shy and retiring or outgoing and effervescent, they're so excited about what they have to offer that they want to make sure people know about it. In fact, they feel eager, almost compelled, to reach out and make contact in whatever ways come naturally to them so people will know about their products and services.

So even if you have no marketing or business background, even if you're starting out in a brand-new community without any existing relationships, even if you're competent but not yet outstanding at your work, you can develop a positive marketing mindset that will enable you to create effective and affordable ways to attract business. By making the following three mental shifts in how you think about getting business, you, too, can project a positive mindset and make getting business easier and infintiely more enjoyable.

))) ILLUMINATING TRIVIA (((

Did you know...

...that Clive Calder and Ralph Simon named their company Zomba, after the then-capital of Malawi, where legend holds that local tribe members were blessed with superior hearing?

❒ ***Think opportunity, not obligation***. Instead of thinking about what a drag it is to have to get business or how dificult, unpleasant, time-consuming, and costly it is to market yourself, shift your attention instead to how eager you are to let others know about what you offer. If you've chosen the right niche for yourself, you obviously like your work and think it's important. You know it's needed and that it improves the lives or the businesses of your customers. Your work is more than a good idea or a way to make some money; it's a benefit to those you serve.

Without the funds to pay for elaborate marketing efforts and the ability to hire top-notch professionals, your own compelling sense of passion for your work will be the most essential element in attraacting business to you. This kind of passion is contagious. It will come through in all your spoken and written communication whether you're introducing yourself or have created a classified ad. So, start to think about marketing as a way to share your enthusiasm for what you do.

❒ ***Think contact, not activity***. Marketing is about making contact with people who need what you offer. It's not about keeping busy. If you're offering a product or service that addresses an unmet need or solves a problem, you probably have a pool of potential customers who need what you have to offer right at this very minute. But chances are they all don't know about you and you don't know about all of them. Somehow you need to find each other. And that's what marketing is about.

Often people ask, "What's the best way for me to market what I do?" They're looking for *the one* steady, reliable way they can count on for making contact with clients and customers. But there is no single business-getting route that's guaranteed to reach everyone. As you'll learn in the following chapter, there is probably a wealth of activities that will work well for you and your business. Finding the ones that will work best for you is an experiment. In fact, *marketing is an experiment*. People who are motivated to make contact with those who need them are always experimenting with new possiblilties to get their message out.

❒ ***Think communication, not manipulation***. Often people think marketing is about being cute and clever, creating a lot of hype or sizzle, especially in the entertainment biz. Worse, they fear it's about being manipulative. Sizzling, cute and clever hype may attract attention, but it doesn't build trust, respect, or value.

Instead of worrying about being cute and clever or manipulative, think about getting your message across. Shift your attention to what it is about that you do that's important to your customers. Think about how you can communicate your message to them in terms they'll understand. Think about how you can help them see the benefits of what you offer.

Managing Your Marketing Programs

Having an organized system in place will make all your marketing and promotional efforts flow more smoothly. Information is your ally as a marketer but if it's not organized it will quickly become your enemy.

The first thing to do is to come up with a list of topical areas or categories of marketing activity you will be engaged in. This may seem like more detail than you need, but information has a way of getting out of control very quickly and the key in business is to keep yourself in the driver's seat, not under the wheels. Here's a list of business marketing categories to get you started:

1. General Business – Under this broad area you create subdirectories for: Planning, Correspondence, Contracts & Agreements, Mail & Postage, Budgets & Financial records, Recording records, Royalty records, Idea file, Copyright forms, Bar codes, ISRCs (see chapter 5, under "Music Metadata") Licenses, Trademark info, Web site info, Manufacturers & packagers, Letterhead, Business support resources, Tax info, Insurance info, Inventory records, Organization memberships, and Subscriptions.

2. General Marketing Info – Subdirectories: Marketing plans, Marketing trends, Market research, Marketing resources, Idea file, Logos & graphics, Media kit, Mailing lists (fans, media, industry – *see next section on building your databases*).

3. Specific Market Info – Subdirectories: Direct to consumer, Film/TV, Terrestrial Radio, Satellite Radio, Online Radio, Distributors, Retail, Record Pools, Catalogs, Print media, Online media, Online retailers, Commercial music users, Touring & venues, Publishers & Licensors, Premiums & incentives, Foreign markets, Video outlets.

4. Graphics & Design – Design ideas, Graphic designers, Photos, Bios, Web site design, CD art, Packaging ideas, Display ideas, Advertising design, Printing vendors.

5. Publishing – Songs & compositions (lyrics, versions, in process), Copyright administration forms, Performing rights, Mechanical licenses, Sampling licenses, Promo & placement strategies, Infringements, Sub-publishers (foreign markets).

6. Sales – Formats & pricing, Distribution accounts, Retailer accounts, Consignments, POP (point of purchase strategies & materials), Listening stations, Co-op deals, Direct sales, International sales, Mail order & catalog sales.

7. Promotion – Release campaigns, Release parties, Street teams, Giveaways, Co-promotion ventures, Sponsorship ventures, Promo novelties, etc.

You will most likely have some additional topics that are specifically relevant to your project that aren't included here. Also, some topics can easily be telescoped out further. For example, under "Web site" you can have subdirectories for Domain names, Artist web sites, Label web sites, Design ideas, etc. Likewise, under "Print media" you'll probably want to include General newspapers, college newspapers, weekly newspapers, General entertainment magazines, Music magazines, Specific writers & editors, electronic newswires, Music publicists, etc.

Once you have your list of topical areas, create *both* a digital folder on your computer *and* a physical folder in your file cabinet for each one. One will complement the other and provide you with a way to save important documents to help all your marketing efforts have the best information backing them up and keep you from going crazy trying to find that design idea you cut out of a magazine two months ago.

Building Your Database of Connections: The Lifeblood of Your Marketing

Marketing and promotion are really very simple jobs. All they require is a little intelligence, some money, a fair amount of tact, a certain amount of *push...*and contacts.

What is your basic marketing goal? Answer: To let John and Jane Public know that you exist and that they should find out more about you. The way to achieve this is through *targeted* marketing and promotion. A target strategy insures maximization of resources; non-strategic promotion, or "shot gunning," can waste gobs of time, money and effort.

There are thousands of companies out there promoting their services and products, but only a handful are doing it effectively. It's the difference between hanging fifty posters that hundreds read and displaying one poster that thousands read. Targeting makes all the difference. So how does one go about it?

The first step is to compile your key contact lists and continue to add and delete from these lists throughout your company's history. They are the "Grand Central Stations" (a phrase you'll se again and again in this book) of all your marketing and promotion, and will allow you to feed the networking that is so crucial for success in today's business world.

There are three separate databases you'll want to develop: a media list, a customer/fan list, and an industry list. Let's look at each.

❒ ***The Media List.*** Newspapers, magazines, radio programs, and television are all driven by common needs: To fill time and space with information of value to their readers, viewers and listeners. They're eager for this information and quite willing, at their own expense, to publish or air it. They need your news.

You can begin this list with the local scene and then branch out regionally, nationally and even internationally, depending on your marketing goals. A good public library is your key resource here. Tell the reference librarian what you're looking for and you'll be guided to the media directories you need. Several good ones are listed in chapter 17. You can find most local media information in the Yellow Pages. Pay attention also to writers and radio D.J.'s who have helped break ground for other independent musicians. When the time is right, you can contact them with a press kit.

❒ ***Fan List.*** This is your grassroots support network. The best way to compile a fan list is at your gigs. Make it as easy as possible for people to join your fan list. Have pens and attractive cards on every table. Make them visible by announcing their existence throughout the night. Designate someone in the band or crew as the "Fan List Manager."

As with all lists, the best way to store them is on a computer with a "contact management" program. One that has been developed with the indie musician in mind is *Indie Band Manager* (http://indiebandmanager.com/). *Outlook* (Microsoft) and *Act!* (Symantec) are two excellent programs. *FileMaker Pro* and other database programs can also serve you well here. A computer will collect, file, and sort thru this information. It can also:

- link information from a message to a certain project or client;
- it will time a phone call and generate a bill;
- it will send you a tickler beep or screen message to remind you of an appointment or phone call;
- it will make connections you might not otherwise make and will save you time by organizing your activities; and *more...*

If you are selling from your web site there are some wonderful and robust shopping cart software products that can help manage your database along with many other marketing activities like order tracking, sales reporting, newsletter management, affiliate selling and more. Two I recommend are Mal's e-Commerce (http://www.mals-e.com) and 1shoppingcart.com. The first is very good and inexpensive; the latter is remarkable and pricey.

Short of creating digital files, simply type the contact names and addresses onto masters that can be duplicated onto self-adhesive mailing labels. This will save you from having to write or type them every time you do a mailing. Speak to a printer about the best way to do this.

❒ ***Industry List.*** Your Industry List will be made up of people and organizations which can promote your music, hire you, use your songs, or book performances for you. This will include club owners, promoters, booking agents, managers of groups who might invite you to be a warm-up act for their group, owners and managers of stores who might stock your record, record distributors, artist and repertoire (A&R) executives at record companies, and publishers and producers interested in buying new songs.

If you're a music production house or a record label, you'll want separate industry databases for such categories as music publishers, ad agencies, manufacturers, recording studios, music libraries, music supervisors, instrument rental services and other vendors.

To obtain these contacts see *The Yellow Pages of Rock* or *The Recording Industry Sourcebook,* two excellent resources for most music industry contacts. More local industry contacts can often be obtained from published lists in local and regional music magazines.

Lists and directories always cost something but they're well worth it. If time is a factor or you don't want to do the research yourself, let others do it for you. No sense reinventing the wheel. These contact lists are an informational goldmine for the independent musician. Whenever you have a gig, send a flyer, postcard or email announcing it to everyone on your mailing list. If you gig more than once a month you may want to do a monthly mailing. Don't forget to include any news about the band. Work to create a buzzzz.

I recommend that you work at least 30 minutes every day on your contact databases. Review them, study them, add to them and increase their value

Your databases can also provide you with valuable insight into your customers' relationship with your company. These are some important behavioral patterns to look for among your customer data. Each one can be set up as a field within your database:

- ❒ Date of last purchase
- ❒ Frequency of & momentum of purchases
- ❒ Monetary value of purchases
- ❒ Response to past promotions (offers, space ads, types of media, telemarketing, catalogs, etc.)
- ❒ Product category & correlation between products purchased
- ❒ Billing & payment patterns
- ❒ Returns, cancellations
- ❒ Seasonality issues

For more on building your mailing lists from other sources, see chapter 6.

Telling the Features – but Selling the Benefits

This might be a good place to discuss the features/benefits aspect of marketing.

People may rationalize their decisions based on facts, but they make those decisions based on emotions. Not the warm, fuzzy stuff of greeting cards, but emotions that allow people to see themselves experiencing the rewards of having taken action. Studies have demonstrated that lacking this emotional connection, people literally cannot decide!

How do you communicate this essential emotional dimension to your customers? You begin by translating features (facts) into benefits (emotional connections). The benefit is not always obvious, so I use the "so what?" exchange to help my clients zero in on the *essential* benefit to the customer.

Do this simple exercise:

Draw a line down the middle of a sheet of paper and in the left column list what's most important about your product. You'll want to list at least three features, but don't list more than six. Focus on what's most important to your prospects rather than just listing specifications.

Now for each item listed on the left, use the right-hand column to write down what you'd say if a skeptical user asked: "So what?" Don't think about it too long - just give a snap answer and write it down. Doing it this way, I've found that I knew things I didn't even know I knew, because it seems to bypass that ultra-logical internal censor most of us have peering over our shoulders.

If you do have to make an entry on the right because the entry on the left didn't already answer the "So what," you're on the right track to finding the message your prospects need to hear for you to successfully market. It may take a few passes, with feedback from prospects if you can get it, but it's worth all the time and effort. I use this technique all the time. I've found that the left-hand list tells you what a product is, but the right-hand column tells you *what it's for.*

And that's what prospects are looking to buy. Here are some samples:

Features	**Benefits**
• state of the art audio gear	• worry-free quality sound for your event
• 30 different styles of music	• full variety for discriminating tastes
• BA in Music w/ MB concentrate; law degree from Suffolk University	• expert counsel you can trust
• flexible hours	• convenience

WORDS THAT PULL LIKE MAGNETS

To get and keep your reader's or listener's attention and interest, work these motivating words into your marketing copy to trigger greater response.

Acclaimed	Discount	Improved	Practical	Striking
Advancement	Discover	Incredible	Prevents	Surefire
Amazing	Easy	Instantly	Profitable	Suddenly
Announcing	Effective	Introducing	Proven	Surprising
Astonishing	Exceptional	Last Chance	Quickly	The Truth
At last	Extraordinary	Love	Recommended	Trusted
Attention	First time	Magic	Reliable	Ultimate
Bargain	Frustrating	Miracle	Remarkable	Valuable
Boosts	Free	Money-Making	Results	Wanted
Breakthrough	Guaranteed	Money-Saving	Revolutionary	Warning
Challenge	How to	New	Safety	You
Choice	Hurry	Offer	Save	Yours

Getting to Know Your Market (s)

Have you ever noticed those small postcard mailers that come with a lot of CDs? They're usually 3"x4" and contain a series of questions in 6 pt. type on everything from where you purchased the CD to what music web sites you enjoy visiting. They may also ask your gender, your age, your annual income and how many CDs you purchase each year. Why? Because they want to know you so they can sell more product to you in the future.

Companies spend millions of dollars each year trying to figure out what makes their customers tick. Known in marketing lingo as "datamining," the music industry has been slow to use this tactic, primarily because its main customers have been retailers, not consumers. Whatever data the industry has gathered over the years, especially though its "record club" operations, it hasn't done much with it. But indie musicians and bands understand the value of this information, and the "mailing list" is one of the primary tools they use to expand their markets.

The logic is simple: know how your customers spend their time and you'll know better how and where to spend your marketing money.

The Net: A Dataminer's Dream come True

Everybody knows by now that the internet has shaken up the music business. But one of the subtler changes has been the amount of raw information that the industry collects – to study the music that sells, and to face up to the music that doesn't.

It's stunning to think about how much music fans are telling us about themselves, in their search queries, the libraries on their hard drives, and the lists they print on their MySpace pages. It's the same kind of quantum leap that we forget to appreciate in, say, web surfing or TiVO, where someone's collecting exponentially more information about you than they ever could before. A business like BigChampagne.com could barely learn more about your online consumption if they had a guy standing over your shoulder.

For example, if you're marketing jazz products you'll want to be aware of the publications *Downbeat, Jazziz* and *Coda,* organizations like the Jazz World Database and various cable TV and radio shows specializing in jazz performance, as well as the hundreds of generalist outlets for jazz music. Likewise, someone marketing reggae-related product will be acquainted with *The Beat, Reggae Report* and *The Reggae Quarterly,* record labels like Mango, Heartbeat and VP, and organizations like Reggae Ambassadors Worldwide. The same thing applies to folk, metal, emo, blues, classical, country, Latin, world, experimental and all other music styles.

Through learning about the who, what and where of your music's audience you also learn about the best ways to reach that audience. This is a fundamental component of marketing. We've already gone over some of this topic in chapter 2 when discussing niches, but let's now go a little further into it.

We've all heard a business owner say, "My product is terrific! It appeals to everyone."

Many of us have also seen small businesses which try to be all things to all people. This is a difficult, if not impossible, bridge to cross.

Targeting your market is simply defining who your primary customer will be. The market should be measurable, sufficiently large, and reachable. When people have choices, they invariably go where they are made to feel special, important, and appreciated. The most effective strategy for leveraging your marketing efforts is to consistently communicate customer-centered information and advice that builds trust and confidence in you, your company, and your products or services.

A great example of this is the online indie music retailer, CDBaby. When I purchased my first CDs from this store my order came with a message on my receipt that said, "CDBaby loves Peter." Now, I realize those who fulfilled my order did not know me from Adam, but nevertheless, this brief "extra value" message works in a subtle way to endear me to the service. CDBaby certainly doesn't *have to* include this message to its customers but the fact that it does tells me the company wants to go out of its way to make me feel special. The new economy requires us marketers to think holistically about our marketing tactics, working from the customer out, not from the medium in.

We already reviewed the three types of general markets in chapter 2. They are the Consumer, Industrial/Business and Reseller markets. Hopefully, by now you are clear which of the three is your *primary* market. Once you understand this you can then begin to focus more clearly on your particular target market(s) within it.

Here are three steps to follow when identifying your target market. They are as follows:

A. Step One: Identify Why A Customer Would Want To Buy Your Product/ Service.
B. Step Two: Segment Your Overall Market
C. Step Three: Research Your Market

STEP ONE - Identify Why A Customer Would Want To Buy Your Product/ Service.

The first step in identifying your target market is understanding what your products/services have to offer to a group of people or businesses. You've already done this in the previous section by identifying your product or service's features and benefits. Review it and then go even deeper.

The way you inventory and describe the benefits you offer customers will also provide you with the vocabulary you need for creating your marketing messages and materials. For example, say you offered a music transcription service that could be adapted to different languages. You describe this feature as "multi-ligual music transcription." That's fine. But the *benefit* of this feature can be described as "customizable to the particular language needs of each client." The word "customizable" (a powerful word in light of recent market trends) can then be used in all your marketing messages to help sell your service.

By knowing what your product/service has to offer and what will make customers buy, you can begin to identify common characteristics of your potential market.

STEP TWO: Segment Your Overall Market

It's a natural instinct to want to target as many people and groups as possible. However, by doing this your promotional strategy will never talk specifically to any *one* group, and you will most likely turn many potential customers off. Your promotional budget will be much more cost effective if you promote to one type of customer and speak directly to them. This allows you to create a highly focused campaign that will directly meet the needs and desires of a specific group. This is called *market segmentation*.

For example, there are many music consumers who desire positive messages in songs as a benefit when purchasing a CD. Rather than targeting *everyone* in their promotional strategy, a record label may opt to target a specific group of consumers with similar characteristics, such as families with young children. This is an example of market segmentation.

Segmentation Pitfall!

The *largest* segment doesn't always represent the *best* opportunity. Often the largest segment draws fierce competition, and consumers in that category may be perfectly happy wth the competitor's offerings. In many cases you'd do better to select a segment the competition has been ignoring. There you'll find consumers who are dissatisfied and underserved – and ready to switch to *you*.

Market Segmentation is the process of breaking down a larger target market into smaller segments with specific characteristics. Each group requires different promotional strategies and marketing mixes (the variety of tools and tactics you chose to reach this segment) because each group has different wants and needs.

Segmentation will help you customize a product/service or other parts of a marketing mix, such as advertising, to reach and meet the specific needs of a narrowly defined customer group.

Larger markets are most typically divided into smaller target market segments on the basis of the following:

1. *Geographic:* Potential customers or organizations are segmented in a local, state, regional or national marketplace. If you are selling music instructional services, for example, you'll most likely need to be located in a fairly well-populated area in order to ensure enough customers to support your company. Or, if you own a retail store, geographic location of the store is one of the most important considerations to make.

Decide if your business is going to do business on a local, regional, national or international level. Identify specific boundaries as to which you will do business. Identify the geographic region your market is located in.

Of course, digital products (like recorded music) have been liberated from geographical constraints thanks to the Internet. The Net enables small entrepreneurs to have the whole world as a market. But even an international reach requires a marketer to have a very local message in order to be effective. Again, high tech requires high touch.

2. *Demographic*: Potential customers are identified by criteria such as age, race, religion, gender, income level, family size, occupation, education level, and marital status. Choose those characteristics of your demographic target market that relates to the interest, need and ability of the customer to purchase your product or service. For example, a target market for a general business band focused on the private party market, would include: Professional married couples approximately 30-50 years old with young children who have an income of over $100,000. Every decision from marketing to design is then based on the profile you develop of your target market.

A demographic for a business would include such factors as customer size, number of employees, type of products, and annual revenue. If you are a business to business marketer for example, you may want to consider segmenting according to your target market's size. A music production company may decide to target only Fortune 500 companies that produce more than a dozen video productions each month because they need high volume accounts to make a profit.

Identify the following demographic characteristics regarding your market.

Consumer Market

Age _____
Income _____
Gender _____
Profession _____
Education _____
Family Size _____
Homeowner _____
Marital Status _____

Business Market

Geographic location _____
Size of Company _____
Annual revenue _____
Number of Branches _____
Number of Employees _____
Industry _____
Age of Company _____
Company mission _____________

3. *Psychographic:* Many businesses offer products based on attitudes, beliefs, and the emotions of their target market. The desire for status, an enhanced appearance, and more money are examples of psychographic variables. The desire to be considered cutting-edge, discriminating and "cool" are other variables. They are the factors that influence your customers' purchasing decision. A seller of high-end audio would appeal to an individual's desire for status symbols. Business customers as well as consumers can be described in psychographic terms. Some companies view themselves as leading edge, high tech, others as socially responsible, stable and strong, and others as innovative and creative. These distinctions help in determining how your company is positioned and how you can use the company's position as a marketing tactic.

The following are some psychographic descriptions for both consumer and business markets. Identify which characterize your target market.

Consumer Market

Lifestyle:
- Fun-Seeking ___
- Family Stage ___
- Trend-Setting ___
- Hobbies ___
- Status Seeking ___
- Sports ___
- Conservative ___

Forms Of Entertainment___
Socially Responsible ___
Environmentally Conscious ___
Publication Subscriptions ___
Family Oriented ___
Technical interests ___
Other ___

Business Market

Business Style:
- Industry Leader ___
- Innovative ___
- Conservative ___

Employee Relations ___
Trade Associations ___
Socially Responsible ___
Business Products/
Financially Stable ___
Services Used ___
Employee Friendly ___
Influencer ___
Publication Subscriptions ___
High Tech ___
Workforce Type ___
Management Style ___

4. *Behavioristic:* Products and services are purchased for a variety of reasons. Business owners must determine what the reasons are, including: brand, loyalty, cost, how frequently they use and consume products, and time of year. It's important to understand the buying habits and patterns of your customers. For example, a consumer does not rush and buy guitar lessons for their child from the first flyer they see. A fortune 500 company doesn't typically make quick purchasing decisions.

Try to answer the following questions regarding your market:

❒ Reason/occasion for purchase?

❒ Number of times they'll purchase?

❒ Timetable of purchase, every week, month, quarter,etc.?

❒ Amount of product/service purchased?

❒ How long to make a decision to purchase?

❒ Where customer purchases and/or uses product/service?

Most businesses use a combination of each of the above to segment their markets. Demographic and geographic criteria will usually qualify your target markets because you need to establish if segment members have enough money to purchase your offering or if they're in a location that's accessible to the product or service. Most businesses then use the psychographic and behavioristic factors to construct a promotional campaign that will appeal to the target market.

Take a moment to decide which segmentation criteria will be most helpful to you in segmenting your target market: Geographic, Demographic, Psychographic and/or Behavioristic.

Next, identify what is most important to your customers. Are they price sensitive? Are they looking for the highest quality? Is great customer service important? Or is location a deciding factor?

STEP THREE: Research Your Market

Where to find the data: You will find loads of market research data in Chapter 17.

Here are some suggestions for conducting your own market research:

❒ *Your current customers* can provide you with insight on *potential* customers and how to appeal to them. You may also discover an opportunity to produce additional products to serve this market or improve on an existing product. Ask yourself: What don't I know about my customers? You need to construct questions that will provide the answer. It can be as simple as asking a current customer: "Why did you purchase this product?" or, "How can this product be improved?" and giving them space to answer.

❒ *If you have a retail outlet*, you have the means of distributing a customer comment card or questionnaire. A suggestion box is also a vehicle for obtaining information about your customers and their wants and needs.

❒ When mailing monthly invoices or statements, *include a questionnaire* and an envelope to return mail it. Those CD questionnaire postcards fall into this category. If you provide an incentive to those who return it, such as a free gift or discount, you increase the chances of getting it back.

❒ *Advertising Representatives*. Most major publications have demographic and behavioristic profiles of their readership. If you're a recording studio, a magazine focusing on regional musicians and bands can provide you with valuable segmenting information. Simply call the advertising department and ask for a media kit.

❒ *Requesting an organization's annual report* will provide you with business demographic information.

❒ *Work with a local college.* If you need help in designing and executing a questionnaire, contact the marketing professor at an area college and offer your business up as a class project.

❒ *Trade associations* can provide valuable information for industries not only on demographic and company size, but competition and trends for growth areas as well. Trade associations usually sponsor trade shows too. For example, a maker of music stands would certainly want to attend the annual NAMM (National Association of Music Merchants) event in California. An American record label seeking to expand its market into Europe, will try to attend the winter MIDEM event in Cannes, France.

By the way, your local librarian can be a tremendous asset at this stage of your investigation. These people are specially trained in the art of tracking down hard-to-find information and will inevitably introduce you to valuable resources you've probably never heard of. Also, public libraries frequently subscribe to online research databases (e.g., Infotrac) that put an enormous amount of valuable information at your fingertips.

Learning to Search Smarter on the Net

The Internet is a godsend to anyone in need of information. And music marketing resources are hyperabundant online. A band could book its own tour by using a mapping site (like Mapquest.com) to plot its route, and then go to UBL.com or Music 411 and pull up promoters, radio stations, press contacts and retail outlets by city, around the country, and around the globe.

But the wild popularity of the Web also has a downside. The proverbial haystack has gotten terribly large, making the needle all the more difficult to find. Know why it's called "*surfing* the Net"? Because it's like riding a rogue wave - you never know where the search engine is going to take you. Unless, that is, you learn a few simple lessons about online information retrieval.

Knowing how to find the information you need online is an acquired skill. When looking for music information its helpful to begin your search with a human-constructed directory like Yahoo.com or About.com. These services have already organized thousands of web sites under topical areas. You can go to Yahoo > Entertainment > Music and locate thousands of music sites organized by category (Artists, Education, Industry Resources, Trivia, etc.). At About.com you'll find the "Musician's Exchange," a rich repository of DIY information organized and edited by "guides" expert in that area.

None of the sites just mentioned are comprehensive so you'll eventually need to resort to search engines to help you find what you're looking for. These can be tricky and you may have been frustrated by a search engine more than once while doing a search. Here are some tricks for producing better search results:

Be specific: Don't type "drums"; type at least three words in your search, such as "1965 Gretsch jazz drum set".

(con't.)

Use "and" or "not". Adding "and" links two terms and focuses a search. Typing "not" narrows a search by excluding pages containing the second search term. Some engines assume you mean "or" if you don't use a conjunction between words. "Or" expands the search, delivering sites with *any* of the words you've typed.

Use quotes: Most engines interpret quotes as "search only for sites with all words exactly as typed". So if you type, for example, *music business resources* you'll get results for every page on the Web with the word "music", "business", or "resources" on it. You'll drown in your results. The correct way to type it would be "music business resources".

Use an exclusion: After attempting a search, you may get dozens of similar sites that have nothing to do with what you're looking for. Exclude these listings by a minus sign followed by the key words you don't want to see. On one search engine, for example,"JAVA" yields 20,000 sites."JAVA-coffee" slices the list to 26 sites.

Directories. As mentioned, a directory search engine clumps thousands of pages together under different categories, from "Old TV Shows" to "Wireless Communications." Use a directory when you're looking for information on a general subject, such as "acoustic guitars," rather than for a specific site, like the Hillar's Classical Guitar page. Several big directories on the Net- Magellan (http://www.mckinley.com) and Point (http://www.pointcom.com) - offer site reviews. The most popular directory is Yahoo! (http://www.yahoo.com), where you'll find sites divided into logical subsections. But Yahoo's content isn't always as current as it could be.

Indexes. When you need specific information on some obscure topic- and you want to blanket the entire Net- a search engine index is the best tool to use. Indexing engines use software programs called robots or spiders that comb the Web, analyzing the text of millions of Internet pages and ranking them according to the number of times a particular word appears. The biggest search engine is Digital's ALTAVISTA (http://www.altavista.digital.com). It gives you the best mileage, hitting millions if Web pages. But Alta Vista's presentation leaves a lot to be desired. It's also tricky to use properly, with poorly explained rules. My favorite in this category is INFOSEEK GUIDE (http://www2.infoseek.com). The millions of listings here are ranked for relevance, and there are cross links to related subject categories. This comes in handy when you go astray. For example, while looking for "Thelonius Monk" you can select the "similar pages; option to locate general jazz sites.

Metasearches. These piggyback on the other search engines. When you type a query, the software goes to several other engines and submits it to each, bringing in more (and hopefully improved) results. Alltheweb.com and Search.com are examples of these metasearch engines. Metacrawler (http://www.metacrawler.com)is one of the best. It submits your query to nine of the top search engines, including Alta Vista, Yahoo!, and Infoseek. The downside: you'll generate redundant listings with this technique.

Specialized search tools. Combing the entire Web doesn't always turn up what you want. You may have to turn to a specialized directory that covers all the sites relating to your particular topic. There are hundreds of such specialized directories. To find them, go to SEARCH.COM (http://www.search.com). Created by folks at CNET, it contains links to over 300 indexes and search engines.

Since each engine has its own peculiar way of sniffing out data, it's a good idea to read the instructions included at each search site. You'll probably end up using only one or two search engines for ninety-percent of your searches. Get to know all that engine's features and read the site's instructions on performing "advanced searches". This will help you know the best way to retrieve the information you're looking for and, in the end, save you hours of grief and disappointing search results.

After identifying and defining the possible segments within your target market, you must face the critical question of whether or not it would be profitable and feasible for you to pursue each identified segment, or choose one or two. To make this decision, you must answer the following questions:

1. What is the financial condition of my company? If you have limited resources at this time, you may want to direct your marketing efforts to only one segment. It would be better to have a concentrated advertising campaign to reach one segment than it would be to advertise sporadically in an attempt to meet two.

2. What segments are my competitors covering? Are they ignoring smaller segments which I can possibly tap? The music production company previously mentioned may decide to pursue small firms because they have many competitors currently serving the needs of larger companies.

3. Is the market new to your company? If so, it may be better for you to concentrate on one segment for now, and expand to others when your initial segment has been successfully penetrated. Developing new markets takes a greater commitment of time, money, and energy.

Important Considerations:

1. If you pursue one segment of your target market and the demand for your product decreases, so will your financial strength. In essence, you are putting all your eggs in one basket along with its inherent risks.

2. When your firm becomes well established in a particular market segment, it may be difficult for you to move to another segment. This may occur due to your market reputation or popularity. For example, if a booking agency becomes known for scoring college gigs, other entertainment buyers may perceive them as only having the expertise to serve that one market.

3. After you have mastered one particular segment, you can then begin to develop another. This strategy of directing your company's marketing efforts at one or more market segments by developing a marketing mix for each specific segment is known as the Multi-Segment Strategy.

The marketing mixes for this strategy may vary by product, price, promotional material and distribution methods. It is not uncommon for a firm using the multi-segment strategy to increase its sales by focusing on more than one segment, since you would have marketing mixes aimed at each segment. Since this strategy would require additional processes, you may incur higher production costs.

Additionally, different promotional plans and distribution efforts will result in higher marketing costs. Make sure the costs don't outweigh the benefits.

Now think about all the characteristics you have identified and start formulating the promotional campaign that will best address this specific target market. Start to formulate a picture or description of your ideal customer. Make sure everything you do from design to message, addresses your market.

Customer Focus:
Making Customers Not Just Sales

For your customers to have a good opinion of your business they need to have a positive experience when they interact with you and your team. Think about the last time you had a negative buying experience. Did the salesperson not have enough information to satisfy your query? Or maybe you were left on hold for too long when you called to place an order or to complain?

Most negative experiences are linked to poor customer service. Good customer service isn't that difficult if you follow these ten rules:

❒ *Commit to quality service.* It should be the focus of the whole team to provide service above and beyond the customer's expectations.

❒ *Know your products.* Conveying knowledge will help you win the customer's trust and confidence.

❒ *Know your customers.* This enables you to tailor your products and services to their needs.

❒ *Treat people with courtesy and respect.* Every contact with a customer leaves an impression - make it positive.

❒ *Never argue with the customer.* They may not always be right but concentrating on solving the problem, rather than laying blame, will encourage the customer to come back.

❒ *Don't leave customers hanging.* Today customers want quicker solutions - 95% of dissatisfied customers will return if their complaint is resolved on the spot.

❒ *Always provide what you promise.* Fail to do this and you loose credibility.

❒ *Assume that customers are telling the truth.* The majority of customers don't like to complain, in fact they will go out of their way to avoid it, give them the benefit of the doubt.

❒ *Focus on making customers, not sales.* Keeping the customer's business over a long period of time is more important than making one big sale. Remember - it costs 6 times more to find a new customer than to sell to an existing one.

❒ *Make it easy to buy.* Keep paperwork and forms to a minimum, make it easy to pay, help people find what they need and explain how products work.

Review the "Ten Demandments of Customer Service" in chapter 3. It's some of the most important information to understand in this book!

Learning From Your Competition

"Stand on the shoulders of those who've gone before you, and you'll see farther." -Anon

Here's my question for you. What happens when customers compare you to your key competitors? Unless you win 100% of those contests, that's a question worth answering.

Let's start with what happens when a prospect calls in. How personal is the attention they receive? If your competitor quickly connects them with a competent sales associate, but your system instead forces them to endure layers of automated phone instructions, only to tell them to leave a message, you've got a problem. Heck, you've got a problem even if your sales people sound too busy to care, or seem unsure of their answers.

Tell me more about your key competitors. What do they talk about? What do they leave behind? Do they make it easy to move along to the next step in becoming a customer, even provide incentives to do so? Do they follow up? How?

Your goal, of course, isn't to mimic that competitor. For all you know, they might be dropping those very items or systems because they failed to produce decent results. Plus, every company is different. It's a mistake – and probably a very expensive one – for a small company to try to sell the same way a huge worldwide competitor does.

But you win when you understand more about what differentiates you from your competitors in your customers' eyes. Who in your company is in charge of knowing your competitors in the same way your prospects do? Without that knowledge, you'll never get closer to knowing why some choose that competitor over you. Or to do something about it.

Comic Relief: Country Song Titles That Never Made It

"I Wouldn't Take You to a Dog Fight Even If I Thought You Could Win"

"My John Deere Was Breaking Your Field, While Your Dear John Was Breaking My Heart"

"I Liked You Better Before I Knew You So Well"

"I Still Miss You Baby, But My Aim's Gettin' Better"

"You May Put Me In Prison, But You Can't Keep My Face From Breaking Out"

A Differentiation Strategy is one of creating a product or service that is perceived as being unique throughout the industry. This has also been called your *USP* (unique selling proposition). The emphasis can be on brand image, proprietary technology, special features, superior service, a strong distributor network, or other aspects that might be specific to your industry segment. In addition, some of the conditions that should exist to support a differentiation strategy include strong marketing abilities, effective product development, creative personnel, the ability to perform basic research, and a good reputation.

Here are some questions to help get you started -

1. What products and companies will compete with you?
List your three major competitors (Names and addresses):

2. Will they compete with you across the board, or just for certain products, certain customers, or in certain locations?

3. Will you have important indirect competitors? (For example, used CD stores compete with record retailers, although they are different types of businesses.)

4. How will your products or services compare with the competition?

Fleshing it out: Use the **Competitive Analysis** table on the next page to compare your company with your two most important competitors. In the first column are key competitive factors. Since these vary from one industry to another, you may want to customize the list of factors.

In the column labeled **Me**, state how you honestly think you will stack up in customers' minds. Then check whether you think this factor will be a strength or a weakness for you. Sometimes it is hard to analyze our own weaknesses. Try to be very honest here. Better yet, get some disinterested strangers to assess you. This can be a real eye-opener. And remember that you cannot be all things to all people. In fact, trying to be causes many business failures because efforts become scattered and diluted. You want an honest assessment of your company's strong and weak points.

Now analyze each major competitor. In a few words, state how you think they compare.

In the final column, estimate the importance of each competitive factor to the customer. 1 = critical; 5 = not very important.

Factor	Me	Strength		Competitor A	Competitor B	Importance to Customer
Products						
Price						
Quality						
Selection						
Service						
Reliability						
Stability						
Expertise						
Company Reputation						
Location						
Appearance						
Sales Method						
Credit Policies						
Advertising						
Image						

Now, write a short paragraph stating your competitive advantages and disadvantages.

))) ILLUMINATING TRIVIA (((

Peculiar Origins of Group Names

THE BEATLES: After the Crickets, because Buddy Holly influenced them so much.
DEPECHE MODE: After a French fashion magazine.
LED ZEPPELIN: The Who's John Entwistle (originally slated, along with drummer Keith Moon, to be a member of Jimmy Page's post-Yardbirds band) joshed that "such a group would go over like the world's biggest lead balloon--a veritable Led Zeppelin".
THE O'JAYS: Cleveland deejay Eddie O'Jay gave them their break, and they named themselves in his honor.
THE POUGES: Short for the Gaelic expression "pogue mo chone", which means 'kiss my ass'.
STEELY DAN: The original Steely Dan appeared in William Burrough's novel "Naked Lunch". A milk-squirting dildo with which lesbians buggered males, its specific appeal to the young Donald Fagan and/or Walter Becker remains lost in the shrouds of time.
UB40: Named after the form English workers have to fill out to receive unemployment benefits.

Developing the Right Mix of Tools & Tactics

Everything we've done so far is "first-stage marketing", the essential foundation stones that need to be in place for successful marketing to happen.

Most of this primary work is designed to help you develop a marketing "mind-set", one that will help you truly inform and render effective your more specific marketing plans.

Once you've reflected on unfolding trends, understand the benefits of your product, discovered and studied your target market, decided on your unique differentiation, and built a strong database of contacts – in other words, developed a clear sense of your niche-focus – your next step is to *communicate* it, that is, actively market it.

With your niche focus you can now decide which will be the most useful, the most effective, and the most profitable means to help you accomplish this. In marketing jargon, this is called deciding on your "marketing mix" – that combination of tools and tactics designed to get your message across to your target audience.

Most of us are not coming at this with deep pockets, nor are we playing with "monopoly money" from a parent corporation. The kind of marketing you will be doing has been given many names: *grass-roots marketing, guerrilla marketing, entrepreneurial marketing, expeditionary marketing, radical marketing*, *touchpoint marketing* etc. No matter what you call it, all of these marketing approaches have the following features in common:

❒ low cost but effective communications
❒ doing more with less
❒ cooperative efforts
❒ leveraging resources
❒ tapping under-utilized resources

❒ using alternative channels
❒ using alternative media
❒ networking
❒ less use of money; more investment of time, energy, imagination
❒ acute focus in terms of products and services

Which Marketing Methods are Best for You?

All marketing activities come down to doing one or more of four things that we've done since kindergarten: WALK, TALK, SHOW, and TELL.

Some of us like to *talk.* For us, marketing activities from networking to making sales calls allow us to talk to our heart's content. Others of us enjoy being in the limelight, up on stage, so to speak. Activities like giving performances, speeches or seminars can be our forte. Still others of us prefer to remain in the background and communicate through the written word in brochures, advertising, direct mail and so forth. Some of us work best one-on-one through others like mentors and gatekeepers. Many of us want our work to speak for itself, and it can. We simply have to find ways to let those who might need or want it experience what we do firsthand through demonstrations, exhibits, or samples.

The best marketing activities will be those that enable you to be most fully yourself. Effective marketing is a matter of identifying what you enjoy doing most, what comes most naturally to you, and what best fits into your schedule and your budget. There are plenty of options for us all.

Marketing Methods Exercise: To find which kinds of business-generating activities are most comfortable and interesting to you, take the following quiz. Check the statements that best describe you and select the activities that would be most appealing and easiest to fit into your schedule and your budget.

Making Personal Contact

___ I like to meet people person-to-person.
___ I enjoy personally letting people know what I do and how I can help them.
___ I work well when I'm the center of attention, even in the spotlight.
___ I feel comfortable and would enjoy using (check any of the following):
    ___ *Direct solicitation: selling in person or by phone or modem*
    ___ *Free consultations: working directly with prospective clients and customers*
    ___ *Networking: making business contacts at meetings and social gatherings*
    ___ *Sales speeches and seminars: selling to a group*
    ___ *Volunteering: contributing what I offer to trade, civic, or business concerns*
    ___ *Walking around the neighborhood: going door-to-door to meet my clients and customers*

Example: Joe Cameron's secret for getting business is breakfast. Joe, an audio engineer and co-owner of a recording facility, woos prospects by inviting them to monthly networking breakfasts he hosts in elegant downtown restaurants. Each month he invites six people who don't know one another. He never gives a sales presentation but, instead, facilitates engaging discussions that highlight his expertise and experience.

Getting Others to Talk About You

____ I feel more comfortable letting other people promote and sell what I offer.
____ I enjoy working through and with peers and colleagues.
____ I like letting others know why they should promote my work.
____ I feel comfortable with and would enjoy using (check any that apply):
 ____ *Gatekeepers and mentors*
 ____ *Gift certificates and coupons*
 ____ *Letters of reference, endorsements, and testimonials*
 ____ *Referrals*
 ____ *Sponsorships, donations, and events*
 ____ *Publicity:*
 ____ *Newspaper*
  ____ *Newsletter*
  ____ *Magazine*
  ____ *Radio and TV*
  ____ *Business and trade publications*
  ____ *Cyberspace*

Example – Glen and Jaya Kemp have a unique niche. Glen provides music backgrounds for Jaya's stories for African-American children. Publicity has been their best business generator. This special husband-wife team has been featured in *Essence, Black Enterprise,* and *Emerge* magazines, appeared on African-American talk shows, and been covered by the *Washington Post,* the *Detroit Free Press,* and the *Chicago Sun-Times.*

What is A.I.D.A.?

Marketing professionals live by the adage, "*Attention, Interest, Desire and Action.*" Known as "AIDA" they find resourceful ways to capture the *Attention* of the reader with a headline or graphic; draw them in with *Interest*-building ad copy; create *Desire* with benefit statements; and then ask for the sale (or a response) with a powerful "call *to Action.*" AIDA is a powerful formula for creating compelling advertising, and with a little work, it can be incorporated into any advertising message. If advertising is part of your strategy, it is well worth the effort.

Telling People All About It

____ I'm good at explaining what I do in terms others can easily understand.
____ I'm good at motivating people with words.
____ I feel comfortable and would enjoy creating (check any of the following):
 ____ *Advertising*

___ *Articles and columns*
___ *Bounce-backs*
___ *Brochures and flyers*
___ *Bulleting boards, tear pads, take-ones, and door hangers*
___ *Card decks and coupon packs*
___ *Catalogs*
___ *Direct mail*
___ *Fax-back, broadcast fax, and E-mail*
___ *Flyers*
___ *Inserts*
___ *Newsletters*
___ *Phone and hold button messages*
___ *Postcards*
___ *Product packaging and point-of-sale displays*
___ *Sales letters and proposals*
___ *Reply cards*
___ *Web site*
___ *Yellow page and other directory listings*
___ *Your own book*

Example – Jim Bernard's company is called, Step Up Productions. A leader and performer in several general business bands, Jim created an inexpensive, 10-page brochure called "Entertainment Planning for Your Wedding" and another called "Entertainment Planning for Your Private Party." These booklets have become his calling card. He sends them to event planners, caterers, banquet hall managers and others who traffic with people who are planning weddings and parties. In this indirect but helpful way, he introduces his own music groups to important influencers in this market.

Tips for Telephone Talk

Unlike face-to-face interactions where the customer can see your posture, gestures and facial expressions, customers on the phone get their entire impression of you strictly from the words you speak and the tone and quality of your voice. How effective is your telephone style?

❒ Does your voice show enthusiasm and interest in what you're doing, or are you coming across as someone using a script?
❒ Do you answer the phone quickly and courteously?
❒ Do you identify yourself to the caller?
❒ How are transfers handled? Do you give your customer the name and phone number of the person you are transferring them to in case of a problem?
❒ Are messages handled in a proficient and professional way?
❒ When you have to put a customer on hold do you always ask their permission? (If a customer does not want to be put on hold, offer to take their number and call them back.)
❒ When using voicemail do you: tell callers the exact information you want them to leave (phone number, customer id. etc.) and explain the details of your particular system? For example, "Please leave your message after the beep, press the # key and hang up when your message is finished." And, do you check your own voicemail message regularly to ensure it is appropriate?

Showing Off What You Can Do

___ I feel more comfortable letting my work speak for itself, and I don't mind finding ways to show it off.
___ I don't mind being the center of attention as long as the focus is on the work I'm doing or have done.
___ I feel comfortable and would enjoy using (check any of the following):
- ___ *Audiotapes*
- ___ *Business cards as samples*
- ___ *Compact discs*
- ___ *Demonstrations*
- ___ *Displays*
- ___ *House parties, open houses, and occasion events*
- ___ *Media appearances*
- ___ *Multimedia Web sites*
- ___ *Photos and portfolios*
- ___ *Radio advertising*
- ___ *Having my own radio show*
- ___ *Samples and giveaways*
- ___ *Television - advertising*
- ___ *Having my own television show*
- ___ *Trade shows and special events*
- ___ *Video brochures*

Example: Erica Retallian deals wholesale in wooden music stands handmade in Indonesia. They are beautiful and functional, and they sell themselves when the right people see them. She makes sure they do so by taking a booth each year at the annual Music Educator's National Conference (MENC) in Virginia and at the National Association of Music Merchants (NAMM) event in Los Angeles. These shows put her products in front of important buyers and boost her credibility in her markets.

Hopefully, you now have a list of possible methods to help market your product or service, as well as some ideas for how to use them.

The Time/Money Marketing Continuum

Once you've settled on the most promising marketing tools for your product or service, you need to then decide how much time, money and energy you will put into each one. Until your sales are well under way, you should be willing to spend at least 60 percent of your time and money on marketing. If you don't have any business yet, you should spend your entire week (if possible) *marketing* until the business you generate starts filling your time.

The measure of a successful marketing campaign is the extent to which it reaches at the lowest possible cost the greatest number of people who can and will buy your product or service. Your goal should be to choose marketing methods that will provide you with the easiest and least costly access to the specific people you want to reach.

Every marketing effort takes a certain amount of time and money. For example, networking is a "high-time, low-money" marketing strategy, while traditional advertising is a "low-time, high-cost" marketing strategy. You need to decide where those precious few dollars will go as you promote your product or service.

Here is a comparison of how some of the various methods and tactics from the list relate on **the time/money marketing continuum**:

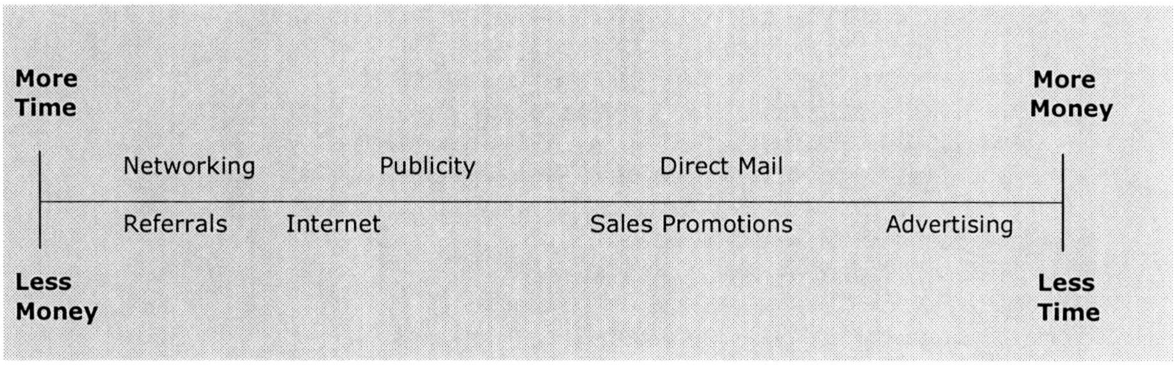

To find the right balance on the time/money continuum, ask yourself:

1. How much business do I need?

2. What can I afford?

3. How much time do I have to invest?

4. How much effort will the activity I undertake require relative to the business it will generate?

5. What will I be motivated to do?

Look at the list below for one hundred possible marketing tactics you can employ. Check the ones that you think would be useful for your marketing campaign

100 Marketing Ideas

Graphical Marketing Tools

❒ Create a Logo that graphically represents my company
❒ Design Stationary including letterhead, envelops, etc.
❒ Design Business cards that communicate your niche
❒ Use Inside signs if my business has a physical location
❒ Use Outside signs if my business has a physical location
❒ Come up with creative Packaging and labels for mailings

❒ Design and display Electronic brochures for digital environments
❒ Develop a general Advertising approach
❒ Use Reprints of favorable media mentions for further promotion

❒ Design Flip charts for instructing clients about your products and services
❒ Take out a Yellow pages ad if appropriate for your company
❒ Conceive a Newsletter that provides useful information while selling your products and services
❒ Design Printed brochures as takeaways or mailings
❒ Write Classified ads for appropriate print or digital media outlets

❒ Design Newspaper display ads for targeted media outlets
❒ Design Magazine display ads for targeted media outlets
❒ Write and send Direct mail letters to your targeted market
❒ Write and send Direct mail postcards to your targeted market

❒ Design a Postcard for postcard deck
❒ Use Outdoor billboards when appropriate
❒ Develop a Fax-on-demand service for inquiries
❒ Show off displays that sell your products and services
❒ Create Audio-visual aids for special presentations
❒ Design Posters
❒ Create an EPK (electronic press kit) for online environments

Internal Marketing Tools

❒ Write a Marketing plan to act as a map that will help you arrive at your business goals

❒ Schedule your goals on a Marketing calendar
❒ Own a Niche and Position your niche in the market
❒ Come up with a catchy, memorable Name for your company
❒ Articulate a unique Identity for your company
❒ Think of a Theme for particular promotions
❒ Provide Hours of operation that meet your customers' needs
❒ Plan Days of operation most serviceable to your clients and customers
❒ Provide Flexibility (e.g. 24 hour service) for maximum customer satisfaction
❒ Develop a Referral program for cross-business promotion
❒ Write Telemarketing scripts for more effective cold calling
❒ Provide Gift certificates
❒ Encourage Word-of-mouth marketing
❒ Develop Community involvement activities to enhance public relations

❒ Show Neatness in both yours and your company's appearance
❒ Provide Guarantees or warranties to alleviate customer reluctance to purchase

❒ Pick a Location that provides easy access to all your customers
❒ Offer Sales training to all staff that need it
❒ Dress in appropriate Attire
❒ Encourage exemplary Service ("going the extra mile")
❒ Follow-up religiously with all initial marketing communications

- ❒ Empower all staff to be marketers
- ❒ Provide a Toll-free phone number
- ❒ Give free gifts that also promote your company (e.g., calendars, pens, etc.)
- ❒ Provide the option of Catalog ordering for your customers
- ❒ Let Speed of delivery, returned phone calls, etc. characterize your company

External Marketing Tools

- ❒ Become involved with a Cause you believe in (e.g. environment, women's issues)
- ❒ Offer free seminars
- ❒ Cross-promote with other businesses (fusion marketing)
- ❒ Write a Column in a publication to position yourself as an expert in your field
- ❒ Write an Article in a publication to further your expert reputation
- ❒ Be a Speaker at a club or organization
- ❒ Mobilize your customers to become a sales force for you
- ❒ Practice good Public relations
- ❒ Develop your Publicity contacts
- ❒ Develop online marketing strategies
- ❒ Conceive and produce a Radio commercial
- ❒ Conceive and produce a TV spot (don't forget inexpensive cable TV)
- ❒ Produce an Infomercial
- ❒ Develop a Movie commercial
- ❒ Produce a Special event
- ❒ Rent or buy targeted mailing lists
- ❒ Develop and nurture your Customer mailing list
- ❒ Put together a Designated street team

Subtle Marketing Tools

- ❒ Practice Sharing with others
- ❒ Make ongoing networking a priority
- ❒ Bring Quality to all you do and offer
- ❒ Provide Opportunities to upgrade your product or service
- ❒ Institute Contests and sweepstakes
- ❒ Conceive and provide Barter options
- ❒ Start a Club with memberships
- ❒ Provide Partial payment plans
- ❒ Practice and maintain a professional Phone demeanor
- ❒ Offer free consultations
- ❒ Offer free demos or tours
- ❒ Offer free samples
- ❒ Use phone on-hold time to communicate your service or product

- ❒ Share past success stories
- ❒ Stress the Benefits of your offering
- ❒ Provide as wide a Selection as possible
- ❒ Give ample Contact time with customers
- ❒ Pay attention to how you say hello and goodbye

- ❒ Emphasize your Competitive advantages
- ❒ Uphold your Reputation
- ❒ Show Enthusiasm (it's contagious)
- ❒ Communicate Credibility
- ❒ Make it easy to do business with you
- ❒ Show Competitiveness
- ❒ Increase your Satisfied customers
- ❒ Use Research studies to support the value of your offerings
- ❒ Seek Marketing insight
- ❒ Gather and use Testimonials
- ❒ Expand Brand name awareness
- ❒ Monitor and assess yourself and those who work for you relentlessly

Building Brand Consciousness & Position

"Style is a word that has no plural." - Auguste Perret, French designer

The first thing you hope will come to someone's mind when they need what you offer is your name or the name of your service, product or company. Major mass-market manufacturers spend millions on developing what is called "brand identity" for their products. As a small or home business, your business name is your brand identity, but of course you probably can't spend millions to make sure it comes to mind. So choose your name wisely.

The word "brand", when used as a noun, can refer to a company name, a product name, or a unique identifier such as a logo or trademark. But branding today is much more than just a company name.

In a time before fences were used in ranching to keep one's cattle separate from other people's cattle, ranch owners branded, or marked, their cattle so they could later identify their herd as their own.

The concept of branding also developed through the practices of craftsmen who wanted to place a mark or identifier on their work without detracting from the beauty of the piece. These craftsmen used their initials, a symbol, or another unique mark to identify their work and they usually put these marks in a low visibility place on the product.

Not too long afterwards, high quality cattle and art became identifiable in consumers' minds by particular symbols and marks. Consumers would actually seek out certain marks because they had associated those marks in their minds with tastier beef, higher quality pottery or furniture, sophisticated artwork, and overall better products. *If the producer differentiated their product as superior in the mind of the consumer, then that producer's mark or brand came to represent superiority.*

Today's modern concept of branding grew out of the consumer packaged goods industry and the process of branding has come to include much, much more than just creating a way to identify a product or company.

Branding today is used to create emotional attachment to products and companies. Branding efforts create a feeling of involvement, a sense of higher quality, and an aura of intangible qualities that surround the brand name, mark, or symbol.

So what exactly is the definition of "brand"? Let's cover some definitions first before we get too far into the branding process.

If you ask ten marketing professionals or brand managers to define the word "brand", you very well may get ten different answers. Most of the answers you receive, hopefully, will at least have some commonalities.

Great Resource!
Branding Glossary

http://www.jaffeassociates.com/Jaffe/GlossaryBranding.php

In my own experience and in my study of brands and branding, there is one definition of "brand" that seems to most succinctly define exactly what a brand is:

A brand is an identifiable entity that makes specific promises of value.

In its simplest form, a brand is nothing more and nothing less than the promises of value you or your product make. These promises can be implied or explicitly stated, but none-the-less, value of some type is promised.

There are some additional terms that go along with branding:

❒ ***Brand image*** is defined as consumers' perceptions *as reflected by the associations they hold in their minds* when they think of your brand.

❒ ***Brand awareness*** is when people recognize your brand as yours.

❒ Brand awareness consists of both ***brand recognition***, which is the ability of consumers to confirm that they have previously been exposed to your brand, and ***brand recall***, which reflects the ability of consumers to name your brand when given the product category, category need, or some other similar cue.

❒ ***Top-of-mind awareness*** occurs when you ask a person to name brands within a product category and your brand pops up first on the list.

Today (mainly because of the Web), branding is *everything*—and I mean everything. Brands are not simply products or services. ***Brands are the sum total of all the images that people have in their heads about a particular company and a particular mark.***

Your goal as a company should be top of the mind awareness based on the delivery of superior and unique service or products. When you hear the marketing term "positioning" think in terms of positioning yourself in *peoples' minds*, not in some external marketplace.

How do you get there? There are many branding strategies, but the one I believe works most effectively is branding through *adding value.*

Building Your Brand Through Adding Value to Existing Products & Services

You add value when you develop a product or service and then add materials, processing or services to create a more valuable end product. You then sell the product in its *value-enhanced* form.

Value may be added by:

- ❒ putting the product through an additional process;
- ❒ combining the product with other products;
- ❒ offering the product as part of a larger package of services;
- ❒ removing something to change the use of the product; or
- ❒ increasing levels of service.

Some examples of adding value include:

1. A student who operated a demo recording business expanded the operation by offering half-day recording seminars and special discounts to clients.

2. A businessman bought large plastic cup lids, licensed CDs, attached them to the lids and marketed them as "LidRocks" at concerts.

3. A music instruction center for kids calls every client's parent to check on the quality of recent lessons (and to promote additional services).

4. A record company creates an appropriate recording or compilation for a tie-in with an environmental organization's benefit project.

5. Here's one from the recent music press: The Marlin Hotel in Miami's South Beach combines a luxury hotel with a state-of-the-art recording studio.

How to add value:

1. Find an existing product or service and think of an additional process, material or service that could be added to create a new product. For example, a product or service may be more successful if an additional element such as packaging or special delivery is added.

2. Identify a process or service which you could provide, then look for types of existing products or services which could be used as a base for your desired operation. For example, provide a compilation CD to an auto dealer to include with all new car sales in a month.

3. Find an existing product which could be changed into a different or improved product by adding or subtracting one or more elements. If additional elements are required, locate a source for these and develop a method of adding them. Conversely, if elements must be subtracted, find a workable way of doing so.

4. Find a customer group which has needs that are not being met by existing products and services. For example, providing iPod owners with a service that loads their CD collections into their players so they don't hav eto spend the time doing it themselves.

5. Find a product which does not work well, or is not well-accepted by a customer group because of its inadequacies. Then improve it by adding or altering elements. For example, adding contact directories to a regional monthly music magazine.

The Power of Linking Up: Discovering Affinity Partnerships

Creative alliances and joint ventures are keys to career and business success today. A joint venture is when two or more businesses come together to work on a project for a set period of time. Well-orchestrated joint ventures can further your chances of increasing sales and profits, save time and money, provide valuable referrals, and increase your market visibility.

Stevan Pasero, discussed earlier in chapter 2, linked up with a marketing expert/ friend and created the executive gift program through which he sold thousands of recordings around the world.

That story illustrates an approach more and more musicians are taking today: to team up with others whose skills complement and enhance their own talents in order to break into an increasingly crowded music marketplace.

Partnering, of course, is nothing new for musical artists. Songwriters collaborate with each other; musicians form "bands" of like-minded players, performers team up with producers, and recording artists sign up with record companies – all in the hope of creating "synergy" where the sum result is greater than the singular parts.

Synergies occur on all levels in the music business. In corporate parlance they have many names: besides joint ventures there're mergers, subsidizations, development deals, limited partnerships, co-ops, and strategic alliances are a few ways they are expressed. Big companies do it all the time in the hope that combining forces will yield new business opportunities. This was behind the Time/Warner merger in 1989, the Viacom/Paramount merger in 1994, and the Disney/ABC and Westinghouse/CBS mergers in 1995. The whole idea here is for media corporations to gather under one umbrella different firms that represent production and distribution interests in a variety of media in order to "cross-fertilize" each other.

Record companies also "merge" in order to acquire additional copyrights, new ideas and hopefully, market share. Sony snatched up CBS Records, BMG purchased both Island and A&M, EMI absorbed Chrysalis and Virgin, Warner Bros. purchased (then sold to MCA) Priority, SubPop and Mammoth, and so on.

There's a lesson in all this for musicians: teaming up can multiply your efforts and move your career in an upward direction more quickly than going at it alone. Traditionally, musicians joined with "professional" teammates like management companies, high-level booking agents and established record labels. This still goes on, but in the DIY era we're increasingly seeing artists and bands avoiding the musical industrial complex altogether and instead finding friends and relatives as viable "partners" in the goal of growing a musical buzz.

The online space, in particular, offers numerous possibilities. Creative alliances can cover anything from trading links to selling one another's products. There are literally thousands of possibilities. Think in terms of what kind of affinity your company's offerings have with others. Here are some suggestions:

❒ The simplest joint venture would be exchanging text links or banners with other related web sites.

❒ Sharing a web site with another business with the same target market. You both will be marketing and advertising the same web site, which means double the traffic. For example, a jazz guitarist can share a web site with a t-shirt company specializing in "jazzy" designs.

❒ Combine your products or services together with another business into one big package. You could split the profits. For example, a general business band can team up with a catering company to offer a package of services for corporate party and event planners.

❒ Do you have a product or service that that you can offer as a free bonus for another business's product or service? For example, a new age artist can offer her CD as a premium to a company that sells aromatherapy products. In exchange ask for a small portion of the profits and/or some advertising space on the company's web site.

Here are some guidelines for developing strong teams and partnerships:

❒ Find someone whose strengths complement your weaknesses and set up a trial period to see if you can work well together. The key is chemistry and chemistry involves experimentation with different combinations of elements until the right formula is found.

❒ Define who will contribute the cash, property, or expertise. Each is needed and each has a value.

❒ Communicate regularly to avoid power grabs and misunderstandings. Talk openly, honestly and relentlessly with your partners. Never let things build up to the point of explosion.

❒ Specify the percentage of ownership each person will have and define how, when, and in what order the profits will be distributed to partners.

❒ Prepare a business plan and financial forecast for the life of the partnership. This provides a map and an agreed-upon route to your goals.

❒ Provide a way to remove or buy out partners who fail to meet their obligations. Shit inevitably happens. People fall in love and leave town, another band snatches your drummer, a job with a steady paycheck becomes just too irresistible – in essence, people change. Prepare for this scenario beforehand and you'll save countless hours of heartache and stress later.

❒ Never forget you're dealing with friends (when this is the case). Don't let the stupid biz stuff and tedium get to you. Stand back from the petty conflicts that inevitably crop up and try to see the big picture."

Lining Up Print & Design Services

Packaging is a message platform to channel your ideas to the consumer fast!. Make your package bold, a "fast storyteller" and reflective of your product's personality. From the moment consumers see your product, your catalog, your envelop, memory connections are built. Consumers have great memories if the imagery you provide is consistent.

Your Graphic Sales Force

The following is a basic inventory of paper and electronic tools you can use for marketing purposes. Not all businesses need all these tools, but it's a good idea to think through which ones you may be using before you make a final decision on an image for your company. You'll want to be sure the look you select is suitable and practical for all possible uses. So, check off from the list below the ones you anticipate using and make it a point to present one coordinated graphic image on them all.

- ❐ Business Cards
- ❐ Letterhead
- ❐ Second Sheets
- ❐ Envelopes
- ❐ Mailing labels
- ❐ Invoices
- ❐ Fax cover sheet
- ❐ Flyers and brochures
- ❐ Samples and giveaways
- ❐ Statements
- ❐ Business checks
- ❐ Trade show booths
- ❐ Product and List Prices
- ❐ Newsletters
- ❐ Presentation packages
- ❐ Press release mastheads
- ❐ Product packaging
- ❐ Point-of-purchase displays
- ❐ Postcards
- ❐ Quote sheets
- ❐ Thank-you notes
- ❐ Service agreements
- ❐ Signs and banners
- ❐ Web page

If for some reason it's not possible, or desirable, for all the elements in your graphic sales force to have an identical look and feel, select compatible alternatives that are as consistent as possible with your chosen graphic image.

Practical Tips On Working With Graphic Artists

Professionally designed printed materials create a successful image, but it doesn't come cheap. One way to make this more affordable is to seek out an art student whose style you like and se if you can work out a mutually profitable exchange. Some tips:

1. ***Know your budget.*** Request written estimates from designers you interview for a particular project (allowing a plus or minus 10% variation). Printing can be complicated and mistakes expensive. If you are unfamiliar with the process, have the artist check blue lines (the equivalent of photo proofs) and handle the press check (verification of colors and alignment as the piece comes off the press).

2. ***Screen artists carefully.*** Ask around for referrals and check the Yellow Pages under "Graphic Designers." Meet with three artists to review their portfolios, but discuss your budget with them on the phone beforehand. Though perhaps awkward, it will save both of you time and frustration if your financial expectations are worlds apart. Ask to see samples relevant to your planned project and make sure the artist was responsible for these samples from concept to execution.

3. ***Give the artist creative freedom.*** Carefully describe the audience you want to reach and the message you want to impart. Show your artist design samples you like then let him or her create. Establish checkpoints along the way so no one is running off in the wrong direction.

TOP 10 GRAPHICS TIPS FOR DESIGNING CDS

1. **Reducing** is good, enlarging is bad
2. **Placement** is everything. Balance and use of space is critical
3. **Choose fonts** with your image in mind
4. **Don't use** more than 3 fonts total in any given design
5. **Use easy** to read fonts that distinguish clearly your name from any product title.
6. **Choose colors** carefully, make sure lettering on colors is easily readable
7. **Work creatively** within your budget, and keep things simple
8. **Put a barcode** on the back cover all recordings intended for retail sales
9. **Use a graphic** artist with CD/Tape design experience.
10. Put artist/band name on the **top 1/3rd of any CDs** or records

4. ***Perfect means professional.*** Proofread! One proofreading tip that works: Hold a ruler under each line as you read. The ruler focuses your eyes on one line at a time and greatly improves your chances of catching errors.

5. ***Approve the design in the early stages.*** Be sure to ask your designer for "comps" before a job is done. Comps are true-to-life renderings of a finished piece. They're usually not cheap but well worth the cost.

6. ***Observe deadlines.*** Give you and your designer enough lead time. Never assign a job without a deadline.

7. ***Pay as you go.*** Never pay an artist the entire amount up front. It's fair to pay one-third at the start, one-third midway through a job, and one third upon completion and delivery. Your contract with an artist is a business agreement. Let mutual respect and fairness prevail.

Great Resource!
Print/Graphics Glossary

http://www.jaffeassociates.com/Jaffe/GlossaryPrint.php

Elements of Online Style

With the growing popularity of online music distribution, there is a massive shift taking place in the world of music packaging and design. Record companies, for example, aren't interested in design in the way they were before. "I'm not sure how valid online artwork will be in the long term," offers James Burton, production manager at Warp Records. "We find that when the music goes online people download what they want (that is, the music). Occasionally, you'll get people who'll see the value of having a well-designed package in the hand, but for others the artwork really doesn't matter," (*Design Week,* 3/4/04).

Burton believes a key way to achieve differentiation in your market is to build a band's brand identity through symbols primarily, allowing a band's meaning to be channelled through a small space.

"Logo design is important. Aphex Twin and Plaid have a logo and this will become very important in the future because as music moves increasingly online you're going to have to separate yourself from other musicians. This will be about distilling ideas into a very small space on a screen, making your MP3 look different," says Burton.

Although MP3 culture is growing, it is part of music consumers' format choice, rather than a replacement for CDs and vinyl. The designers applying themselves to MP3s are seeing this as a new challenge, rich with opportunities, not one that cannibalizes existing music package design.

Creating a Marketing Budget With What You've Got

Say you have $1000 reserved for your marketing campaign. How are you going to spend it?

The answer, of course, depends on many factors, including the size, age, industry and target market of your business. While no rules of thumb exist for marketing all businesses, the following is intended to give you ideas on how to determine the optimal marketing budget. The goal here is for you to think through the best methods to effectively reach your target audience for the least amount of money. See how Evie Eclectic used her money to work out a marketing budget in the Case Study at the send of this section.

A common method of establishing your budget is to estimate what your competitors are spending and then try to match it. You do this by monitoring the ads they place, the promotions they mount, and the special events they sponsor. Not a precise method, but it does provide you with a "ball park" estimate. You must be careful if you do this, not to simply copy what may be the ineffective spending habits of other businesses. Use an estimate of your competitor's promotional budget more as a guide than as a rule.

The more precise way to determine your budget is to first assemble a list of the marketing methods you would like to use to meet your objectives. Draw these methods from the 100 Marketing Tools list from earlier in this chapter. Then, based on actual rates for print and broadcast advertisements and estimated costs for sales promotion and publicity, assign each activity a dollar value. Assess your list and begin scaling it down until you have a reasonable budget that falls within the $1000 range.

You will need to do some research in your local area to find out, for example, how much a classified ad costs in your daily newspaper, or a display ad in your local music magazine. Depending on your mix of methods, you'll want to check out the costs associated with promoting at a music conference or designing a banner ad for a targeted web site. Your local reference librarian can point you to all kinds of advertising rate information.

Remember, airing television and national print advertising may not be the best options for you at this time. It is better to implement a variety of techniques rather than spend your promotional dollars on *one* type of promotion. Why? Because promotion isn't a science. It may take you several months to a few years to discover the most effective mix established for your company. You will constantly need to evaluate how you are allocating your budget and make adjustments as you go along.

Once you begin generating increased sales you can increase your promotional budget. Don't be afraid to start small - just remember to be consistent. Consistency will become a major factor in how successful your promotional efforts will be.

Establishing an effective promotional mix will not be effective, however, when resources are allocated only from time to time. For your marketing message to be received and eventually acted upon, marketing must occur on a regular basis. Consumers rarely take immediate action and have to be reminded of your message again and again, before they will be moved into action. To do this, you must make a commitment of your resources and this should be reflected in your budget.

Here's a case study to help give flesh to these ideas:

CASE STUDY: Evie Eclectic recently produced a recording that falls within the New Age genre. She also has a keen interest in music therapy and the power of music to both raise consciousness and provide healing. As Evie ponders the Time/Money Marketing Continuum and the 100 Offline Marketing Tools list, she accepts the fact that she only has about $700 she can put towards marketing right now.

She considers the possibilities within this small budget:

• PHASE ONE: Evie brainstorms on the different kinds of outlets she can sell her recording in. She realizes she can direct-sell her CD to fans, family, friends, new age music lovers, body workers, and libraries.

To do so she will have to:

- ❐ write out a basic CD marketing plan
- ❐ design and test-mail 100 targeted one-sheets about the CD to regional body workers and libraries
- ❐ come up with various length descriptions about the CD for different occasions
- ❐ evaluate distributors she will pursue and/or figure out how she will distribute the product independently
- ❐ throw a new release party at the large home of a fan where she performs pieces from the CD

Associated costs: mainly time, except for postage and envelopes, copying ($5) and food/drink for the party ($200).

TOTAL COSTS SO FAR:	$245.
BALANCE:	($455.)

• PHASE TWO: Evie develops and offers a free 2-hour workshop on vibrational sound healing. She hopes to use these freebies as testing grounds for more developed seminars later and as springboards for developing school programs, as well as an outlet for selling hers' and others' recordings.

To do so she will have to:

- ❐ see what kind of competition there in this area
- ❐ develop the workshop
- ❐ secure a space in which to hold the workshop
- ❐ get the word out through targeted media

Evie does some research and decides it is cost-prohibitive to rent out a space for a workshop. She begins brainstorming on possible partners. She decides to team up with a continuing education organization and offers her course through its own catalog of offerings. The organization also assumes the responsibility for publicizing the event. Now space and advertising requirements are met. Evie does, however, need to attend other similar workshops in order to know how to differentiate her workshops from others. She decides to attend two other workshops she reads about on the Internet. Both are being offered in a nearby city and are relatively inexpensive. She studies the way the workshops are described, and reads the brief biographies of the workshop leaders, as well as the testimonies of people who attended previous workshops.

TOTAL PHASE TWO COSTS: $100.
BALANCE: ($355.)

- PHASE THREE: Evie decides to use the remaining balance to:

  ❒ design and print both letterhead and business cards for her fledgling company, and

  ❒ purchase a software program to enable her to develop a web site.

These will help her make a creative and professional impression in all her communications. Since professional graphic artists are very expensive, she uses the graphic tools in her word processing program to experiment with different design elements for the letterhead. When she settles on one she likes, she takes a crisp hard-copy master to her local printer who shows her the many kinds of paper she can choose to print the letterhead on. She picks one and has 250 sheets printed.

For her business cards she visits Vista Print (http://www.vistaprint.com) online to try out some business card designs. This company offers the first 250 cards for free, except shipping.

Evie has a brother who offers to help her out when it's time to design her web site. She bought a software program he recommended to help her map out the basic elements of her site.

TOTAL PHASE THREE COSTS: $120.
BALANCE: ($215.)

As you can see, through creative planning, linking up with others and frugal shopping, Evie was able to accomplish a lot with her $700 and still have money left over.

TAX TIP: HOW TO DEDUCT UNSOLD INVENTORY

Did you press 1000 and sell only 200?
Unsold inventory of CDs, tapes, sheet music, instruments, and related products can be worth a federal income tax deduction when a business donates them to charity. Regular (C) corporations may deduct the cost of the inventory donated, plus half the difference between cost and fair market value. In other words, deductions may be up to twice cost. S corporations, partnerships, and sole proprietorships earn a straight cost deduction.

A free guide is available that includes step-by-step instructions on the donation process, as well as a formula for calculating your company's potential tax savings. To receive a copy, call the nonprofit National Association for the Exchange of Industrial Resources: 800-562-0955, or visit its website at http://www.naeir.org

Marketing Wisely

Here are some summary tips to help you in all your market planning.

❐ **Find time to strategize** - Set aside time each week to think about new ideas and initiatives for your company. Brainstorm with your staff or other business associates. Read business publications, visit websites or go for a walk. By challenging your mind and getting out of the daily routine, you will probably come up with creative approaches and new ways to solve problems, capture customers or just bring a better quality of life to your business.

❐ **Stay focused** - Know what you want, choose how you are going to get there and don't allow yourself to be distracted. Share your vision with your team and encourage them to adopt it as their own. Make sure you understand their role and the benefits they'll enjoy through their efforts.

❐ **Market in new media and keep the old** - Take the time to learn how to really use web technology and learn the deeper features of your most used software programs. Technology gives you the reach and efficiencies of a larger company. Remember, as you add new media to your marketing mix, don't abandon traditionally effective tools. One message delivered in multiple ways can grab the attention of customers and potential clients.

❐ **"Fusion" marketing is the name of the game** - Partner with affinity companies so that you can share information, clients and opportunities. For example, if you run a booking agency, think about cross-marketing with a wedding planner, a caterer or tourism bureau. Link to each other's websites and explore ways to market in traditional media as well. You'll increase the service and excitement you currently offer your customers. Build those relationships to build your business.

❐ **Stay abreast of the news** - Take the time to read newspapers, magazines and visit news and information sites on the Internet. Information is power and can positively affect your business by helping you to provide value to your customers, inspiring new ideas and leading to prospects. See "General Industry & News Reference" in chapter 17 for some resources to hep with this.

One piece of marketing that isn't discussed in this book is setting up your company as a legitimate business entity. That topic is thoroughly covered in my book, ***INDIE POWER: A Business-Building Guide for Record Labels, Music Production Houses, and Merchant Musicians***. Check it at: http://www.mbsolutions.com/books

CH 5

PUTTING YOUR ONLINE MARKETING TOOLS TO WORK

"Music can be made anywhere, is invisible and does not smell." - W.H. Auden

The Internet will easily be your best marketing tool as an indie artist or company, so get ready for another full chapter of insights and strategies to help boost you towards success.

Digital Democracy & Info Empowerment

With the Internet, the information explosion of the past few decades has finally found a technological partner. Entertainment conglomerates and arts-grant bureaucrats still hold the strings to attractively fat purses. But their power is being tempered by the reach of the Internet and the resourcefulness of creative minds paired with cheap, versatile tools.

Publishing in all its forms has been revolutionized by the Net. It's often been said that "freedom of the press belongs to those who own one." The Net enables *everyone* to own the press. Rather than competing with other media outlets for the public's attention, the media is suddenly competing with the *public itself.* Individuals can decide *on their own* what's important and what's not, set up their own information "filters" (rather than rely on the editorial judgment of faceless media conglomerates), and get closer to sources of information than ever before.

This potentially seismic shift isn't just limited to how works are created. Already, digital technology has caused sweeping changes in how people gain access to creative works.

Music downloads are the most prominent example, but the growth of broadband Internet has also made it possible to distribute everything from books to digital artworks online. It's not a surprise that so many competitive groups have entered the market given the fact that online music shopping has taken off.

Music has certainly played a key role in this space. Reported music subscription sales are expected to grow from $313 million last year to $890 million in 2009, while individual digital downloads are anticipated to reach $1.7 billion is 2009 (Jupiter Research), compared to $358 million in 2005. Warp Records and NinjaTune are two UK independent labels whose online sales campaigns are so effective that more units are sold through their websites worldwide than from their entire UK retail distribution!

Independent musicians have long turned to the Internet in their struggle for recognition outside traditional industry channels such as radio and MTV. Now, in the wake of the dot-com bust, many are discovering that savvy online marketing may never catapult them to stardom – but it *can* give their careers an important lift. I recently read a story of how Death Cab for Cutie's Ben Gibbard discovered an artist named Devin Davis on a site called *Music for Robots* (http://www.music-for-robots.com). He dug Davis's music and began an email correspondence, which eventually led to Gibbard inviting Davis to open a show for his band. Serendipity.

You never know who is watching or who is listening on the Net.

BTW, see chapter 10 for an exploration of Internet Radio and its potential for promotion

The Internet and the 'Long Tail' Market

Outfits that have sprung up to peddle creative works on the internet – whether just through online ordering or through actual electronic delivery – have discovered something surprising: A major portion of sales go to obscure, niche works that were difficult or impossible to find before the advent of the Web and its unlimited "shelf space."

The theory of the Long Tail is that our culture and economy is increasingly shifting away from a focus on a relatively small number of "hits" (mainstream products and markets) at the head of the demand curve and toward a huge number of niches in the tail. As the costs of production and distribution fall, especially online, there is now less need to lump products and consumers into one-size-fits-all containers. In an era without the constraints of physical shelf space and other bottlenecks of distribution, narrowly-targeted goods and services can be economically attractive as mainstream fare.

This phenomenon shows consumers' increasing power to bypass hyped-up hits and follow their own tastes. It also promises more financial support for artists working on the fringes.

For a great article on this Long-Tail phenomenon and how it relates to music, check out: http://www.wired.com/wired/archive/12.10/tail_pr.html.
The author's ongoing blog covering the Long Tail can be found at: http://longtail.typepad.com/the_long_tail/

Designing & Promoting Your Web Presence

The biggest pitfall facing new online marketers is inexperience in both web design and layout and lack of marketing experience. As over 100 years of marketing trial and error has proven, bad or poorly designed sales copy *does not sell*. Even the best product with lousy copy will do worse than a terrible product with outstanding sales copy.

The first thing you need is a web site, a multimedia representation of who you are. Your Web site construction costs can range from free to well over $10,000, depending on the information included, the complexity of the design and who does the actual coding of your site.

There are plenty of web designers for hire and costs are far-flung. But if you're a band on a shoestring budget, and nobody in the band feels ready to tackle HTML, you're going to have to find an economical solution. One idea is to tap into the talent of your fans. See if there is someone on your mailing list who would like to help you create your band's site in exchange for a lifetime free pass to your shows and copies of your CDs. Or, look into art schools with New Media Design or Computer Graphics programs. Students in these programs are often looking for opportunities to grow their portfolios. For a quicker solution tap Craig's List (http://www.craigslist.com), an international collection of local community classifieds and forums.

The Basics of Web Site Design

But let's say you decided to go it alone and design your own Web site. Besides the web development sites listed in chapter 17, here is a primer on the basic requirements for effective web site design. Here's what you'll need:

- ***A computer and a modem.*** Minimally, use a Pentium II or PowerMac with at least a 56 Kbps (kilobytes per second) modem. Anything less powerful can make cruising the Web and downloading data feel more like creeping in rush-hour traffic. The newer cable modems and DSL (digital subscriber line) are *very* fast so consider these more expensive options too.

- ***An HTML editor.*** A top-notch HTML (hypertext markup language) editor will give personality to the text of your Web page. HTML is essentially plain ASCII text with embedded codes that enable you to create links, fill-in forms and clickable images – all elements of a great Web page. More on this in a moment.

- ***A Web Browser.*** Almost any browser will do – Netscape's "Navigator", Microsoft's "Explorer", Apple's "Safari" – even the ones built into one of the commercial online services, such as AOL or CompuServe. The only requirement is that the browser includes an option that allows you to view files stored on your computer's hard drive before you add them to your Web pages.

• ***Graphics software.*** If you want your Web page to get noticed, it has to have attractive graphics. You'll either have to create them yourself or find a good clip art program. Many of these come on CD-ROMS and are in the public domain so you won't need to obtain permission in order to use them. Another good, fee-based online source is http://clipart.com. You'll also need a graphics converter program, such as HiJaak Pro, to convert images you've created into GIF and JPEG formats that Web browsers use.

• ***A PPP or SLIP connection and server space.*** A PPP or SLIP is your connection to the Internet's World Wide Web. You can obtain a SLIP or PPP connection through an Internet service provider, such as Earthlink, Netcom, or AOL. This is the most expensive part of setting up your Web page, so shop around. These can also provide server space for your home page once it's created. They thus become the "host" to you, the "client". Search out and critique potential hosts using http://www.budgetweb.com. See below (*"Finding a Host for Your Site")* for more information on site hosting.

• ***Master of your own domain.*** You also want to obtain your own domain name, such as www.MyCoolBand.com. It may cost you $70 for the first two years and $35 per year thereafter (though there are cheaper, less reliable options), which is chump change, so I highly recommend it. Pick a domain name that you can yell into the mic at the end of a set, or tell all your drunken fans, and have a good chance that they will be able to remember it the next day. Also use the nifty look-up feature at http://www.internic.net to verify that nobody else has taken your domain name.

Do not mistakenly go to www.internic.*com*, who will cheerfully charge you $200 so you can fill out the same form on their site, which they automatically forward to www.internic.*net* with $75. Their profit: $125. They are raking in the dough from the uninformed, so beware. An even easier service is provided by http://register.com, and if money is a big issue, check out http://godaddy.com.

New Domain Names Ease Congestion

The Internet Corporation for Assigned Names and Numbers (ICANN), which manages the domain name system, opened up seven new top-level domains (TLDs) towards the end of 2001.

So, in addition to the familiar *.com, .org, .net, .edu* and. *mil,* you're starting to also see:

- .info for general use
- .biz for businesses
- .pro for professionals, such as physicians and lawyers
- .aero for the aviation industry
- .museum for, well, museums
- .name for individuals
- .coop for business cooperatives

• ***Finding a Host for Your Site.*** You can have your site hosted for free on services like Yahoo! Geocities (http://www.geocities.yahoo.com) or FreeServers (http://www.freeservers.com), but you won't get your own domain name. Instead, your name will be tagged onto the host's domain name (e.g., http://www.freeservers.com/MyCoolBand.html). This is due to the extra maintenance of unique domain names on a server. Another option is to pick a hosting company and pay them to host your domain. Fees range from $10/month up to $500/month, and it is not the case that higher-priced hosts are always better. You just have to do a lot of homework to figure out who's good. $25-40 /month is about average. CDBaby also offers hosting through its service HostBaby.net for $20/month and includes a suite of web design tools for web site creation.

One good way to find inexpensive providers is to use http://www.budgetweb.com. It also provides all sorts of other criteria to help narrow your search. A feature you definitely want on your site is RealAudio and/or MP3 streaming so that your music files can be heard. Visit each of the suggested hosts and verify their price. Pay careful attention to the different "packages" they offer, since some of the low-end packages won't actually have all of the features you asked for. Also, see if they have any music clients. Check out their web site and verify that their music servers are not dog-slow. Contact these clients, and find out how satisfied they are with the host. Ask: Is the customer service efficient? Is tech support available? Have there been any breakdowns and for how long?

• ***Other Features & Resources.*** There is a lot of help out there for amateur web page designers. Keeping updated on the cool tips and tricks requires a little more effort, but you can learn a lot by seeing what other Webmasters are doing on their pages. Getting involved in message boards and forums, or utilizing the resources mentioned in Webmonkey (http://www.webmonkey.com/) will also go a long way toward helping you keep up with developments in HTML authoring.

DIY Web Design. If you've been hesitating setting up a web site because learning HTML is about as attractive as sticking your head in a beehive, take heart! The past few years have seen a flood of "HTML Editors" come to market and their target market is *you*. No need to learn HTML coding or any of the other cryptic formatting commands early web authoring demanded. If you can handle word processing, you can now author your own web pages including graphics, audio and even video. Drag-and-drop commands and WYSIWYG (what you see is what you get) interfaces go a long way toward making web design a snap. Some are "freeware" (like "Page Spinner"); others are packaged by software companies (Claris "HomePage", Adobe "PageMill", Microsoft "FrontPage", etc.). Any of these programs will do the job, and for well under $100. So what are you waiting for?

There are also free templates and utilities designed to help musicians create a web site. Two of the best are bandzoogle.com and hostbaby.com. Check them out!

Adding Sound. You'll want to include "sound files" of your songs on your web page. There are two ways to deliver music on the Web. The first is to make your song into a downloadable file. There are four file types: wav, aiff, au, and MPEG3 (aka as, MP3). The sound quality for all file types is decent, with MP3 being practically CD quality. To convert your music to one of these types of files, use CoolEdit (http://www.syntrillium.com) or Sound Forge XP (http://www.sonicfoundry.com). The downside is the user has to wait to download the file, which can sometimes take a while.

INDUSTRY FACT:

Radiohead made its whole album available for streaming two months before its official release and it still achieved higher than expected record sales.

To avoid making the user wait, you can "stream" your audio by using software like RealAudio, QuickTime3, LiquidAudio, or Netshow. The sound quality will suffer slightly but the music starts to play at the click of a button, so it's a sacrifice a lot of Web site owners are willing to make. Having *both* a streaming *and* a download option is probably the smartest approach. For further information on constructing a killer web site, see chapter 17 for a list of online Web Site Development Tools.

Once you've finished your masterpiece, you'll then need to transfer the files you created to your host's Web server. This usually means that your host opens an account on its file server for you. Then you use the Internet "ftp" (file transfer protocol) function to upload your home-page files to the Internet provider's computer. *Voila.* Your home page lives.

You can also put your home page on other servers as well. The benefits of going with a commercial music site provider (like garageband.com, for instance) are many: you get a built-in music-loving audience, Web design expertise, in-house familiarity with the online music market, and relatively inexpensive disk storage space for your data and sounds.

A Dozen Design Tips for Creating Great Web Pages

With these foundations in place, you can now design your killer web site.

1) ***Get organized.*** Start visualizing your Web page before you ever turn on the computer. Think about what you want to put on your home page, what you want the reader to get out of it, how the information will relate, and how you want everything to look. Some Web experts recommend creating a storyboard or flowchart - small sketches of each page in outline form - before you start writing. I like to use the "journey" metaphor when designing. Take your visitor on a journey into your story.

2) ***Take a look at other web sites.*** No sense reinventing the wheel. Check out which sites you like the best, put them in your favorites file, and then study them. What features make the site easy for you to use? What content appeals to you? What designs do you like best? Select the best elements of your favorite sites and incorporate those features into your own site.

3) ***Add value.*** Don't waste people's time with a page that provides only a list of links to other Web sites, unless, of course, that is your purpose. You should think about providing content that is of value to your site visitors. For example, if you're an avid blues lover and want to create a Web page on the subject, tell visitors where the best blues clubs are in your area and provide directions. *Pull* people in with useful information.

4) ***Keep it simple.*** The home page is to the rest of your Web site as a book's cover is to its contents or as the front door is to a place of business. The design should

be bold and understandable at a glance. Don't clutter it up with unnecessary details or over-complicated layouts.

5) ***Get visual.*** Use imaginative layouts and good-looking typography to give your Web pages a unique and identifiable look. Graphical content should be of some practical value. Avoid empty window dressing. To save time, many users set their browsers to ignore graphics; all they see is text. It's essential that any important messages or links contained in graphics be duplicated in textual form. Test-drive your page in text-only mode to make sure it works. You may also consider creating a "text only" version for visitors who prefer this option.

6) ***Observe limitations.*** Many people have "technologically challenged" hardware. The World Wide Web becomes the World Wide Wait when huge graphics or audio files are downloaded for viewing. Keep graphics to no more than 50k and your site will be a delight to visit.

7) ***Make it easy to navigate.*** One of the home page's primary roles is as a navigational tool, pointing people to information stored on your Web site or elsewhere. Make this function as effortless as possible. Also, don't bury information too deep in the page hierarchy. Stepping through five or more links can get pretty tedious. Finally, don't leave your visitors looking for bread crumbs to find their way to you. Provide a clear e-mail gateway so people can contact you if they wish.

8) ***Include the essentials.*** Here are a few things most every home page should have: a header that identifies your Web site clearly and unmistakably, an e-mail address for communicating and reporting problems, copyright information as it applies to online content, and contact information, such as mailing address and phone number.

9) ***Make it fun***. What causes people to come back for return visits? According to IntelliQuest, 56% return to entertaining sites, 54% like attention grabbing sites, 53% extremely useful content, 45% information tailored to their needs, 39% imaginative sites, and 36% highly interactive sites.

10) ***Be sure to title your home page*** with a headline that will attract the most viewers to your web site. Many search engines use the title as one of their main ways of selecting sites to show to requesters. The first paragraph of text after your title is also often used by search engines to rank listings, so be sure your first paragraph contains key words about the contents of your site. As a matter of practice, you should add proper titles to the rest of your pages as well. Follow the same basic principles for all your pages.

11) ***Visit Dr. HTML*** (*http://www2.imagiware.com/RxHTML*) for a free testing service that will test a single URL and report back to you on spelling, form structure, link verification, and other aspects of your web page. Your entire site can be checked for a fee. That will cost about $25 per 50 pages, which is a good deal.

12) ***Keep it fresh.*** Visitors could get jaded if your Web site never changes. Encourage return visits by giving them something new to look forward to. Include your Web site in your established publicity program, so that new information (such as press releases), appears concurrently on your Web pages.

There are certain things you can do in the design phase of your web site that will help to maximize its visibility to Web surfers and searchers. Be sure to read about these in the section of this chapter titled, "Advanced Marketing Techniques" so that they can be incorporated into your site design.

See chapter 6 for some powerful ways to make your web site more interactive.

SPECIAL CONSULT

For those who already have a web site --
Web Site Tune-Up: Improving Your Website for Optimal Performance

Those who already have a web site will want to constantly improve it. Below is a procedure for rating the functionality of a web site. It is a good starting point for recommending design changes, marketing advice and overall improvements for the performance of web sites.

1. Rate overall web site design and functionality:

View web site, going through several pages, looking for:

__ An immediate understanding of what the site is about.
__ Aesthetically pleasing design.
__ Consistency in design.
__ Interesting content.
__ Ease of use / navigation.
__ Check spelling.
__ Check keyword incorporation in text on page.
__ Open all links to check validity, mail to, graphics and URLs.
__ Navigation links to other pages of information within the site.
__ Fast-loading pages.
__ Hyperlinks should be 'above the fold,' meaning visitors should not have to scroll through boring ad copy before they find a link to more information with in the web site.

2. Check site traffic:

__ View web site stats, if available (ask your server-host about these).
__ Check site with Alexa to see if it has been rated, approximate traffic, and number of pages. Alexa is a free web utility that provides info about web sites including popularity, number of pages, freshness of content and related web sites. It is available free at http://www.alexa.com. You may need to upgrade your browser for optimal performance.

3. Check site ranking:

__ Go to http://www.aadsoft.com/agentwebranking/ranks.htm, do a free position check by keyword and URL.

4. Web site check:

__ Run free web site check at WebSAT (http://zing.ncsl.nist.gov/WebTools/)
__ Print summary report and analyze.
__ Print specific problem areas.

Here are some typical problems, and some solutions:

❒ Browser Compatibility - Recommend redesign and checking the site in several different browsers. A free utility is available at http://www.anybrowser.com
❒ Register It Readiness (Meta Tags) - Recommend addition of meta tags and/or modifications of the existing tags.
❒ Load Time - Recommend less graphics or compression of gifs and jpegs.
❒ Dead Links - Recommend freshening of the content of the pages, getting rid of stale or dated content.
❒ Link Popularity - Recommend reciprocal linking.
❒ Spelling -Get a spell checker or hire a new webmaster that can spell
❒ HTML Design -If you are using a WYSIWYG editor and haven't learned HTML and call yourself a web site designer then I have no sympathy for you. Learn HTML or hire a programmer that can write and read code from scratch!

__ View source of the page to see if meta description and keywords have been included in the header of the document.
__ View source on several pages to see if keywords are coded with in the site and if keywords are unique for each page of the web site. Check page titles for uniqueness and incorporation of keywords and key phrases within the title.

Remember your visitors are coming in with different browsers, computers, platforms and modem speeds. You can't please everyone, but you have literally a few seconds to make your impression. Professional design, fast loading pages and interesting content can mean the difference between a visitor that clicks and one that clicks away.

Branching Out Into Ecommerce

Determining the Purpose of Your Site

A fundamental question to answer before you create your Internet strategy is: what is the purpose of my web site? Here is a detailed list of the possibilities. Not every feature or function will apply to your particular business. Go through it and note those you'd like to implement in your own web site. Many of these features will be part of your overall site design, so be sure to work through these ideas first, *before* designing you site.

Selling

- Online store
- Customer access to online catalogs, with changing prices, features, and details; information constantly updated
- Online order taking
- Inexpensive communication with new potential customers, worldwide
- Electronic distribution of software, publications, and music
- Guidance to potential purchasers
- Open communication channels
- Avoidance of purchase orders for continuously supplied goods
- Contact with more customers; enhanced telesales capability

Product Design

- Better knowledge of available components and of vendors' information, worldwide
- Knowledge of low-cost facilities in distant countries
- Links to suppliers for joint design
- Access to remote knowledge sources
- Ability to search for information, worldwide
- Literature searches; vast amounts of literature accessible online
- Knowledge interchange with communities of common interest

Marketing

- "Micromarketing" linked to individual requirements, tastes, and profiles
- Fast user community feedback: product reviews, information about problems, suggestions and concerns, worldwide
- Data for market research; knowledge of related products
- Knowledge of customer wishes
- Continuous forecast of sales from dealers; worldwide facilities; better production planning; less inventory stockpiles.

Support to Customers

- Online guidance to users
- Faster problem resolution
- Fast access to expertise
- Customer newsletters, online
- User community interchange of product knowledge and guidance on product use
- Online answers to frequently asked questions (FAQs)
- Customer tracking of orders and delivery

Manufacturing

- Better selection of suppliers; identification of low-cost components, worldwide
- Direct communications with suppliers
- Online forecasts and tracking to lower inventory
- User-group discussions of problems and solutions

Expertise

- Membership of special-interest communities
- Communication of specialist knowledge; spreading of knowledge
- Exchange of experience
- Ability to search for relevant experience, literature, data, or technology

Human Resources

- Electronic resumes
- Access to many education resources; self-education
- Knowledge of job opportunities within your company
- Empowerment of employees
- Use of remote contract employees (virtual teams)

General Administration

- Company wide e-mail
- Savings in telecommunications cost for some operations (shared lines, fast message relay, fewer phone calls, worldwide e-mail the same cost as local e-mail)
- Flexible work arrangements, virtual offices, telecommuting, and location-independent work
- Connectivity of diverse hardware, software, and networks
- Electronic money transfer (using PayPal or similar high-security interaction)
- Closer, fast-response, links to business partners; greater diversity of business partners, worldwide
- Use of education and training facilities on the Internet (including CD-ROMs with Internet access)

Value Streams in General

- Small, empowered teams with access to the resources they need; teams that are smaller, self-sufficient, less dependent on other departments
- Virtual operations (virtual corporation) in which external resources are used as though they were internal
- Value-stream teams that are scattered geographically
- Access to specialized expertise, bulletin boards, and remote computers
- Direct contact with value-stream customers
- Instant response to value-stream customers or users

Practice Good NETiquette

Message boards, forums and mailing lists are very sensitive about blatant self-promotion so you need to tread carefully here. The quickest way to make a bad name for yourself on the Net is to send obnoxious e-mail or news. This is called "spamming" the Net and usually results in being "flamed" (being sent nasty or insulting messages for your violation of "cybermanners"). So mind your netiquette. Here are some good ways to do this:

- Before posting a message, make sure your post has a point to make. If you do not have a point, there is no need to post because it will waste other people's time, bandwidth, and disk space. Also, when responding to a message, if you include a copy of the original message, trim it down to the minimum needed. Again, no sense wasting bandwidth.

- Know the difference between the address you use to get on or off a mailing list and the address you use to send messages to the list itself. ***(con't.)***

• Read a mailing list or newsgroup for at least a week before you try to send anything to it so that you understand what topics it covers and grasp the level of discussion.

• Most lists and groups have an introductory message, and most newsgroups periodically post FAQ (frequently asked questions) messages that introduce the topic and answer the most common questions. Before sending in your question, make sure it's not already answered for you.

• If you are arguing with someone on Usenet, keep to the facts and avoid personal insults. If you are angry, wait until you cool down to post your response (it may even be a few days). If you cannot cool down and must send something, do it in e-mail and keep it private instead of using Usenet.

• Include a short signature file that contains at least your name and your email address. You can also include a brief "marketing" sentence about your music or company, like "Organically-grown electro-acoustic improv" or "The Best in Audio Mastering".

See http://usenet.com or http://groups.google.com

The Nuts and Bolts of Ecommerce

Whether your e-commerce operation involves selling an entire catalog of items, a small collection of goods or even just one product, the simple reality is that unless people buy the items for sale on your Web site, you won't make any money.

And while the last few years have done a lot to make consumers more comfortable with the idea of shopping online, a significant effort is still necessary, on your part, to convince potential customers that they will be doing business with a secure and trustworthy operation.

Because you'll have to employ some form of remote payment, you'll need to do business with some type of transaction-processing business. Even more than your customers, your billing solution partners will demand some assurance that your operation is secure before they involve themselves in your transactions.

To put it simply, in the e-commerce business, securing trust in your company is essential to your success. Trust is as important to a potential customer's purchasing decision as the products you offer. And an essential element of building that trust, with both customers and partners, is the assurance that your e-commerce operation meets the demanding security standards required of organizations handling sensitive financial data.

How Web Page Traffic Is Measured

There are several ways to measure traffic to a Web site, including hits, impressions on page views, and click-through. While each of these terms describes a way to measure the number of visits to a site, there are significant differences in what they measure.

Hits

Each Web page is really a document made up of various elements that might include text, graphics, sound, animation, and even video. Each of these different elements is stored in a separate file. Every time someone visits the site all the files that compose the page are sent and each of these files counts as a hit. So, for example, if a Web page that consists of two graphic files, a text file, and the instruction file for how to put it all together is accessed, that page would be counted as four "hits". The server is aware of how many times it sends out each element and keeps a count, which is easily accessible and usually provided without charge to the Web page owner by the ISP.

Impressions or Page Views

Another way to measure Web site traffic is to count "impressions" or "page views." Each time all the elements of a Web page are transmitted to a user, that counts as a single "impression" or "page view." Obviously, tracking page views or impressions is a little tougher than simply tracking hits because you have to correlate the information about each page more carefully. But it more clearly reflects the actual number of visits to a site.

Click-Throughs

Web pages can and should be designed so the visitor can select another Web page or Web site from the page he or she is currently viewing. This is called a "link." The number of times a visitor clicks on the links on the Web site is called a click-through. Click-through numbers are considered the most valuable way to measure Web site traffic because they are seen as active requests for material and therefore show more involvement on the part of the person visiting the site. Click-throughs tell you, for example, which pages of your site are most popular, etc.

Setting up an Online Store

A big part of building trust with your customers is your presentation. That they're even browsing your online store is a good indicator that they're familiar with the possibilities of online shopping and are prepared to consider buying. What you do to convince them, and the effectiveness of your efforts, may be the deciding factor in a possible sale.

The shopping interface you introduce to customers is arguably the most important piece of your e-commerce site's presentation. A familiar, easy-to-navigate interface can go a long way toward establishing the trust you're after. Seasoned online shoppers will know what to expect from an e-commerce site, and meeting those expectations is a good way to gain their confidence. Novice surfers will probably be more comfortable if your online store closely resembles the major e-commerce interfaces they might have encountered.

Building a storefront compatible with your customers' expectations is one of the more obviously beneficial features of using an e-commerce software product such as those provided by Miva (http://www.Miva.com), BizCrafter (http://www.BizCrafterCorp.com) or eCartSoft (http://www.eCartSoft.com) to build your site. Another good and inexpensive one is Mal's eCommerce (http://mals-e.com/). Most of these programs will help you to build a simple, effective and familiar shopping interface that can include pictures, shopping cart functions and a number of useful security features.

In addition to helping you build an attractive online shop, most e-commerce software has features allowing it to help manage your inventory, interact with your payment processing systems, simplify your relationships with suppliers and affiliates, and even promote your site.

E-commerce software can usually be purchased online from the maker. But it is also quite often included as part of a specialized e-commerce package from any of the many Web hosts that support such operations.

Finding a Commerce-Friendly Web Host

If this is one of your first efforts at building an e-commerce Web site, it's a safe bet that you'll be outsourcing most, or at least some, of the site's technical operations to a Web hosting company. This is by no means a bad thing, and in fact can free up your time and IT resources, allowing you to focus on the operations of the business itself.

More than simply freeing your time, however, many Web hosting companies have plans tailored specifically to the needs of customers developing or operating e-commerce Web sites. A few hosting companies offering enhanced e-commerce features include, Interland (http://www.interland.com), ValueWeb (http://www.ValueWeb.com) and Global Internet Solutions (http://GISol.com). You can also use the rich rack of all-in-one services offered by http://CDbaby.com, which includes a hosting service known as hostbaby.com.

These commerce-friendly hosting plans often include a software license for one of the storefront building programs with your monthly fees, as well as a number of other support services designed to provide you with a secure platform from which to do business.

While software and services may be convenient, there are other reasons why a host that understands e-commerce is critical to your business. A good e-commerce host will already have the means in place to secure your online transactions with protocols such as SSL (see more on this in the next section). It may be able to process transactions for you, or help you set up a merchant account. And, most importantly, it will have the service level guarantees suitable to the high demands of your e-commerce operation.

Of course, in addition to the products and services they provide, it's hard to argue against the value of experience. And a Web host well versed in e-commerce should be able to help you by answering whatever questions you may have.

Securing Information Using SSL

At the core of any e-commerce operation is the financial transaction between Web site and consumer. One of the most common methods for accepting payment from your customers is via the submission of credit card information online. But by accepting your customers' credit card information through your Web site, you are also accepting the responsibility for the security of that information.

The standard protocol for securing communications on the Web is Secure Sockets Layer (SSL). Developed by Netscape Communications Corporation, the SSL security protocol provides data encryption, server authentication, message integrity and client authentication for TCP/IP connections, allowing client/server applications to communicate in a way that prevents eavesdropping, tampering or message forgery.

To establish an SSL session with a customer's browser, your server has to be able to generate a public key and a private key and have them authenticated by a certificate authority, such as VeriSign (http://www.VeriSign.com), Thawte (http://www.Thawte.com), Tucows (http://www.Tucows.com) or InstantSSL (http://www.InstantSSL.com). Your Web host may include an arrangement with one if these authorities, or may allow you to use its certificate.

KEY RESOURCE: Internet Marketing Glossary
Following chapter 17

Processing Transactions

Once your customer is willing and able to give you his or her credit card information, you still have to make arrangements to be able to process the transaction and receive your payment. Obviously, credit card processing is a complicated process, and a number of organizations can be involved, from both your bank and the user's bank to a credit card processing company and the credit card communications network.

Your involvement in the processing operation will vary according to how much of the responsibility you want to outsource. It can be as simple as employing a "buy button" solution hosted by a third-party provider (like, for example, 1shoppingcart.com), where all you have to do is include a piece of HTML code on your site and the processing company will send you a check. But keep in mind that the more responsibility you take on yourself, the smaller percentage of your profits you'll have to hand over to service providers.

In a more hands-on solution, many of the storefront-building software solutions include tools and ongoing support services to handle payment-processing functions. Your Web host may have already set up this sort of pre-arranged processing option. For storefronts not equipped to provide payment processing, there are service providers, such as IBill (http://www.IBill.com) or CCBill (http://www.CCBill.com), designed to do just that. These providers charge a scaling service, which can reach as high as 15 percent, for their services. And these charges can be avoided by setting up your own merchant account.

If you decide to handle most of the processing yourself, saving many of the fees associated with outsourced payment processing, you'll have to enable your Web server and applications to send and receive information from the credit card network. To do this, you'll have to obtain your own merchant ID and terminal ID, numbers that will identify you and the source of your transactions.

These IDs can be obtained from a merchant bank by applying for a merchant account enabled to receive payments by credit card. The merchant bank will have relationships with acquiring banks that can handle both credit card processing and Internet payments. Once the merchant bank supplies you with merchant and terminal IDs, you'll use these numbers to configure your payment software or provide them to your outsourced processor.

There are plenty of responsibilities beyond security involved in running an e-commerce Web site, not including managing the supply chain relationships and inventory and, of course, fulfilling your customers' orders. But, when dealing with the sensitive data involved in processing customers' credit card information, there can be no question that earning the trust of your customers through a comprehensive and responsible approach to security *should* be a primary concern.

The State of Micropayments

The ability to make small online payments (known as micropayments) is a dream which predates the commercialization of the Internet, but is only now starting to come to fruition. Various payment systems are now emerging to facilitate micropayments, which are both fuelled by and fuelling the trend towards paying for online music. In addition to the well-established PayPal, there are the likes of Bitpass (http://www.bitpass.com), Peppercoin (http://www.peppercoin.com), Earthport (http://www.earthport.com), Metacharge (http://www.metacharge.com) and Yaga (http://www.yaga.com). The list of featured sites mentioned at http://www.bitpass.com/share includes a number of musicians and labels who are trying out Bitpass' micropayment technology while it's in beta.

Email – Your Best Friend in Marketing

Email provides quick, nearly free communication with large numbers of people. The benefits are clear:

• *Low cost*: You may pay monthly charges to get access, but the money you save on fax and mailings by using the Net instead will more than make up for these fees.

• *Extremely fast delivery*: Most email arrives at its destination (around the corner or around the world) in seconds.

• *Permanent records*: A copy of all your email messages will be stored on the server host of your email program, for as long as that server is in existence.

• *Flexibility*: It's not unusual to send a two- or three-word email message. Email provides the considered thoughtfulness of mailed correspondence with the quickness and informality of a phone call.

Make that Sig file Work for You

This was a musician's sig file in an email message sent to me:

What would you get if you combined Yanni, Hans Zimmer, and Kitaro, threw in a dash of Pink Floyd, set to simmer, and served it for dinner? Click here: http://www.kellykendall.com to find out!

I clicked!

• *Ease of communication*: Replying to an electronic letter is simple and fast.

• *Ease of replication*: Because email is digital, you can replicate a message as many times as you'd like. A band with 100 fans can alert them to a surprise performance and encourage the 100 to forward the message to three friends each, bringing the total distribution to 400 people in minutes!

5 Tips for Networking Online

1. Never confuse advertising with networking. While there are ways to advertise online both for fee and for free, when networking online, you must exercise restraint in promoting yourself. People are looking for ideas, advice, colleagues, and help. Most people resent a sales pitch or even a self-serving promotion.

2. Think collegial and interactive. Just as face-to-face networking is a two-way process among colleagues and peers, so is online networking. Visit newsgroups and forums and join Internet mailing lists that relate to your field, reviewing ongoing conversations and think about how you could join in the dialogue and make a contribution based on your expertise and your curiosity. Asking good questions is a contribution, too.

3. Visit promising sites often. Just as attending in-person networking meetings regularly is important, being visible online regularly is also important. You don't build relationships by dropping a message here and there and rushing on to other sites. You will develop online business through establishing ongoing relationships.

4. Provide personal responses. The more personal you can make your communication the better, so respond to concerns and queries of particular individuals whenever possible.

5. Provide valued information. When leaving messages for an entire forum or newsgroup, focus on tips, trends, new information, or recent discoveries you've made in your work that would be of high interest and practical use to others. You might want to post a tip sheet, your newsletter, or segments from your informative booklet if you have one. Just be sure the information you post is informative, and no more than subtly 'promotional.'

Preparing Your Music for Digital Distribution

Intro: The Digital Content Landscape

For digital distribution to be deemed acceptable by the recording industry, it must minimally represent an "end-to-end" solution.

It must -

1. Move the music, artwork and liner notes,

2. Copy-protect the music,

3. and Register the royalty responsibility,

all the while maintaining CD-quality sound. This has presented an enormous challenge to the record industry and complete solutions are only slowly beginning to manifest themselves.

Digital distribution goes way beyond merely selling audio downloads. It includes everything from software distribution and eBooks to ringtones and digital film. It's sometimes difficult to get a handle on this hydra-headed phenomenon so let's first get a quick overview of the digital content landscape as it looks today (3/06).

First, there are the **Digital Music Warehouses**. These are the core of the digital media business. They hold licensed content in various formats for distribution to media and retail businesses. The main players are:

- ❒ MusicNet (owned by WMG, BMG, EMI, Real Networks & Sony)
- ❒ On-Demand digital (owned by LoudEye Corp.)
- ❒ ReddotNet (owned by Alliance Entertainment Corp. - mainly kiosks)
- ❒ Digital Distribution Domain (owned by DX3 Technologies)

Next are the **Independent Aggregators**. They play a similar role as the warehouses but for smaller artists. Aggregators take your tracks, negotiate the content license agreement with the digital music services, collect royalties, make sure the services pay up and send labels and artists royalty checks with sales reports. New ones are popping up all the time, but the main ones include:

- ❒ IODA (Independent Online Distribution Alliance)
- ❒ DRA (Digital Rights Agency)
- ❒ IRIS (IRIS Distribution)
- ❒ CDBaby (supplies downloads to bigger sites like iTunes, etc.)
- ❒ Rightsrouter (started by AIM, the Association of Independent Music)

Then, there are the **Digital Jukeboxes**, commercial jukebox systems for restaurants and bars. They include:

- ❒ ECast (software platform: music, films and games)
- ❒ TouchTunes (complete dedicated con-op music system)
- ❒ NetMusic (owned by Ultimate Jukebox Inc., also owns Audio Lunchbox)

Satellite Radio is beginning to reach the larger markets owing to deals with auto manufactures. The stations make their money through subscriptions and sales of receivers. The main players are:

- ❒ XM Radio (USA and borders)
- ❒ Sirius Radio (USA and borders)
- ❒ WorldSpace (South America, Europe and Asia)

Also in the radio realm is **Internet Radio**, programmed audio streaming on the Web. There are thousands of Net radio outlets – some on dedicated players; some free; some by subscription and some on retail sites (like iTunes). Niche programming is its forte. Here are three of the bigger ones:

- ❒ Live365.com
- ❒ SHOUTcast
- ❒ Radio Paradise

Peer-to-Peer (P2P) Networks use standard Internet protocols and some add-on software to transport files between web users. Any digital content can be distributed using P2P. There are many but the biggies are:

- ❒ Gnutella
- ❒ Grokster
- ❒ iMesh
- ❒ KaZaA
- ❒ Morpheus
- ❒ BitTorrent
- ❒ eDonkey
- ❒ LimeWire

USING PEER-TO-PEER TO GENERATE MONEY & PROMOTE YOUR ACT

Already mentioned in Ch. 3, check out **Weed** – a type of digital rights management that allows artists to monetize music sales within P2P systems.

http://weedshare.com

Navigating through all the options for distributing your music digitally can become overwhelming. Here are some of the best options available today for independent musicians and composers:

❒ **Artist Download Sites**. Thousands of do-it-yourself (DIY) artists distribute their music directly to their fans via their own web sites.

Of course, distributing your music digitally from your own web site means you've set it up so it's possible. This will often mean a greater financial investment in your site design in order to accommodate this feature.

❒ **Community Download Sites**. Many DIY artists use community sites based around genre and geography commonalities. They provide a sort of shared commons, a retail portal, and forums for communication. Some examples are: http://myspace.com, http://cdbaby.com, http://friendster.com, and http://tagworld.com.

Music Metadata: Getting the Right Coded Information into Your Music

If you plan on releasing your music on the Net, through satellite radio, or via music services like Muzak, you'll need to understand the following.

A lot of information on a music CD isn't music. Some of it is codes that help trace the uses and sales of your music online. Without them there is a good chance you'll miss out on royalties owed you.

The four important codes you'll need are:

❒ **UPC (Universal Product Code)** - This is also known as a "bar code" and is attached to nearly every packaged product available in retail stores. Each product has a unique 12-digit number, encoded in the bars, which are scanned upon purchase and allow for the tracking of inventory and sales.

Nielson Soundscan collects UPC sales data form over 14,000 outlets in the U.S. and Canada to compile its weekly list of music sales, which are published online (www.soundscan.com). See chapter 9 for more on obtaining a bar code.

❒ **ISRC (International Standard Recording Code)** - The ISRC is the international identification system for sound recordings and music DVDs. Each ISRC is a unique and permanent identifier for a specific recording, to help identify recordings for royalty payments. It is assigned *per track*, not per CD. It's smart to identify your recordings this way. They are embedded in the metadata of your CD during the mastering phase. For further information on ISRCs go to: http://www.riaa.com/

❒ **CD Text** - CD Text is information about the release that can be encoded as a separate file on an audio CD. It stores such information as the album title and song titles. When playing back an audio CD containing CD Text information on a CD Text-enabled player (usually an LCD screen), the listener will be able to read this information on the display panel. It's displayed only on CD or DVD players, not on the desktop of most computers. Since its part of the *Red Book* standard CD Text info can be entered onto a CD master quite easily using the "table of contents" in the appropriate CD subchannel.

❒ **CDDB (CD Data Base)** - A database for software applications to look up CD information over the Internet. It was designed around the task of identifying entire CDs, not merely single tracks. The identification process involves creating a "discID", a sort of "fingerprint" of a CD created by performing calculations on the track duration information stored in the table-of-contents of the CD. There are alternatives to Gracenotes's proprietary CDDB. These include FreeDB, MusicBrainz and All Media Guide's AMG LASSO. To submit to Gracenote's database go to: http://gracenote.com

and read the FAQs under "Company Info".

MAIN PLAYERS IN ONLINE INDIE RECORD RETAIL

DISTRIBUTOR	OWNER OR RELATED	FORMAT / PLAYER
CD Baby	CD Baby	CD
The Orchard	The Orchard	CD, MP3, WMA
Ampcast	Ampcast	CD, MP3
ARTISTdirect	Distributor BMG, sister-Label: iMusic	MP3
Audiogalaxy	Audiogalaxy	MP3, Real, WMA
EMusic	Vivendi Universal Net	MP3
Epitonic	Sputnik7 LLC	Mp3, WMA, Real
MP3.com	CNET	MP3
Music Rebellion	Music Rebellion	MP3
Vitaminic	Vitaminic, Buongiorno	MP3
Wippit	Wippit	MP3, WMA

MOSTLY MAJOR ONLINE RECORD RETAILERS

DISTRIBUTOR	OWNER OR RELATED	FORMAT/PLAYER
MusicNet@AOL	Group included WMG	MusicNet
buyMusic	BuyMusic	WMA
iTunes player	Apple	AAC, iTunes
Launch	Yahoo	Napster
Listen	RealNetworks	Real, WMA, Rhapsody
MusicMatch	MusicMatch	WMA
MusicNow	FullAudio, Charter Communications, Clear Channel, Earthlink	WMA
Napster 2	Roxio based on PressPlay (Duet)	Real, WMA

What You Can Expect to Be Paid for Downloads

While iTunes initially paid indies almost half of what the majors made, today (4/1/06), iTunes is finally paying indies a wholesale price-per-track of about .65-.70, just a few pennies less than the majors. There's strength in numbers, and thanks to aggregators like CDBaby, indies are starting to get their due.

If you distribute your music through CDBaby.com, you can see a fairly comprehensive chart of the retailers CDBaby distributes to and what each one pays at: http://cdbaby.net/dd-partners

Affinities & Affiliates: Finding Online Partners to Help You Sell

The Net easily allows you to find and link up with businesses your company may have an affinity with. For example, a client of mine who specializes in producing recordings of traditional Irish music discovered all kinds of affinity partners, ranging from gift shops to Irish tour companies. With each one she created a media swap where she displays banner ads or links to their sites in exchange for the same at theirs. Within a month of initiating these exchanges her business doubled!

These online "joint ventures" are all about related businesses teaming up and combining skills, products, services and resources to create new streams of income and profit. One great way to profit through joint ventures is to seek out products or services that would benefit your visitors, and then approach the companies that provide those products or services. Ask them if you can recommend their product or service on your site for a portion of the profits. Most companies will gladly agree to this arrangement - after all, there's no risk for them since they only pay you when you refer a paying customer.

Affiliate programs are similar to "affinity marketing" but are also a bit different.

An ***affiliate program*** (also referred to as a *reseller* or *associate program*) is a way to get other people to promote your product or service. For every customer your affiliates send to your site, you pay them a commission. Your affiliates send visitors to your site using banner ads, text links, letters of referral, and other methods of promotion. Then you track these visitors using special software. For every visitor who decides to buy, you pay your affiliate a commission.

❐ **Recommend affiliate products.** Recommending affiliate products creates a "no-risk" partnership that allows you to promote another company's products or services on your site to earn a percentage of their sales. As one of the company's "affiliates" or promotion partners, you earn a commission each time someone you've referred to their site makes a purchase. To advertise their wares, you might post a banner on your site that links to the affiliate program's site, or you might publish an article about the company and their products in your newsletter.

❒ **Start an affiliate program.** With your own affiliate program, you can recruit an army of people (your affiliates) who will recommend your product on their web site for a percentage of any sales they refer. You have the power to exponentially increase your income as more and more affiliates sign up and you continue to teach your existing affiliates how to increase their commission checks (and your income).

Advanced Online Marketing Techniques

Internet marketing has quickly developed a sophistication that allows the online businesses to get a helpful peek into how people shop, what they're most interested in, and what works to make sales. Unfortunately, this book can't probe the depths of all these tools and services. So, instead, I've opted to cover a few newer tools below, and then to include an annotated "Resource List for the Advanced Internet Music Marketer" in Ch 17, "Further Resources to Fuel Your Music Marketing."

❒ Podcasting

As its name suggests, a podcast is a combination of an iPod (or some other form of a portable music device) and a broadcast. It is essentially a radio show that is frozen and time-shifted. Podcasting makes audio files available online in a manner that allows these files (often in MP3 format) to be automatically downloaded to a subscriber's computer (or portable music device) at the user's leisure.

Forrester Research estimates 300,000 podcasts will be available by year's end, growing to 13 million in 2009. The number of podcast *listeners,* however, is more difficult to track. Bridge Ratings, which does radio-audience market research, reports that 5 million radio listeners downloaded at least one podcast in 2005. It expects that figure to at least double in 2006.

SEARCHING FOR THE PERFECT PODCAST

Check out Podzinger, which uses speech technology to convert to text the contents of 60,000-plus podcasts. Since it can search through the text of podcasts, it can better determine the relevance of search results to help you find what you're looking for. Narrow searches work best, as I discovered when I tried the site. Searching for "electronic music" pulled up 2010 results. Searching for "house music" pulled up 93 results. Searching for "drum and bass", sorted by relevancy, pulled up 48 good options.

For those unable to afford the multi-million-dollar price tag of a broadcast tower and FCC license, podcasting offers a fun, low-cost (sometimes no cost) and easy way to create and publish audio material for a potentially huge - like international - audience using downloadable audio files like MP3.

Listeners benefit from podcasts, as opposed to traditional radio broadcasts or streaming internet programs, in that content can be "time-shifted." This is just a fancy way of saying that audience members can download a podcast featuring a mix of their favorite music and then listen to it using their computers, digital audio players, cell phones, PSPs or PDAs whenever they get a free moment.

Software called "podcatchers" can be easily programmed to continually search the internet and find listener's favorite shows and then download updates automatically. It's sort of like a Tivo, but without the costly subscription service. Again, testifying to podcasting's popularity, Apple has included a podcatching function in the latest version of its iTunes software (beginning with 4.9).

How can you use podcasts? Indie warrior, Gilli Moon offers these suggestions from her trove of podcast wisdom:

• "You can have it embedded in your own artist website, your MySpace.com page, anywhere you can manipulate the html code of a webpage you host on the Internet.

• Fans can listen to your podcast either through the Internet, there and then from your webpage, or download the mp3s to their computers through a podcatcher download the podcast to their ipods through a podcatcher subscribe to the RSS feed so that every time you as the podcast host change your show, it automatically updates on their computer or ipod (this is the coolest part!)

• Fans can also take the html code of your podcast and put it on their sites, thereby adding to the ultimate goal of spreading your music far and wide," (Source: http://www.gilli.net/article-podcasting.htm)

Right on sister.

❐ **MP3 Blogs**. MP3 blogs – weblogs that present audio files from their host's collections, one at a time – are another opportunity for music promotion. Nobody's sure who came up with the first MP3 blog, and the evolution of the form was gradual enough that it's hard to pinpoint the date of its origin, although it was probably in 2002.

As recently as July 2004, there were perhaps two dozen music blogs. Now (3/06) there are well over 1000, with more appearing every day from all over the world, specializing in everything from hard-core punk to pre-World War II gospel. Music blogging has developed into a subculture with its own unofficial leaders and unwritten rules, and it's becoming a significant force in the music industry, which mostly seems to be smiling on the phenomenon.

There's a relatively standard format for MP3 blogs that's unofficially evolved: one or two songs a day, each one accompanied by a paragraph or two about the song or the artist. Some bloggers also include photographs or links to places where their readers can buy the CD on which each song appears.

Most focus on little-known musicians or rare and out-of-print recordings; few will post something that's already a huge radio hit or by a very famous artist, and it's frowned upon to post more than a single song from a given album.

Of course, one of the first questions a lot of people ask about MP3 blogs is if they're legal. The answer is that it's a gray area, and MP3 bloggers tend to work form the principle that it's easier to get forgiveness than permission. None has been sued, and nobody's yet talking about suing them. In fact, Universal Music Group's European division is paying Matthew Perpetua, the 25-year-old curator of Fluxblog (fluxblog.com), to be a talent scout (he sends them an annotated CD-R of his favorite new music once a month)!

All a prospective blogger needs is a site, a way to host the files, and a way to get the word out. The site is easy enough: free services such as Blogger.com provide the basic setup for a lot of music bloggers. The word can spread through friends' links, or through clearinghouse "metablogs" like MP3blogs.org. And YouSendIt.com – originally intended as a free tool for emailing large files – has also become a favorite resource for nascent MP3 bloggers.

Record labels could easily get in on the action to promote their back catalogs with blogs of their own. "Labels don't seem to get that websites have to be updated constantly," says Perpetua. "You want to encourage people to keep coming back to them. People would visit a Blue Note Records blog every day." (Source: *LA Times*, 7/3/05).

❐ **The Power of Familiar Association**. While digital distribution has opened the floodgates of music discovery, many independent artists are having trouble cutting through the clutter.

Certainly stores like MusicMatch, Napster, iTunes and MSN Music have helped to proliferate independent catalog online, but how does a music fan find that hidden gem?

Derek Sivers, founder of independent online CD retailer CDBaby, relayed some interesting discoveries at a conference I attended last year. While combing through download logs from various digital music stores, Sivers was surprised by some of the top sellers. Many of the most successful digital artists were unknown even to Sivers, who spends a considerable amount of time reviewing top bands on his site.

Upon closer examination, Sivers made an important connection: almost all of the artists in question had covered well-known songs, causing them to appear next to searches for major artists like, for example, Morrissey, Bob Dylan and the Rolling Stones. "People would discover the band by listening to a cover song, then get interested and check out the album," said Sivers. Meanwhile, some of the top artists on CDBaby failed to get major attention on stores like iTunes, with few signposts or recommendations guiding the casual user.

The tale is another accidental discovery to crop up in digital music, almost making a mockery of more complicated recommendation and discovery engines.

But in the wilder P2P space, bands have used similar tactics to gain placement next to superstar acts. That includes changing titles to match a popular group, with many downloaders willing to give a relative unknown a chance.

Meanwhile, Sivers pointed to a wide range of clever ways to get discovered online. Understanding the psychology of the online music fan is key, with some users only listening to bands recommended by friends, while others only interested in discovering something on their own. For Sivers, such distinctions are essential for the savvy artist to understand, with different sites offering specific types of users.

Search, test, reflect and use what you learn!

Summary:
A 17-Step Internet Marketing Plan Checklist

To conclude this chapter, take a moment to walk through the Checklist below and see if you've taken all the essential steps for developing your Internet strategy. It's not the be-all and end-all of Net marketing and promotion, but it'll provide some important benchmarks to ensure you're on the right tracks.

- ❒ Develop clear sales & marketing objectives.
- ❒ Write and create a site that sells.
- ❒ Register domain name.
- ❒ Arrange reliable, cost-effective hosting.
- ❒ Setup secure credit card capability for online, real-time, international sales.
- ❒ Setup a proven, effective search engine strategy in the html codes.
- ❒ Post the site correctly.
- ❒ Manually index individually with the Big 8 search engines.
- ❒ Automated indexing with 400+ specialized search engines and directories.
- ❒ Automated posting to all related NewsGroups and Mailing Lists.
- ❒ News release to music editors via email and fax.
- ❒ Search strategy to contact organizations, associations, distributors, retailers online.
- ❒ Immediate personal response mechanism to each new prospect and customer.
- ❒ Maintain automated customer and prospect email database.
- ❒ Email monthly merged automated newsletter to all prospects and customers.
- ❒ Consider potential affiliate program to pay commissions on referral sales.
- ❒ Consider potential Internet advertising campaign on websites and publications.

CH 6
Marketing Direct to Fans & Customers

"The best way to send information is to wrap it up in a person."
- Robert Oppenheimer

"There is no such thing as 'soft sell' and 'hard sell'. There is only 'smart sell' and 'stupid sell'."
- Charles Brower, American Advertising Executive

Direct marketing is probably the most familiar marketing ground for most musicians. You direct market when you play a gig, talk with fans, mail out your tour itineraries, and call an agent. It's the most *direct* route to your market.

Direct marketing can be geared to your already loyal fans or to people who are *likely* to take an interest in what you're about. We'll be focusing on the second group in this chapter – how to market to those who are likely to dig what you're about. *Finding* these people is the challenge; they need to be sorted out from the masses; but how? Though performing falls under direct marketing as well, we'll devote the whole next chapter to that topic.

We're going to look at the process for getting a qualified, targeted list of people to approach with your music in a moment. First, let's take a look at a direct marketing approach that also sorts out prospective buyers but with a more "shotgun" style.

Differences Between Direct Mail and Mass Media

Direct mail	Mass Media
1) You target your prospects and send your ad only to those consumers.	1) You reach all consumers who read a publication, tune in to a broadcast, or see an outdoor ad.
2) You can personalize each marketing message.	2) You can target your message but it is very difficult (and expensive) to personalize it.
3) You determine your format and length, and can include samples, reply cards, or any other items you feel will inspire a response.	3) You fit your message into available ad units.

Street Team Marketing: Mobilizing Your Fans

Street team marketing is probably the most familiar form of direct music marketing.

Many marketing professionals in the entertainment industry have come to realize that a fan base that loves a movie or band will gladly share their experience with their friends. This is a far more effective means of grass roots marketing - using genuine, committed fans that are driven by the belief in the music/artist. In return, give this core fan base t-shirts, and make them feel part of the band and instrumental in their growth. It's a win/win.

Traditionally a few fans would attend gigs and hand out fliers. Digital street teams have become a huge marketing tool during the last few years, especially in the US. At the initial stage, a band will get, say, 10 to 30 fans to spread the word electronically – via e-mail & text-messaging, and hence build a community.

The traditional work of street teams can be difficult to measure, i.e. distributing fliers, etc. However the use of technology makes tracking and logging street team activity far easier, and hence quantifiable and justifiable to the artist's team. Depending on your style of music, artists should seriously consider this cost-effective form of grass roots marketing, before hiring publicists and other marketing reps.

What kinds of data and information are artists and labels seeking to collect about an artist's fan base? Core things are e-mail address, country and mobile. Gender, address, and age are often collected as well, depending on the requirements of a band, and how general or niche a market they are targeting. Campaigns typically encourage people to re-register in order to maintain a current and reliable e-mail database, by offering incentives in order to achieve this.

Making this as easy as possible is a key to success. Incorporating ideas of devoted fans so that they can share their experience around your project is a valuable way to build trust and expand reach.

To help us understand how a street team campaign works, let's look at a case study involving Interscope artists Queens of the Stone Age, compliments of Universal Buzz Intelligence.

Interscope was challenged with launching the second QOTSA album "Lullaby to Paralyze" to an established fan base while crossing over the band to a larger mass audience. In particular, they sought to engage the college aged audience to drive album sales and tour date attendance.

Universal Buzz devised a lifestyle and relationship marketing campaign that impacted college campuses and those key neighborhoods within walking distance in 18 regions nationally. Working with the community in each city, UB hosted a listening party at all-ages lifestyle destinations prior to the release of the new album. Each party included the enter-to-win contest for the giveaway of a digital music player pre-loaded with the new QOTSA album. Promoted in conjunction with local media outlets, record stores and boutique outlets the parties were an opportunity for fans to gather and share their enthusiasm for "Lullaby to Paralyze".

More than 25 successful listening parties were completed introducing the album to thousands of existing and new fans nationwide. The album debuted at #5 in the Billboard sales charts during its first week of availability.

IM: A Taste of Super Distribution

Perhaps one of the biggest issues to come out of the entrance of Microsoft and Yahoo! to the online music business has been the sales potential of song sharing via instant messaging (IM). While IM software already lets people listen to online radio, new versions are letting people share and interact with one another's digital play lists.

"One of the most powerful sales motivators is word of mouth," says MusicNet's Mark Mooridian. And, that's basically what you get with IM. "It's an immensely powerful tool," he emphasizes, adding that the industry term for this type of marketing is *Super Distribution*. "What that means," says Mooridian, " consumers help to increase and distribute sales by sharing with others."

Super Distribution comes out of the IT world and was first coined back in 1989. At its root is the understanding that electronic objects are fundamentally unable to monitor their own copying, but are trivially able to monitor their use - a definition that seems to be finding its way into legal peer-to-peer (P2P) distribution models of which IM song sharing is an extension.

Are these signs of a changing landscape? You bet they are. Models from the IT world are making their way into traditional sales models and staking their claims.

Street Media

Street Media includes a number of guerrilla media tools and tactics that can be used to create brand awareness on the street and through lifestyle avenues. These include:

❒ **Guerrilla Media Placement (GMP):** Wild Posting, Sniping, and the use of non-traditional Outdoor Media Vehicles. Street Attack executes GMP campaigns using promotional materials including:

- Static Clings
- 11" x 17" Posters
- Large Format Posters
- Sidewalk Chalk/Decals
- Stickers

❒ **Lifestyle Media Placement:** Targets specific lifestyle venues, retail outlets, and colleges to align brands and products with specific consumer interests. Marketing materials such as posters, samples, stickers, and demo CDs are placed in high-visibility areas where consumers can see and take leave-behind materials.

- Colleges
- Cafes, bars, venues
- Music/DJ/Gear shops
- Skate/surf shops
- Pop Culture shops
- Clothing Boutiques

❒ **Graffiti Murals:** Legal graffiti advertising media brings unique street-level presence to outdoor ad campaigns. Using legally leased wall space, graffiti artists spray-paint murals integrating brand logos, product images, and ad creative. Mural advertising is a great way to bring "street cred" and "street buzz" to traditional media campaigns.

Many indie labels like Relapse Records and Drive Thru have very strong street teams that market their new releases for them, for only the cost of the occasional free promo CD to members, and free concert tickets. Street Team duties often include fliering for local shows, distributing newsletters and magazines, and even taking store inventories of local record stores.

The Proper Care & Feeding of a Street Team

❒ First, decide on what your goals are going to be. Is it to make people aware of an event?, Bring visibility to a band's name?, Drive people to your web site to listen to your music?

❒ Next, choose your take-away. What do you plan on leaving with people? Will it be a postcard? A flier? A promotional novelty? A demo recording?

❒ Tap your fan base for team members. Which fans have shown the most interest in your music? Which ones are always at your gigs? These are the people you want to reach out to for help.

❒ Decide together with your team when they'll be going out, for how many hours, and which areas they should cover on the street.

❒ Finally, decide on a meeting time to re-assemble and review how things went, what can be improved for next time, and to schedule the next promotion.

❒ Oh yes, and bring some kind of treat/reward for your teammates. After all, they've worked hard on your behalf and faced a lot of rejection and disinterest during the promotion. Pizza always works.

Building Your Database List by List

Mailing Lists

Unlike retail operations, where you can set up shop in a popular area and wait for consumers to come in, direct mail operations must actively solicit potential customers. If you plan to do any advertising via the mail or telephone, you will need to rent lists - names, addresses and phone numbers of consumers who are likely to buy your products.

Because of years of market research it is relatively easy to obtain strong, qualified lists of very specific buyers. You can get mailing lists of musicians, music educators, music executives, music schools, music retailers *and* music buyers.

For example, you can obtain mailing lists from the Hugo-Dunhill List catalog (http://www.hdml.com) of people who have purchased music through the mail in the past year, broken out -

- By Genre
- By region
- By income
- By job function
- By age

Even more targeted lists are available from any number of relevant businesses like, for example, music magazines (e.g., *Performing Songwriter*), music organizations (e.g., Music Educators National Conference), music trade shows (e.g., SXSW in Austin, TX), and music directory publishers (e.g., Music Business Registry). Their subscriber and member lists become very valuable assets over time and a number of them develop an additional revenue stream by making these lists available to others for a price.

A mailing list can make or break any direct-mail advertiser. Good lists are worth more to you than a doubling of your ad budget. Mailing lists can also be rented from list brokers. You can find them in your local telephone directory or online under "Advertising-Direct Mail." Lists are available in almost any imaginable category. The one-time rental fee for these names is usually between $35 and $80 per thousand.

Selecting the Right List for You

Use the "RFM formula" to assess and select a list: R stands for recency, F for frequency and M for money. Because people and businesses move and their economic status's change, recency is vital to the success of a list. Frequency refers to how many times the people on the list responded to similar offers. Money refers to how much they spent.

You can target an audience more effectively with a mailing list than with any other medium. Say you advertise on the "Tonight Show." You'll automatically get millions of viewers. But what kind of viewers? Are they mail order buyers? They could be teens, the elderly, married couples or singles. There is little selectivity in this kind of medium. On the other hand, you can rent a mailing list of people who bought, say, concert tickets through the mail. So, you ultimately achieve selectivity in marketing.

A mailing list is often expensive. When you are advertising in a mass medium like a newspaper or magazine and you pay $10,000 to reach one million readers, you are reaching one thousand readers for $10 - or a cost per thousand (CPM) of $10. A mailing list by itself can often run to $80 per thousand names. (The more specific the buyers on a list, the higher the cost. More on this later.) Also, you should plan on a minimum purchase of 2,000 names.

Normal direct response rates (that is, how many people actually respond to your offer) are 1-3% and the more niche-oriented the list and product, the higher the rate. I've seen some targeted direct mail campaigns achieve rates as high as 10%, but this is rare.

Is Your Business Suited to Direct Mail?

The more of these following criteria your business meets, the more likely direct mail will work for you. If you meet very few of these criteria, you should look to other methods.

1. Is your market easily definable using finite demographic parameters?

2. Can you actually reach your potential market through a third-party delivery system, such as the U.S. Postal Service, UPS, or Federal Express?

3. Is your prospective customer likely to have purchased a similar product or service as a result of direct mail in the past?

4. Is your product or service one that can be sold without discussion or demonstration?

5. Is your product or service sufficiently visually oriented for the potential buyers to understand its value clearly from a mailing?

6. Is your product or service one that is conducive to impulse buying?

7. Is your product or service highly discounted compared with those of your competitors?

8. Is your product or service one wherein a mistake in purchase will NOT affect the buyer or his company in an especially negative way?

9. Is your product or service one that lends itself to on-the-spot decisions?

10. Can you afford what it takes to produce a sufficiently impressive package to get your prospective purchase?

11. Can you afford either the money to buy appropriate lists or the time to

create one sufficient to make mailing worthwhile?

12. If you are selling to consumers, can you afford to send your package to enough people that a 1 percent return would be profitable?

13. If you are selling to businesses, are you willing to do the follow-up telephone calls needed to make sure your mailing was received and to discover potential interest?

Mailing List And Direct Mail Handlers

You can go direct to a magazine or organization to inquire about list availability, or you can use a *list broker*.

The list broker acts as a purchasing agent. The broker is commissioned by the person who already owns the list. Here is an example of how a broker works: If you're going to publish a cookbook and you want to rent a list of the people who purchased the Betty Crocker Cookbook through the mail, the broker will contact Betty Crocker (or its list broker) and obtain the list for you. If the list is $50 per thousand, that's what you pay. The broker gets her commission from Betty Crocker.

Mailing list brokers have specific requests you must provide in order to use their lists or their services. They will ask for the following:

- ❒ A sample of your product.
- ❒ Your business plan and objectives.
- ❒ Samples of direct mail advertising already generated.
- ❒ A review of your testing tactics.

Many list brokers will also require a copy of the piece you are mailing before giving you the final go ahead. This is done to insure that the list is not being used for inappropriate purposes like fraud or hate mail.

Most list brokers suggest that you stick with one broker throughout your whole marketing campaign. This way, the broker can help you plan your long-term advertising and marketing goals, and avoid redundancies.

Sometimes you may deal directly with list owners, which are people or companies that compile, promote and, hopefully, maintain the integrity of the lists for rental to others. List owners will not let you use the list if they feel that your offer will be offensive to those on the list, or if your offer might be too competitive with whatever product they may be selling. List owners frequently ask to review the material beforehand.

Often a mailing house will handle the distribution of your direct mail materials once they're prepared. Some of the time-saving and cost-saving functions a "mailer" will perform include:

- ❒ Folding your material
- ❒ Inserting it into envelopes
- ❒ Affixing mailing labels
- ❒ Running the material through a postage meter
- ❒ Stamping on a bulk-mail permit (if not preprinted on the envelopes)
- ❒ Sorting the material by zip code (required by the Postal Service)
- ❒ Delivering it to the post office

All this is done for a few cents per piece. (Most mailing houses have a minimum charge, no matter how many pieces you give them). You can find these types of services in the Yellow Pages under "Mailing Services".

> ***TIP:*** *Labels, managers and artists should try to find out from their fan base what other artists their fans are listening to, and then market their product to this wider potential fan-base.*

Types Of Lists

In general, there are two types of mailing lists:

- ❒ Compiled lists
- ❒ Buyer (or House) lists

A *compiled list* is put together out of directories – car owners, boat owners, license holders, etc. They are people who are on the list for demographic reasons, such as people who live in the suburbs of Manhattan who make over $40,000 a year; people who are between 25 and 40 years of age; people who are born in the month of March; people with the last name of Fox, etc. They are not necessarily mail order buyers.

The other type of list is the *buyer list*. These names can be your gold mine because a buyer list is made up of people who have purchased through the mail. They can be people who have bought the latest Coldplay album, people who have bought a music instruction book, people who have purchased sheet music through the mail, etc. As discussed earlier, those who have recently purchased a product like yours through the mail are most likely to do it again.

A buyer list is different from a compiled list because the people are established mail order purchasers – a better bet for your marketing plan.

List brokers will be able to assist you in either compiling a list or acquiring one from another source. Many times they have the ability to tailor a list for the market you are interested in pursuing. Their fee is approximately 20 percent of the cost to rent the list from a list manager.

QUESTIONS TO ASK WHEN SELECTING A LIST BROKER

1. What sources do you use for your lists?
2. Why do you use these particular sources?
3. How often do you use them?
4. What accuracy rate do you guarantee?
5. How often are your lists updated and corrected?
6. How long have you been in business?
7. Are your lists qualified - that is, have the people on them bought similar services or products by mail?
8. Can any of my criteria not be met by your lists? Which ones?

Other Factors In Selecting A List

In addition to the RFM (recency, frequency, money), demographics and psychographics are crucial. Following up on chapter 4, you must look at the income, age, gender, education, type of residence, occupation, ownership of credit cards - in short, the demographics - of potential buyers when you're selling a product. The list owner should be able to break down the list you're renting according to some or all of the above variables, plus such factors as location (states and zip codes).

Again, the more defined the list, the higher the cost. But in return for that cost, you should be able to elicit a higher response rate.

Psychographics is a relatively new factor in list selection. The theory behind psychographics is that you can determine more about a person by habits than income. For example, political conservatives are more likely to be hunters than those leaning more to the left. If you're looking for a list, and the owner says there is a psychographic profile, get it. See if these habits match those of your prospective buyers.

You also need to know who else is renting the list. Like the way a business owner looks at a magazine to see who's repeating their advertising, mail order operators want to know who else is making money with a list. These are likely to be people with similar products of people who are using the list quite often. Any list owner will be more than happy to furnish a usage history for prospective list renters.

You should always ask for a list that has been "cleaned." A dirty list has a lot of old names. Every piece that goes out third-class mail does not get forwarded if the addressee has moved. If it doesn't get delivered, it's money down the drain. And while each mailing piece may cost only 25 to 30 cents, if you're mailing a thousand pieces a month - 10 percent (no delivery) of that is 100. That's $40.-$60. you're throwing out. Get a list that has been cleaned within the last six to seven months.

Can I Use the List Again, and Again and...?

Remember, when you get a list, you are renting it for a *one-time use*, because a lot of other people will be using it. Always ask who else is using it. Also, beware of using a list more than once and thinking the broker will never know. A standard broker practice involves "seeding" or "salting" - sprinkling a rented list with fake names and addresses in which direct mail pieces ultimately end up back in the hands of the broker. If the broker sees that you've used the list more than once, you will not be able to rent a list from the broker again. However, once a person from a list responds to your ad in any way, the person can (and should) be added to your in-house mailing list.

Because good mailing lists are essential for the success of your mail order campaign, carefully check out any list as much as possible. Buy only from established brokers or owners. Ask how many times the list has been rented in the previous six months, and get the names and telephone numbers of some of list's previous users. Call them and ask what their response rate was with the list. How many (if any) pieces were returned because of bad addresses? Was the list worth the money they paid?

Getting Your Product into Mail Order Catalogs

When you make your music available in an online store, you're, in a sense, placing your product in the site's "catalog". But there are also mail order catalogs go to people who purchase goods through the mail. These range from the huge department store tomes (J.C. Penny, etc.) to niche lifestyle catalogs (like those put out by PBS and its various affiliates).

There are two ways to get your product into someone else's catalog: You can contact catalog companies yourself, or you can work through a catalog broker.

Do It Yourself

Look through the *Directory of Book, Catalog and Magazine Printers* by Ad-Lib Publications and the *National Directory of Catalogs* by Oxbridge Communications (they should be available at the library) to find catalogs that carry products similar to or compatible with yours. Call these companies and find out if they would consider carrying a product like yours. If so, ask them for their policies and procedures for submitting new products. Follow these carefully. Usually they will involve sending product descriptions, samples, and pricing information. Once you have submitted the requested materials, follow up repeatedly.

Use a Broker

Product brokers will find catalogs for you that will carry your product(s), for which they charge either a fee or commission. Catalogs that want to carry your products will usually charge you for ad space or will buy the product from you at wholesale prices. Some companies will drop-ship your product, meaning they will take the orders and pass them on to you for fulfillment.

Each catalog has its own procedure for contacting and reviewing your product. Getting into catalogs is often a long, tedious process but if your product is selected it can mean large revenues.

The Words You Use:
Tips for Writing Effective Direct Marketing Copy

Effective direct marketing depends on the kind of words (or "copy") you use to get your message across. Your words need to be compelling, engaging, personal - and should include a *call to action* ("Order Now!", "Call now!", "What are you waiting for?", "Quantities are limited!").

As DM Consultant Ruth Evans says, "Brand advertising copy seeks to change what you *think*. Direct marketing copy seeks to change what you *do*." Here are five tips for getting people to change what they do when encountering your direct marketing.

1. Make Every Word Count: Reading is hard work. Every word should add value to the reader. This doesn't necessarily mean that short copy wins over long copy. You could have seven pages of very hard-working words that culminate in the reader being sold, whereas half that many words would not have done the job. The copy should be as long as it needs to be to get the job done right.

2. Testimonials: Having others say good things about you, your products or your services is so much more believable than your own self praise. Famed Direct Marketer Jay Abraham said if he had only one tool to use in direct copy, it would be the testimonial.

3. Action Words: Use *action* words. This seems obvious, but I'm shocked at how often I see passive copy, which only telegraphs that the writer isn't a hard core believer in the product or service he/she is writing about.

4. Ask Questions? Absolutely. People are programmed to answer questions. It's a great involvement technique.

5. Authenticity: Don't be too slick. Let your personality come through. People like authenticity. This is probably why the old Carvel ice cream commercials and those SBLI Insurance spots are successful - they come off as being authentic, as opposed to Madison Avenue slick.

Some Ideas to Make Your Website More Interactive

Your web site gives you a direct connection with your fans. Unlike TV, films and radio (which are *uni-directional*), the Internet is *bi-directional.* This is why the Internet is such a radical departure from everything that preceded it, and also why it's such a potentially powerful tool in the hands of musicians.

When people arrive at your landing page, you have their attention for about 5 seconds. That's it – a very short window of opportunity. That's why it's crucial to have something at your site that magnetizes visitors, keeps them interested, engaged – *and* willing to return.

Here are four ideas to bring more interactivity to your web site and make your fans love you even more:

❐ **Set up a discussion board.** Ideally, what you want to do is start an ongoing conversation with your fans. Having a message board enables this conversation and helps establish a lively and loyal online community. You're essentially saying, "you're ideas and input is important to us – come closer." Fans can interact with each other and the band if they wish. This is the online equivalent of talking to the crowd between sets at your gigs.

Once your fans are aware of the board, they will come back to see if they've had response to their post and what other posts may have been put up. If you want to set up your own message board on your website, the easiest method is to install someone else's software. You can install or use most of these for free or for very low rates. Check out these to start with: www.bravenet.com or www.webcrossing.com.

❐ **Create a band blog/journal.** There's a good reason magazines like *People* do so well. Fans like to feel they have a personal connection with the artist. Fans are fervently curious and want the inside scoop. This is a place to provide that for them.

A band blog gives fans an almost real-time feel for the band's day-to-day activities, thoughts and plans. It gives artists an opportunity to share the less visible aspects of the band. It can also be set up to integrate with IM and other text messaging services so that you can broadcast messages to fans at a moment's notice. They can also be set up so that fans can respond to your journal as it develops.

Two popular, easy-to-use blog-creators are typepad.com and livejournal.com.

❐ **Give fans a page of their own.** A page dedicated to your fans, including pictures from shows and prize giveaways to be determined, will be visited often. Fan photos from shows and both candid and live band shots can also be included. Photos can be scanned from prints, taken with a digital camera, captured from video, or delivered from the film processing plant already on a CD. You can announce at shows that you've been taking pictures and they need to check out the website to see if their photo is there. Everyone likes sharing their claim to fame with friends.

You can tease your fans with "members only" areas on your website. This site feature will be possible only if your web host has provided you with a secure server feature. You can then put web content in areas that are password-protected, and only people who have registered with your site, or purchased a subscription, or have been given a "secret password" from you, can access it.

❒ **Start a "Fan of the Month" contest.** Each month take entries for why your fans think they are fan of the month. Urge them to be creative in their submissions, stretching the truth of why they should be chosen. The fan of the month can also have reign over the fan page, telling you what you should do to it. If the fan wants it pink that month, then pink it is! Contests are another good and fun way for growing your mailing list. And they keep people coming back to your site.

Of course it takes a lot of work, time and effort, sometimes even some cash to develop a site that communicates like this. But when you think in terms of the life value of your potential fan, it makes a lot of sense to go out of your way to make your visitors feel really special, delighted and willing to talk with you.

Simply because there are so many voices trying to be heard on this global forum, you will need your fans or customers to help you get noticed. The more personal relationships you build online, the farther the word of mouth spreads.

Direct-Selling Your Merchandise

The Rolling Stones' tongue logo. The dancing bears of the Grateful Dead. These graphics have become familiar to us all after seeing them repeatedly on those respective bands' merchandise. If you're a performing artist or band, you have a golden opportunity with each show to introduce the audience not only to your music but also to your branded merchandise ("merch" in industry lingo). From thrash punk hovels to arena concerts, artists often earn the bulk of their revenue from merch sales. Having a good selection of merchandise is important even when playing in small clubs.

Merchandise will earn you money, foster a sense of belonging among your fans, and get you talked about. Any personalized product, beyond officially released recordings, is merch.

At the core of your act's identity is the way you choose to represent yourself. Think long and hard about this because it's the most important thing in the whole merchandising process.

What to sell? Well, besides your CDs, other possibilities include T shirts, caps, condoms, pens, hoodies, beanies, bumper stickers, lighters, bottle openers, key chains, shot glasses, autographed photos of the band, sweatshirts, bandanas and more. These items usually fall under the marketing category of "advertising specialties" or "promotional novelties" and there are plenty of companies supplying them.

	Brunetto T-Shirts www.brunettotshirts.com	**Café Press** www.cafepress.com	**Contagious Graphics T-Shirts** www.contagiousgraphics.com/teeShirts	**Distroy** www.distroy.com
Available Merchandise	T-Shirts	Any	T-Shirts, Posters, & Stickers	T-Shirts
Available Colors	Up to 4	All	8	All
Set-Up Costs	None	None	$15.00	None
Minimum Quantity	12	None	24	None
Online Store Provided	No	Yes	No	Yes
CD Packaging Available	No	Yes	No	No
Handles Payment Transaction	No	Yes	No	Yes
Handles Fulfillment	No	Yes	No	Yes
Manages All Returns & Exchanges	No	Yes	No	Yes
Percentage Markup/Profit for Vendor	None	Base Price for Each Item	None	None
Premium Services Available	No	Yes	No	No
Promotion of Your Store	No	No	Yes	No

	Paw Media www.pawmedia.com	**Print Mojo** www.printmojo.com	**Spreadshirt** www.spreadshirt.com	**Zazzle** www.zazzle.com
Available Merchandise	T-Shirts & Mouse Pads	Clothing Apparel	Clothing Apparel	T-Shirts, Posters, Cards, & Stamps
Available Colors	All	8	All	All
Set-Up Costs	None	None	None	None
Minimum Quantity	10	24	None	None
Online Store Provided	No	Yes	Yes	No
CD Packaging Available	No	No	No	No
Handles Payment Transaction	Yes	Yes	Yes	Yes
Handles Fulfillment	No	Yes	Yes	Yes
Manages All Returns & Exchanges	No	Yes	Yes	Yes
Percentage Markup/Profit for Vendor	None	None	None	None
Premium Services Available	No	No	No	No
Promotion of Your Store	No	Yes	Yes	No

If you're going to sell merchandise at shows you'll need several items to make it a smooth affair:

• **A sales rep:** this will sometimes be a band member or a fan or roadie, who greets the potential buyers and controls the sales transactions. Some bands give the rep a commission, say 5%, on all sales.

• **Sales table**: longer is better for accommodating more people and spreading out your wares.

• **Solid color tablecloth** that complements your CD colors and that will 'lift' your merch off the table rather than have it lying flat.

• A bowl of individually wrapped **candies** (required!).

• **Flyer displays** that say what is available along with pricing. You can get plastic-coated easel boards that hold your flyer and stand up on the table for easy viewing from stores like Staples or Office Depot.

• A method of getting names & email addresses for your **Mailing list**: Depending on the crowd you're playing to, you can perhaps have a bowl with a sign that says, "Mailing List...Drop Your Card In", instead of having people write on a list.

• **Postcards** people can take away with them that invite them to your web site.

And this leads to all the online possibilities for merchandising and the companies that can help you get your merch line together. In general, there is usually no channel for music fans to buy band goods unless they attend a concert. If you want a piece of tour merchandise, it's only on sale one day at one venue. But with the internet bands have the opportunity to offer everything they sell through their web sites 24-7, and many companies have appeared so help facilitate your operations.

There are literally hundreds of merch vendors supplying everything from printing to web-based storefronts, complete fulfillment to unlimited color selection. To help you sort through the many choices I distilled a ton of information down to a few highly-rated choices on the charts on the previous two page.

The Best of the Rest

❒ **Brochures**. Leaflets, fliers, or other descriptive circulars; these are particularly useful for service businesses. Brochures can be very expensive, so if you do decide to use one, make it a "keeper" by offering information and tips that are valuable to the reader.

❒ **Coupon books.** Ever thought that coupons were only for groceries? Think again! In these money-conscious times consumers are turning to coupons for all kinds of services to help cut costs and make ends meet. A friend of mine uses the "Yellow

Coupon Book" in his region to offer discounts to his music instruction company, The Music Connection. He says these were crucial in establishing his business. Just be sure not to send out coupons too often or people will just wait for your coupon before making a decision to buy and you'll miss out on a lot of full price sales!

❒ **Advertising specialties**. Print your promotional message on anything from a mouse pad to a baseball cap, from a sticker to a coffee mug. A client of mine, Amalgam Entertainment, supplies all his retail accounts with bags that have the Amalgam logo and web address printed on them. They get free bags and Amalgam gets all that exposure for its products which that retailer carries. It's a clear "win-win" for all.

❒ **Bundling and Inserts**. Include your flyer or brochure with another company's product. I did this early on with my company. I made a deal with a local music magazine to insert my brochure in all 10,000 distributed magazines one month. What I was offering (resources and consulting for musicians) had an affinity with what the magazine was offering (musician news and stories from around the region). Make sure your item has a connection or affinity with the distributed vehicle so that your message gets across to your target market.

❒ **Samples**. Every one likes to get something for nothing. Giving away freebies creates a positive experience in the mind of the potential customers, thus making your business memorable. I've been doing this for ten years now, sharing free infoletters (*Music Biz Insight* and *Music Career Juice*) each month, as a way to educate music entrepreneurs and at the same time promote my products and services. These, combined with the content of my web site, now generate 99% of my business. Giving is receiving.

❒ **Trade Shows**. Exhibiting products at trade shows is an important sales tool, even more important in some categories than advertising and direct mail, according to a survey by Deloitte & Touche.

The survey of 6,000 sales and marketing professionals found that exhibitions are more effective than advertising and direct mail alone in:

- generating leads,
- introducing new products,
- taking orders,
- promoting brand image and
- generating new markets.

What else do you need to know?

Perhaps owing to the schmooze factor, the music and entertainment industries hold hundreds of trade shows and conferences each year.

❒ **Cable TV advertising.** More than any other medium, TV can generate an emotional reaction in viewers – and with the average household watching seven hours of TV *every day,* you are guaranteed an audience. Of course, network TV advertising is prohibitively expensive for most grass roots marketers. But with the explosion of cable TV, you now have a situation where it's a buyer's market as cable stations compete for smaller pieces of the viewer pie. With programs like Comcast's "Spotlight", for example, you can purchase 30 second spots for as little as $15 a piece. Plus, they will even produce the commercial for you *and* set up ordering and fulfillment services as well. In addition, cable advertising lets you target specific audiences and test market in micro markets throughout different regions of the country. Though not an appropriate medium for every product or service, cable TV is certainly worth looking into if you have the right offer.

All of these are forms of direct marketing – ways to directly reach your target market. We covered mobilizing your fans with street teams, building qualified mailing lists, and also ways to communicate your direct message through both traditional and electronic channels. Now we'll turn to marketing your music through live performances – one of the most powerful ways to get your message across in the arena of music.

))) ILLUMINATING TRIVIA (((

Did you know?...

It took the mail order catalog industry a hundred years to represent 4.5% of retail sales. It took online retailers only six years to accomplish the same feat.

Source: NARM Research Briefs (narm.com)

CH 7
Marketing Through Live Performances

"The whole idea is to deliver what money can't buy." - Bruce Springsteen

You've been calling a club for weeks, and you finally get the booker on the phone. Don't celebrate yet– the real work is still ahead. That crucial conversation you're about to strike up is an art that requires skill. Luck and talent won't help you much on the phone.

What you say and how you say it is as important as what you shouldn't say. By understanding the needs of the market in which you're, you can anticipate a booking agent's response and turn a "no" into a future opportunity.

While the recording industry continues to slump, the concert touring industry annually turns a profit. The pristine, unmediated dynamic between musician and audience seems to never lose its demand, providing that visceral experience music lovers crave. While Elton John and Dave Matthews fill arenas, smaller "jam band" circuits continue to buzz in mid-size venues, generating sizeable revenues for all involved.

On the local level, it's a bit of a different story.

Understand the Venue Business

The current club scene is experiencing a bit of a slump owing to competing entertainment options (like those amazing *home* entertainment systems) and some anti-drinking legislation. Despite the woes, however, the clubs still provide a crucial outlet for bands to hone their performance skills and catalyze local, regional and national followings. So how does one go about getting club gigs?

First, it's a fact that selling your band on the phone is a tough proposition. Try to realize the volume of calls clubs receive, then imagine the booker's frame of mind. You want exactly what 100 bands a day want. What makes *you* worthy of the coveted slot?

DIFFERENT LEVELS OF MUSIC TOURING ACTS

	NEW OR LOCAL ARTISTS	MID-LEVEL ARTISTS (MULTI-STATE TO NATIONAL)	NATIONAL HEADLINERS (NATIONAL & INTERNATIONAL)
PLAYERS	❑ Band or artist ❑ Agent (not likely) ❑ Fans	❑ Band or artist ❑ Agent ❑ Tour manager ❑ Fans ❑ Roadies ❑ Concert promoter ❑ AFM	❑ Band or artist ❑ Agent ❑ Tour manager ❑ Concert promoter ❑ Advance person ❑ Fans ❑ AFM ❑ Road manager & crew ❑ Sound tech. ❑ Light tech. ❑ Instrument tech. ❑ Tour publicist ❑ Tour accountant
VENUE SIZE	❑ Small clubs ❑ Self-produced shows ❑ 5-300	❑ Medium to large clubs ❑ Mid-size concert halls ❑ College auditoriums ❑ 300-3,000	❑ Large concert halls ❑ Stadiums ❑ 10,000-100,000
CD SALES LEVEL	❑ 0-100 units	❑ 1,000-10,000+ units	❑ 30,000-1,000,000+ units
AVERAGE REVENUE PER PERFORMANCE	❑ $0-$1,000	❑ $1,000-$3,000+	❑ $40,000-$1,000,000+

Before you call, do some market research. Make sure your music is compatible with the club's entertainment focus. For clubs you're unfamiliar with, use *The Musician's Atlas* (see chapter 17) to get some intelligence on the venue. Check the local entertainment guides for info on who's booked where. Also, make sure to space your gigs out in a local area, keeping at least three weeks between gigs. If possible make a personal contact first. The music business like most businesses is *relationship*-driven. If you can meet someone eye-to-eye, you'll have a head start.

When you call, keep your tone friendly and relaxed. Get right to the point. Bookers are busy. They need to know exactly what you want right away. Get a feel for each person's style. Be very clear about the date you want, thank them for their time, and leave a number. It's important to specify a particular night. That way, if your date won't work, there's a chance to ask what date will.

Instead of too-frequent callbacks that can irritate the booker, tell him or her you'll call them back in a couple of weeks. Then use that promise to launch the next conversation. Don't vent your anger on the booking agent. Remember, they're in control and you're not. You're in a buyer's market. The only control you have is your following. If you're trying to develop a club following, incurring the wrath of a booker could be a terminal setback.

Even in music meccas like L.A., the club circuit is small. Bookers and managers know when a band can draw a crowd. When you get to that point, a club that turned you down six months ago might call *you*.

But, nine times out of ten, clubs won't call you back. Accept this as the way it is. Be persistent, however. Give them a few weeks to hear your material, then call at least once a week, depending on the response. If they say they haven't got the CD by then, send another. Even when a booker is curt and abrupt, make a point of ending on a polite, friendly note. Cultivate a calm, hang-tough approach.

REAL NAMES OF REAL BANDS

- Alcoholocaust
- Apocalypse Hoboken
- The Boxing Ghandis
- Brady Bunch Lawnmower
- Bulimia Banquet
- Cap'n Crunch and the Cereal Killers
- Cindy Brady's Lisp
- Four Nurses of the Apocalypse
- Gefilte Joe and the Fish
- Headless Marines
- Hindu Garage Sale
- Hitler's Bikini
- Kathleen Turner Overdrive
- Lawn Piranhas
- Lesbian Ninjas
- Mao Tse Helen
- Max Roach and the Holders
- Mussolini Headkick
- My Dog Has Hitler's Brain
- Norman Bates and the Shower Heads
- Not Drowning, Waving
- Phenobarbidols
- The Pro-Midget Mafia
- Psychic Buddhist Gorillas
- Pungent Frustration
- Reluctant Stereotypes
- Roid Rogers and the Whirling Butt Cherries
- Sandy Duncan's Eye
- Screaming Headless Torsos
- Smegma & the Nuns
- To Live and Shave in LA
- Tragic Mulatto
- Trotsky Icepick
- The Well Hungarians
- Zombies Under Stress
- Zulu Leprechauns

Talking Business

Your job is to convince the booker that it would be to the club's advantage to have you play there. How do you communicate this?

First, emphasize the crowd you will draw. Even if it's just fifteen people, let them know. Second, stress the uniqueness of your music – what makes it stand out from the rest? Third, let the booker know about your promotional plan for the show and all the *free* publicity the club will receive from your mailings, flyers, radio announcements and newspaper calendar listings. Show them you are organized, professional and thinking ahead. This alone will set you apart from the crowd.

Should you send a contract when you secure a date? Most clubs operate strictly on verbal agreement. Usually this is okay. As you get more popular it becomes easier to secure written agreements with clubs. Early on, however, there's little you can expect in the way of formal contracts.

Remember, a club is a *business.* It has to make financial sense for them to give you a gig. Bands that haven't got any notoriety yet should get some college airplay in the vicinity of the clubs they want to play first. You have to respect the club's position; if no one's ever heard of you, how can they make money off the show?

Here are a few ideas for how you can work together with clubs to bring in larger crowds.

❑ Hook up with local promoters; there are dozens of promoters that would love to promote a club once a week.

❑ Call local record labels, record stores, magazines, newspapers, radio and TV stations and see if they want to have a night at the club. Lots of radio stations promote clubs to their listeners and are always looking for new venue to affiliate with. Labels are always renting clubs to showcase their bands to the local media.

❑ Call all the above people and talk to the promotion departments, especially at radio stations. See if you can send them tickets to your show. Make it a habit of mailing them tickets.

❑ Bundle your show into a package. Team up with two other acts, come up with a theme, and then approach the booker with your ideas. The club gets a fully packaged night, along with the followings of each act and the revenue this brings. Done creatively, you can probably get your pick of the night if done enough in advance.

❑ Set up a contest with the club, like a legs contest (girls or guys), or during intermission announce, "The first person to the bar with red underwear gets a free CD." Bands can donate CDs and tapes; clubs can donate free drinks. The point is to give everyone a good feeling about that club and that band.

❑ Run co-op ads in local magazines and newspapers advertising the show and the contest. Give the ads some pizzazz. Include coupons for free admission or a free drink with admission. This will make your ad a hundred times more effective and bring in a lot more people.

❒ Encourage the club owner to have his employees to put names on the clubs guest list. Their friends will add to the clubs regular crowd. Request that the band have an unlimited guest list. This will make the job of getting all their fans to your club easier.

The lesson is: *Don't start until you're ready.* Make sure your vocals are strong, your arrangements tight, your equipment adequate and your promotion happening. Jumping the gun and taking gigs for which you're not ready can take months - even years - to repair. As the saying goes, "You never get a second chance to make a first impression." Prepare and come out strong.

))) ILLUMINATING TRIVIA (((

Did you know...

...one of Bob Dylan's first recording gigs was playing harmonica on a Harry Belafonte album in 1960? The pay was $50.

Source: *The New Book of Rock Lists* by David Marsh

Beyond the Clubs

When most musicians think of "getting a gig," nightclubs are what usually come to mind. After all, clubs provide local forums for you to sharpen your stage act and spark that grassroots buzz so crucial for moving up to the next level of success. But clubs are not what they used to be and for some very good reasons.

First and foremost is population changes, or in marketing lingo, "demographics." Generally speaking the largest portion of club-goers today are people in their twenties. There are approximately 46 million twenty-somethings in America at present - a large pool for sure. But just ten years ago, when the "baby-boomers" were clubbing, there were 76 million of *them*.

In other words there were 30 million *more* potential club goers at that time. Correspondingly, the club scene was a lot healthier. Where are these 76 million now? Home raising families and grooving on their home-entertainment centers (*Note:* This is slowly changing as baby boomer *offspring* begin reaching college age. *That* population is over 85 million strong!).

While that's probably the most significant reason for a shrinking club scene, there are others as well. The lion's share of club profits are derived from bar receipts and people today are drinking less alcohol. Related to this are the numerous drunk-driving laws and drinking-age requirements, which have further eroded club profits and kept people home.

The heightened awareness of alcohol-related dangers has also affected liability insurance requirements for club owners. My father, for example, had a live entertainment club in Arizona that was put out of business because the state legislature (albeit controlled by a conservative Mormon majority) upped the liability requirement for all Arizona bars (to the tune, for my Dad, of $24,000 per year!). While it hasn't gotten *this* bad in most other states, liability insurance does account for a big chunk of a club's expenses – one most musicians rarely consider when negotiating fees.

But lest we start pitying the clubs for trends they can't control, it is also important to acknowledge how little clubs provide in terms of comfort, adequate ventilation, respect for musicians and general cleanliness. These too have kept potential patrons away. To battle shrinking profits clubs have resorted to everything from mobile DJs to karaoke. These are some of the real factors affecting *your* attempts at securing club gigs. So where else can musicians find performing work?

If you like to perform but feel a bit jaded on the club scene you're in luck. There are literally hundreds, probably thousands, of hidden gig opportunities awaiting your act's performance. Besides a chance to play, these jobs will usually pay you more than a club date and also allow you to reach audiences who probably wouldn't set foot in most clubs.

))) ILLUMINATING TRIVIA (((

Did you know...

Elvis Presley was tossed out of the "Grand Ole Opry" in 1954 after a show for a perceived lack of talent. He was also turned down by Arthur Godfrey's "Talent Scouts".

Getting Ready

Non-nightclub gigs tend to require a different standard of *professionalism.* You're aiming higher and dealing more with the "suit-and-tie crowd", so your presentation has to really shine. What does "professionalism" look like? Many things. First, the person that books your act should be a good communicator - someone who can succinctly and effectively deliver your sales pitch over the phone or on paper; has a high-functioning answering machine and upbeat message; possesses "people skills"; and is able to negotiate contracts and mediate between band members. With these skills you'll make great headway. Without them you're sunk.

Professionalism also means having all your "marketing communications" ready to go: promo kits, sales letters, business cards, contracts, confirmation letters, photos, testimonials from others you've worked for, demo tape, mailing labels, envelopes, etc.

While we shouldn't judge a book (or, in this case, a band) by its cover, in reality *we do.* First impressions stick and they're very hard to unglue, especially in the unforgiving world of business. Opt for the very best materials you can afford. Be sure your materials have a clear theme and that all contact information is clearly displayed on every component in the package. And keep good records!

Unlike club gigs, these will usually require written contracts between client and performer. In fact, you will find that some of these events will require two contracts--one from the client, and one from you.

Performance Contract Essentials Checklist

Regardless of the type or size of performing group, there are a number of standard elements that all contracts should contain:

1. The date of the agreement.
2. The artist's name, address, phone and fax number, and primary contact person.
3. The presenter (thereafter referred to as "employer") name, address, phone and fax number, and primary contact person.
4. The date and time of the performance, including number and length of set(s), and duration of breaks between sets.
5. The location of the venue where performance will take place.
6. The artist's fee, plus the time and manner of payment (check, cash, etc.); whether there is a deposit required; and a guarantee that there will be no taxes, union charges or other surprise deductions from the fee when it is paid.
7. Any technical requirements regarding stage size, lighting, sound and dressing room amenities.
8. Arrival time, set-up time and the time for sound-checking.
9. An "Act of God" clause which releases the artist from liability for failure to perform if such failure is caused by an event beyond their control. Such clauses are referred to as "boilerplate" (standard legal clauses common to most time-sensitive agreements).

Of course, what's standard for bands may not be for presenters. They may want the contract to include other "essentials" (from their perspective) such as a clause about decibel levels or a "radius clause" wherein your group can't play within three or five miles of his club within 30, 60 or 90 days. The latter, however, usually happens with clubs and only when the group has a large following.

You might also want to find out if the venue is liable for any damage to your stage-equipment by customers during your hours of employment (as stated in the contract) or any damage to the customers if, say, a speaker falls on one of them. If the club isn't liable, you'll want to check your own insurance coverage. You are ultimately responsible for your own equipment.

Contract Riders

The above are the nine essentials of a performance contract, also known as the "contract face." That should suffice for most gigs. Any additional requirements fall under the heading of "Riders" - supplemental attachments to the standard contract face.

Contract riders can range from such simple requests as a meal and beverage for band members all the way to the picayune, like the removal of brown M&Ms from the mix (I kid you not)!

Riders are vital unless you wish to exist solely on the presumed generosity of club owners and concert promoters. On the other hand, you can't expect a club or a promoter to provide what you need unless they know what it is. It's best to make the rider part of the contract so you have only one document to sign.

The information you need in order to access these gigs won't be found in most gigging and club directories. Your public library will be the key resource in digging out these hidden opportunities. Libraries are repositories of useful information. Get to know the reference librarian. This person will be your guide through the many directories you're likely to consult.

As you find potential clients for your services, add them to your database. Software programs like *Act!* and *Indie Band Manager* help you manage your contacts. If you prefer hardcopy make copies of the **Booking Research Worksheet** at the end of this chapter and use one for each contact. Putting them in a 3-ring binder will keep them organized and handy.

Where to Look for and What to Do

What follows is a list of gig possibilities with information on how to access them. It's not a complete list. Hopefully you'll be able to add your own ideas to it as you brainstorm with your band mates. The gigs I'll be discussing cover a wide spectrum and won't apply to every musician. Some will match your act perfectly and others you'll want nothing to do with. A few may require more music than you have right now. But that doesn't mean you can't be preparing for them in the days ahead.

Associations. Check out the multi-volume *Encyclopedia of Associations* and you'll find over 25,000 associations (read, similar interest groups) in the U.S. Start with topical associations that strike your interest: environmental, arts, religious, media, educational, computer, medical, social service, science fiction, etc. Virtually every association sponsors state, regional and national meetings and conventions, and many of them hold dinners, programs, dances, or fund raisers that need music.

Call them and ask for two things: First, request they send you information about their association with a calendar of the coming years' events (you will have, of course, already done some research on the Web) and, second, the name of the association's Entertainment Coordinator or Chairperson of the Entertainment Committee. When you reach the entertainment person (after you've studied the information sent to you) be ready with a sales pitch tailored to their own special interests. The key is to create a "tie-in" with what they're all about. Begin with local associations and branch out.

Businesses of all kinds are possibilities for a wide variety of music work. Though business events are often booked by entertainment agencies or public relations firms, many are open to outside suggestions. Businesses need music for any number of functions including ground-breaking ceremonies, grand openings, seasonal sales, trade shows, promotions and retirements, company milestones, Christmas and New Year's Eve parties, and fashion shows.

I once played a reggae gig for a Caribbean travel agency at a bridal fashion show in the Providence Civic Center in Rhode Island. Our job was to provide background music to entice brides to choose the Caribbean for their honeymoon spot. We were literally put behind a curtain, out of sight. So we just jammed some reggae grooves for two hours and walked away with $1500! This, and a few other gigs like it, helped us finance a recording we were making at the time. Can your act fit in with any of these events? Businesses are everywhere. *The Yellow Pages* is your best source for ideas. The possibilities are endless.

Non-profit Organizations sponsor all kinds of events that need music. Again, begin locally with a directory from your public library and scope out those organizations you resonate with. There are as many non-profits as there are associations so it's a wide-open field. Don't forget civic orchestras, historical societies, health organizations and foundations - all of which may sponsor dinners, dances or shows to benefit a cause. Some of these will be non-paying (basic freight and technical costs excluded), but what is lost in cash can be gained in publicity and important contacts. As with the business and association gigs, these jobs often lead to repeat business for your act.

Conventions make up one of the largest, fastest growing markets in contemporary America. Just about every business, industry, government agency, social group, and professional association has, at the very least, an annual meeting or conference to discuss common interests, socialize with colleagues, make useful contacts, and plan for the coming year. And they all hire musicians for entertainment. Try to find out if there will be a particular theme for the convention and then tie-in your act with that theme.

The people you want to contact for these gigs are Events Planners. They specialize in organizing all the different components of a successful convention. Most work through entertainment companies but isn't that what you are? Again, the way you present yourself makes all the difference. There's a great annual resource called *Meeting Professionals International Directory* (214-712-7700, TX) that will give you the contact info on these people. You should be able to find it in a large public library. See also the *Yellow Pages* under "Convention Services and Facilities".

Country Clubs need music for an astounding variety of occasions. They have regularly scheduled dinners, dances, parties, athletic events as well as more specialized "theme" parties, seasonal activities and shows. When you think of "clubs", however, don't limit yourself to just the big country clubs. Include every organized group you can think of, and you'll expand your market to include all kinds of non-public but well-paying gigs. Since country clubs are often linked to golf courses you can find a complete national list of them in a directory called *Golf Courses: The Complete Guide to over 14,000 Courses Nationwide.*

Park Programs abound, and local government agencies are often in control. Begin with the "Recreation and Park Departments" in your region. If you want to check out parks programs outside your region consult *The Municipal Executive Directory* to put you in touch with key people in parks and recreation departments. Other government-sponsored work can include inner-city festivals, cultural enrichment programs, officers and NCO clubs and even foreign tours. Some of this information can be found through the mayor's office in the city of your choice.

Cruise Lines. Want to spend the winter jammin' on the warm waters of the Caribbean? Then perhaps cruise line work is for you. According to the Cruise Lines International Association (CLIA), the cruise industry is one of the fastest growing categories in the entire leisure market. The industry has tripled in size every ten years! New employees are needed to support the growing cruise vacation business, and this includes a wide assortment of musicians. Cruise lines rely on entertainment agents such as Marcelo Productions out of Miami (305-854-2228) and ProShip Entertainment out of Quebec (514-485-8823), who regularly hold auditions in various cities. Players should be able to read as well and have a wide repertoire to draw from. Salaries range from $350 to $500 per week and include food, lodging and transportation to and from the ship. For inside information on this job option see *How to Get a Job with a Cruise Line* by Mary Fallon Miller (see chapter 17).

Hotels are a prime market for musicians and not just GB (general business) acts. Hotel-sponsored parties are frequent and a variety of music is sought for these. Much of this work comes through word of mouth. If you have a good relationship with the catering or sales staff, you'll get these jobs. A full list of a particular city's hotels can be obtained from that city's Convention & Visitor's Bureau or Department of Tourism.

Private Parties are another specialized but excellent market to pursue. Since many of these are held in well-to-do homes it is important that you be able to relate socially as well as musically. How do you find out who's throwing a party? One way is to contact party organizers and caterers. Send them your business cards, letting them know what you can offer their clients by way of music. Stay in touch. You never know what will turn up.

))) ILLUMINATING TRIVIA (((

Did you know...

...that Stephen Stills flunked an audition to be in The Monkees? – he joined Buffalo Springfield instead.

Public Relations firms and Advertising agencies can be good music clients because they are involved in creating and staging all kinds of events. A band I was playing with was approached by a PR rep for McDonalds to see if we'd be interested in performing at the grand opening of one of their restaurants. It's nice when they come to you, but you can also go to them. Whatever your musical specialty, you should let all the advertising and PR firms in your area know, so when they need your type of music they'll know where you are. Remember, public relations and advertising people thrive on innovation and are open to suggestions for new or unusual uses of music. Therefore, when talking with these firms, let creativity rule. Make suggestions that are too unusual to present to other clients, and you'll be treated as a kindred spirit.

Schools offer a broad market for all kinds of music, whether elementary, high school or college. Colleges, in particular, are rich with playing opportunities. They should be viewed as small cities with scores of events happening each week throughout the year. If you're serious about playing the college circuit you should definitely check out NACA (The National Association of Collegiate Activities, 3700 Forest Drive, Ste. 200, Columbia SC 29204, 800-845-2338). NACA holds annual regional conferences (read trade shows) where musical acts can exhibit their wares for the hundreds of college talent buyers passing through. Live showcase opportunities are also possible and, if you're liked, can result in "block bookings" along the college touring circuit. To book yourself at colleges, call the student activities office and find out who is responsible for hiring entertainment at that school. Call that person and inquire about specific events during the upcoming year that might be appropriate for your style of music.

For music opportunities on the elementary, middle, junior high and high school levels, check out *How to Make Money Performing in Public Schools* by David Heflick (Silcox Productions, PO Box 1407, Orient, WA 99160). Heflick discusses what schools are looking for, developing a program, how arts commissions work in relation to schools, promotion, scheduling, performance, payment and follow up. An excellent handbook.

These are just a few of the thousands of "non-nightclub" opportunities available to performing musicians. Musical jobs are literally all over the map and there's no reason you shouldn't enjoy the rewards of these less-common jobs. With the current slump in the club scene and surplus of willing bands, these lesser-known jobs should be all the more attractive.

Just to repeat and underscore, most of these jobs will bring you in close contact with the professional business world. The musician who can communicate on the same professional level will be the one who builds the bridge that gets the gig.

CHEEKY ADVICE FOR PERFORMING BANDS

- ❒ Never start a trio with a married couple.
- ❒ No one cares who you've opened for.
- ❒ A string section does not make your songs sound any more "important".
- ❒ If your band has gone through more than 4 bass players, it's time to break up.
- ❒ Don't say your video's being played if it's only on the Austin Music Network.
- ❒ Never name a song after your band.
- ❒ Never name your band after a song.
- ❒ Drummers can take off their shirts or they can wear gloves, but not both.
- ❒ It's not a "showcase"– it's a gig that doesn't pay.
- ❒ Playing in Albany, Springfield and St. Albans doesn't mean you're on tour.
- ❒ Although they come in different styles and colors, electric guitars all sound the same. Why do you keep changing them between songs?
- ❒ If you use a smoke machine your music sucks. Ditto a light show.
- ❒ Remember, if blues solo's are so difficult, why can so many 16 year olds play them?
- ❒ If you ever take a bad publicity photo, destroy it. Otherwise you may turn up in places like The Boston Rock & Roll Museum (www.dirtywater.com)

Now let's look at ways you can get the most promotional mileage out of every gig you play.

Making the Most of Every Gig

One of the keys to music business success is the ability to maximize limited resources. This simply means making the most of the time, money and effort available to promote your career. Though your resources are meager it's what you do with them that really counts.

This principle applies to every aspect of a musician's life, but I want to focus on just one of them: *How to get the most out of every gig you play.*

Gigs are one of the most potential-rich avenues for bands and musicians in terms of networking and exposure. Yet few take full advantage of the opportunities they present. *Each gig should be seen as an occasion for expansion of your music and performing skills, your fan base, your media contacts and industry relationships, etc.* What follows are 12 ways to get the most out of every gig.

You've just booked a gig at a new club and it's two months away. Let's look at some of the things you can do *now* to maximize this performance before, during and after the show.

Marketing Before the Show

1. ***Find out all you can about the room you're going to play.*** Know the stage size, what times bands are expected to sound check, begin and end playing and whether there's a dressing room or not. Find out about the sound and lighting system if it's provided and talk to the sound person. If possible, ask other bands who've played the room for tips and pointers. Remember, you're there to perform a show, not worry about all these details. Get the right information before the gig and you'll have that much less anxiety during the gig.

2. ***Rehearse your show straight through*** as if it were the real thing. Pay attention to your stage *presence* as well as your stage sound. Practice any movements or dance steps you're planning to use at the gig. You may also want to hold a full dress rehearsal and have someone snap some digital photos or shoot a low-budget video of the group to see what the audience will see. This is always educational (and often humbling!). Remember, you're trying to make the *most* of this gig.

3. ***Publicize the show***. To save money, all of the following can be done electronically, but hard copy still creates an impression. So if the budget allows for it, print up a bunch of flyers with all pertinent information, including contact number. You're competing with a lot of other events so you want your flyer to stand out. Use colorful paper and eye-catching graphics. Seek the advice of a friend who's an artist or go the extra distance and have a full professional create a killer gig poster for your act, leaving a blank space at the bottom for all relevant info.

Once you have your flyer in hand it's time to send it out. First, send it to the club you'll be playing. This tells the club that you're serious about packing the room. Second, send it to all music writers in the local media. To obtain this information, check out the Further Resource section in chapter 17.

The next list you want to assemble is that of local radio. Most stations have local concert listings as part of their news segment and you'll want to target a flyer to each. College radio stations will be the most receptive. Be sure the station receives your notice at least a week before the show. If the gig is extra-special (i.e., a high-profile showcase-type room), you may also want to send out personal invitations and free tickets to local music industry representatives (record or ad execs, booking agents, personal managers, entertainment attorneys, radio personnel, etc.). Remember, think ***maximization.***

Besides your mailings, you'll also want to post your flyers in music stores, hangouts, inside the venue (don't forget the bathroom stalls!) and on all community bulletin boards in the area. Remember, it's illegal in many cities to hang posters on public property, with fines ranging from $50-$500! So keep your nose clean.

If you want to save money on the mailings, you can have your flyer reduced to one-quarter its size (from 8 1/2 x 11 to 4 1/4 x 5 1/2) and printed on postcard stock. This lowers your postal rate about $.27 per piece. If you're doing huge mailings on a monthly basis, check with the post office about a "bulk-mailing permit" for additional savings.

Marketing During the Gig

At last, the night has arrived. You walk into the club, greet the sound engineer (you already know each other), park your belongings in the appropriate space, and proceed to set up on the familiar stage. Smooth. Now here are a few more things you can do to make tonight's show a standout:

4. ***Have a banner with the band's logo*** hung up behind the act, high enough to be easily read by all (for good prices on banners try ASAP Banners (http://www.asapbanners.com), Artist Promo (http://www.artistpromo.com/band-stage-banners.htm) or Jakprints (http://www.jakprints.com). You'd be surprised how many people will see and hear your act and never know *who* you are. A visible banner solves that problem.

5. Place ***"table-tents"*** with band information, perhaps some lyrics and gig schedules on each table around the club. Use sturdy, post-card stock for best results.

6. ***Set up a visible area for merchandise*** (CDs, T-shirts, bumper stickers, etc.). The person (non-band member; though a band member or two should be there when available to interact with fans) running the merchandising can also oversee the new fan mailing list. A longer table is better for accommodating more people and spreading out your wares. Use a solid color tablecloth that complements your CD colors, anything that will 'lift' your merch off the table rather than have it lying. Make sure there are plenty of writing instruments and paper on hand. For more merchandising ideas, see chapter 6.

7. Have plenty of ***business cards*** with contact person's name and number in the pockets of all band members and support crew. Distribute them liberally.

8. When you're on stage remember to ***make your show visually as well as aurally stimulating***. You're on display and all your clothing, colors, movements and

lines should blend with the music you're playing. Give the people what they want – a feast of sight and sound. This is an essential part of "working the crowd."

Marketing After the Gig

You just had a great gig! Congratulations. A lot more people know about you now than before this evening. There's a small buzz brewing and now it's time to follow it up.

9. But first, before you leave the club, ***try to secure another gig*** with the owner while you're fresh in his mind. At the very least, seek a verbal commitment and call within a few days to confirm and formalize it.

10. Before leaving the club ***make sure the dressing room (if there is one) is in the same condition you found it in***. While this may sound trite, it's a basic human consideration and will speak well of your act.

11. ***Strike while it's hot!*** As soon as possible, follow-up on any industry contacts made at the gig. Call and thank them for coming to the show. Build rapport. Network.

12. Finally, ***send a personal letter to all new fans***, thanking them for coming to the show and informing them further about the band and other ways they can support you (for example, calling club owners, calling radio stations to request your song, purchasing your music at local retail outlets, telling their friends about you, etc.).

More and more, we are seeing the smarter bands being brought home because they know how to organize publicity, work the radio, boost promotion and generally maximize and optimize their limited resources. After all, why should one gig equal *one* when it can equal *ten*? Maximization is the key. Go for it!

Bringing It All Home: Organizing a House Concert

House concerts are a long-standing tradition on the folk and acoustic circuit but can be used by any act if the appropriate setting can be found. They are usually organized by the artist in conjunction with a fan who would like to host the event at their home. In general, you may need to provide a bit more hand-holding to the host, but you'll be dealing with a lot less politics than with the club scene.

Here are some tips for making a house concert work for you:

- ❑ Presenting a house concert is like planning a good party. You need space, performers, an audience, goodies and promotion.

- ❑ The space can be a large living or family room in the host's house. Arrange the seating with an aisle for audience and performers to get in and out easily. Maximize the space and make sure lower seating is up front.

- ❑ Moderate amplification is usually fine and pay attention to the room's acoustics. Wood is great but lots of glass can make the sound brittle.

❑ Make sure parking is adequate and have someone outside directing people where to park if necessary.

❑ Try to get performers a 'Green Room' where they can change their clothes, prepare and unwind.

❑ Think about having an opening act to warm things up. Split bills need to be worked out beforehand so that logistics flow smoothly and all monies are accounted for.

❑ Speaking of monies, house concert tickets are often priced higher than club tickets since there won't usually be bar receipts to supplement the door admission. I've paid up to $25, and for national acts, I've heard of prices as high as $75 per person.

❑ Offer tasty treats or even suggest people bring a dish for a potluck. But be careful with serving alcohol. Keep it to beer and wine and remember liability. Coffee, tea, decaf, juices, seltzer, spring water are all standard fare at these events.

❑ Always have a merchandise table both for merch sales and for people to sign up for your mailing list.

Tech and the Touring Band

Tech help on the road. Thanks to portable technology, a band's grueling 3-month cross-country concert trek has become a bit more bearable. Wireless communication – via vice, email and chat – lets rockers stay in touch with their girl (or boy)friends and families back home like never before. Digital cameras and video camera help chronicle tour high jinks for later DVD release. Microscopic computer recording rigs allow musicians to work on new albums from hotel rooms, and digital music players provide an opportunity to bring thousands of CDs' worth of music on a bus that's often too cramped for the band members alone.

Guerrilla Gigging?

Punk is back, and its got a laptop. A new breed of alternative rocker is once again giving the finger to the corporate music machine, thanks to an arsenal of do-it-yourself new media.

Organizing using the Web, cell phones and instant messaging, upstart guitar bands are staging secret, spontaneous concerts at unconventional venues in the latest online music craze, dubbed "guerrilla gigging."

Guerrilla gigs came to prominence when London-based band, The Others, commandeered two London Underground trains to perform an impromptu set for 200 fans in the summer of '05. While better-established bands might have needed several months and a costly marketing campaign to pull it off, The Others summoned the crowd in just a few hours, with a cryptic message to the band's Web forum members to meet at a local pub.

Once assembled, fans used SMS messages to tip off friends across town before moving to a nearby train station to pack an eastbound train for a furious 30-minute set – belted out using a megaphone while onlookers crowd-surfed in transit.

While free concerts are not new, unknown acts' recent success in distributing music, building a fan base and calling ad hoc performances online eschews the marketing channels of the increasingly risk-averse major record labels, whose support was traditionally seen as critical to finding fame.

The thrill comes from just "playing for the hell of it," according to Art Brut guitarist Chris Chincilla, who uses an iBook G4 to burn CD-Rs and posts to his band's forum to announce short-notice guerrilla gigs at venues like funeral parlors and galleries. "You never know what to expect. You can arrange a last-minute gig the day before, put it up on your web site, send it out to the mailing list, and there will be hundreds of people there," he said.

"Sometimes the music industry doesn't want to help, so you just do it any way you can. We use SMS, email, mailing lists, message boards, my Sony Ericsson T68i and technologies like MSN Messenger and iChat; then people pass details on to other people to spread the word."

The emerging phenomenon is a perfect example of technology mobilizing cultural collective action, according to Howard Rheingold, whose book, *Smart Mobs: The Next Social Revolution*, examines how mobile devices help conjure public congregations out of thin air.

"Just as the Fender guitar was the enabler for the rock 'n' roll revolution," he said, "the mobile phone plus online communication mean that flash mobs, spontaneous gigs and other forms of self-organized entertainment are going to continue to break out and transform the way people get together to meet, entertain and make art."

BOOKING RESEARCH WORKSHEET

Package Out: Follow-up Call: ______________________

Date

Name of Club/Facility ______________________

Address ______________________

Phone Number(s) ______________________

Fax ______________________

Contact Name ______________________

Musical Style Preferences ______________________

Set Structure ______________________

Budget Information ______________________

Booking Procedure ______________________

Past Acts ______________________

Room Capacity ______________________

Stage Size ______________________

Sound System ______________________

Monitor System ______________________

Soundperson Name ______________________

Lights ______________________

Dressing Room ______________________

Standard Amenities for Bands ______________________

Additional Notes ______________________

____

____

____

CH 8

Marketing to Producers & Record Labels

> *"All the inspiration I ever needed was a phone call from a producer."*
> - Cole Porter

This book is written primarily for artists and industry careerists of an *entrepreneurial* bent. Most of you have either abandoned the notion of "getting signed" to a label or you never embraced the notion in the first place. You're aware (sometimes painfully aware) of the typical inequities of signing over your creation to larger companies. You've seen great talent have the life sucked out of it as it came up against the impatience of bottom line demands.

But, of course, the record industry is not all one monolithic Goliath bent on destroying the art of David. There is a great variety once you move away from the multinationals towards the fringes and corners of the industry, and these "off-the-mainstream" companies can indeed serve as creative partners in your career.

))) ILLUMINATING TRIVIA (((

HE'S A (RIPPED OFF) SOUL MAN

Testifying before California's Senate's Judiciary Committee, singer Sam Moore, formerly of Sam and Dave, recalled learning in his 50s that his retirement fund would be $67 a month because his record label never reported income to his pension fund.

The Current State of the Recording Industry

It's clear from all indications that the recording industry, as we've known it, is on the decline. Sales of physical recordings (essentially, CDs), after a light increase in 2004, fell another 7% in '05, making it five out of six years of declining sales. More importantly, the number of *multi-platinum sellers* have also been declining for five straight years, lessening the revenue available to record company divisions across the board.

Since the entire infrastructure of record company culture is built on a business model that demands the sale of physical product for profit, we can expect a continued decline in company revenue. It's important to remember: the whole dynamic of physical music distribution is changing. What we're really seeing is the *atrophying* of distribution and its replacement with *access* to music.

So what does this mean for music-makers looking to partner up with record companies and producers?

Though the *record* industry part of the music business has been the most hard hit in recent years, producers and labels are nevertheless always on the lookout for great songs and great talent, for these continue to make the whole industry go 'round, both in the core and peripheral parts of the business. There may be fewer signings at the major label level these days, but there are still opportunities both inside and outside this space. Indie labels in particular continue to show strength and creative development as they sign and produce new sounds for our listening pleasure.

Perhaps you have songs, beats, arrangements, demos or master recordings you'd like to pitch to producers or record labels. Maybe you would like to get on a compilation CD a record company is planning to release. Or perhaps you play an unusual instrument or possess a unique vocal style a producer may find useful for upcoming recording projects.

Let's look at some ways you can interact with producers and labels to help forward your career and business.

Your Demo Recording/Calling Card

Ideally, you want to *attract* the attention of producers and labels by first creating a buzz in your regional market. You do this primarily through your performances and your fans. But, just as with most things in the development of music careers, you must first create some success on a smaller level before magnetizing the attention of various movers and shakers who can take you to that higher level you aspire to.

This means recording a demo that you can sell at shows, get some radio airplay and reviews with, and send to potential producers or labels.

For those with the goal of attracting these entities, a demo recording is your calling card.

Fortunately, recording technology is now so good and so accessible, it's become fairly easy to either create a master-quality demo yourself, or find someone you know who has the gear and can record you and your band for a reasonable price.

But remember, if your demo isn't excellent it will do more harm than good. You never get a second chance to make a first impression. Everyone today expects professional-sounding recordings because they're accustomed to high-fidelity sound – it's not the exception but the rule. The standards for recorded sound are still set in the media capitals – New York, Los Angeles, and Nashville – and those standards apply to your demo just as much as to a pop record.

Another caveat: Just because you *can* create a recording (demo or CD), doesn't necessarily mean you *should.* The market is saturated with musical product right now that is *not* ready for prime time. These thousands of half-baked efforts are clogging up the pipeline and making it harder for more complete efforts to shine. Don't release music into the market until *it's* ready and *you're* ready.

Though the ins and outs of recording music is way beyond the scope of this book, there are two bits of information I'd like to offer that will serve you well:

1. Modern recording technology has afforded anyone with a modicum of musical ability the ability to arrange, record, edit, mix and master a demo recording from the desktop with relative ease.

Machines cannot make good music, but they can make good music sound great with the right combination of tech savvy and good ears. While there's no reason you can't do it all yourself, it is advisable to have another musician acquainted with the gear to give their input and provide some objectivity in the process.

2. The key ingredient to a successful recording experience is pre-*production* – Spend the requisite time trying different arrangements and sounds, rehearsing, reviewing, and rehearsing some more until you've got the song exactly the way you want it recorded.

How many songs should you include on your demo? The general rule is three, and be sure to front load it with your *best* song first. You want to grab and hold the listener's attention from the get-go.

Of course, the earlier you can get a producer involved with your project the better. ***Producers can help bring out the best from your music, and their connections can often move your music into larger spheres of influence.***

What Producers Can Do For You

A producer may or may not have a sensitive musical ear, or great business abilities, such as that of raising money. He may or may not be wise enough to surround himself with people who have the talents which he does not possess. He may or may not be personally involved in the lives and life-styles of his artists.

However, the one thing that all highly successful producers do have in common is an almost unfailing instinct for producing a highly commercial and profitable product that will attract one or more segments of the buying public.

A producer can provide you with a trained, objective ear that isn't boxed in by personal emotional investment. He can see and hear the music more clearly and that's what you want.

Let's see what a producer typically does when working with an artist signed to a mid-level record deal. Though varying, record producers are usually responsible for:

1. creating a budget for the production with the artist;

2. applying for compulsory licenses for songs, when necessary;

3. selecting and scheduling time in the studio;

4. renting extra instruments and equipment;

5. obtaining a contractor for extra (union or non-union) musicians, if necessary;

6. completing union and record company paperwork;

7. maintaining accurate records of names, timings, and so forth for label credits and conveying this information to the record company, when applicable;

8. seeing that all bills are paid in a timely manner;

9. managing each recording project to ensure that it stays close to its budget; and,

10. keeping the 'bird's-eye view' of the project through overseeing and orchestrating all the various elements of the recording process.

This list depends, of course, on how much the artist is involved in the production, engineering, and business aspects of the project. Artists often appropriately get "co-producing" credit on a recording as they are often in the best position to contribute musical, arranging, and sound recording ideas to the recording project.

Too, most recording artists reading this book aren't signed to a mid-level label and are doing most of the production work themselves. But, to the extent you are using a producer, you need to determine which items from the above list are relevant to your particular project.

Another great value in working with a producer, it that he is very often connected to labels and other parts of the music business, and can serve as a bridge to wider pastures for artists.

But how do you find them?

))) ILLUMINATING TRIVIA (((

Did you know?...
...that from 1983-85 Neil Young deliberately withheld his hit material from Geffen Records until his contract ran out as retribution toward David Geffen for suing Young for not delivering "commercial" albums?

Finding the Right Producer

Producers come in all shapes and sizes with a vast range of production "styles" – from micro-management to laissez-faire.

Depending on where they fall on that continuum, producers can be perceived as the Svengalis of the business – responsible for transforming raw talent (or lack thereof) into artists and hit-makers, or as Zen Masters – unobtrusive in the process of letting the particular genius of their musicians shine through.

A producer's role is often determined by the style of music they're producing. As Moses Avalon states in his illuminating book, *Confessions of a Record Producer:* "In rock, the members of the band are the songwriters and the instrumentalists, and the producer has a more passive role, but in R&B and rap, the dynamics of the producer's role are more intricate. They usually write all the music and do all the arranging of the rhythm tracks. Then they find a vocalist, who will be the artist to sing the lyric track".

You need to determine what producer style works best with you and/or your band's style of music and personality.

Producers are not always easy to locate. If you're looking for a producer for a recording project you want someone whose work you already resonate with. Phil Ramone or The Neptunes may be out of reach for now, so concentrate on those who have produced recordings you dig from the indie music world. Their names are easy to find on a recording's liner notes.

Then find the contact info for the artist whose recording you like and make contact, inquiring how you can get in touch with that particular producer. Most indie artists or their managers are accessible and willing to provide this information. Same with the label. You might also ask them about their own experience with that producer: Was it a positive experience? Negative? Why? Is there any advice they'd like to offer to someone considering using the same producer?

You can also try "googling" the producer's name to see if he or she has a web site, or shows up in message boards, news articles or blogs. Another resource you can consult is ProductionHUB, Inc. (http://www.productionhub.com), an online resource and industry directory for film, television, video and digital media production.

A good print directory, co-published by The Music Business Registry and RPM direct, is the annual *Producer & Engineer Directory.* Check it out at http://www.rpmdirect.com.

One-time record producer Moses Avalon also offers a full-spectrum producer/artist matching service that I think is a good idea for serious artists with the budget to afford it. Contact him at http://www.mosesavalon.com.

Once you've located a producer that seems like a good match, use the following guidelines to help make a decision whether to move forward with this person or not:

❒ Is he a good communicator? - The psychology of the producer/artist relationship is as crucial a factor as the musical dimensions when a recording project is undertaken.

❒ Is the producer a musician? - This, of course, isn't essential but it does allow for more affinity and common language ground to work on. Musician/Producers will often bring musical ideas about arrangements, harmonies, instrumentation and other musical nuances that can greatly improve the sound of a recording.

❒ Is he also skilled as an engineer? - A producer who knows his way around the gear has a distinct advantage over one who doesn't and, in the end, can save the whole production project a lot of time.

❒ Is he very "hands-on" or more "let the artist do his thing"? - Again, this is a question of style and your own comfort level.

❒ What role does the producer see himself having in the *pre*-production phase (rehearsals, selecting musicians, etc.)?

❒ Is he a "signature sound" producer (one who leaves a strong, individual sonic stamp on all the recordings he produces) and is this sound what you really want?

How Producers Get Paid

Producer fees are all over the map. As with artists, producers often have a built-in reluctance to discuss money or anything businesslike. Some producers, therefore, have their own manager (if available) to discuss money matters. If that is the case, you'll be negotiating with the producer's rep.

Most producers working with already signed artists, usually ask for a cash advance against sales royalties. However, unless you already have a major-label contract, this arrangement is pretty unlikely. You can't really offer a producer sales royalties if there's nothing to sell.

Most mid-level producers charge an hourly or "project" rate for their services. In the Boston area, up-and-coming producers usually charge between $300 and $2000 per song, depending on how much they contribute to the project and how much marquee value their name has. Hourly rates vary between $50. and $150.

A producer may also ask for a percentage of your record company advance, *if* the demo they produce gets you a deal. This figure is typically 3-5% of the gross advance payment. But, again, everything is negotiable in this business.

The Artist/Producer Agreement

A production agreement doesn't have to be a scary thing. It's simply a tangible document that spells out the responsibilities of a creative collaboration. Any contract not built on a relationship of trust isn't worth the paper it's printed on. As long as you feel there is integrity and ethics in your relationship with your producer, you're on a good track.

Below are the points you will want to clarify *before* sitting down with your producer to work out an agreement. Once you've worked out the main outlines, you'll then bring this to your attorney who can create an agreement document you and the producer can sign.

A **Sample Producer/Artist Agreement** can be found at the end of this chapter.

These are the *Basic Contents of a Producer/Artist Deal Agreement:*

- the number of tracks to be recorded;
- the advance (or, in this case, down payment) per track, or the overall advance for the entire project;
- the date on which the advances will be paid;
- statement of copyright ownership of sound recordings (that would be *your* company, most likely);
- the royalty rate (if any), along with any escalations in this rate and whether the rate is to be calculated at that rate by reference to the wholesale or the retail price;
- the recording budget should be specified but it should be stated that the producer will have no responsibility for any excess costs, unless they have been incurred because of willful neglect or default on his part.
- the credit requirements: on liner notes, etc;
- when pre-production will commence.

(For further helpful guidance on these kinds of agreements, see to Avalon's *Confessions of a Record Producer,* 2nd. Ed., chapter 14, especially the budget information on pp. 134f.)

What is a "Production Deal"?

This is a different sort of deal. It's where the producer signs you to *his* production company, records you and then shops the recording to the label he is "signed" to, or seeks a deal with a label on the artist's behalf.

Marketing Your Music to Record Labels

"If an album fails to create immediate excitement, word comes from on high to shift manpower and marketing dollars to a different project. This syndrome, far more than substandard royalty rates, is what devastates artists."
- Danny Goldberg, former president of Mercury and Warner Bros. Records

The title of this book is *Indie* Marketing Power. It's whole approach is doing it yourself in the context of things *indie*, apart from the "musical industrial complex" (that is, the major label system).

If you're interested in trying to obtain a major label recording contract, you're probably reading the wrong book (though I hope, by now, you've been converted)! There are plenty of places online that can help you groom yourself for *that* goal. Starpolish.com and Garageband.com are two that immediately come to mind.

To get my own philosophy on the major label system, please refer to an article I wrote titled, *"The REAL Reason Major Labels Suck (for Artists)"* at:

http://www.mbsolutions.com/articles/companies_suck.html

If, however, you're interested in marketing to indie labels, then you're in the right place. By the way, I'm not advocating that all indies are virtuous while all majors are evil. Some indies have screwed artists as much as their multinational counterparts have. But in general you'll find more personal attention at an indie, as well as more commitment to you and your music.

Of course, this assumes you know *who* you're dancing with.

Indie labels are a richly diverse group of companies, spanning every music style from a capella to zydeco. Their business structures are diverse too, from full-corporate subsidiaries to solo micro-business. Defining them inevitably remains difficult.

Some indies with minority or majority ownership by major record companies are classified as "independents" thanks to their use of independent distribution (i.e., national and regional distributors NOT owned by the major labels).

Others are distributed by majors, but remain fiercely independent in terms of spirit and ownership.

The rest (most, I'd say) are very small, often artist-run music production/ marketing companies doing the best they can in a tight music marketplace within their niche.

Indie market share in the U.S. is about 25% (most surveys say 20%, but they don't account for "under the radar" sales that occur at performances and through direct mail). Indie market share is even higher in other countries like Japan where indie product accounts for well over 50% of all record sales.

Today, unlike a few decades ago when the majors competed directly with the independents, absorbing them when they became successful, the majors cooperate with the independents, pursuing "joint ventures," or equity deals, partial ownership, and distribution deals.

Finding the Right Label Match

How do you find the right record label for your project? Start with those recordings in your collection you really like. Not just the music, but the packaging, liner notes, graphics and how they were displayed at the store (if that's where you bought it).

Here's a trick I use regularly: Go to one of the bigger record chains that carry indie product. Seek out the buyer in your style category. Often, there are buyers specializing in particular genres like classical, country, pop, R&B, world, folk, etc. Ask this person which indie labels *they* would recommend, particularly the labels that put money into promoting their releases at the retail level.

Why ask them? Because they are on the front lines of record sales and if you're going to sign with an indie label, you want to be sure the label is doing its job where it really counts.

Once you've narrowed your target list down to several indies you'd like to approach, follow these guidelines:

❒ ***Get the Info***. Visit the label's web site and get a sense of it's size, staff, mission, catalog and release schedule. Google the label name to see if there have been any stories written that mention the label and its artists. Look for a link to "submission guidelines" at the label's site. Read these carefully and follow them to the letter.

If you can speak with one of the label's artists or the artist's manager, you'll hopefully be able to get some insider knowledge about the label and whether it's a good match for your project.

Also, remember that every business is becoming a music business. Toyota has started a record label, as has Artois Brewery in Europe. Your label partner may end up being way outside the orbit of the traditional record industry and you needn't limit yourself to traditional players any longer.

❒ ***Fully assess your assets***. A label is usually *only* interested in an artist if that artist is already generating a measurable buzz in the marketplace. Be sure to *realistically* assess your impact: How many fans are on your mailing list? Where are you playing? What's the turnout at gigs? How many reviews and stories have been written about you? Which and how many stations are playing your tunes, both online and at terrestrial stations? It's important to make a full inventory of your achievements before approaching a label. If you're creating a buzz, chances are the label has heard about you already.

❒ ***Be professional***. No one will want to sign you unless you're going to make them money. As such, you and your band must be confident, experienced, dedicated, and have it together (in other words, you must look like you will bring in money). Unless you're the next Beatles, there are a thousand other bands like you - so make yourself stand out from the rest by being professional from the beginning.

❒ ***Become solicited***. Wouldn't it be nice if all you had to do was get an address, slap a label on the demo package with "Attention: A&R" and just wait for the offers to roll on in? Yes, Dorothy, it sure would be. But it's time to come back to planet Earth and realize that getting heard at all (much less by the right people) takes as much effort and planning as writing and performing songs. There are several steps that you should go through when attempting to have your band seriously considered by an A&R representative.

Once you have a qualified list of record labels that you are interested in sending your demo package to, call each and every one of them *prior* to mailing anything and verify that:

- They are accepting unsolicited demo submissions;
- They are interested in your style of music;
- You have the correct name/address (and correct spellings!) to send the package to. Labels will often supply you with a secret code to include on the mailing label to alert them to solicited packages.

))) ILLUMINATING TRIVIA (((

Did you know...

In protest against the pressure from his record company (Chess) to "go electric," Howlin' Wolf gave his second electric album in 1968 the unwieldy title, "This Is Howlin' Wolf's New Album - He Doesn't Like It - He Didn't Like His First Electric Guitar Album Either"?

❒ ***Prepare & send your promo kit to a person***. I like to think of your promo kit as your "graphic ambassador", the one that goes before you representing you to your target market.

The promo kit should be a tightly constructed sales pitch. There should be no confusion about what kind of band you are. Image must be crystal clear – it needs to shine through all the separate parts of the package, unifying printed, photographic, and audio materials. In fact, it is advisable that when constructing your kit you begin with the photo. Use it as the tone-setter for the entire project.

The package should have a cover letter, demo CD, band biography, band photograph, and press clippings. With all of these things, how do you make it attractive? I have five words for you: KEEP IT SIMPLE BUT CREATIVE. Label people are busy and the quicker they can get through your materials the better. They see so many mediocre packages that when a truly creative presentation crosses the desk, they tend to pause a little longer and take it in. Try to stand out from the crowd, both in your music and in the way you "wrap" it.

If the label prefers to visit your web site instead, then point the rep to your EPK (electronic press kit) online. If you want to see what a good EPK looks like, visit Sonicbids at http://www.sonicbids.com.

❐ ***Patience & Follow-up.*** Now what? Wait. If you do not hear anything in 4-8 weeks, make a follow-up phone call. Ask for the person who you addressed the package to. If he or she is unavailable, or if you simply addressed the package to the A&R Department, speak with the secretary. Verify that they received your package, if they had a chance to review it, and their reactions.

Now take a deep breath and brace yourself. If they 1) didn't like the demo, 2) blow you off, or 3) never got it - do not overreact. Thank them for their time, hang up the phone, and gripe to a friend. There are literally thousands of record labels in the U.S. alone; don't waste any more of your time on one that's not interested in your band.

Does this mean you should never send them another package? No. After about 6 months to a year, if you have a new recording (or other significant change in your demo package) and still feel that label would be a great business partner, give them another call. You never know; they may like your new stuff, or they may be trying to change their image.

Remember too that in this difficult climate where CD sales are on shaky ground, labels are becoming increasingly risk-*averse.* So hang tough.

Kinds of Label Deals

What can you expect if the label shows interest? There are several different kinds of deals a record label can offer you:

1. Demo Deal: This is a short-term, low-risk recording agreement between an artist and a record company that isn't sure it wants to sign the artist. A label rep (usually from A&R) may advance a little cash to record a demo of one to two songs which is then handed over the company. The company will "hold" the demo for 30-90 days while it considers whether it wants to sign the artist. Most of the time, if the label passes, artists can take these same recordings to shop for another deal.

2. Development Deal: Development deals are more binding and normally last longer. The idea of a development deal is to provide the A&R person with enough time to work with the artist on developing songs, live shows, etc. while under a low-cost, low-pressure environment. These operate the way A&R used to operate before the record business became the multi-billion dollar business it is today. With a development deal, you can take a band that has lots of potential but still needs time to grow, and try to work towards improvement. You have access to more money and time than with a demo deal, and it's all done under the company's radar with no major expectations.

The development deal involves more money too (anywhere from $15,000 to $75,000, usually) and more time (three months to one year). Due to the fact that there is more money involved, there is a more binding contract involved too.

3. License (P & D) Agreement: "P & D" stands for *p*ress (i.e., manufacture) and *d*istribute, and there are two basic forms this kind of deal can take:

• A signed independent label (that is, a subsidiary to a major or large indie record company) signs recording artists to recording contracts, produces the recordings and the graphics and *delivers the master* to the major label. The major label then presses and packages the records and distributes them through its distribution system; or,

• An indie or single record artist *licenses the master* to a label (usually a foreign label) for pressing (often also re-packaging) and distribution through their system.

This is the most common form of a deal when working on a compilation music project, like those you find on the retail counters of Pottery Barn, Victoria's Secret and Starbucks (though Starbucks is increasingly moving towards signing their own artists to its Hear Music label).

THEMED CD COMPILATIONS

As mentioned in chapter 3, the compilation has emerged as a vital force in the record market, thank to companies like Rhino Records and other of its ilk. Have you noticed all those compilations on the counters of lifestyle retailers Pottery Barn, Restoration Hardware, Williams-Sonoma and others? One man - Rock River Communications' Jeffrey Daniel - usually chooses the music. If mixing tapes is an art, then Daniel is the most popular artist you've never heard of: his branded compilations have sold nearly 5 million copies. Rock River's annual wholesale revenue is about $8 million, on par with a midsize record label.

4. Types of Deals Between Labels:

• The major label will create a spin-off label and send it through both the major and independent distribution networks, with the new label referring to itself as an independent, even though it is entirely owned by the major (e.g., Sony's label 550 Music - Celine Dion - is an example);

• A major label will buy part of an existing and successful indie label but will send the records exclusively through independent distribution networks (e.g., Warner Bros. did this with Tommy Boy Records - Coolio, De La Soul), also known as an "equity deal."

• A different form of the equity deal where a major buys into an indie and sends the records through the major distribution network. The relationship between BMG and Zomba (Backstreet Boys, Britney Spears, R. Kelly, etc.) fits this model.

• The major label will purchase all or half of an existing indie *distribution* company, in order to gain access to the indie marketplace through smaller retail outlets (e.g., Sony/RED, EMI/Caroline Distribution, Warner/ADA, etc.). Finally, sometimes a major will merely launch its own "indie" distribution arm.

It's a confusing landscape to map, because a label, by definition, is considered "independent" if it is *distributed* through independent networks rather than by the majors (this is how both *Billboard* magazine and Soundscan count indie product in their respective tallies). A label can be partially owned by a major and access larger amounts of capital investment, but still be considered an indie. That was the case with Tommy Boy before Warner purchased the remaining ownership in the company.

Then, of course, there is the standard *Recording Contract....*

The Most Important Points in Every Recording Contract

It is beyond this book's scope to explicate *all* the nuances of recording contracts, but I thought a list of contract essentials would be helpful at this juncture, just so that you have the 'lay of the land' if and when you have the opportunity to consider signing one of these documents.

TIPS FOR SELECTING A MUSIC LAWYER

Of course, you NEVER want to sign *any* contract until your music lawyer reviews it. For tips on selecting an appropriate attorney see:

http://www.mbsolutions.com/articles/selecting_entertainment_attorneys.html

Before signing a record contract, every performer must know the answers to the following questions, since they will have a substantial effect on the direction of his or her career.

- ❐ *Time Limit (aka, "term"):* How long will the contract last?
- ❐ *Options:* How many times may the contract be renewed, for how long, and by whom?
- ❐ *Recordings and Releases:* How many sides will a artist record, and does the record company have to release the finished recording commercially?
- ❐ *Royalty Clauses:* How much money does an artist receive from the sale of singles, albums, CDs, videos, and any other formats?
- ❐ *Reduced Royalty Clauses:* How much does an artist receive from the sale in foreign countries, record club or television album collections, radio station promotional copies, and low-priced budget albums?
- ❐ *Record Company Deductions from a Performer's Royalties:* What expenses do record companies deduct from a performer's earnings?
- ❐ *Escalating Royalty Clauses:* Are there ways to guarantee that as an artist becomes more successful, royalties will be automatically increased?
- ❐ *Costs of Packaging a CD, Tape, or Other Recording:* How much money do record companies deduct from an artist's royalties for the cost of album covers, special inserts, and tape, CD, digital compact cassette (DCC), minidisc (MD), or video containers?

- *Free or Discount Recordings:* How many recordings can a company give away for free or at a discount without paying royalties to the artist?

- *Returns and Reserve Accounts:* Since an artist is not paid for CDs and other recordings that are returned for credit, how much money can be withheld from royalties in anticipation of such returns?

- *Advances:* When do record companies give cash advances to artists? What criteria do they use?

- *The Recording Artist as a Songwriter:* Do record companies pay lower songwriter royalties to artists who perform their own songs (they'll often try to - usually offering 75% the statutory rate)?

The most important thing to remember when trying to obtain a recording contract is: the more you bring to the table in terms of self-made success, the less the company can take away if and when the deal ends.

Success, in terms of revenues and numbers of fans, provides the artist with the leverage needed to negotiate the best deal possible for all parties involved.

Key Activities for Marketing Your Own Record Label

We've been discussing how to market yourself or your music to record companies, but what if you're a record label or music production company looking to market *itself*? I know a lot of my readers have small labels and production houses they'd like to see become more visible in the marketplace.

I asked my associate Keith Holzman, industry veteran and author of *The Complete Guide to Starting a Record Company,* to check in and share some of his hard-won wisdom on how a record company or production company can best promote and market itself to its market.

Of course, the *best* way to market your company is to effectively market your artists. Afterall, this is ultimately what you want your market to respond to. Here are Keith's suggestions:

- Market your label by marketing your new releases in a thorough and professional manner.

- The most important activity is to develop a comprehensive marketing plan — and then execute it.

- The marketing plan is a road map for handling each and every release. It will vary based on the needs of the project.

❒ It should encompass needs of all "departments" in terms of actions to be taken and budgeting for them:

- Publicity for the artist and project;
- Radio play for those releases where airplay is possible and valuable;
- Planning of Artist Tours, and support, where possible;
- Use of Retail Marketing Specialists when appropriate;
- Use Street Teams when appropriate;
- Preparation and distribution of promotional video, when applicable and affordable;
- Post a page or more on company's web site for each project;
- Set up for Online sales.

❒ The marketing plan should be on a "phased" or "stepped" basis. If phase one is proceeding well, then start phase two at the appropriate time. If a phase is not working well, then figure out why and re-try it or switch tactics.

❒ In the case of a label with a very small staff, hire professional specialists for Publicity, Independent Promotion, etc., on a project by project basis.

❒ Determine timelines for all events — working back from proposed street date.

❒ Prepare a One-Sheet for distribution purposes.

❒ Prepare a Press Kit — electronic or one to be mailed two to four months prior to street date.

❒ Determine the best time for starting an airplay campaign.

❒ Determine best times for an artist to hit the road.

❒ Coordinate touring with local radio and press well in advance. Try to get artist interviews to air or be published a day or two prior to performance, but also try to get press and radio to see and review performances.

❒ Consider advertising only for established artists, and then use sparingly.

❒ Pitch artists and releases where most appropriate for the intended audience — particularly for "niche" artists.

❒ Consider non-traditional retail for non-traditional artists.

❒ Be prepared to revise and update a marketing plan as necessitated by events as they occur. It's a road map, but it's not written in stone.

I would also add to Keith's list the pursuance of publicity stories about the label and its team in the entrepreneurial business press. Progressive magazines like *Business 2.0*, *INC.*, *Entrepreneur* and *Wired* are always on the lookout for interesting company stories from the entertainment sector and this can help increase the value of your company beyond just the recording industry.

SAMPLE PRODUCER/ARTIST AGREEMENT

AGREEMENT made as of the day of , 2 ________ , by ________________,

individually and collectively p/k/a (hereinafter referred to as "Artist"), and ____________________________________ (hereinafter referred to as "Producer").

W I T N E S S E T H

WHEREAS, Artist desires to engage Producer for the purpose of producing certain master recordings embodying Artist's performances; and

WHEREAS, Producer is capable of and desires to provide his services with respect to such master recordings;

NOW, THEREFORE, in consideration of the mutual promises and covenants contained herein, the sufficiency of which is hereby acknowledged, the parties hereto agree as follows:

1. TERM

The term of this Agreement shall commence as of the date hereof and shall continue until such time as Producer shall have completed all of his services hereunder. Producer shall, at all times, diligently, completely and to the best of the Producer's ability, perform the services required to be performed by Producer hereunder.

2. SERVICES

During the term hereof, Producer shall serve as the individual producer to supervise, direct and produce master recordings embodying the performances of Artist (the "Masters"). Producer shall also perform services as engineer and Producer shall be paid $ per hour (or, per track) for said engineering services. Said engineering fee shall not constitute an advance against any royalty payable under this agreement.

3. RECORDING

(a) Recording sessions for the Masters shall be conducted by the Producer at such times and places as shall be mutually designated by Artist and Producer. Each Master shall embody the performance by Artist of a single musical composition designated by Artist and Producer.

(b) As between Artist and Producer, Artist will pay the following costs of recording in respect of Masters recorded hereunder pursuant to a written budget approved by Artist and Producer: studio rental, engineering fees, tape editing, mixing, equipment and dubdown, instruments, musicians, vocalists, conductors, arrangers, orchestrators, copyists, travel, transportation of instruments and other similar costs in connection with the production of the final Masters, producer's fees, expenses and all other costs and expenses incurred in producing the Masters hereunder from time to time until the delivery by Producer to Artist of the tapes referred to in paragraph 3(c) hereof, and which are customarily recognized as Recording Costs in the phonograph record industry.

(c) Producer shall deliver to Artist for each Master, a two track stereo tape, and all multi-track master tapes (including, but not limited to, any twenty-four-track master tapes). All original session tapes and any derivatives or reproductions thereof shall also be delivered to Artist, or at its election, maintained at a recording studio or other location designated by Artist, in its name and subject to its control.

4. OWNERSHIP

As between Producer and Artist, all Masters produced by Producer hereunder from the inception of the recording thereof, and all other reproductions made therefrom, together with the performances embodied therein and all copyrights therein and thereto, and all renewals and extensions thereof, shall be entirely Artist's property, free of any claims whatsoever by Producer or any other person, firm, or corporation representing. Producer and Artist shall have the absolute rights to reproduce, exploit, distribute, sell, publicly perform and/or grant any and all such rights to third parties; provided, however, that nothing contained in this sentence shall be construed to relieve Artist of Artist's obligation hereunder to pay fees and royalties to Producer. As between Producer and Artist, Artist shall accordingly, have the sole and exclusive right to copyright the Masters, or other reproductions, in Artist's name, as the owner and author thereof, and to secure any and all renewals and extensions of such copyrights (it being understood that for such purposes, Producer shall be Artist's employee-for-hire). Producer shall, upon Artist's request, execute and deliver to Artist any assignment of copyright (including renewals and extensions thereof) in and to the Masters as Artist may reasonably deem necessary, and Producer hereby irrevocably appoints Artist as Producer's attorney-in-fact for the purpose of executing such assignments in Producer's name. Without limitation of any of the foregoing, Artist and/or Artist's designees shall have the exclusive worldwide right in perpetuity to manufacture, sell, distribute, and advertise phonograph records or other reproductions (visual and non-visual) embodying such Masters, to lease, license, convey or otherwise use or dispose of such Masters by any method now or hereafter known, in any field of use, to release phonograph records or other reproductions embodying such Masters under any trademarks, trade names, or labels, to perform such phonograph records or other reproductions publicly, and permit the public performance thereof by radio and television broadcast, or any other method now or hereafter known, all upon such terms and conditions as Artist may approve, and to permit any other person, firm, or corporation to do any or all of the foregoing, or Artist may refrain from doing any and all of the foregoing.

5. CREDITS AND PRODUCER'S IDENTIFICATION

(a) Artist shall have the worldwide right in perpetuity to use and to permit others to use Producer's name (both legal and professional, and whether presently or hereafter used by Producer), likeness, other identification, and biographical material concerning Producer for purpose of trade in connection with the Masters hereunder. Artist shall not use any picture or other likeness of Producer or biographical material concerning Producer without Producer's prior approval. Artist shall use its best efforts to cause appropriate production credit to be given to Producer on single record labels, and in liner notes on back covers or on inner sleeves of albums and cassettes embodying Masters recorded hereunder. Artist shall use its best efforts to cause Producer to be given credit as the Producer of the Masters in all paid advertisements of one-half (1/2) page or more placed by Artist or under Artist's control or by a third party record company in so-called "nationwide" trade and consumer publications as follows: "Produced by. Mixed and recorded by ." No inadvertent failure on Artist's part to fulfill any obligations under this paragraph shall be deemed a breach of this Agreement, with the understanding that Artist will use its best efforts to correct any such inadvertent failure on future runs after Artist has been notified by Producer in writing of any such failure.

(b) If requested, Producer shall make available to Artist photographs and biographies of Producer to use in connection with the exploitation of the Masters recorded hereunder.

6. PRODUCER'S FEE AND ROYALTIES

In consideration for Producer's services hereunder, Artist hereby agrees to pay Producer as follows during the term and after the term hereof:

(a) ________________________________ dollars ($_________) payable on commencement of recording.

(b) ________________________________ dollars ($_________) payable upon completion of recording.

(c) A royalty of ________ percent (______%) of the suggested retail list price in respect of net sales of phonograph records or their equivalent (e.g., cassettes, CDs, etc., hereinafter "Records") derived from the Masters produced hereunder; provided, however, that the royalty payable to Producer hereunder with respect to any Record embodying any of the Masters together with other master recordings shall be computed by multiplying the otherwise applicable royalty rate by a fraction, the numerator of which shall be the number of Masters embodied on such Record and the denominator of which shall be the total number of royalty bearing master recordings embodied on such Record.

(d) Royalties shall be payable to Producer hereunder as and when royalties become payable to Artist pursuant to the terms of the Recording Contract, provided that no royalty will be payable to Producer until the Record Company or Artist, as the case may be, has recouped its Recording Costs from Artist's royalties (Note: This is usually the practice with independent artist projects; However, when artists are signed a producer will sometimes seek to insert a "Letter of Direction" clause which demands payment go directly from label to producer and not through the artist first). After such recoupment, Producer's royalties will be computed retroactively and paid to Producer at the next regular accounting period, from the first record sold. Royalties shall be paid to Producer prior to recoupment of any tour support costs, video costs and other advances that are not Recording Costs.

(e) Producer's royalties hereunder shall be subject to the same escalations and reductions as may be provided in the Recording Contract. For example, with respect to the sale of Records other than sales through normal retail distribution channels in the United States ("Other Sales"). Producer's royalties hereunder shall be reduced in the same proportions as the royalty payable to Artist by the Record Company with respect to the sale of Records through normal retail distribution channels in the United States is reduced for such Other Sales. All royalties payable to Producer hereunder shall be computed in accordance with the terms and conditions set forth in the Recording Contract, and shall be subject to the same deductions and exclusions which the Record

Company shall apply to Artist in computing its record royalties pursuant to the terms of the Recording Contract.

(f) Artist agrees to use all reasonable best efforts to have royalty payments required hereunder made directly to Producer by the Record Company after recoupment of Advances.

7. ACCOUNTINGS

Artist shall account to Producer no less than semi-annually, but in no event more than thirty (30) days after Artist receives accountings and remittances from the Record Company pursuant to the Recording Agreement. Said statements shall be accompanied by payment of accrued royalties, if any, earned by Producer hereunder during the applicable accounting period,. less all advances and charges under this Agreement, along with copies of any and all statements received by Artist from the record company which reflect such accrued royalties. Artist agrees to use all reasonable efforts to cause the record company to account and remit directly to Producer all monies due and owing the Producer under the terms of this Agreement. Producer shall have the right to examine Artist's books and records pertaining to the subject matter hereof at the place where such books and records are normally maintained. Such examination shall take place upon reasonable notice to Artist and not more frequently than once during any twelve (12) month period.

8. WARRANTIES

(a) Producer warrants and represents that Producer is not under any disability, restriction or prohibition, whether contractual or otherwise, with respect to his right to execute this Agreement and perform its terms and conditions and with respect to his right to convey to Artist the rights herein conveyed. In this regard, Producer warrants and represents that no selection produced by Producer hereunder is or shall be subject to any restrictions, pursuant to any other agreement which Producer is otherwise bound.

(b) Each party hereto (the "indemnitor") hereby indemnifies and holds the other party hereto (the "indemnitee") harmless against any and all liabilities claims, demands, loss and damage (including reasonable attorneys' fees and court costs) arising out of or connected with any claim by a third party which is inconsistent with any of the warranties, representations, covenants or agreements made by the Indemnitor herein, and the Indemnitor agrees to reimburse the Indemnitee on demand for any payment made by the Indemnitee at any time after the date hereof with respect to any liability or claim to which the foregoing indemnity applies and which has been reduced to a final

Judgment or settled with the mutual consent of the parties, which consent shall not be unreasonably withheld. The indemnitee shall notify the Indemnitor of any claim, demand or action for which the Indemnitor may be liable, and the Indemnitor shall have the right to participate in the defense of such claim at the Indemnitor's own expense, with an attorney of the Indemnitor's choice.

9. ASSIGNMENT

The services under this agreement are not assignable by either party without the prior, written consent of the other party.

10. NOTICES

Any notice to be given under the terms hereof will be properly given if mailed by prepaid postage, certified mail, return receipt requested, or telegraph, to the parties at the following addresses:

PRODUCER:

ARTIST:

or at such other address as either party may hereafter advise in writing. Except as otherwise provided herein, such notices shall be deemed given when mailed or delivered to a telegraph office, all charges prepaid, except that notice of change of address shall be effective only after the actual receipt thereof.

11. FORMAL AGREEMENT

This Agreement incorporates, replaces and supersedes all prior oral agreements between the parties hereto with respect to the subject matter hereof. This Agreement sets forth the entire understanding and agreement of the parties hereto with respect to the matters contained herein. This Agreement may not be altered or modified except upon agreement of the parties hereto in writing, and all rights and remedies shall be cumulative and not limited by specification. All signatures at the foot hereof shall make this a valid, binding and enforceable agreement between the parties hereto.

12. RELATIONSHIP OF THE PARTIES

Nothing herein contained shall constitute a partnership or a joint venture between the parties. Neither party hereto shall hold itself out contrary to the terms of this paragraph, and neither party shall become liable for any representation, act, or omission of the other party contrary to the provisions hereof. This Agreement shall not be deemed to give any right or remedy to any third party whatsoever unless said right or remedy is specifically granted by all parties hereto, in writing, to such third party.

13. ATTORNEYS' FEES

In the event of any action, suit, or proceeding arising from or based upon this Agreement brought by either party hereto against the other, the prevailing party shall be entitled to recover from the other its reasonable attorneys' fees in connection therewith in addition to the costs of such action, suit or proceeding.

14. GOVERNING LAW

This agreement shall be construed in accordance with the laws of ___________(state)____________________ governing agreements wholly executed and performed therein.

IN WITNESS WHEREOF, the parties hereto have executed this Agreement under seal as of the day and year first above written.

____

"Producer" (SS#)

____

"Artist" (SS#)

CH 9
Marketing to Distributors & Retailers

"The best ad is a good product." – Alan H. Meyer

When the self-titled debut from Clap Your Hands Say Yeah landed on the *Billboard* Top Independent Albums chart in August of 2005, the group accomplished the feat without a label or distributor. Instead, the band took its album directly to indie retailers, finding a national distributor in Junketboy, a company owned by the Coalition of Independent Music Stores. Now, the dance-rock act is finding that with a well-timed tour and a wealth of Internet buzz, a record label may not be all that important.

The five-piece, led by eccentric singer Alec Ounsworth, has sold 12,000 copies of its debut, according to Nielsen Soundscan, fulfilling most orders itself from a Brooklyn, N.Y. apartment.

The band eventually signed a U.S. distribution deal for the album with Warner Music Group's Alternative Distribution Alliance (ADA), which gave it access to larger retailers. ADA president Andy Allen calls his company's one-off deal with CYHSY highly unusual. "Other than [jam band] O.A.R., who we've had a long-term relationship with, we've never actually done a deal directly with a band," Allen says.

Tapping into the Web-savvy audience that catapulted the Arcade Fire to the top of the indie community, CYHSY began selling its album to non-New Yorkers via its Web site. When sales started to take off, the band enlisted the help of online retailer Insound, where the act has been the top seller since June 2005.

Of course, being without a label offers some challenges. "We're paying a little over $1 per CD, so I can't order 5,000 CDs until I get my money for the CDs I just sold," band manager Nick Stern says. "Since it takes three weeks to print the CDs, there's been a lag in getting CDs out to stores." (Source: *Billboard* September 27, 2005).

The above story illustrates new approaches bands are taking to secure retail presence today. While an increasing amount of music is being sold via the Net, through both online retailers and as digital downloads, most CDs still get into peoples' hands through "brick & mortar" retailers.

You should note that CYHSY was picked up by a distributor only after attaining regional recognition. You need to see getting distribution as an amplification of your efforts that are already in motion. Before expanding into distribution, your band or act must warrant broader distribution and you must possess the means to press enough records to keep product in stock.

How can you get your music into all the appropriate retail outlets so that people can purchase it? Before we answer this question, it's important to first understand who the players are and how the "terrestrial" music distribution system works.

The Major Label Distribution System

After 50 years of trial and error, even major labels are still trying to figure out a better distribution system. Until about 1950, only a handful of companies were in the recording business. Each had its own procedure for delivering its products to customers. With the rapid proliferation of labels in the 1950s, newcomers to the market often lacked an understanding of the essential need for a national network of distributors to get their products to retail outlets. Smaller labels would seek larger ones to distribute their records. Other new labels contracted the services of the growing number of independent distributors that were setting up operations in most markets.

The major company players in the record distribution system are BMG Distribution, EMI Music Marketing, SONY Music Labels, WEA Corp. Distribution and Universal Music & Video Distribution.

Each one divides the US into 5-8 regions and then divides each region further into local markets, which includes roughly the top 20 markets nationally. Each major distributor has branch offices in each of these cities and employ between 20-30 people each. Here's how each is structured:

ORGANIZATIONAL CHART OF A
MAJOR LABEL BRANCH DISTRIBUTION CENTER

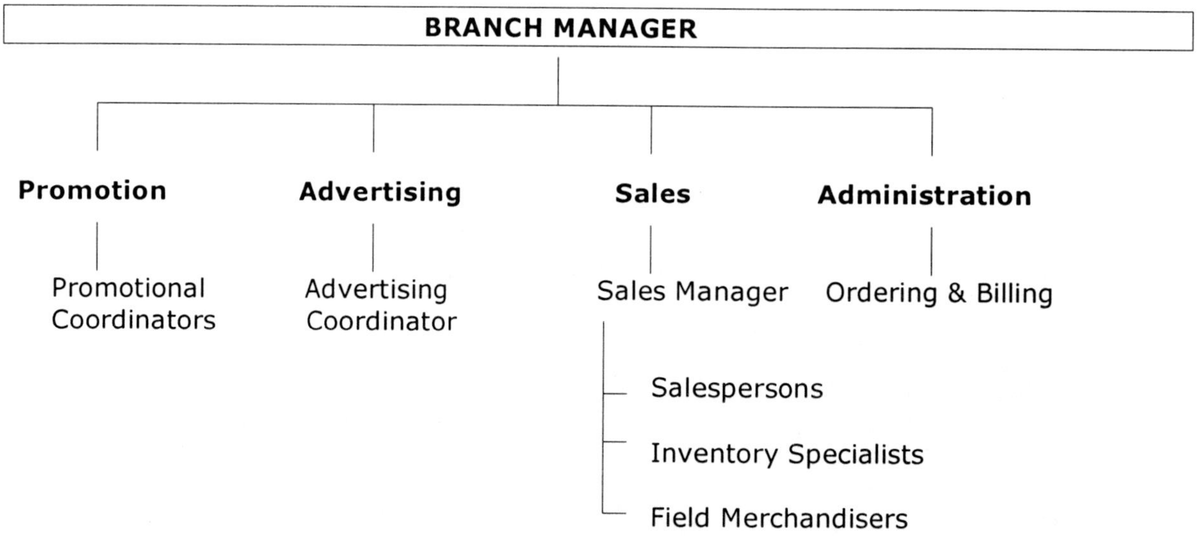

Distribution begins at the manufacturing plant (most major label companies own their own) where the record is produced as a retail product. These are also located around the twenty or so major metropolitan hubs for quick and efficient distribution to retailers. A record distributor receives finished musical product – such as CDs, Dual Discs, and videos from the record company – and is responsible for selling and delivering it to retail stores and online outlets. The parent company for most major labels also owns a distribution company to handle the needs of all the company's owned and affiliated labels. Independent record companies either align themselves with a major distribution company, or contract with an independent distributor to deliver their product to retailers.

View form the Ground: From their branch offices, the majors send sales personnel to show catalogs, create interest in new releases, offer purchase incentives, and take orders from retailers. The label's pressing plant or regional warehouse ships the goods to the retailer. Field merchandisers call on dealers to set up in-store displays and provide point-of-purchase materials (including posters, mobiles, and promotional paraphernalia). Inventory specialists visit each store to see how the products are moving and give advice on reorders. In addition to distributing records by the major's own artists, they have distribution arrangements with some independent companies and provide the above services for their products as well.

Independent Music Distribution

In contrast to these giants, there is a network of self-funded independent labels which operate on limited budgets. These labels rely on distributors such as Red, Caroline, INDI/Alliance, Navarre and Koch to get their CDs into major chains like Musicland, Tower and Warehouse (in addition to smaller stores). By housing and shipping product, these distributors act as the middlemen between the labels and the stores.

By and large, indie distributors have a much smaller overhead of costs and therefore can be less concerned with turning huge profits. Keeping an eye on the numbers, they're typically very dedicated music fans as well, working extremely hard for minimal financial gain. The competitive and trend-based music marketplace forces indies to diversify their companies in order to turn a profit. This can mean working simultaneously with vastly different genres of music and as many different labels as possible, or expanding operations to include a label, mail order, and a retail store. It's challenging, but artists and labels working with an indie distributor can expect to deal with people who are passionate and knowledgeable about music.

Major vs. indie distribution is probably best defined by what it's not. If you're not distributed by one of the majors, it's considered indie; it's simple as that. But many would question whether ownership plays a role in it. For example, Alternative Distribution Alliance (ADA) is 95% owned by the Warner Music Group, which is definitely one of the majors, but it is an independent company. It does its own shipping, its own collecting, and it works with primarily independent artists. Sometimes an indie distributor can be defined as working with, in most cases, developing bands or niche-oriented bands, whereas a major distributor can be defined as working with new bands, developing bands, and huge superstars like Clapton or Madonna and that type of thing.

As mentioned in chapter 3, there's a movement underway to redefine what "indie" is in the retail /distributor sectors. It's being led by Don Rose, president of the newly minted

AAIM (American Association of Independent Music), which contrary to the Billboard/Soundscan approach, wants to count all indie product distributed by majors as *indie* market share (of course, the majors want to count all this product for *their* market share).

Another player in the distributor-retail picture is the *One Stop*. One stops are called one-stops because an account can come to one vendor and virtually pick up every record that's released in the industry. They are essentially, *sub-distributors,* buying in bulk from the majors and selling in small numbers to "mom & pop" stores. There are stores that choose just to buy from one source. They pay a little bit of a premium to do so, but in some cases they get better service, overnight delivery, and other extra values. Plus, they only are taking one phone call and they can buy virtually every record released in the industry from that one place. So a number of labels rely on one-stops to get to those stores that they don't get to directly or those stores that choose not to buy from everybody.

Distribution Arrangements & Pricing

There is a wide range of distribution arrangements. Most of the national independents work around a straight distribution fee. In some cases, the distribution arrangement may include manufacturing, where the distributing company pays for the manufacturing/packaging of the music product and recoups its investment out of sales revenue.

The distribution company charges a fee of, in some cases, as low as 18 percent all the way up to 30 percent of the sales of the record. If discounts or advertising dollars are used as a marketing tool, the distributor may participate based on an agreed-to formula, or the label may fund that entirely out of its share. So in most cases, an independent label should be seeing around 80 percent of the wholesale cost of a record. These days, a suggested retail list price (SLRP) of $15.98 wholesales for anywhere from $10.30 - $10.70. That's the wholesale value. So the label should be seeing from the distributor approximately 20 percent less. The 20 percent is what the distributor keeps.

The other accounting mechanism that a distributor may employ is a *returns reserve*. A returns reserve is really in place because it's assumed that a certain percentage of what labels ship is going to be returned to the distributor. Remember, most distribution agreements are really consignment agreements. There's rarely, if ever, an advance payment for CDs. A label is only paid if the product sells through at retail.

The national average for returned product is about 20 percent. Therefore most distributors will keep about 20 percent in reserve. And what that means is that instead of paying the label 100 percent of what's due them the month you sell the record, you would withhold 20 percent of what's due for some period of time, assuming that it may come back or be returned by the retailer.

Most good distributors have a formula in which they give that money back to the label over some period of time. The label can, of course, spend that money in a way to help sell those records, so it's in the best interest of both parties to get that money back to the labels as soon as possible.

For an independent label that may only put out six to eight records a year, there is going to be dips and peaks in their cash flow, and the returns reserve can level that off a bit. You always want a situation in which the distributor owes the label money. You don't want a situation in which the label owes the distributor money. That's basically a negative cash flow situation, and it's just not very healthy. So the returns reserve is something that can smooth that out a bit.

Music Retail Players

Needless to say, record retail has experienced the one-two punch of both declining CD sales along with mounting competition from online retailers for a good seven years now. This has made it increasingly difficult for record retail to survive, much less thrive, in this environment. According to the organization, Almighty Insitute of Music Retail, independent record stores declined by almost half over the last ten years – from 5000 in 1996 to 2800 today.

Notwithstanding, most CDs are still purchased at bricks & mortar retailers, and the main retail players are continually seeking ways to reform their business structures to keep this so.

Here are the main players in the music retail field today:

❒ ***Record Chains.*** These are the 800-lb gorillas and include: Musicland Corp. (based in Minneapolis, MN) with over 1200 stores, including Sam Goody, Harmony Hut, Musicden and Media Play outlets. Next is Trans World Entertainment (Albany, NY), owner of 900 record stores under names like F.Y.E., Coconuts, Strawberries, Planet Music and Spec's Music.

Smaller record chains include Tower (100 stores in US), Virgin, HMV, and even smaller regional chains like Massacusetts-based Newbury Comics (20 stores).

In an effort to shore up laging sales, the chain stores are combining their inventory of CD's etc. with related products like computer software, multi-media products, videos, books and magazines, and even home electronic equipment and appliances.

❒ ***Mom & Pop Record Stores.*** Once the main avenue of recorded music to the public, the privately owned mom-and-pop record stores have, for the most part, given way to the chain stores and the discount merchandisers. However, because the stores carry a smaller inventory, sell less product, and use the one-stop middleman distributors, the average cost of the CDs to the public are habitually priced higher in order to produce a profit.

❒ ***Discount Merchandisers.*** These are the entertainment superstores, and include Circuit City, Target, Best Buy, Wal Mart and The Wiz. Of course, many other retailers have entered the music market as well, like Borders Books & Music, and Starbucks.

Mass merchandiser stores offer the top-selling 10 or 15 albums in the pop, country, and R&B styles and depend on high turnover for volume business. They sell for less because they get it for less due to volume purchases. In fact, these stores often price music product so low, they don't make any profit. Thus, music is used as a "loss leader" – designed to lure shoppers in in the hope that they'll purchase more profitable items like stereo equipment and TVs.

These stores usually have their music departments serviced by *Rack Jobbers*. Being a hybrid of intermediary distributor and retailer, rack jobbers buy from the label and sell directly to the public within department stores, supermarkets, drug stores, and other outlets.

The rack jobber either has a consignment arrangement or rents space within a large store, and independently sets up and maintains display racks within each store. Some huge department store chains (like Sears) have so many stores that they buy records in large quantities and ship them to their individual stores which maintain their own record departments, thus eliminating rack jobbers.

Rack jobbers play an important role in the distribution system because they specialize in retailing beyond the sphere of music specialty stores, and thus help to get records to a wider audience.

FACT: *Wal Mart is now the world's largest music retailer and, next to the Government, also the largest employer in the United States.*

Retail Monitoring & Soundscan

Soundscan started in the early 1990s as an inventory tool for retail stores and record labels. When a retail store swipes the bar codes of CDs, Soundscan keeps count of how much CDs are bought for each album, label, and artist. Soundscan is owned by VNU, a Dutch information and publication company which also owns *Billboard*, BDS, and EMIS. Soundscan gets its money from subscriptions and licenses from entities like *Billboard*.

Many indie labels question how much their CDs are being monitored in comparison to major label products. Soundscan keeps close count on all CD sales, but major labels do have a priority when it comes to checking out charts on particular area retail stores, artists, and label sales overall. Indie labels can get reports for Soundscan but are limited to 20 titles of their own products at any given time.

Many in the music industry continue to be concerned about disproportional numbers in Soundscan monitoring. Some retail stores have been found to scan bar codes for higher number counts on certain CDs, but Soundscan monitors this very closely and calls attention to outrageous numbers. Technology and good service has been Sounscan's trademark. In the near future, Soundscan has also recently set up a program to be able to keep count of digital downloads via internet sales. Also, scan cards will be distributed to customers to keep count of their purchases so labels will know what the right tools and products in the right areas.

To register a work with Soundscan or to obtain more information on its products and services, go to: http://www.soundscan.com/register.html

Or write:
Soundscan
220 North Central Park Avenue
Hartsdale, NY 10530
914.328.9100

It is free to have your music listed with SoundScan, but they charge you to *retrieve* the data.

Putting Together Your Distribution & Retail Strategy

Here are some pointers for setting up your own distributor/retail strategy.

1. Get a Barcode.

If you plan on selling recordings and you would like those sales to show up in SoundScan reports, you will need to obtain a Universal Product Code (UPC), which is kind of like a bar-coded social security number for your releases.

Most music chains no longer carry non-UPC products (because they can't scan them at the cash register), and major label A&R departments conduct much of their market research on unsigned bands and indie labels by checking Sound Scan sales on the retail level.

"It's a great idea to put a UPC on your CD," says Kevin Williamson, VP of A&R at Atlantic Records. "A UPC helps tell the truth concerning how many [CDs] are actually being sold. It can also really help a band to attract interest from us. That's a way we found Hootie& The Blowfish. Our research saw that their self-released CD had already sold thirty to forty thousand units on the local level."

A UPC consists of twelve digits: The first six numbers uniquely identify your band or organization, the next four (which you choose) specify the release, the following number corresponds to the format (CD or cassette), and the last number is used to check that the scanner read the product correctly.

If you'd like to receive an application for a UPC or need more information, contact the **Uniform Code Council at (937) 435-3870** or online **http://www.uccouncil.org**. (The UCC is a non-profit organization dedicated to standards development and maintenance for automated product identification and electronic data.) The UCC will mail you a membership application or you can download it from their Website; once you've sent in the $500 fee, it should take between ten to fifteen business days to process your application (although an additional fee of $35 will shorten the turn-around to four business days). Thankfully, after the one-time membership fee, you can use the six-digit organizational number on any subsequent release without further costs.

An Alternative (read, Cheaper) Way to Get a Barcode –

CDBaby.com is a popular online retailer of indie product. If you're a member of CD Baby, and you're not planning on releasing hundreds of differenet recordings, they can get you a barcode for just $20. Here's how this works according to Derek Sivers, founder of CD Baby:

"When you register with the Universal Code Council in [Ohio], and pay them $500, what you're actually doing is registering your COMPANY. Once you do that you can release 10,000 products under that company registration.
But most of us independent artists are only going to release a few records - and paying $500 wipes out all the profit you'd make from your first 100 album sales.

So - CD Baby paid the $500, and can give you your own unique UPC Barcode for only $20. It will be entirely yours for all eternity. When your CD is scanned by Tower Records or Amazon, ***it will show up on the register as YOUR Album, YOUR Band, YOUR Record Company***. The only place you will be "tied" to CD Baby is in our records here in Portland [Oregon]. Nowhere else.

We will send you a BITMAP graphic [of the barcode]. You or your art designer can import this graphic into your album art, or make stickers from it.

If you want to do this, you need to be a CD Baby member. I know it's a chicken & the egg thing. ("How can we be a CD Baby member if we need a UPC code for a CD that won't be out for 2 months?") So go sign up now, submit your CD to CD Baby in advance, we'll send you your UPC Barcode now, and mark you down as pre-paid for the future when your CDs get back from the factory!

See - by law, we can't just hand out barcodes to anyone who asks. These are meant only for people who are a paid member of CD Baby. To be a member, you have to fill out our submission form, send us some of your CDs, and pay the $35 setup fee.

If you don't have your CDs yet, you must fill out the submission form NOW - giving us all the information possible, pay the $35 setup fee, and send us your CDs as soon as they're back from the factory. We can still give you the barcode now. It takes 1-2 weeks for us to give you your own UPC Barcode. Please don't call us in a panic, needing it in 4 hours . We email you a BITMAP GRAPHIC file, which you can either place into your album art, or print onto stickers. We don't do the printing for you. We just email you the unique UPC barcode graphic.

If all is understood, please submit your CD to CD Baby first. Then, when done, pay for your $35 setup and $20 barcode." Good deal. Thanks Derek.

2. Create a Distributor/Retail One-Sheet

A one-sheet gives both distributors and retailers a quick read on all the pertinent information about your recording. Its purpose is to convince them that this is a release to push because it has good planning and marketing behind it. A sample from artist-owned Feather Records, can be seen on page 199. Here are all the possible elements to include on your One-sheet.

- ❒ Record company logo (if any) and contact information.
- ❒ Album title and artist name (and logo, if available).
- ❒ Product catalog numbers and UPC numbers for all formats (CD, tape, and so on).

r each format.

and to radio.

;t and the album (including all note-worthy

es of any well-known participants, whether

isicians).

vious sales.

cord of previous sales.

audience, and size of following.

ce plans to support the release (including schedule).

ding independent promotion) and schedule.

ule.

nedule.

l promotion plans and ideas.

ors that will be handling the product.

ng web sites.

GREAT RESOURCE

Distribution Handbook

yeusa.com/services_handbook.php

Redeye Distribution prepared this handbook for its artists and labels who have product ready for retail distributon. It covers everything from set-up to follow-through, and even includes some pertinent sample documents, like Soundscan Reports and Tracking Reports.

NOTE: Redeye is moving increasingly towards strictly digital distribution.

3. Employ Grassroots Retail Promotion

If you have your discs in record stores, then you can *maximize* their presence by following this advice:

❒ Target stores near important venues, especially college areas.

❒ Call stores, ask to speak to the manager or buyer. Briefly make that person aware of your product. Offer to send promo copies and a one-sheet. Also let them know which suppliers (i.e., distributors, one-stops, etc.) are carrying the line.

❒ Send stores promo copies (2 each), one-sheets and any other P.O.P. (Point of Purchase) materials you have available (posters, T-shirts, stickers, etc.) Make followup calls a week after mailing to see if they received the package.

❒ Always contact retailers one week prior to performing in their area. Get names of store personnel who might like to see the show. Make a guest list.

❒ If at all possible, visit the store on the day of the gig with posters, T-shirts, etc., and make friends. Remember their names. Double check the guest list.

❒ If you have radio interviews arranged the day of the show, be sure to give the store(s) a free plug when you mention the album.

❒ If the store personnel do show up at the gig, treat them royally...buy them a drink and be sure to plug the album and the store from the stage. Example: "Here's our new album (hold up a copy of the album), it's called, 'Sick and Phat', and it's available right around the corner at MoJo's Records!"

❒ Send friends/fans to stores to purchase copies of the album.

❒ If an important store is not carrying the record, have friends, family members and fans call once a week to ask for it. Chances are if they hear about it enough, they'll eventually stock it.

❒ Be sure to keep your distributor informed of all press items, radio airplay, TV appearances and other helpful news... especially all tour dates and itineraries. Fax tour schedules to them monthly.

❒ Don't worry about **listening posts** unless you have thousands of dollars to spend. These are bought and paid for in the same ways the big labels lease out the best store real estate (windows, end caps, counter displays, etc.)

Summary: Treat retailers as your best friends because they are your best friends! You simply cannot sell records without them, unless you want to be selling records off the stage the rest of you career. One enthusiastic store clerk can sell as many copies of your records as a spin on the radio! In-store play is every bit as important as radio play; in the absence of radio play, it is one of the only avenues open to you for exposing and selling your music.

4. If you can't get distribution, do consignments deals.

Go into the record store and fill out a consignment form. If it's a chain store ask to speak to the Consignment Buyer; if not just speak to whoever is at the counter. You can generally only put 5-10 CDs in the store. It's up to you to periodically check the inventory. If they sell out, collect a check and re-supply the store. If your CD is only selling 1-3 copies a year, the record store will tell you to take them out of the store. The price of the CD is negotiable between the store and the artists. Consignment deals differ with each retail outlet. Keep track of all transaction with a *Retail Tracking Form* (see page 197).

5. Don't limit yourself to just music retail.

When considering potential retail partners, don't just think record or even just entertainment stores. Think about which retailers your work has an *affinity* with. For example, one client of mine took his Irish folk music and consigned it to Irish-themed gift shops. Another, a New Age/electronica composer, found a number of affinity retailers in the health food, massage therapy and Yoga studio markets. Museum gift stores, airports, book stores, art galleries, grocery stores, mall trollies, sporting venues, and outdoor festivals are all possibilities.

Distribution Contracts

Many factors go into a distribution contract that you have to check thoroughly and pay close attention to. As with all contracts in the music business, have your attorney review it. Here are the main points you need to be aware of:

- ❐ **How much money** you are getting paid for each CD sold after CD gets sold and marketed?

- ❐ **Distribution fee:** How many fees are being paid to the distribution company?

- ❐ **How is the distributor handling discounts** on your merchandise to accounts (record stores). Does it come out of your pocket, does the distributor pay, or do you both pay, and are you paying more than the distributor?

- ❐ How much is the **return's reserve?** This is how much the distributor holds for themselves for protection of your product being returned to the distributor's warehouse.

- ❐ **Breech and cure period.** If you have a two year contract with a distribution company and after the first year, you feel as though they breached contract, the distribution company has a year to "cure" the contract by showing that their service will get better.

- ❐ **Coop and other charge backs**. When are these deducted?

- ❐ **Who owns the inventory, you or the distributor?** If you want to switch distributors and the first distributor owns the inventory, you as a label have to buy back the inventory.

- ❐ **Non-exclusive arrangements.** Can the record label sell records without using the distributor or do all records sold have to go through the distributor? Be careful with this because a lot of times, you will not have as much priority in the distribution company if you have non-exclusive rights.

- ❐ **Digital rights.** Some distributors are beginning to make the assignment of a label's digital distribution rights a condition of the distribution deal. This is a tough one because in assigning these rights your label will often get better terms and service. However, if the distributor goes under, your digital distribution rights can be sold and then held in limbo. In my humble opinion, it's probably better to use a service like the Orchard, IODA or CDBaby for your digital distribution.

Retail Trends to Watch

• Traditional record retail stores that are making it are doing so because they've gone the direction of **"retail as theater"** (Newbury Comics is a good example of this) and as segmented boutiques (department stores did this years ago).

• Many large chain stores are now featuring local, regional, and national **artists in concert at their stores**. This trend is not solely the domain of the chains however. Enterprising independent stores have found that specializing in one or two genre of music, and featuring live performances by those artists in their stores, is an effective method to attract customers (Borders, Tower, HMV)

• In many urban and suburban shopping centers, large chain stores now charge large sums of money to record labels to **"buy" or "lease" promotional space in their stores.** What was once a free service, is rapidly becoming a lucrative source of extra income to a music retailer. Table space, window and in-store wall displays, newsletter space, and the aforementioned listening posts can generate fees ranging from a couple hundred dollars to several thousands of dollars. For example, during the holiday season Trans World charges labels upwards of $70k per title to lock up coveted locations within its stores.

Online Music Retail

With the rapid growth of peer-to-peer services and the emergence of pay-per-song and subscription sites, it is hardly surprising that the music industry has paid considerable attention to the competitive impact of music being made available online (for free, through piracy, or commercially).

There are dozens of websites using different combinations of the above strategies – StarPolish, BeSonic, IUMA, Vitaminic, etc. But the bottom line with these sites, despite the possibilities they encourage for the future, have one glaring problem: if a band is not on their charts (if they have charts) or other form of page real estate, how will it get heard? At each site you have the online version of a warehouse-sized flea market CD stall with thousands and thousands of CD's with names you've never heard before.

With that said, CDBaby and Amazon are probably the two best online retail options for independent artists. They both have strong brand recognition and well-oiled operations. In addition, CDBaby offers impeccable customer service and dozens of resources to help independent musicians grow successful careers.

❒ **CDBaby.** CDBaby is the premiere indie superstore on the Internet. They advertise that they get over 150,000 hits a day. You send them CDs and they will do order fulfillment for you. They have a one-time set up fee of $35 for each title you want them to sell, and they take $4.00 for each unit sale. They will email you with the sales information for every CD that's sold, and send checks out on a weekly basis. You start by sending them 5 CDs. Their digital distribution service comes free with membership. URL: http://www.cdbaby.com

❐ **Amazon.com.** Amazon.com has been selling independent music for a number of years now. At this time, they are offering two different programs for independent musicians: "Amazon Advantage," and "Amazon Marketplace". The Amazon Advantage program handles all order fulfillments through Amazon.com. This program takes a 55% commission. You must submit a CD for consideration and acceptance into the program. Your CD will be listed on Amazon.com, one of the biggest online stores there is – they have a customer base of 45 million people. Amazon Marketplace is an alternative to the Advantage program, where you provide order fulfillment and shipping. They take $0.99 plus 15% commission per item sold. They will also give you a credit towards shipping.

There are dozens more online retailers who will gladly take on your product. My advice, however, is to stick with the two above options. The only exception to make is if you find a retailer that specializes in your particular genre of music (say, for example, hip-hop, women's music, or dance). It would make sense to place your CD there as well. Most retailers do not require exclusivity when it comes to physical product.

However, for digital distribution to work effectively, an exclusive agreement is often required. CDBaby encourages it, as does The Orchard. Check this feature out thoroughly before signing on.

Don't be confused by all the different options available to you. Remember, you can always start small, with little or no investment, and grow your e-commerce solutions as your volume grows. You never have to bite off more than you can chew, and the beauty of the Internet is that you can start out with very modest resources.

SAMPLE RETAIL TRACKING FORM

ARTIST:_________________________ **TITLE:**________________________________
LABEL:________________ **DATE:** _______________

STORE	LOCATION	IN STOCK	COPIES SOLD	COMMENTS

Digital Formats Continue to Bless Indie Labels & Artists

Independent artists continue to benefit from the digital revolution, which has leveled both the promotional and distributional playing fields. The result is a lot more choice for music fans, who are now discovering artists across a number of new outlets. "When you give consumers the option of choice, they tend to exercise it," said Jim Griffin, CEO of Cherry Lane Digital, during a Digital Music Forum panel Wednesday. Suddenly, labels are able to bypass expensive retail access points like endcaps and coveted terrestrial radio spins, while more affordably targeting interested buyers online.

Meanwhile, the independent sector is grabbing a big piece of the action. David Pakman, head of independent online retailer eMusic, pegged the independent sector at a 27 percent market-share in the US, a figure that factors in major label distribution arrangements. Pakman noted that the independent sector is "the only area that is growing in terms of revenue and market share," while observing that the "independent artist has always been afforded advantages online that he has not been given in a traditional retail environment". Others took the concept further, shunning more established promotional and distribution outlets. "An endcap in Tower Records doesn't work, a single on K-Rock doesn't work," said Michael Hausman, an artist manager and co-founder of SuperEgo Records. On the subject of iTunes, Hausman was quick to call Apple a friend. "iTunes is a great account," Hausman said. "It pays, and offers an outlet."

Source: *Digital Music News*, 3/2/06

SAMPLE DISTRIBUTOR ONE-SHEET

FEATHER RECORDS
New Release Information

TWO TRU - Shadow Language

16 Adult Comtemporary songs

Lauren delivers another solid CD...she never disappoints the listener! In this coupling with Cindy Brown on the Two Tru CD she will not disappoint her many fans. After the first playthru I found myself anxious to go back to the first track to listen to the whole CD again. The material is fresh and refreshing, and the delivery defies comparison to other performers, as each track demonstates the meld of these two artists to the material. It exemplifies the inherent qualities of this genre. In other words..."It can't get much better than this!"
Reviewer: Alan Hartwell/Concert Producer

What a beautifully recorded disk! Great variety of textures. obviously done with great attention to the details. Fine packaging as well. I have it in the car CD player and am enjoying it whilst buzzing around town.
Reviewer: Dan Jackson

Great vibe, creative arrangements, stellar performances, rich vocal work, top-shelf production....A standout recording for '04!
Reviewer: Peter Spellman, Music Business Solutions Director

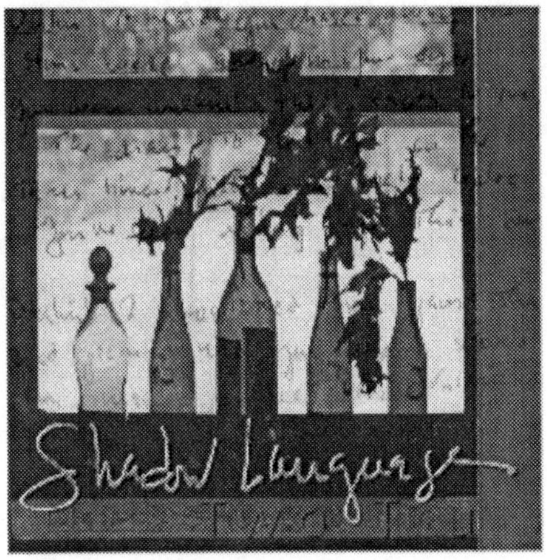

produced by	LAUREN PASSARELLI & CINDY BROWN
mastered by	JONATHAN WYNER, M-WORKS

Distributed through CDbaby.com and most online music download sites.

P.O.Box 230132
Astor Station
Boston, MA 02123

www.feather-records.com
anyone@feather-records.com

Catalog # CD-0401-2
UPC code CD-7-66477-0401-2

LAUREN PASSARELLI	guitars, vocals, bass, drums, percussion
CINDY BROWN	keys, vocals, percussion
JOHN METTAM	drums, percussion
JEFF SONG	bass, cello
MARK KOHLER	drums, percussion
SANDRA KOTT	viola
KIMBERLY RULLO	drums
SARAH BURRILL	vocals
ACE BAILEY	drums
THADDEUS HOGARTH	harmonica
LENI STERN	guitar loop
TOMMY MOORE	bass
JEFF LANDROCK	keys

CH 10

Marketing to Radio

"It makes no difference how good you are. If you're not exposed to the public enough, then you're dead." – Johnny Shins, American musician

Radio was invented around 1906 and was initially in the hands of amateurs. Afraid of it getting into the wrong hands, the federal government took over all radio operations during WWI. This constrained radio for a time and it had to wait until 1920 to develop further. Early radio acted like today's TV in peoples' lives. People tuned in for all kinds of dramatic programming. Radio and silent films were the mass entertainments of the day. When sound was added to films and "talking pictures" were born, dramatic programming moved increasingly to movie theaters and *music* took its place as radio's primary content and draw.

Radio is still the most important vehicle for breaking new acts, though this is changing, especially in the wired 12-25 year-old demographic. According to a study by Soundata in 2003, radio was the number one influencer of musical purchasers (incidentally, the other influencers went as follows: 2-browsing in store; 3-word of mouth; 4-MTV; 5- concert; 6-newspaper; 7-VH-1).

In the US, indies have over 80% of the releases every year and 30% of digital radio plays, according to Soundscan. But in traditional radio broadcasting, indies come in at 5%. Why? Because there's a log jam at radio and a serious weighting towards the majors: 4 labels control 95% of radio spins! This makes traditional terrestrial, commercial radio a virtual closed door to indies. More on this later.

Context:
The Culture & Dynamics of Radio Today

Today, there are about 12,313 radio stations in the U.S., with 39% being AM (amplitude modulation) stations and 61% FM (frequency modulation). They fall into two primary camps: **Commercial** (10,207 stations) and **Non-commercial** (2,106 stations). Non-commercial include both college and non-commercial public radio stations. The FCC (Federal Communications Commission) sets aside a segment of the FM broadcast band (88 to 92 megahertz) for schools, colleges, civic entities, and others who devote all or part of their programming to education, the arts, and other kinds of non-profit enterprise.

Of course, there are also satellite and internet radio stations, two growing media we will look at later in this chapter. And last but not least, pirate radio continues to do its subversive thing, while neighborhood micro-stations now have FCC-sanctioned liscenses for local narrowcasting.

Radio divides itself by "format" (see chart below) and this is determined by the kind of audience the station is trying to attract.

RADIO'S MOST POPULAR FORMATS (2004)

Rank	Format	# of Stations
1	Country	2088
2	News/Talk	1224
3	Oldies	807
4	Adult Contemporary	692
5	Hispanic	628
6	Adult Standards	497
7	CHR (Top 40)	491
8	Sports	429
9	Classic Rock	425
10	Hot AC	399
11	Religion	347
12	Soft Adult Contemporary	336
13	Rock	273
14	Black Gospel	253
15T	Classic Hits	237
15T	Southern Gospel	237
17	R & B	207
18	Modern Rock	189
19	Contemp. Christian	167
20	Urban AC	128
21	Ethnic	102
22	Alternative Rock	99
23	Jazz	90
24	R & B Adult/Oldies	66
25	Gospel	64
26	Pre-Teen	60
27	Modern AC	51
28	Variety	36
29	Classical	32
30	Easy Listening	18

The average person spends 22 hours per week listening to the radio. About 70% of radio listening takes place outside the home and most of that is during commuting time. For advertisers, radio can be extremely effective in pinpointing a market. Mutual fund companies tend to advertise on classical music stations, to which affluent listeners flock; promoters of skateboards find an eager audience listening to modern rock stations.

It's good to be reminded that Radio is not in the *music* business, it's in the *advertising* business. The primary function of a radio station is to gain an audience. It does this through public services, contests, on-air personalities, news, special features - and the music it plays. Radio stations "deliver" demos (demographics) to advertisers so that they can purchase commercial airtime for their clients' products and services. The most important demographics are considered to be age, sex, and income bracket. Once those parameters have been established, the station can more accurately recommend ideas for station programming, general format, scheduling, and advertising policies.

Trends in Traditional Radio

With the passing of the 1996 Telecommunications Act Congress eliminated most restrictions on broadcast mergers. Over the next twelve months more than 4,000 of the country's 11,000 radio stations changed hands and more than 1,000 corporate mergers were proposed in broadcasting.

This arrangement reflects a fundamental shift of power in the music business. In the past, powerful record companies were accused of bribing deejays operating at small, independent radio stations to influence what songs were played. This practice was known as "payola" and it was finally outlawed in the 1960s.

Trend: Pay to Play in a New Way

Radio's current buzz phrase is "new revenue streams" and the music industry is a very large and juicy target. Labels are purchasing airtime from radio stations to create infomercials in order to advertise their product more directly. Some labels have also decided to buy radio stations in order to have complete control over music programming.

Industry mergers have moved the balance of power to radio groups, which today have the collective clout to launch a song simultaneously in scores of markets across the country - or consign it to oblivion. In a quest to create new revenue streams, Clear Channel Communications will soon launch its own record label and sell music on the Internet. "We have this giant distribution system in place," says John Madison, senior VP of operations at Chancellor. "It only makes sense that we would consider expanding into the record business. Having our own record label would give us more control over the content we pump through the distribution channel."

Programming is also being affected by these new power blocks. It's common now for the parent company to produce one general show which is distributed to all its affiliate stations while allowing room for local customizations. The local DJ has little or no say in music selections and Music Director positions at local stations are gradually being phased out.

Technology is also driving new developments in conventional radio. Radio is on the verge of facing the kinds of challenges that print and television have been facing for years. Satellite radio in particular is opening new avenues to a now limited and local-driven single market. And reports indicate that Internet radio is already impacting radio listening behavior as well (see the end of this chapter for more on Internet radio).

Payola, though in a different suit, has also made a comeback. Advertising rate cards are now available that sell airplay slots to record companies and others who can afford it. In one case, a document obtained by the *Los Angeles Times* showed that Chicago radio station Q101, owned by Emmis Communications Corp., explicitly promises radio airplay as pat of a promotional package. "For $3,500 you will receive 30 guaranteed spins the first week...20 guaranteed spins the second week,,," and so on.

College radio, on the other hand, is *music*-minded to the extreme. Freed from commercial constraints and funded by school budgets, college radio has unbridled license to indulge every musical taste, and it does.

There is a synergistic relationship between the record industry and radio - they need each other. Radio needs the music produced by record labels to attract an audience, and the labels need radio because this exposure creates a demand for recordings that result in sales.

Words of Wisdom -

"The minute you go into writing, if you're thinking about radio, you're in the wrong place. Radio is in a different business from us. They sell advertising space and we make music. Occasionally our goals converge, but not often."

- Glen Ballard, producer

How the Radio Charts Work

The "charts" found in trade magazines are important to the recording industry because they provide a weekly barometer on how well singles and albums are doing in the national market. A "chart" is a numerical ranking of current releases based on sales and airplay over a one week period of time.

The charts influence a wide spectrum of players in the mainstream music biz:

❒ for **those who work in promotion and sales**, the charts are a quantification of how well they do their jobs;

❒ for **booking agents and concert promoters**, the charts indicate who is hot and who is not, and thus determine value in the market place for personal appearances;

❒ for **publishers and songwriters**, the charts indicate the acceptance of their copyrights in the marketplace and allow them to project their projected earnings;

❒ for **record labels**, the charts are the measuring stick whereby they measure their successes and failures relative to other labels in the marketplace.

Sales and airplay is where the difference between various charts come into play. The singles charts (in *Billboard*) are based on *airplay* while the album charts are based on *sales*. These two categories, single releases and album product, are the two essentially different types of charts, although there are charts for a number of different kinds of music.

The way charts are compiled is called the "methodology" and the methodology differs between competing trade magazines. The two most important trades are *Billboard* and *Radio & Records*. Others include *Hits*, *CMJ*, and *The Friday Morning Quarterback*.

After 1990, *Billboard* created a new data collection company, **Broadcast Data System (BDS)**, to collect information about what is being played on radio stations. It collects this information through computer sampling, monitoring, and identifying each song played via an encoded audio "fingerprint".

Another monitoring service new to the scene is **MediaGuid**e. A joint venture between royalty collections agency ASCAP and the ConneXus Corporation, MediaGuide monitors over 2,500 colleges, non-commercial and commercial radio stations across the United States, as well as over 4800 Internet radio stations.

MediaGuide is hoping to offer serious competition to Nielsen-owned Broadcast Data Systems, which has become a de-facto monitoring favorite for many radio stations, labels, and royalty collection firms. The company, which boasts a superior digital fingerprinting technology, also aims to become closely involved in the lifecycle of artist careers. That is good news for indie artists, who can use MediaGuide to track their overall radio impact across a large number of stations, through its Artist Monitor service. Definitely check this out if radio is a part of your marketing program!

Radio & Records (known in the biz as *R&R*), a competing trade magazine, continues to rely on verbal and written reports from 250 CHR (contemporary hit radio) station playlists. These stations are divided into three groups, the most important being the "Parallel Ones" (or P-1s): about 62 stations across the nation that regularly reach a million or more listeners.

Each week these stations, and the less influential P-2s and P-3s, report to *R&R* which new releases they have added to their playlists – thus forecasting potential hits. The resulting chart published in the weekly *R&R* influences other radio stations to play the same records.

Chart Limitations

There are several problems with the charts, but two are most noticeable and underline their limitations:

❒ Charts are *inferential* computations, which means that a small sample is taken in order to determine a large number. Unlike pollsters, who use a random data base, chart compilers use a fixed database (and, thus, subject to both vast inaccuarcies as well as corruption).

❒ Because of the technology used, the reporting stations are in major urban markets. While this represents approx. 75% of the U.S. population, the other non-represented areas indicates the potential for chart inaccuracy. The PROs (performing rights organizations - ASCAP, BMI & SESAC) compensate a bit for this with their own random sampling of station airplay, which usually turns up some interesting data, particularly regarding "oldies".

College Radio

Back in the '70s - what many call the format's true "heyday" - most college stations were ignored by record labels, and much of the music that was wanted for a station was either purchased or serviced to the station after numerous attempts. But while servicing may have been a problem, many were content with the fact that the format was indeed a true alternative to the legions of AOR (album oriented radio) stations that dominated the commercial airwaves. Stations were relatively untouched by the giant corporate music monster, allowing them to blossom and develop their own styles and sounds.

There was still a sort of innocence to the format. That, however, is not the case today.

Since the late 1980s, more and more college stations have become marketing outlets for labels to promote their "product." College radio is now viewed as a "tool" that will gain their acts "credibility," perhaps making the transition to the next level—commercial radio—a little easier. Sadly, many college stations have accepted this role and lost sight of what the format represented in its glory days, when stations usually opted to play music that, compared to the standards set in the '70s, was rather tame. Today, many share artists with the local commercial Alternative station, and their play lists mirror those of MTV.

But college radio is still the most promising radio outlet for independent artists. Over the course of the last fifteen years major labels have increasingly recognized college radio as a crucial talent source and as an important vehicle for breaking new bands into the mainstream. Jane's Addiction, Smashing Pumpkins, Dave Mathews and, more recently, Basement Jaxx, Daft Punks and Chumbawamba all got their first radio break at colleges. In fact, at a recent music conference in Texas, a major label rep told me that he now looks primarily to college radio deejays to provide the A&R service of scouting out new talent.

Since college stations receive dozens of CD and tape submissions weekly you'll have to work smart to ensure that your music gets to the right person and that they will give it a chance for some airplay.

Mapping Out Your Radio Strategy

Getting the right information is your first task. There are literally hundreds of college radio stations in the U.S. alone. You'll want to *target* your efforts. To begin, pick a small number of stations (twelve or so) in a fifty mile radius of your base and concentrate on these.

You probably already have a pretty good idea which local stations would be receptive to your music. Contact these first. Identify yourself as a musician with a new release. Find out the names of the Program Director, the Music Director and deejays who have shows that play your style(s) of music. Commercial radio formats are quite formal and inflexible. College radio, on the other hand, is much less formal and its eclectic programming allows for a mix of formats or styles. But you should know generally where your music fits in with a particular station's programming.

The key person on your list will probably be the Music Director (MD) since this is the person who often determines what gets played. But this isn't always the case. When you call the station ask for the name of the person who should receive your music. Be sure to get the correct spelling of that person's name.

RADIO CONTACT INFORMATION

Two good sources for radio personnel, addresses and phone numbers are ***The Yellow Pages of Rock*** and ***The Recording Industry Sourcebook***. One or both of these can be found in a well-stocked city library in the Music Reference section. On the Net you can find a fairly comprehensive college radio list at **http://www.jett.com/collegeradio/clgradio.html**. Unfortunately, current radio personnel are not included. Always call the station to confirm and update directory information.

You also want to find out if the station is a "reporting station," that is, one that sends its play lists to the trade magazines that publish radio charts (see list of radio trades in chapter 17).

Radio Syndicates are another option. These are radio programs that play on numerous local stations each week. These include shows like "Echoes", "Midnight Special", and "The Sheriden Gospel Network." Visit each program's web site for "submission guidelines". See the Resource chapter at the end of this book for a list of radio syndicates in the U.S.

Keeping things organized is critical. Write down all information in a notebook as well. Provide a separate page for each station. Keep a phone-log for every station you contact and note all the names of those with whom you speak. A sample radio phone-log sheet can be found on the next page. If you have access to a computer, store your data in a database file for easy retrieval. Once you've compiled a list of stations you're confident will give your music a hearing you're ready to put a package together to mail out.

The Radio Mail-Out

Which format is most appropriate for radio airplay? By far the best is CD. Second best is vinyl (yes, vinyl) and, only as a last resort, cassette (though tape players are going the way of the MacPlus). The reason for CDs is the ease with which a song can be cued and the general durability of the product. Some stations may prefer DAT (digital audio tape) or reel-to-reel, but these are the exceptions.

Even though you'll be submitting a sound recording containing numerous songs you'll want to *select the one song you deem best for radio and push that one*. MDs and deejays are busy people. Make their jobs easier by telling them which cut to play.

The person receiving the package is going to want current information about the artist or band. You should include a brief cover letter referring to your initial phone conversation, a biography, photo (best to incorporate onto bio) and any favorable press about the act. Make each piece graphically interesting. Talk to printers for ideas (see, "Practical Tips On Dealing With Graphic Artists" in chapter 4).

Also include mention of any other stations that have agreed to play your music as well as information on the record's availability in local stores. Make sure your name and address are on every item in your package.

RADIO COMMUNICATION LOG SAMPLE

STATION CALL LETTERS **STATION FREQUENCY**

WATTAGE **TRADE REPORTING**

STATION OWNER

STATION ADDRESS

STATION FAX #

STATION EMAIL

STATION WEB ADDRESS

PROGRAM DIRECTOR

MUSIC DIRECTOR

KEY DJs:

Name	**Show**	**Date/Time**
Name	**Show**	**Date/Time**

COMMUNICATIONS LOG:

Date	**Outcome**

Remember MDs receive tons of new music – *twenty to fifty* full-length CDs each week! One way to make your recording stand out is to enclose something unique in the package like a hip calendar with your logo printed on top or some other promotional novelty that will make your name memorable. Be creative. You're aiming for attention.

Another important item to include is a *DJ Response Card*. It's an easy way to get *some* feedback from the station. I use printed postcards, self-addressed and stamped. On the card you print three questions: Will the record receive airplay at your station? Which cuts? Would you be interested in an interview with the artist? At the bottom leave room for "Comments" (to be used in subsequent promotion), their name, station address, phone number, and best time to call. The rate of return for these cards is about 30%. They can provide crucial feedback for your ongoing radio promotion. A sample response card can be seen below.

DJ RESPONSE CARD
(also called "Radio Bounceback Card")

Side 1

Thank you for taking the time to listen to **"Only When I Breathe"** from **Amanda Hunt-Taylor.** Please answer the following questions so we may service you better.

A stamp is already attached to make it as easy as possible for you. Thanks again!

Will this CD receive airplay at your station?
I so, which cuts?
Would you be interested in interviewing Amanda Hunt-Taylor either in- person or by phone? In person __________ By phone __________
Would you like to receive upcoming releases and news from Amanda?
What trades does your station report to?
Comments?

Your name ________________________________ Phone # __________________________

Side 2

WMUS
100 Radio St.
New York, NY 11223

Stamp

Your Return Name, Address
and Phone Number

Follow-up all positive comments with a phone call. Use this to remind them of your recording. Tell them of other stations' response to it and any current information about your act. People talk. Work to create that buzz. Any invitations for interviews (in studio or over the phone) should be followed up on immediately and scheduled preferably in tandem with an upcoming gig in the area.

Maximizing Your Radio Airplay

Whenever you release a CD locally, your radio promotion should be tied into your other efforts encompassing retail presence, performances and publicity. This four-prong approach ensures the greatest amount of exposure for your music. Here are some additional ways to maximize your college radio airplay:

❒ **Know the rules.** Most program directors and music directors accept calls only during specified hours. Ask their assistants for their "call hours," and call then and only then to pitch your material. These call hours apply to everyone – major labels, indie labels, independent promoters – so be prepared to be put on hold for an extended period of time. Call once just to make sure the PD or MD received your package. Don't bug them before they've had a chance to form an opinion!

❒ **Push a single.** Because of the sheer quantity of music at college radio stations and the natural time constraints of student deejays, it is wise to make their job easier by telling them the cut you want played. Some will ignore your choice and make their own selection, but most will take your lead and play that cut. Having a single repeatedly play over several weeks is often more effective than airing multiple cuts. Your single should be the strongest song on the CD and should not exceed 3 1/2 minutes.

❒ **Requests.** This should not be underestimated. Without getting obnoxious about it you, your brother, your mother, your boyfriend/girlfriend, your Aunt Sally and your band mates should all be on a "request schedule" - each person taking a different day to request your song. Even if the song isn't played when requested you've filled an ear with your act's name and song one more time each time.

❒ **Give thanks.** Send a letter to thank the radio station for playing your song. This proves you were actually listening, which will encourage them to play it again.

❒ Ask the MD about **other opportunities** for bands and artists at the station – live music weeks, benefits, annual fund-raisers, etc. Get involved!

❒ **Radio PR.** In exchange for airplay mention the station with thanks in all your promotional literature. Tell the Station Manager and MD you will do this. It can't hurt.

❒ While working a college station, try to **network** yourself into the school's entertainment scene by contacting those who hire talent for various events and mention you're getting airplay at the college's radio station. You can locate these entertainment buyers through the student activities office.

❒ Provide the station with **giveaways**. Records, CDs, tapes, T-shirts, tickets to shows, whatever. Station personnel love this.

❒ **Continue scouting out key stations**. Subscribe to a national publication specializing in your music style to see what radio stations in your region are industry leaders. Make sure you send your record to them as well. For example, if your music is primarily acoustic, then check out *Dirty Linen* out of Baltimore. If it's thrash rock look into *Maximum Rock N Roll* out of Berkeley, CA. If it's world music then check out *Rhythm Music* out of NYC.

❒ If you really want to make a splash on radio you can **hire an independent radio promoter**. Independent promoters know the ins and outs of breaking a record on radio and can save you a lot of time trying to go it alone. More importantly independent promoters already have relationships with MDs and deejays. Getting a record played is a lot easier for them than it would be for you.

Independent promoters aren't cheap (going rates are from $200 - $500 per week for a 6-8 week period, not including product and mailing costs) and should only be considered once your distribution lines are established and you have money in the bank. You can find promoters in the *The Yellow Pages of Rock* and *The Recording Industry Sourcebook*. Of course, as with most things in this business, word of mouth is your best bet for referrals. Be sure to ask the promoter for references from recent clients so you can hear from artists themselves about their service and effectiveness.

❒ **Leverage your assets.** Be sure to include a list of all radio stations that play your music in future press kits.

Internet Radio

Internet radio (also called "streaming audio"),resembles real radio in every way save one: the sound comes through computer speakers instead of over the airwaves. Users download a piece of software known as a "player," which acts like a tuner on a conventional stereo and allows them to access audio streams on the Internet. Accordingly, Web radio has grown from 178 stations in 32 countries in August 1996, to more than 4000 stations by mid-2005. Arbitron, radio's audience measuring service, has expanded its service to now include Internet radio. That information is coveted by advertising firms, the financial engine behind conventional radio, and may lead to new interest in Net radio.

In appearance and feel, Internet radio is similar to regular radio. Instead of turning a dial, you enter a URL. Anyone with a broadband Internet connection can hear CD-quality audio, better sound quality, in fact, than with traditional FM radio. Even dial-up users can get sound quality roughly analogous to AM radio. Another key difference is that under federal law, Internet radio stations are responsible for paying per-performance royalties for each track they play that they do not own the rights to. Regular radio stations are not responsible for per-performance royalties on sound recordings.

Part of the attraction of Net radio springs from real-world radio's current straits. As related earlier, consolidation has largely left over-the-air radio in the hands of multi-station networks, with computer-generated play lists, controlling consultants and fierce competition for ratings. The results are cookie-cutter programming and stifled innovation, leaving a prime opportunity for competition on the Net. On the Net you'll find such idiosyncratic radio shows as "Sweet and Soulful Motown," "80s Funk," "Evening

Melancholy[vocal jazz]," and "Smooth Jazz Piano & Keyboard." Narrowcasting, but global.

Internet radio operates on a different, radically decentralized model: individual DJs decide what music they like and what music to play. And music fans listen; they even pay a premium to listen to ad-free content.

Internet radio also makes it simple to track listening behavior, accurately gauge total listener-hours and gather demographic data on listeners. For example, you can easily use the Live365 web site to see which stations are playing your music and how many listening-hours they have had over the past month – valuable information you could never obtain from traditional radio. Plus, webcasters are obligated to identify song, artist and album when playing a recording and radio shows get archived for up to two weeks. Many also link the album to Amazon.com and other retailers so that people can purchase the music they're listening to.

Such Net radio companies as Broadcast.com (http://www.broadcast.com)and major players such as Spinner.com (http://www.spinner.com), Imagine Radio (http://www.imagineradio.com) and the aforementioned Live365 (http://www.live365.com) are building a strong presence. They offer artists and genres not heard on conventional radio, commercial-free programming, and the ability to break down the geographic boundaries of conventional radio. Particularly in music selection, such features are a big change and play very nicely into the segmentation tendencies of today's music market.

Podcasting, another form of Internet radio narrowcasting, is explored in chapter 5.

The Revolution in Radio

Bill and Rebecca Goldsmith are making a living from an idea that would probably get you laughed out of business school: running an Internet radio station commercial free. From their home in Paradise, California, in the foothills of the Sierra Nevada, they operate Radioparadise.com, a format-busting station that spins a tasteful mix of music ranging from the Beatles to Norah Jones to the Strokes. Fewer than 5,000 listeners tune in during peak times, but fans like it so much, they sent the couple $120, 000 in contributions last year, covering the cost of bandwidth, song royalties and other expenses and leaving enough to support a "comfortable lifestyle," says Bill Goldsmith, who quit a 30-year career in FM radio to run and DJ his homegrown version.

Source: *Time Magazine* April 19th, 2004

Satellite Radio

When it was announced in October 2004 that shock jock Howard Stern would be jumping from free AM/FM radio to pay satellite radio, it brought instant attention to the young medium. It took four years to sell a million VCRs, three years to sell that many

CD players. DVD caught on faster - a million units sold in just over 2 years.

Satellite radio has beaten them all, signaling a million subscribers within 23 months. Only satellite dishes reach critical mass faster, says Clayton, former head of DirecTV. He estimates the market for satellite radio to be 3 1/2 times larger, considering all the cars, trucks and boats out there.

You can think of satellite radio services like Sirius (which signed Stern) and XM Radio as something like a combination of satellite broadcaster DirecTV and premium pay channels such as HBO, says Michael Harrison, publisher of *Talkers,* a trade magazine covering the radio industry. Like DirecTV, these companies bounce their signals off satellites to beam high-quality digital service coast-to-coast. Like premium channels such as HBO, they offer exclusive ad-free programming (well, for the most part).

A look at satellite radio:

❒ **Two players.** The entire satellite radio "industry" is made up of only two companies – XM Radio, which started broadcasting in 2001 and has 6 million customers, and Sirius, with 4.2 million subscribers since going live in 2002 (figures are as of 3/06). Neither makes money, but they continue to have investor interest. Both predict double-digit growth throughout the first decade of the 21st century.

❒ **Something different.** Similar to the way FM radio grew against dominant AM radio, satellite radio is becoming known for "edgier" alternative programming. In addition to Sirius and Stern, XM has signed "Opie & Anthony," New York DJs who were kicked off the air due to their raunchy antics. Also, in sports, Sirius has an exclusive National Football League package, and XM offers NASCAR.

❒ **Start-up costs.** Potential subscribers have to start by purchasing special receivers and attennas. The sky's the limit for fancy gear, but a typical start-up package sells for about $150 at retailers such as Wal-Mart, Sears, Best Buy or Circuit City. Units are available for homes, cars and boats, but each unit takes a separate subscription. Some portable units can move from car to home and back again.

❒ **Subscription costs.** Besides harware, consumers also have to subscribe to either XM or Sirius. The services and their gear are "mutually exclusive." Sirius goes for $12.95 per month or $142.50 for a year. XM costs a flat $9.99 per month. Subscribers who want to hear Opie & Anthony pay an additional $1.99 per month.

❒ **Niche programming.** The companies are creating an array of channels to appeal to every taste. As of December 2005 XM offers 122 channels: 68 commercial-free music channels; 33 news, sports, talk and entertainment chaneels; and 21 weather/traffic channels. Sirius offers 120 channels: 65 commercial-free music channels and 55 channels fo sports, news, talk , entertainment and weather.

❒ **Getting into the dashboard.** Sirius has exclusive deals to offer its gear and service as original equipment in DaimlerChrysler, BMW and Ford Motor models. It expects to be offered in over 80 vehicle models this year, as well as Hertz rentals. XM's biggest partner is General Motors, and it is working with Acura, Audi, Nissan and Toyota to ofer service in more than 100 models this year, as well as Avis rentals.

Making contact:

1. First, determine which satellite radio stations are appropriate for your style of music
2. For Sirius, send your submissions on CD to:
   SIRIUS
   Attn: Music Programming Dept.
   1221 Avenue of the Americas
   New York, NY 10020
3. For XM, Go to the XM web portal and find your target stations. Look for instructions on how to submit music for airplay on that particular show.

iPODS OVER THE RADIO

A whopping 85 percent of music listeners between the ages of 12 and 24 would rather listen to their MP3 players than to terrestrial radio broadcasts, according to a recent finding by Bridge Ratings. The audience measurement firm also found that internet music delivery mechanisms rank higher with this age group than traditional radio. The statistics were a part of a joint study with USC on the listening habits of the "iPod Generation". The report, titled "How to Make Music Radio Appealing to the Next Generation," polled 2,000 younger listeners across the United States. Survey participants all grew up with the internet, which included easy availability to music in digital formats.

The results also showed a growing disconnect between AM/FM radio and Generation Y. "While it appears that the next generation has responded negatively to traditional radio, the reasons are rooted in radio's abandonment of the 12-24 year old over the last 10 years," explained Bridge Ratings president David Van Dyke to Mediaweek. "This age group appears to want radio to step up, change for the better and challenge them with a new way of presenting radio that is customized for their lifestyles and tastes."

These statistics also show the erosion of terrestrial radio as the primary promotional tool for the record industry, an interesting twist as the industry continues to grapple with new digital delivery mechanisms. Bridge offers several recommendations to pull this young audience back into traditional radio, though newer mediums are now successfully competing for the ears of record buyers. That does not yet include satellite radio, which was only adopted by 2 percent of the survey respondents.

Story by news analyst Richard Menta. (*Digital Music News*, 2/06).

Future Radio

It's clear that radio is going through one of the most fundamental changes in history since the dawn of stereo FM signals in the 1960's.

There are radios and tabletop stereo sets on the market that can connect to the Internet without a computer and stream audio from Internet radio stations. Add in support for Wi-Fi networking - essentially equal to an Ethernet port without a chord -and you have a radio that can go anywhere in the home and play sound from anywhere in the world without regard to the broadcasting station's location. You may live in San Francisco and listen to state radio from Beijing or London or Bombay as easily as you do local radio, just as long as those faraway stations stream their programming online.

Take it a step further. Wi-Fi is limited by how far a network signal can reach –generally a few hundred feet from the access point or hot spot. Now imagine wireless Internet connections that aren't as limited by distance. The new buzz is surround WiMax, a Wi-Fi-like networking technology that could boast a range of up to 30 miles from its source. Suddenly, every radio station in the world that broadcasts on the Internet will be reachable from nearly anywhere in the world where there's WiMax coverage. A wireless Internet connection will be an expected feature, not a curiosity found only on a few high-end models. Radio will be a global medium once again.

HD Radio – the HD stands for "high definition" just like its TV counterpart – is already available in about 100 radio markets in the united States. It promises to make some improvements that radio has long needed: AM will sound as good as FM and FM as good as a CD, proponents say. AM may once again be suitable for music, and not just the constant chatter of talk radio hosts.

HD Radio will cause the most change in the FM bands. Under plans now being tested by the National Public Radio, FM stations will be able to broadcast more than one program at a time on a single radio frequency. Tune in to a given station, and you'll have the choice of listening to its typical programming on what's being called the "A" channel. Don't like it? Switch to the "B" channel, and hear something else without having to change stations.

For example, there are markets where there's no longer a classical music station. A public broadcaster could offer that on a secondary channel in addition to its regular programming. They could also "counter-program." A station that does jazz all day and then switches to news in the afternoon, can continue to offer jazz on the secondary channel later in the day, and vice versa. Other ideas include programming the secondary channel in languages other than English. Some think this has the potential to reach entirely new audiences. Time will tell.

Radio Continues to Morph, But Who's Winning?

Terrestrial, online, satellite, HD, and mobile-based platforms are all clamoring for the next-generation radio listener, part of a battle royale of new models. But is this a one-horse race? During a panel discussion at the Digital Music Forum recently, Motorola iRadio executive LaSean Smith characterized the debate as "academic," and pointed to a co-existence of various models moving forward. "Fed-Ex and the post office co-exist," Smith said, referring to just one example in the larger marketplace.

The recently-launched iRadio is a mobile-based listening experience, which uses a Bluetooth-enabled phone to port music and radio stations across a variety of platforms. Amazingly, new experiments like those make earlier entrants like satellite radio seem quite established, though both XM Satellite Radio and Sirius Satellite Radio are just ramping past 10 million subscribers collectively. Jon Zellner, a senior vice president of programming at XM, pointed to a continued transition to the satellite format, driven by an appetite for targeted, premium stations. Meanwhile, the concept of radio itself is continuing to morph, and new formats are attracting a more hands-on listener. "Consumers are used to an incredibly passive experience, and they still are - but now, that is starting to change," Zellner said.

Also embracing the newly-active listener is online radio, which pushed the concept of genre-specific stations early on. Jack Isquith, an executive director at the AOL Radio Network, pointed to a "narrowcasting" approach that minimizes station branding. That leaves more room for advertisers to position their messages, which is ultimately the end game for AOL. Meanwhile, radio executives also discussed the podcasting phenomenon, though it is unclear what that will mean to advertisers over the long haul. Isquith pointed to initial interest from advertisers based on press-driven hype, though now the larger question is whether the format will remain attractive over the next few years.

Source: *Digital Music News*, 3/2/06

A Quick Note About Radio Advertising

This is the hardest form of advertising to make work. There are always more radio than TV stations in a city. People normally listen to the radio while they are otherwise occupied. You also don't have the ability to display any pictures with radio.

On the plus side, radio can expose you to people that you may not be reaching with your other advertising. For some of you, this will be important enough to justify all the difficulties associated with radio. Some potential music-related businesses that may do well are music instruction services, audio recording services, record stores, and instrument retail. Radio is also good for getting the word out about a particular music event or concert.

I strongly urge you not to try to buy radio time yourself. My first suggestion is to go to a buying service. Television buying services may or may not buy radio time. An advertising agency would be my second choice. Radio spots can cost anywhere from $10 - $2,000, for a single 60 sec. spot. The price goes up in proportion to the size of the audience. I would stay away from spots costing more than $125 unless you are in a major city. In a big city I'd go up to $200 a spot. Radio spots are normally 60 sec. This is the only format you should use until you are more experienced with radio.

For the production of the spot, you should go through the radio station itself. The station will have the technical equipment and the talent to generate the spot. There are radio commercial production shops around the country that make spots too. Many of these shops will turn out high quality work but you'll pay more. Negotiate. You could easily be charged $1000 for a good spot. Always try to purchase the spot as an outright purchase with no royalties attached.

I tell my clients to focus on the morning and afternoon drive time slots. These are your commutes when lots of people are in their cars listening to the radio. Go after stations with traffic updates. Sometimes these stations have helicopters reporting on the traffic conditions. These drive time spots enable you to reach a nice cross section of the working population. In general, you will be missing the young people under 18, the elderly, the disabled, and the bedridden. But there are specialty shows that reach specific audiences. Phone-in talk shows are effective. Some cater to women, some to men, and some to everyone. Phone-in shows will generate a lot of interested respondents that typically have a very low conversion rate.

Radio listeners tend to increase in the warm months. People are on vacation engaging in outdoor activities. I would suggest that you keep your radio advertising expenditures to about 15% - 20% of your total advertising outlay.

A good catchy telephone number helps people remember it. Make sure you have a big Yellow Page ad. This is the first place a listener will go to find you, if they forget your name or number. You can always include something in your Yellow Page ad like "As seen on TV and Radio." Try to include something in your Yellow Page ad that will cause the reader to associate this ad with all of your other ads.

Don't advertise on the same radio show as your competitors. This will dilute your results. If you are spending big bucks on a radio station and some competitor starts to advertise on the same station, they will be getting some people that will confuse you and them. In other words they'll be benefiting from the interest you've been building with all of your advertising. This tactic also works in reverse and applies to other advertising mediums such as print.

CH 11

Music Marketing thru B-2-B Licensing

"Research men in advertising are really blind men groping in a dark room for a black cat that isn't there." - Ludovic Kennedy, British Journalist

To say the least, distribution channels and methods are changing in the music business, with the greatest growth opportunities shifting toward partnerships between artists and labels on one hand, and corporate brands and marketers on the other.

Music has accompanied just about every product that's come to market since the 1930s. This is because product manufacturers learned early on that music, especially familiar music, adds a strong emotional connection between the familiar sounds and the product. And this business use of music hasn't slowed one bit. In fact, some of the most fertile areas of music usage today are in the Business-to-Business realm.

Business-to-business (hereafter referred to as B-2-B) marketing means your company sells, licenses and publishes your music to other companies. The end users are businesses, not individual consumers, as when you sell a CD at a performance or out of a retail shop. As CD sales decrease and consumers increasingly opt for subscription music services, as physical music distribution shifts to music access, artists are increasingly looking outside of album sales for revenue and looking to exploit all rights as a brand to the business community at large.

Today there are more sponsorship deals by way of brands, advertisements, TV and films (synch deals) which can help break an artist, than ever before. Such is the market for breaking artists through commercials and advertisements, that some ad agencies are now acting as publishers for music used in commercials, and I imagine some will soon be launching their own record labels as well. All of which is reflective of the trend where every business is becoming a 'music business.'

TYPES OF MUSIC LICENSING USED IN B-2-B MARKETING

There are seven distinct types of music licenses:

1. Synchronization (when musical compositions are used in "timed-relation" with audiovisual works)
2. Mechanical (music without any synchronized or visual accompaniment)
3. Public performance (performed commercially and to the public)
4. Master recording (reproduction of a musical composition of a particular artist)
5. Adaptation (when alterations or modifications are to be made to a particular work)
6. New media (for distribution on new media including CD-ROM)
7. Print licenses

THE MAIN PLAYERS IN MUSIC LICENSING

- Writer(s)/Composer(s)
- Recording Artist(s)
- Music Publisher
  - ▼ Administrative Publisher
  - ▼ Co-publisher
  - ▼ Sub-publisher
- Record Company
- Mechanical Rights Organizations (e.g. Harry Fox Agency)
- PROs
  - ▼ ASCAP
  - ▼ BMI
  - ▼ SESAC
- Clearance Houses
- Music Supervisors
- Misc. Licensing reps (e.g. music libraries, etc.)
- Ad agencies

The Many Business Outlets for Original Music

As the whole business world goes multimedia, its need for audio in all its manifestations increases. In response to this need, numerous kinds of music suppliers have emerged: jingle houses, music libraries, specialty labels, even individual artists (think Moby). Sometimes these suppliers deal with companies one-on-one when brokering deals, more commonly companies hire agents of various kinds to facilitate the process. These "agents" can be music supervisors, music specialists at libraries, composer representatives, producers, or ad agency staffers with a focus on music content.

Some examples of business uses of music might include:

- Piped in music at a department store via a music service like DMX;
- A smooth jazz CD added to a wine-themed gift basket;
- On-hold music for a telcom;
- Placement of an original song as background music for a TV show;
- Providing ringtones to a cell phone provider;
- Having your composition play when a visitor lands on the home page of Volkswagen's web site.

Each of these examples reflect a great variety of potential markets for music providers. Each market has its own procedures, protocols, values and expectations - in short, its own culture. Only by understanding these "cultures" will you be able to successfully market your music to them.

This book cannot address every one of the potential B-2-B markets in detail, but it will focus instead on several and also provide some basic guidelines to help you understand how best to approach these markets. Half the battle in marketing is having the best information and so I also point out further resources in chapter 17 to help you develop a detailed, customized plan of approach for a particular market segment you may wish to pursue.

In this chapter we'll briefly focus on the following markets:

❒ Commercial jingles/Ad agencies
❒ TV/film
❒ Business music services

- ❒ Interactive Game Market
- ❒ Premiums & Incentives
- ❒ Ringtones

For each one I will first provide what I call "Context" (cultural framework) and, second, "Approach" (practical guidelines) suggestions.

A Quick Note on Using Third Party Music Licensing Services

With the explosive rise of indie music and the Internet there has been an equal explosion of music licensing services to hit the scene. Indie 911, Agoraphone, Primary Elements and VersusMedia are just four of these services. Recognizing the value of the content in its online store, CDBaby has also branched into this part of the biz, licensing tracks for its thousands of indie artists. Each of these "indie consolidators" are set up to take your tracks and license them to media producers in all markets including Film, TV, Radio, Telephony (music on hold), Advertising, Web, Interactive and Game productions.

Most of these are non-exclusive deals (meaning you can be licensing the same tracks to more than one service at the same time), allow you to retain full ownership, and pay you a 50% commission on each licensing fee. This is certainly fair since they act as your publisher, "booking" your track with a specific music user. They do the work of building bridges to the producers who can use your tracks. Fees are generally on the low end, anywhere from $50. - 300. per license.

As with any music service, the proof is in the pudding. Before signing on with any of them, ask about "success stories" they've been part of and also ask for some references of composers who they've worked with. A large piece of working with these companies is trust because you *never* fully know how much money your songs and tracks are earning under their negotiations. So make sure you speak with enough people and get enough questions answered to your satisfaction before signing on.

Commercial Jingles

The word "jingle" describes an advertiser's audio image – a short custom-made melody with original lyrics about a product specifically designed to catch and hold a consumer's attention. To a great extent, this has become "old-school" as licensing familiar tracks from pop catalogs is on the ascent.

Context

• *Pop advertising.* There was a time when rock gurus like Springsteen and Dylan ritualistically shunned the advertising world. These days, the very opposite seems to be true. BB King is pitching Whoppers for Burger King (through Lowe, New York), 'NSYNC is peddling sloppy joes for Chili's (GSD&M, Austin) and everyone from the über-hip to the down home - Garth Brooks for Dr. Pepper (Y&R, New York) - is getting in on the act.

• *Original masters.* For the past decade the art of the jingle has lessened in importance, as advertisers have turned to classic songs to tie consumer goods to a hip, nostalgic image. Bob Seger belts out "Like a Rock" for Chevrolet. James Taylor's "Shower the People" sells MCI. And most recently, Bob Dylan's "Love Sick" is an invitation to shop at Victoria's Secret.

THE SELLING POWER OF SONG. Los Angeles-based Cynthia Sexton, senior VP of visual marketing and licensing, Astralwerks, Virgin Records, says, "Advertising has become an integral part of our business. In the past two years it is one of the areas that has been exploding. The money [in our business] is not what it used to be. And there is more money in advertising than in licensing to film and TV. Subsequently artists are lending themselves to sponsorship and product endorsement."

• Known, original songs can be used in two ways in commercial jingles: 1. Derivative Use = a new version of a previously established song; or, 2. Integral Use = the original version of the song is used.

• *Costs up.* Licensing original songs isn't a cheaper path, though. Whereas an original jingle may command about $10,000, negotiated rates for licensing songs in commercials can reach up to the millions of dollars for a superstar's version, although competition is starting to drive prices down.

• *Local and regional businesses*, however, continue to depend on the 30-second jingle spot and so provide the most promising avenues for the beginning jingle composer.

• *Ad agencies become publishers*. Specially created songs for national companies are increasingly being owned by the ad agency and considered works for hire under copyright law. In other words, the agency owns the publisher's share of the copyright, while the composer or music production house retains the writer's share.

• *New uses for commercial jingles.* New outlets for commercial jingles continue to multiply with in-store video monitors, 800 phone order lines, outdoor video screens, online ads, handhelds, etc.

TYPICAL FEES FOR THE USE OF POPULAR SONGS IN COMMERCIALS WILL DEPEND ON

- The past and present popularity of the song
- The type of media campaign being planned
- The territory involved
- The nature of the product or service being advertised
- The music budget
- The length of the song being used
- Whether master recording rights are also being requested
- Whether total advertising exclusivity as opposed to product exclusivity is being requested
- Whether present or future promotion of the song might be diluted because of the commercial tie-in
- The importance of the song to the message of the campaign
- Whether the agency wants to alter the original lyrics

Approach

• *Don't re-invent the wheel.* Study the way other jingle houses are doing it. Visit their web sites, listen to their jingles, observe who their clients are.

• *Do it better.* Corey Bauman, a student at Berklee College of Music I knew, wanted to break into the jingle business. He listened to jingles of local Boston companies, recorded them for analysis, then created his own better jingle. He'd then go to the business and play it for them, offering his version at "student prices". After a month he was selling his jingles for $1000 a piece.

• *Know your buyer.* Before approaching a business, learn everything you can about it. Read its own marketing information to get a sense of what its vision for itself is. Research the media to see where the business is popping up in the news. All of this will provide clues and ideas for how to best tailor your message.

• *Know your rights.* Selling your jingle as a work for hire is one thing – it's a simple exchange of the song for money and that's it. Short of this you're into the cryptic land of music licensing which means you'll need to bone up on its many aspects: copyright, master use, synch rights, derivative rights, etc. The more you understand how rights work the better the deals you will be able to negotiate, both in the short and the long term.

))) ILLUMINATING TRIVIA (((

Did you know...

Grammy winning lead singer, Jimi Jamison of 80s band "Survivor," sings the vocals for the Bud Light "Real American Heroes" commercials?

TV/Film Markets

Context: Film

• Music and film (whether in theaters or on TV) have been intertwined since the earliest days of the cinema. Film music is music, primarily instrumental, which works in conjunction with dialog and image to establish the mood and tone of a movie. Classical, jazz, electronic – regardless of genre, any material composed or scored expressly for use in a motion picture can be defined as film music.

• A soundtrack album, on the other hand, is not necessarily film music, as many of the songs which make up the record (as with those for *American Graffiti*, *The Big Chill*, *Napoleon Dynamite* and so forth) were not originally intended for use in the movie, and other times (as in *Batman Forever*) don't even appear in the actual feature at all.

• Over the last few years, as entertainment conglomerates have acquired both record labels and film studios, the bond between the film and music industries has tightened. Motion picture soundtracks have become a magnificent cooperative marketing opportunity for movies and music, in which each drives sales of the other.

• It is usually the director of the *film* who decides on the music used in the production. The director works through a network of music supervisors and music editors to find the music he requires for the production.

Context: Television

• TV production moves at a quicker pace and, while still requiring scoring, more often uses already recorded songs and compositions in its many shows and programs.

• Each year over 5000 individual series episodes are produced for the ABC, CBS, and NBC television networks, the Fox, UPN, and WB networks, first-run syndication, pay television, cable services and PBS.

• In addition, many movies of the week, miniseries, and one-time specials add to the annual total of television production.

• Production costs for an individual television episode can range from $750,000 to $1 million for 1/2 hour network shows and from $1 million to over $2 million for 1-hour shows.

• Since network license fees normally cover only between 60-80% of production costs, production companies must look to future local television syndication, cable and foreign television sales, home video, and in certain cases, foreign theatrical distribution merely to recoup.

• It is usually the producer of the TV production who decides on the music used in the production. The producer's staff works through a network of music supervisors and music editors to find the music he requires for the production.

Approach

• Understand how music supervisors work. The music supervisor has come to be the person responsible for all the musical elements - technical, creative, and administrative - that are exclusive of the score and its production. As described by music supervisor Mark Roswell, ("Sleeping with the Enemy", "Wild at Heart"), "We provide a service to the director to find source songs that are right for the film. To do this we follow the same instinct - creativity - as the composer, but with an entirely different execution."

Another music supervisor, Barbara Jordan, says there are many more opportunities for beginners writing these generic background songs for movies than in getting songs cut by top recording artists. "For consideration by a Dolly Parton or a Whitney Houston, you need to have a song that is nearly perfect because you're competing with top-notch songwriters for a limited number of cuts. But there are many more opportunities for placement of songs in film and TV, and it's not as critical that these songs be 'perfect.' They just have to set the right mood."

• As with jingles, don't make a move until you understand the publishing intricacies of film/TV music: "synchronization rights", "performance rights", "blanket rights", "public domain rights", etc..

• As with everything in music, business is driven by relationships. So first, think of all the people you know or know of, even remotely connected to the film and TV industries. Start networking with these people: this means reaching out with polite, purposeful letters, emails, faxes and phone calls. Ask questions, read online and offline, and respond.

WHAT CAN A TV COMPOSER EARN IN PERFORMANCE ROYALTIES?

Scenario:

A composer has 15 minutes of background music in each of 66 episodes (3 seasons) of a 1-hour primetime network television series. All 66 episodes are repeated once (for a total of 132 airings), and the show is sold to foreign countries and eventually widely syndicated on U.S. local television stations.

Possible composer royalties might be as follows:

U.S. network TV airings	$316,000
Foreign TV performances	$196,000
Initial-year U.S local TV Performances	$110,000
Total perf. right income	$622,000

• Have your presentation (message, business identity, demo tapes, etc.) ready for the asking. TV and film producers need *both* songs *and* instrumental music.

Visualizing a Music Licensing Negotiation

SETTING:

Office of the Vice President of Business Affairs from a major music publisher receives a call from a music supervisor. The conversation goes something like this:

THE PHONE CALL:

MUSIC SUPERVISOR: Hi, this is the music supervisor from CSI Miami. We'd like to use the song (Name of Composition) in a scene for an episode in which two of the characters find themselves in a singles' bar.

PUBLISHER: How would you like to use the song and what rights do you need?

MUSIC SUPERVISOR: The use will be a 2 minute background vocal, as we'll be using (Name of Performer's) record on a jukebox. There is a possibility that one of the characters may also sing a few lines either while the record is being played or a couple of scenes later. For your information, I'm getting a fee quote from (Name of Record Company) so we can use the master recording with his actual performance. For the use, we'll need a worldwide price quote for the following media:

1. A 5-year free television license
2. An option or a 5-year renewal
3. An option for a life-of-copyright free television license
4. Options for a pay television license for both 5 years and for life of copyright
5. An option for all television rights for life of copyright
6. An option for home video buy-out
7. An option for theatrical use outside of the United States
8. An option to use the song in television promos for the series

PUBLISHER: That's quite a laundry list. When do you need the quotes?

MUSIC SUPERVISOR: Well, we're really under the gun. The scenes are being filmed tomorrow and I need your confirmation whether we can use the song and how much it will cost almost immediately, so we can know whether we'll have to go with another song.

PUBLISHER: Okay. Let's go through the list: $950 for the 5-year free TV license and $1,200 for the 5-year renewal. Life-of-copyright free television will cost $3,000. Pay TV for 5 years will be $1,500 and for life of copyright $4,500. All television life-of-copyright will be $8,500. Home video will be $4,500. Foreign theatrical will be $5,000. And television promos will be an extra $500.

MUSIC SUPERVISOR: Thanks. A couple of the fees seem a bit high, but between you and me, they all fit in with our budget. I'll send you a letter confirming our understanding and, if the song is used, I'll request a license.

THE LESSON: Be smart, have hope, but don't hold your breath. Move on...

• Network around film schools, find the most talented director and offer to put your music on his movie. The UCLA Graduate Film Students Program approached Warner Bros. Records for someone to score first-time director Jeff Fines' "No Easy Way," and ended up with American Music Club Mark Eitzel.

• Take a movie by a director you'd like to work with and create your own score for it. When Robert Rodriguez first asked Los Lobos to do the score for his movie *Desperado*, he suggested they get a tape of his first film, "El Mariachi," and put their own music to it as an exercise.

• Find out who the leading film and video editors are and send them your music. Editors often put their own "temp" music track on films they're working on to liven up the cuts and sometimes they and the directors become so enamored of it, they end up using the music and the final score.

• Learn how to work with music software. We've come a long way from the first synthesized movie soundtracks, but now everybody is using a PowerMac, MIDI sequencers and *ProTools*. Get used to it.

• Let your publisher, ASCAP or BMI know you are interested in film work. Performance Rights agencies are in touch with the film community and know if a movie is coming up that is looking for someone to do a soundtrack.

• Establish a distinct musical identity, but be prepared to abandon it in favor of diverse vocabulary. Sound like yourself. Artists like Hispanic-American Los Lobos and Irish-American Seamus Egan originally broke into films of very specific ethnic genres but have managed to convince directors they can either work outside that style or make the style work apart for its normal connotations.

• Be able to work as part of a team and accept direction. Your typical modern pop artist is used to being his own boss, answering to no one and having absolute creative freedom. In movie, TV or commercial soundtrack work, the musician must answer to a director, a producer or a client.

• You must communicate with people who know nothing about music. Says Lobos' Steve Berlin, " You have to forge a new language to reach that common ground."

• Deadlines, deadlines, deadlines. A rock star can work on a record for as long as he wants. Soundtrack and score composers are working on strict timetables. Usually, they need it "yesterday."

Background Music Services

Context:

"Background music," "mood music," "elevator music," "wallpaper music," "Muzak" – all of these terms have been used to describe a type of music which seems to be ever-present as we go about our daily lives. We hear it at the supermarket, at the dentist office, at restaurants, on the phone, perhaps even in our own workplace.

The sickening pabulum some of us grew up listening to in our dentist's waiting room has today morphed into a rainbow of music offerings. The company Muzak itself offers dozens of styles to suit any environment. It's no longer "one size fits all". You can get "tropical", "urban", "exotic" , "latin," even "sexy" too.

Every day, Muzak (founded in 1935) is heard by 100 million people, the equivalent of more than a third of the U.S. population. Today's Muzak is played in the Gap, McDonald's and Barnes & Noble and in homes via the Dish Network, to name a few.

"Audio Architects", who act as the firm's DJs (in fact, many *are* club DJs), design 74 music programs in 10 categories. The music is changed monthly, but the songs' order changes every day, so no two days are exactly the same. The programs are delivered to 350,000 locations primarily via satellite but also through CDs, tapes and other methods. Charges average $65 a month per location. Muzak controls 70 percent of the marketplace when it comes to businesses that subscribe to music services.

> Muzak's competitors include DMX Music, Music Choice, PlayNetwork and IBN. Although Muzak does not consider satellite radio firms to be a threat to its business. But the fact that Starbucks signed a deal with XM satellite Radio in 2004 makes people wonder how many other retailers will soon opt for this as well.

What accounts for this outpouring of musical sound? What do the people who pay for a background music service hope to accomplish? One answer is that they hope to run a smoother operation, have fewer problems to deal with, and increase profits. This is based on a premise (partially proven through controlled experiments) that music can perform certain psychological or therapeutic functions - that music can have an effect on human behavior.

Background music is the most familiar type of "business music." However, another trend is what is called "foreground" music, which has different uses. The musical repertoire used in foreground music is similar to the music heard on the radio.

And each of the business music services is a signatory company to the PROs (ASCAP, BMI and SESAC), so each play of music generates performance royalties for the copyright owner, just like in radio and TV.

Approach

• Visit the web sites of each business music service before submitting material. Try to get a sense of the various genre categories they use to slot the music they use in their service. Does your music correspond with any of the music styles they employ?

The two biggies are:

http://www.DMXMusic.com
http://www.Muzak.com

• Look for "submission guidelines" on each respective site. For example, DMX requires at least two copies of your CD, and firmly states that DATs, cassettes and vinyl will not be accepted.

MUZAK: For submission guidelines call 800-331-3340

))) ILLUMINATING TRIVIA (((

Although there is an elevator in Muzak's North Carolina headquarters, it does *not* have a speaker.

Interactive Game Market

In the last twenty years video games, or interactive entertainment, have taken the world by storm. Since the U.S. release of the Nintendo Entertainment System in 1985, technology and consumer demand have created a console war that is still red hot.

"If you're over 35, chances are you view video games as, at best, an occasional distraction...If you're under 35, games are a major entertainment and a part of life. In that sense, they are similar to what rock 'n' roll meant to boomers."
– *USA Today* (11/17/04)

Context:

• U.S. computer and video game software sales grew four percent in 2005 to $7 billion – a more than doubling of industry software sales since 1996.

• Seventy-five percent of American heads of households play computer and video games.

• In 2005, more than 228 million computer and video games were sold, almost two games for every household in America.

• The average game *player* is 30 years old and has been playing games for 9.5 years.

• The average game *buyer* is 37 years old. In 2005, 95 percent of computer game buyers and 84 percent of console game buyers were over the age of 18.

• Eighty-five percent of all games sold in 2005 were rated "E" for Everyone, "T" for Teen, or "E10+" for Everyone age 10+. For more information on ratings, see http://www.esrb.org.

• Eighty-seven percent of game players under the age of 18 report that they get their parents' permission when renting or buying games, and 92 percent say their parents are present when they buy games.

• Forty-three percent of all game players are women. In fact, women over the age of 18 represent a greater portion of the game-playing population (28 percent) than boys from ages 6 to 17 (21 percent).

• In 2004, 19 percent of Americans over the age of 50 played video games, an increase from nine percent in 1999.

• Forty-two percent of game players say they play games online one or more hours per week. In addition, 34 percent of heads of households play games on a wireless device, such as a cell phone or PDA, up from 20 percent in 2002.

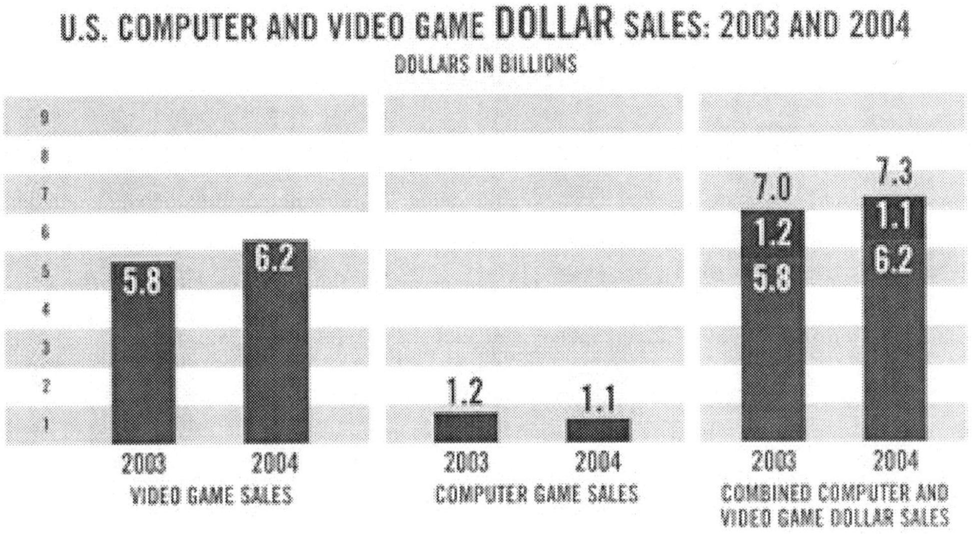

Source: The NPD Group / NPD Funworld® / TRSTS® and NPD Techworld®

• Music in games, originally created by in-house composers, is moving in new directions. Recent games have licensed singles by popular artists, and some have even contracted bands and artists to produce original work for a game, similar to a movie soundtrack.

• Because of the extreme stylistic diversity from game to game, the game composer is often hired on contract to a game company for a specific game, although there are also many full-time audio people who compose music in addition to other duties. Different projects have widely differing musical needs, ranging from orchestral to techno to pop-punk, and there continues to be a need for synthesized music for handheld systems like Game Boy.

• In a market where there are hundreds of thousands of people competing for jobs and only 100 or so good jobs to be had each year, you can see the kind of odds that you're really looking at and it's no wonder that established composers want to protect their odds by not introducing more evolved competition into the marketplace. As a result, you will experience a very aggressive lack of concern for your talent. The more talented you are, the more of a threat you are and the more resistance you will meet from your competitors. This is often an unspoken aspect of the industry as it is shameful behavior, but if you're looking for the truth, this is the very foundational aspect of the struggle of young game composers.

• Since games have replaced radio for the younger demographic in terms of exposure to new artists, game publishers are increasingly paying *less* for music uses. Videogame publishers increasingly are bartering prime position on top titles for free music from hot acts.

• The next step will be videogame sponsorship of tours featuring a game's music acts. Midway has taken a step that way, financing music videos that incorporate bands Adema and Dry Kill Logic and game footage. The game discs also feature the videos as added content.

RESEARCHING THE INTERACTIVE GAME MARKET

Finding free research on the gaming market is difficult. Here are some research firms that cover the game industry (and related industries), for a price:

- *Alexander & Associates - www.alexassoc.com*
- *Cahners In Stat - www.instat.com*
- *Datamonitor - www.datamonitor.com*
- *DFC Intelligence - www.dfcint.com*
- *IDC - www.idc.com*
- *Jon Peddie & Associates - www.jpa.com*
- *NPD - www.npd.com*
- *Yankee Group - www.yankeegroup.com*

As for free research, industry organizations are your best bet. The Entertainment Software Association annually releases a "state of the industry" report, which is available on their site at http://www.theesa.com. That usually has data on the overall size of the game market in the United States, which may be of value to you.

You can also try the International Game Developers Association, which has some free research available at http://www.igda.org/Endeavors/Research/research.htm.

Approach

• The best game composers, whether contract or full time, need to be able to write music in any style needed by the game, and must be able to work with the latest composing and recording software. For cost reasons, most game music is created using synthesizers or samplers, but whether it's real or electronic, a background in instrumental performance will help you create the richest quality of music. And for almost any style you compose in, you'll need training in cinematic scoring, since game music needs to generate emotional reactions much like film music. So your demo CD should reflect this diversity of style.

• Spend your time focusing on what makes you special and what you can offer to the world of games. Maybe it's a certain groove that you specialize in, or perhaps you have a unique way of using an orchestra.

• Once you have a product that separates you from the crowd, then you have to get yourself heard. Networking is key. There are many venues for doing this and you don't always have to be the most obnoxious person in the crowd to make this happen. Meeting the people that make decisions about music is the only way to do it. Try to attend at least one big game confab each year. Here are the top three in the U.S.:

1. Electronic Entertainment Expo (E3) http://www.e3expo.com	May
2. Game Developer's Conference (GDC) http://www.gdconf.com	March
3. SIGGRAPH http://www.siggraph.org	July

• Keep in mind that after discovering the people you think can help you, they've already got established relationships with composers they already think are great, so you have to approach them carefully. Everyone loves good music and if your stuff is great, then you'll quickly gain respect and maybe opportunities. But you have to make sure that when they take the time to stick your CD in their player, it's going to stand out from the last dozen he listened to that day.

The Premiums & Incentives Market

In 1998, California musician Doug Robinson recorded a CD of smooth jazz piano tracks. Using a contact he had made in the advertising industry, Doug was able to sell his CD to a pharmaceutical company that was looking for a "thank you" gift to give to physicians who gave the company's new drug a try. The company bought 50,000 CDs from Robinson in one single day!

Stevan Pasero, who we met in chapter 1, did the same with his "executive gift" program and Apple Computer. The opportunities are there and the market is big. Companies like Pasero's focus on strategic planning for music/brand integration. Based on the trend where every business is becoming a music business, it should come as no surprise that an increasing number of brands are focusing on music-based marketing as a core driver of long-term brand value. "Emotional" and "experiential" are the watchwords of the marketing world, and music is a medium that creates deep, personal and lasting bonds with listeners.

Context:

The use of products as promotional items, giveaways, special incentives and premiums has grown into a $38 billion dollar a year industry in the U.S. How often have you received a gift from a company for subscribing to a certain magazine, or for making a large purchase the previous year or for using a certain financial service? Though the gifts' quality varies, they nevertheless work to establish goodwill between customer and company. And that's the point.

A whole industry has grown up around this market which does nothing more than purchase the appropriate premium and incentive items for any given promotion. Music, of course, makes a great gift and represents over 20% of all premium and incentive gift-giving. All the major record labels have "specialty marketing" representatives whose sole job is to create compilation CDs and other music formats for this market.

Approach:

• First, think about who might want to use your music. Is it country? Maybe you can approach John Deere Tractors. Is it reggae? Perhaps a cruise company specializing in Caribbean tours. The possibilities are endless! Remember, while price, service, packaging, etc. are important in this market, the key ingredient is the motivational value to the target audience. What are this audience's needs, attitudes, desires, habits? What motivates them to take action? The more insight you can bring to these questions, the better your chances are of landing a deal.

• Next, you have a choice of approaching the company's incentive buyer yourself or hiring a sales representative specializing in this market. Either way, you should be creative and benefit-oriented when presenting your product – clearly and convincingly pointing out how your music can help this business, that it is a lasting gift, that your style of music is perfect for its potential customers, etc.

• To find out the names of company incentive and premium buyers check out The annual ***Buyer's Guide***, available through *Incentive Magazine* (http://www.incentivemag.com). A large public library should have it.

The Ringtone & Phone Wallpaper Market

Context:

• The ringtone craze may have started with mainstream artists, but the concept is now hitting the indie market in a major way. In August 2005 independent digital distributor Digital Rights Agency announced a dedicated ringtone store called Bliptones, available at http://www.bliptones.com. Master ringtones purchased through the Bliptones site will initially be downloadable by customers of AT&T, Bell Canada, Cellular One, Cingular, FIDO, Rogers AT&T, Sprint and T-Mobile. "By building the Bliptones brand through online and offline marketing and making it an outlet exclusively for our clients, we are providing our labels with an important leg-up in the mobile entertainment market," said Digital Rights Agency managing director Tuhin Roy.

• In any new media there are three potential 'victories' to a content owner: revenue, promotions and co-op marketing. It is unlikely that an artist will capture all three, but two at a time is definitely possible. Artists, signed or otherwise, can utilize both their content and their audience to create additional value. This can be realized as increased revenue, rewards to fans, CD Buyers, concert goers, giveaways, and more. Mobile content is not rocket science, it is just another way for artists to connect with their fans

• As the ringtone space grows, the mix of consumers and ringer types has started to evolve. While a good pop hook can always catch someone's attention, consumers also look at ringtones as a way to define themselves. That plays well for independent labels, which have some of the most dedicated fans and tap into niche lifestyles.

• Meanwhile, a rapidly expanding ringtone market offers a good way to bring visibility and revenue to lesser-known artists and labels. But it's also about independents getting a seat at this all-important table. "We are excited to enable our label clients to add ringtone delivery to their websites," said Bryn Boughton, chief marketing officer of IRIS, "because it is important in establishing the role of independent labels in this emerging market."

• Other indie players are also pushing into the ringtone space. Recently, digital content distributor IRIS Distribution launched a service that allows artists to layer ringtone sales into their existing websites. That solution, along with the Bliptones store, were launched with the help of Xingtone, an LA-based firm that also markets software that creates ringtones from CD tracks. Meanwhile, longtime indie distributor The Orchard is currently selling ringtones through over 150 different mobile outlets, Sprint, Dwango and Zingy.

• Keep in mind that downloading is easier in Europe and Asia than it is in North America. Why? Because in these foreign places, a consumer simply has to push a five-digit code to get the song, and a keyword to activate the loading process. The wireless companies here are a little slow on the uptake. Cingular and Sprint are supposed to have their key code in operation shortly, while Verizon Wireless is set to get theirs by summer 2006.

Approach:

• Any of the following services can help any indie artist start selling/promoting ringtones of their music:

Digital Rights Agency (http://www.digitalrightsagency.com)

The Orchard: Mobile Partnerships (http://www.theorchard.com/marketing/orchard_mobile_partners.htm)

Xingtone (http://www.xingtone.com)

IRIS (http://www.irisdistribution.com)

Bandaidonline.com (http://www.bandaidonline.com)

Primetones.com (http://www.primetones.com)

Look for any "rules for submission of materials" links at the above web sites and follow them to the letter. You may want to test the market first yourself. Keep these guidelines in mind:

• Be aware that your mobile carrier may charge you for transferring the ringtone to your phone.

• Make sure your phone can use MP3 ringtones - as of May 2005, there are over 150 mobile phones that support mp3 ringtones.

Determining How Much to Charge for a Licensed Track

When the call comes in from an ad agency, TV producer, film director or music supervisor, and you are trying to decide how much to charge for the use of one song, you need to consider a number licensing parameters, including:

❒ How the song is used (vocal performance by an actor on camera, instrumental background, vocal background, visual performance by a band in the background of a scene, theme, under the opening and/or closing credits).

❒ The overall budget for the film or commercial, as well as the music budget.

❒ The stature of the song being used (current hit, new song, famous standard, rock 'n roll classic).

❒ The duration of the use and whether there are multiple uses of the song.

❒ The term of the license (2 years, 10 years, life of copyright, in perpetuity).

❒ The territory of the license (the world, universe, specific foreign countries).

❒ Whether there is a guarantee that the song will be used on the film's soundtrack album.

❒ Whether there is a change in the original lyrics.

❒ Whether deferred payments are being offered if a film breaks even or makes a profit.

❒ Whether the producer requests and exclusive hold on the song or places restrictions on its use in other motion pictures or commercials.

❒ Whether the producer also wants to use the hit recording of a song, rather than rerecording a new version for use in the film.

❒ Whether the motion picture is a dramatization of the events described in the song.

❒ Whether the motion picture uses the song as its musical theme as well as its title.

❒ Whether the motion picture is over budget at the time a song is requested.

❒ Whether a number of songs from the same publisher are contained in the film.

❒ Whether the film producer wants a share of the publishing income or a co-ownership interest in the song.

These are the kinds of questions negotiators ask when the call comes in. No fees are "written in stone". The parties go back and forth in a sort of see-saw until an agreement is reached. Prices are also affected by various union standards such as those of AFTRA (American Federation of Television & Radio Artists) and SAG (Screen Actors Guild). Such song negotiations occur hundreds of times every day around the world. Don't worry. The more you do it the easier it becomes.

Hey, no one said this business was gonna be easy!

Setting Your Fees

Use these guidelines to determine how much you should charge for your work:

• "Work for hire" rates should be based on what you would like to earn per hour plus all expenses related to the project (i.e., demo fees, phone calls, mailings, etc.).

• When estimating a project, provide a range to the client (for example, $1700.-2000.) and try not to go beyond it. As with almost every estimated job, add an additional 20% to whatever you come up with to cover unforeseen changes that may have to be made.

• As with all work for hire arrangements, make sure to get a formal letter of agreement up front, signed and dated by both parties.

• Try to establish a "minimum fee". It's often not worth getting yourself and your equipment all set up for a 15-minute session. Decide what your minimum should be and stick to it, even if you have to bill out your hourly rate for a 10 minute re-mix.

According to the *Film and Television Music Salary & Rate Survey,* other pay factors may include:

• Publishing (ownership) that composer retains (see below).
• Composer's participation in soundtrack album royalites (guaranteed inclusion of score cuts, etc.)

• Deferred compensation agreements based on distribution and/or profits of film.

• Some film and multimedia projects may also pay a percentage of profits or a per-unit "bonus" based on units sold (for CD-ROM games and interactive projects).

Publishing Rights. If you retain all or some of the rights to the work, then things can get more complicated. But your creative fee for the project shouldn't change. This is because, even though you may see synch and performance royalties, that is *additional* revenue *on top of* the original time you put in to the project. Plus, composer royalties are very often meager (especialy for instrumental music), or so difficult to monitor, that it is advisable to get as much money up front since this may be the only substantial money you'll see.

If this is an area you plan on exploring, then be sure to join The Film Music Network (http://www.filmmusic.net) for further guidance and opportunities.

An excellent directory of music licensors to business can be found at:

http://www.business.com/directory/media_and_entertainment/music/

Explore some sites to get an idea of what the competition is doing and they present themselves online. Stand on the shoulders of those who've gone before you, and see farther!

CH 12

Marketing to Music Publishers

"You write a hit the same way you write a flop." - William Saroyan, Writer

In 2001, EMI Publishing, owner of the copyright to the song "Have Yourself a Merry Little Christmas", collected over $2 million in revenue from the song. Not bad for a tune written in 1944! This included:

❐ performance revenues from all the radio airplay the song received, plus its use on TV shows such as "ABC World News Tonight" and "General Hospital";

❐ The song also earned money from mechanical royalties when recordings were sold. Many artist released recorded versions of the song, including Natalie Cole, Melissa Manchester, Amy Grant, Vince Gill, Shawn Colvin, and Grover Washington Jr.;

❐ The song was also used in several movies that appeared that year, with a synch right being negotiated between the publisher and the movie company (usually about $25,000 per license);

❐ Additional mechanical royalties were paid by the record company that released the movie soundtrack. If the movie is shown on TV, the television station must pay a performance fee when the movie was broadcast. If the song is used in a commercial, the company using the song must pay the music publisher, and so on...

It goes without saying that the *uses* of a song (as opposed to the *sale* of recordings) is the *real* money maker in the music business. This brings us into the very complex, sometimes arcane, world of music publishing.

The Song Makes the Industry Go 'Round

The writer is the first link in the music industry food chain, the earth from which everything springs. The writer faces an empty page and from the factory of his or her mind creates words and music that weren't there before.

But once that song is written, and assuming the writer wants to move it beyond the four walls of his bedroom, the next step is *publishing* it.

In all styles of music, the big-name publishing companies are no longer dominating the industry. Writer-producers who do most of their production work at home aided by MIDI and ProTools studios have pop hits on a regular basis with a variety of artists.

A Song's Income*

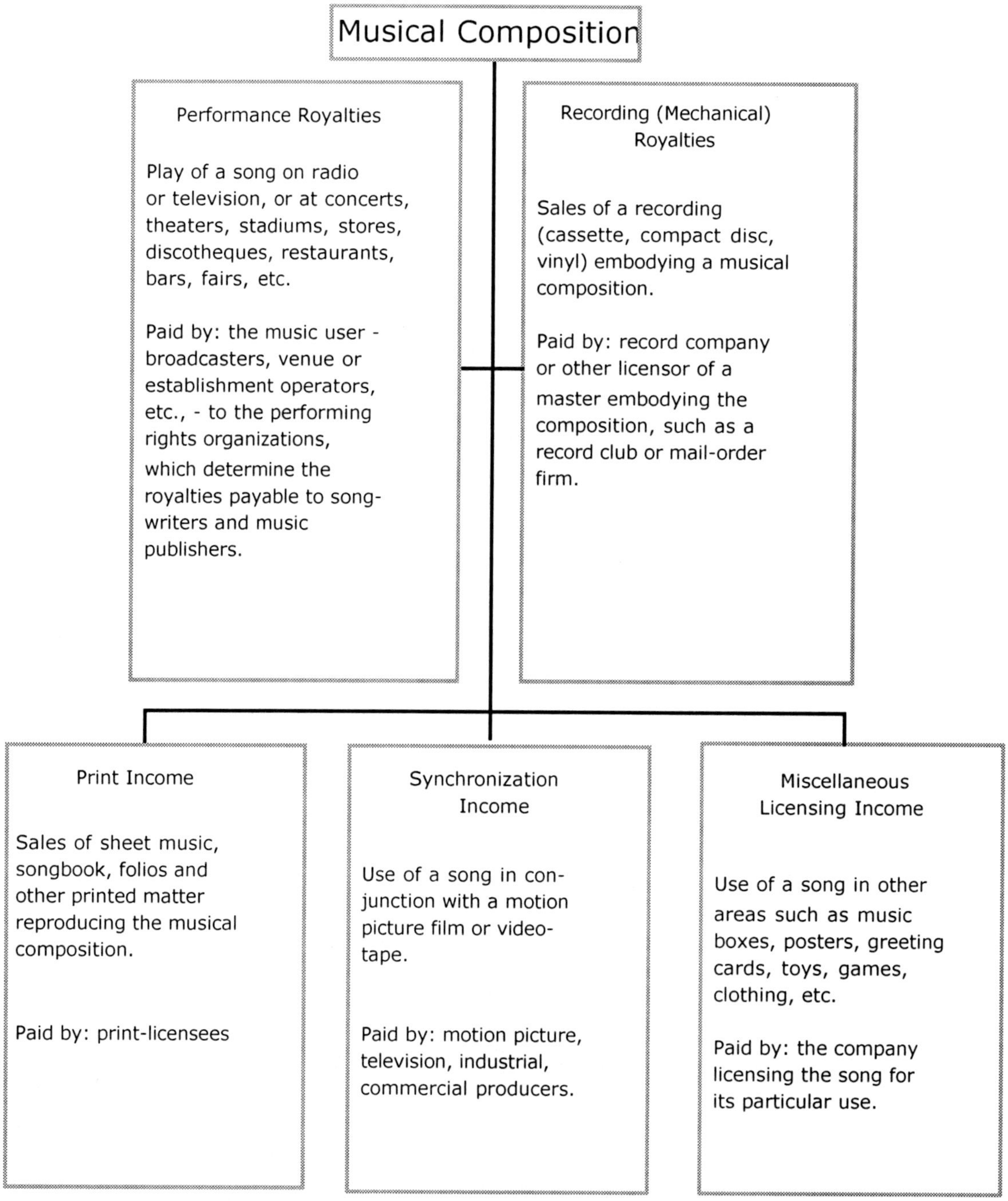

Musical Composition
Performance Royalties
Play of a song on radio or television, or at concerts, theaters, stadiums, stores, discotheques, restaurants, bars, fairs, etc.
Paid by: the music user - broadcasters, venue or establishment operators, etc., - to the performing rights organizations, which determine the royalties payable to song-writers and music publishers.
Recording (Mechanical) Royalties
Sales of a recording (cassette, compact disc, vinyl) embodying a musical composition.
Paid by: record company or other licensor of a master embodying the composition, such as a record club or mail-order firm.
Print Income
Sales of sheet music, songbook, folios and other printed matter reproducing the musical composition.
Paid by: print-licensees
Synchronization Income
Use of a song in con-junction with a motion picture film or video-tape.
Paid by: motion picture, television, industrial, commercial producers.
Miscellaneous Licensing Income
Use of a song in other areas such as music boxes, posters, greeting cards, toys, games, clothing, etc.
Paid by: the company licensing the song for its particular use.

*Performance royalties are paid by the performing rights organizations (ASCAP. BMI and SESAC) directly and seperately to music publishers and songwriters. All other income is paid directly to the music publisher, which in turn remits the appropriate earnings to the songwriter.
Reprinted with permission from the 1992 Songwriter's Market (Writer's Digest Books).

As the chart on the previous page illustrates, the chain of economic benefits that starts with the songwriter or composer is a long one and has a positive economic impact on a great many people: the artists and musicians who perform the works, the technicians who record them, the retailers, both traditional and online who sell them, all those in the live concert industry, from road managers to janitors at theaters and arenas, the workers who manufacture instruments and electronic equipment, the technology wizards and entrepreneurs who develop ways for more people to access music more easily than ever before.

And with...

- Hundreds of television production companies churning out thousands of series episodes and specials,
- over 500 motion pictures being produced ever year in the United States alone,
- satellite television,
- the internet,
- $38 billion of prerecorded records, tapes, and CDs being sold annually throughout the world,
- colorization of the old television series and movies,
- the emergence of digital recording and downloads,
- advertisers using hit songs to sell their product,
- Broadway and road shows opening their curtains to over 1.2 billion yearly,
- cable and wireless technology taking over the world,
- the growth of paying per-viewed programming and the success of pay television series channels,
- the introduction of fiber optics and interactive media,
- VCRs, DVD's, Computers, game consoles, and digital technology having become a staple of ever home,
- and the emergency of high-definition television as a reality...

...with all these developments, ***music publishing*** has reasserted its place as a cornerstone of the ever-expanding and enormously profitable business of entertainment.

Music publishing can get very complicated very quickly. We can't cover the subject in its entirety (see chapter 17 for plenty of supplemental material) but I'll provide the essential outlines anyone with an interest in marketing their songs needs to understand for getting them into the music marketplace today.

But first, some context.

Context:

❒ **Music Publishing is the sleeping giant in the record world.** It takes people a while in this business to realize that the real money isn't on the *record* side, it's on the *music* side. Records go up and down the charts, but the publishing goes on forever (well, almost forever).

❒ **There are approx. 70,000 music publishing companies in the US alone**, though a great many of these are largely inactive. In fact, only a few hundred publishers have songs on the U.S. charts each year. Anyone can set up a music publishing house, but the value of a publisher lies in how effectively they are able to "exploit" their copyrights. With the rise of the "digital common" along with the "every business is a music business" trend, many businesses are beginning to develop music publishing subsidiaries. From radio stations to ad agencies, airlines to online licensing services – they are all waking up to the riches that lie within music.

❒ **Types of Music Publishers:** There are essentially four different kinds of music publishers –

1. *The Mega Pubs* – These are the major publishing companies affiliated with a multinational record or film company (such as Warner/Chappell, EMI, BMG, Sony/ATV, MGM, Rondor, Jobete, Famous Music, etc).

2. *Major Affiliates* - Independent publishing companies, fully staffed, whose "administration" is handled by a major record or publishing company (e.g., Quincy Jones Publishing admin. by Warner/Chappell; or, Interscope Music, administrated by Universal).

3). *Stand Alones* - Publishing companies not affiliated with a major but who do their own administration – that is, collect their own money, do their own accounting, etc.

4). *Writer-publisher owned companies* (e.g., Bruce Springsteen, Bob Dylan, Sting, Diane Warren) - They pocket the lion's share of the publishing and pay a 5-8% admin, fee to a major company to handle the paperwork, typically known as an "administration deal".

))) ILLUMINATING TRIVIA (((

Did you know...

...that for five years Bob Dylan did not publish songs in order to avoid sharing an exorbitant percentage of the income with his manager Albert Grossman?

Rockonomics: the Money Behind the Music by Marc Eliot (1989, Franklin Watts), chapter 11.

❒ **Publishing is the "real estate" of the music business**. It can be subdivided into many smaller pieces and owned by many parties. In this scenario, the publisher is similar to a landlord or managing agent, who exploits the property and receives money from those using the property, and then distributes the income to the owners.

❒ To most people the term "music publishing" connotes a business concerned with *print* music. And, in fact, this was what early music publishing was. However, over the years the importance of popular sheet music sales has declined in inverse proportion to the success of recordings.

In fact, most music publishers today don't manufacture product in any physical form, nor do they sell product directly to consumers. Instead, music publishers *license* other companies *the rights* to use, perform, copy, and sell songs in various types of media. It's primarily a B-2-B (business to business) rather than a B-2-C (business to consumer) kind of business.

It might have been a logical step for music publishers to issue music on records, but, as things unfolded, *record companies* emerged to "publish" recorded performances by musicians and singers. That meant that record companies had to obtain permission from the music publishers who owned the songs performed by the recording artists.

The upshot was that, instead of selling product per se, music publishers began dealing in *rights*, and so it remains primarily a *service*-based business.

❒ **Since most music publishers, then, have no physical product, *copyrights* constitue their sole stock in trade.** Copyrights are intangible assets (i.e. they don't have physical properties you can see or touch). Music publishers "rent" the rights to intangible properties (songs) to *users*, such as record companies, artists, record producers, broadcasters, film producers, ad agencies, software developers, etc. The users can make physical copies of the songs and sell them to consumers (after paying the appropriate licensing fee, in this case, a mechanical license).

❒ A newer trend in publishing is the signing of writer/performers to **"Development Deals."** More and more publishers are providing the service of artist development that record labels have relinquished. For example, the band Everclear signed a publishing contract with Rondor Publishing and Rondor helped promote the band to *CMJ*, an influential industry trade magazine. They also helped the band buy new equipment and offered some tour support. This was Everclear's "back-way" into visibility and, eventually, a recording contract.

❒ Until the 1960s the work of music publishers involved signing songwriters and then placing their songs with singers who would use them for commercial recordings or public performances. The publisher would then receive an income from sales of the recordings and sheet music, and revenue from performance rights.

The emergence of rock music radically changed the relationship of publishers to popular music production. In the Tin Pan Alley tradition there was a clear cut distinction between writers and publishers on one side, and performers and record companies on the other.

The success of artists such as the Beatles and Bob Dylan and the emergence of the rock aesthetic that placed great emphasis on individual expression, resulted in performers increasingly writing their own songs. And so it remains today.

What Music Publishers Do

The essential gig of the music publisher is to be an *agent for songs*. Towards this end, and depending on his company's size and scope, a publisher is inevitably involved in most of the following activities:

❒ Copyrighting musical compositions in the United States and making sure that songs it represents are also protected in foreign countries.

❒ Securing records, television, and motion picture uses and inclusion of songs in Broadway, Off-broadway, and regional stage productions.

❒ Arranging for the manufacture and distribution of sheet music, folios, songwriter compilations, and other music oriented books.

❒ Securing uses of songs in televsion and radio advertising commercials.

❒ Suing infringers of musical compositions and negotiating settlements, when appropriate.

❒ Properly registering songs with The Harry Fox Agency, ASCAP, BMI, SESAC, and all other representatives and collection agents (both domestic and foreign) so that royalties can be collected for record, tape, and CD sales as well as for radio and televison performances.

❒ Staying abreast of all new developments and formulating policies and procedures dealing with such new areas so that songs are not only used but also earn maximum compensation.

❒ Promoting the creation of new songs by helping to support and develop promising writers.

❒ Negotiating fees for all uses of music and efficiently issuing appropriate licenses.

❒ Making sure that all payments from licenses (record companies, video cassette distributors, television, and film producers) are paid on a timely and accurate basis.

❒ Providing correct information to and effectively communicating with all representatives in foreign territories so that said representatives remain aware of all current developments with respect to a publisher's catalog.

❒ Giving potential users prompt and correct information on songs being considered for usage so that decisions can be made quickly by potential users.

❒ Promoting legislation affecting the music/entertainment industries and the protection of the rights of creators.

❒ Creating interest in songs and their writers by the creation of special projects such as commemorative stamps, anniversary albums, single writer folios, and compilation hit promotional albums for radio stations, producers, recording artists, film producers, television companies, and all other users of music.

❒ Keeping track of motion pictures, television shows, commercials, and video projects in pre-production, production or post-production so that compatible songs can be submitted to producers for possible inclusion in said projects.

Adapted from the very informative, *Music, Money & Success* by Jeff & Todd Brabec (2002, Schirmer).

How Publishers Build Their Catalogs

Acquiring marketable copyrights is a prerequisite for successful publishing. The sum of a publisher's copyrights is called its "catalog."

Publishers build their catalog through the following methods:

❒ ***Individual song agreements*** - signing songwriters to one-song deals;
❒ ***Exclusive agreements*** - acquiring temporary management of copyrights;
❒ ***Co-publishing agreements*** - acquiring part ownership of songs;
❒ ***Subpublishing*** - acquiring temporary rights to foreign catalogs or songs;
❒ ***Purchase*** - buying existing copyrights.

Publishers try to make acquisitions on market-oriented principles. In other words, there should be no acquisition without a clear plan for "exploitation" (this is publishing lingo for "effectively marketing" not "exploitation" in the sense of "unjustly taking advantage of").

Acquisition of quality copyrights nearly always requires a captial investment, whether an "advance" or an outright purchase.

))) ILLUMINATING TRIVIA (((

Did you know...

In 2003 Mike Batt, a British producer, put a minute of silence between tracks on an album by The Planets, and was sued by the representatives of John Cage's estate. He had to pay out over $200,000 to settle the matter.

Copyright 101 Review

Before tackling some strategies for exploiting your songs, let's do a quick review of the meaning of "owning a copyright".

First, a work is copyrighted when it is fixed in some type of medium. In a sense, then , a work is "copyrighted" when it is created (drawn, filmed, played, written or recorded). You do not obtain a copyright from the Library of Congress in Washington, D.C., you merely *register* your copyright there.

A copyright gives the owner five exclusive rights. The owner can:

(1) **Reproduce** the work: make and sell the work in any form;

(2) **Distribute** copies of the work: one illustration of this would be a record company that hires a plant to manufacture their CDs. The plant gets the right to reproduce the songs (#1 above), but not the right to distribute copies of them;

(3) **Peform** the work publicly: it doesn't matter whether the performance is by live musicians or a DJ playing records, you get to control this right;

(4) Make a **Derivative** work: a derivative work is a creation based on another work. An example is a parody lyric set to a well-known song (e.g. "Gangster's Paradise" which Weird Al parodied as, "Amish Paradise"). The new work is called a derivative work because it's *derived* from the original. By the way, Weird Al did not have to obtain the permission of the original writer and publisher to create these derivations because parodies fall under "fair use laws". Al, however, takes it upon himself to request permission. If he doesn't get it, as in the case with Eminem, he doesn't go forth with the parody.

(5) **Display** the work publicly: this doesn't really apply to music; it's the right to put paintings, statues, etc. on public display.

Length (or, duration) of copyrights. Copyright protection begins on the date of creation and, in most cases, lasts for the lifetime of the author plus 70 years. So if you single-handedly write a song in 2001, and die in the year 2080, the copyright will last until 2150.

What about songs written before January 1, 1978? These originally fell under the Copyright Act of 1909 which gave the song 28 years of protection with the right to renew it for another 28. The copyright Act of 1976 extended the life of pre-1978 copyrights to 75 years from the date of creation.

For an easy-to-follow chart on the length of copyrights go to:

http://www.unc.edu/~unclng/public-d.htm

What Can & Cannot Be Copyrighted

The following works can be copyrighted:

- Musical compositions
- Recordings of musical compositions
- Arrangements of musical compositions

- Works of literature
- Recordings of works of literature
- Adaptations of works of literature (e.g., screenplays)
- Logos (trademarks)
- Original pictures
- Original photographs
- Original illustrations
- Film, video and animation.
- Software
- Clothing and product designs.

The following works cannot be copyrighted:

Any idea, procedure, process, system, method of operation, concept, principle, or discovery - regardless of the form in which it is described, explained, illustrated, or embodied - in an original work, cannot fall under copyright protection.

For example:

- An improvised speech where a recording or prewritten script doesn't exist;

- Titles, names and short phrases (unless these items form a part of a trademark);

- Ideas, methods and procedures (unless protected by patent);

- Lists of common information (such as calendars, or items taken from public domain sources).

Of course, as with all matters of "intellectual property", there are many grey areas, many exceptions to the rule, and many complicated scenarios that can twist your mind like a pretzel. I would point you to chapter 17 for plenty of further resources to satisfy your intellectual property curiosity.

))) ILLUMINATING TRIVIA (((

Did you know that...

...John Fogerty's "The Old Man Down the Road" sounded so much like his Creedence Clearwater Revival hit "Run Through the Jungle" that he was sued for copyright infringement of his own song by CCR's label, Fantasy Records?

Registering Your Copyrights

It is *not essential* to register your copyrights with the government's copyright office but it is *advisable.* Registration creates a clear paper trail in the event of an infringement on your copyright. Plus (and this is ultimately most important), formal registration allows you to collect statutory damages as well as attorney fees from the infringer when you win your case. 'Nuff said.

There are five music-relevant copyright registration forms obtainable from the Library Of Congress. They are:

- Form PA (Performing Arts))
- Form SR (Sound Recording)
- Form TX (Non-dramatic literary works
- Form VA (Visual Arts)
- Form CA (Corrections & Amplifications)

A CD project can easily involve every one of these forms. For example, when the tracks were just "unpublished" songs on a rough lead sheet, you could have registered each one with form PA. When the tracks were recorded, you could have filed an additional SR form to register the sound recording version of the songs registered under the previous PA form.

You may have some special liner notes written for the CD which can be registered using form TX, and the CD graphics registered using the VA form.

What about the CA form? Well, listen up and save some dough.

A person may register as many songs as they wish on a PA or SR, call it "The Collected Works of Joey Singer", Vol. 1", and be granted full copyright protection for each song listed on the form. This is great because for one $30 fee each song gets protected.

But what if someone hears one of these songs and wants to cover it? How will they be able to find it in the Copyright Office records?

"They won't", says Page Miller, a senior copyright information specialist in D.C. "This is why we created the CA form." The CA (Corrections & Amplifications) form allows you to "amplify" your PA or SR filing so that each of your songs can be individually indexed at the Copyright Office.

Now if a band or artist wants to cover a song you've written or recorded, they would be able to look up your name as the song's copyright owner. If the song in question was merely one of, say, ten songs registered on a PA or SR form, it would be protected but it would not allow a person to find it in a copyright search. A CA form registration has nothing to do with giving the song additional protection, *it just provides a tracking path to the song's author.*

You file the CA after you receive your registration number back from the first filing. The total process can take several months.

So for a total amount of $60 ($30 for each registration) you can register and protect all your songs, and provide a tracking route to them as well.

Office of Copyright Contact Info:

Download any form you'll need at: http://lcweb.loc.gov/copyright/forms/

If you want to speak with an Information Specialist at the office of Copyright call: 202-707-5959

Recording Copyrighted Songs

Copyright law gives the owner of a copyrighted song the exclusive right to make the first sound recording of the song. However, once the song has been recorded and distributed to the public, others are entitled to make their own recordings of that work. How so?

In the early 1900's, the disruptive technology was player pianos. Manufacturers of player piano rolls purchased a single copy of the sheet music of a song, hired someone to record the music and then sold these mechanical reproductions to consumers. The songwriters held that this was copyright infringement, while the piano roll manufacturerers pointed out that they had paid the appropriate copyright fees when they purchased the sheet music. As often happens, lawsuits flew.

Though the Supreme Court found in favor of the piano roll manufacturers, it invited Congress to consider new legislation on the issue. Congress responded with the Copyright Act of 1909 which created a new form of intellectual property known as "mechanical reproduction rights".

So now if you want to record a previously published song, you *do not* need to obtain permission from the copyright owner directly. The law does, however, require you to make account to the copyright holder and to pay fixed rates per song for each record manufactured and sold. This is accomplished through the issuance of a compulsory "mechanical license".

There are three ways to get one:

1) First, find out who owns the copyright on the composition by contacting BMI (212-586-2000 or http://www.bmi.com), ASCAP (212-621-6160 or http://www.ascap.com) or SESAC (800-826-9996 or http://www.sesac.com). Armed with this info, you can contact the publisher and negotiate your own rates.

2) If you don't want to negotiate your own rates, contact the **Harry Fox Agency** (http://nmpa.org/hfa.html) which is authorized to issue mechanical licenses at the statutory rate of 9.1 cents per song up to five minutes. Songs over five minutes are calculated at $0.0175 per minute, per song. To figure out your royalty fee, multiply the cost per song by the number of units manufactured [E.g., one seven minute song on 1,000 CDs would cost 1,000 x (7 x $0.0175) = $122.50].

STATUTORY ROYALTY RATES
(or, "Mechanicals")

As of January 1, 2006 the statutory mechanical rate is as follows:

9.10 Cents for songs 5 minutes or less,
or,
1.75 Cents per minute or fraction thereof over 5 minutes.

For example:

5:01 to 6:00 = $.105 (6 x $.0175 = $.105)
6:01 to 7:00 = $.1225 (7 x $.0175 = $.1225)
7:01 to 8:00 = $.14 (8 x $.0175 = $.14)

In some cases, Harry Fox does not administer publishing rights, and you must find the individual publisher who owns the publishing rights. This can often times be much more difficult, especially with defunct and obscure record labels. Again, if you have the original release, you can look in album credits for publishing information. If you do not have the original recording, a good place to start is the All Music guide (http://www.allmusic.com). This website can help you find album and/or song credits for many artists, even those on small independent labels. Once you contact a publisher, you must prove that you have begun the process of obtaining the proper mechanical license, and you intend to complete the transaction. In some cases, the publisher may give you written permission with out any fee. In either event, it is recommended that you obtain written permission on company letterhead.

3) If you can't afford the standard fee, contact a group like the Volunteer Lawyers for the Arts (call 215-545-3385 for the chapter nearest you). They can often help negotiate reduced royalties for schools and non-profit groups.

The Growing 'Public Domain' Catalog

"Public domain" refers to the status of a work having no copyright protection and, therefore, belonging to the world. When a work is "in" or has "fallen into" public domain it means it is available for unrestricted use by anyone. Permission and/or payment are not required for use. Except with respect to certain foreign-originated works eligible for restoration of copyright, once a work falls into the public domain ("PD"), it can never be recaptured by the owner.

This is very siginificant because we are just now beginning to see some early rock music entering the public domain. For example, Elvis Presley's, "That's All Right" is soon to enter the public domain in Great Britain, followed by other milestones of popular music as Britain's fifty-year protection period comes to an end. Naturally, rights owners are outraged, regarding it as a "wakeup call" for Britain to adopt something similar to the

1999 Sonny Bono Copyright Extension Act (this extended U.S. copyrights by 20 years, from 50 to 70 years).

New material added to PD songs makes these compositions eligible for copyright to the extent new material is added and the public domain portion is not resurrected. "New material" includes editorial revisions of old lyrics, new lyrics, changes in melodies, arrangements, and compilations of versions of the same song.

New copyrights based on public domain material, make it possible for writers and publishers to receive performance monies, and mechanical license fees from record companies. In his book *Music Publishing* (MIX Books), Tim Whitsett tells the story of Warner Chapell's commissioning of new arrangements of Gilbert & Sullivan operettas they owned the copyright to in order to continue collecting a degree of royalties on these copyrights.

WHEN WILL A WORK PASS INTO THE PUBLIC DOMAIN?

See the easy-to-follow chart at:

http://www.unc.edu/~unclng/public-d.htm

'Clearing' a Song

Determining the copyright status of a song can be tricky. The most reliable method is having a copyright attorney or professional music clearance agency make the determination for you. If you decide to conduct the research yourself, there are several resources available to you.

If you can verify through a reliable source that the song was published prior to 1923, you can conclude that the song is currently in the public domain. The reliable source might be records maintained by the United States Copyright Office, or original sheet music or a music book that includes the publication date of the song.

Unfortunately, **there is no "official" list of songs in the public domain**. There are unofficial lists such as the *Mini-Encyclopedia of Public Domain Songs*, published by BZ/Rights & Permissions, Inc., a clearance service (Contact BZ at 121 West 27th Street, Suite 901, New York, NY, 10001, 212-924-3000/Fax: 212-924-2525). Not all compilations are created equally so exercise caution in selecting the lists on which you rely.

The Copyright Office located in Washington, D.C. maintains records dating back to 1891. Records from 1978 through the present can be accessed through the Copyright Office's website. The Copyright Office does not maintain a list of public domain works. Instead, you can use their records to determine the song's publication date and whether the song's owner adhered to the formalities required for maintenance of the copyright.

You can conduct the search yourself, or the Copyright Office will conduct the search for you for a fee of $65 per hour. If you can't get to Washington, D.C., libraries throughout the country have copies of the Copyright Office's records catalog. The Copyright Office's Information Circular No. 22 provides information on searching Copyright Office records. The information circulars are available online.

Other databases and sites on the internet may also be helpful. Public Domain Info (http://www.pdinfo.com/) is a good site with which to start. It contains helpful articles, a listing of public domain songs, and links to other resources.

Each of **the performing rights societies** -ASCAP, BMI, and SESAC - as well as the Harry Fox Agency maintains an online catalog of songs which you can search for free. Although these databases won't tell you whether a song is in the public domain, they will give you general copyright information on the song such as the identity of the writer and music publisher.

ALTERNATIVES TO TRADITIONAL COPYRIGHT

The Creative Commons (.org)

"Digital Environmentalism," the movement spearheaded by Stanford professor, Lawrence Lessig that is fashioning a new understanding of what the public domain—the "commons"—might be. The great achievement of the environmental movement was its ability to convince a swath of the population—consumers and industrialists alike—that they all had a stake in this thing called "the environment," rather than just the small patch of land where they lived.

Similarly, digital environmentalists are raising our awareness of the intellectual "land" to which people ought to feel entitled.

Lessig proposes "flexible" copyright arrangements based on how the Creator would like to his or her work to be used, rather than having it dictated to the user by law.

Performance Rights (ASCAP, BMI & SESAC)

Another exclusive right you get as a copyright owner is the right to perform your composition in public. These are known as *performance rights* and each user needs your permission to play the song on the radio, TV, and many other venues including, Amusement Parks, Arenas, Auditoriums, Bowling Centers, Colleges & Universities, Convention Centers, Country Clubs, Dance Studios, Festivals, Health & Fitness Centers, Hotels, Music In Businesses, Nightclubs, Racetracks, Resorts, Restaurants, Retail Stores, Shopping Malls, Sports Bars, Stadiums, Taverns, Theme Parks, Water Parks, and Web Sites.

Now what's the problem with this logistically? Correct – a million separate licenses. So out of this situation developed the *blanket license* and *performing rights organizations (PROs).*

Essentially, the PROs go to each publisher and say, "Please designate us as your agent for the performing rights in *all* your songs. We'll then go to the people who want to use the songs (radio stations, nightclubs, etc.) and give them a license to use *all* the songs of *all* the publishers we represent. For each license we will collect fees, divide them up, and send you your share."

And this is what happens, for the most part.

The license that the PROs give each music user is called a *blanket license* because it "blankets" (covers) all of the compositions they represent. In other words, in exchange for a fee, the user gets the right to perform all the compostions controlled by all the publishers affiliated with the PROs. The fee can range from a few hundred dollars per year for a small nightclub to millions of dollars per year for televsion networks, all based on brain-deadening formulas applied to adjusted gross receipts.

ASCAP or BMI?

A common question among songwriters and musicians is whether there is any difference between BMI and ASCAP. Generally, both organizations offer similar payment rates and follow similar rules. If you have a hit song, you'll probably receive the same income from either organization. Some differences are as follows:

1. ASCAP charges annual dues ($50 for publishers and $10 for writers); BMI does not charge annual dues but charges publishers a one-time fee of $25.

2. BMI surveys various "low-wattage" college and public access stations.

3. ASCAP and BMI both offer instrument insurance, and medical and dental insurance.

4. ASCAP has a credit union which offers financial benefits.

Performance Rights Societies Overseas

BMI and ASCAP are affiliated with foreign performance royalty organizations and will collect fees when your song is played in foreign countries. As a general rule, songs earn more per play when played in foreign countries than when played on stations in the U.S. Why?

Because many foreign stations (for example, the BBC in Britain) are *national* stations and broadcast to the entire population of the country. For example, one play on the BBC in Britain may result in a payment of several dollars (vs. several pennies in the U.S.). In addition, the surveying techniques on these stations may be more precise.

In many cases, these performing rights societies are allied with or part of the local mechanical rights society. Such is the case with SACEM-SDRM in France, JASRAC in Japan, and GEMA in Germany. While foreign performing rights societies are operated similarly to their U.S. counterparts, there are some individual differences.

For example, in Germany GEMA collects performance income on a per-patron royalty basis in movie theaters for the music contained in a motion picture soundtrack. In Japan, due to the tremendously high cost of an album (well over $25), there is a huge industry devoted to renting records so that they may be taped by a customer in his home (or frequently in the store). JASRAC collects a portion of the rental fee which it distributes to publishers as a rental copyright royalty (which is really a mechanical royalty, however the "reproducer" is a private party and not a record company). All of the foreign performing rights societies have mutual collection agreements with one another.

Thus, PRS (UK), SACEM (France), GEMA (Germany), JASRAC (Japan), etc. all account to ASCAP and BMI, which in turn account to their members

TYPES OF ORGANIZATIONS
EXEMPT FROM PRO LICENSE REQUIREMENTS

Certain groups in the U.S. do not need to obtain performance licenses to play songs. These include:

1. religious organizations (during worship only)
2. non-profit educational institutions
3. record stores and other establishments where the primary purpose of playing the music is to sell it
4. government bodies (state and federal)
5. state fairs and agricultural events
6. certain veterans and fraternal organizations during charitable social functions (added in 1982 in a last-minute legislative session)
7. various "non-commercial" and charitable performances that have no admission charge, commercial intent or paid performers
8. movie theaters

So far we've looked at the two largest generators of music publishing income – mechanical and performance royalties. There is a third that is on the increase, and thes are synchronization (or, synch) royalties.

Sound Exchange & The Digital Performance Right

The record industry, represented by the RIAA, has tried several times over the past sixty years to amend the copyright laws to create an excusive right of public performance *for sound recordings*. European countries have had this right all along, but in the U.S. record companies were too late to the negotiation table to obain it earlier last century. Subsequently, whenever a *recording* is performed (say, via radio) record companies do not receive a cent. Publishers and writers *do,* owing to the performance right in the underlying *composition*, but recordings (i.e., embodiments of the underlying composition) did not. And so it has been.

In 1995, as Internet radio stations (webcasts) began to multiply, the labels achieved a partial victory by getting Congress to establish a sound recording performance right for *digital* transmissions by enacting the **Digital Performance Right in Sound Recording Act (DPRSRA).**

And then in 1998, Congress enacted the **Digital Millenium Copyright Act (DMCA),** under which eligible services may secure a statutory license for the use of sound recordings instead of having to negotiate with individual artists and labels. It covers public performances by four classes of digital music services:

- *Eligible nonsubscription services* (i.e., noninteractive webcasters and simulcasters that charge no fees). [Note: "Noninteractive" means not allowing on-demand or personalized programming].
- *Preexisting subscription services* (i.e., residential subscription services providing music over digital cable or satellite television).
- *New subscription services* (i.e., noninteractive webcasters and simulcasters that charge a fee).
- *Preexisting satellite digital audio radio services* (i.e., XM and Sirius satellite radio services).

The last category of satellite radio, which specifically includes XM and Sirius, are not technically "webcasts" because these services are delivered through satellites directly to devices that play the transmissions, not through the Internet. However, it makes sense that satellite radio is covered by the DMCA's compulsory license provisions because satellite radio is noninteractive and delivered by digital transmission.

Who Collects the Fees? Just as the PROs appeared to collect licensing fees and pay writers and publishers, **Sound Exchange** emerged as the entity to do the same for sound recording performance monies. Originally a division of the RIAA, it's now an independent, nonprofit performance rights entity jointly controlled by artists and sound recording copyright owners. The US Copyright Office has designated SE to collect and pay out fees derived from the statutory license for digital transmission of master recordings provided under the DMCA.

Fees are split 50/50 after an administrative deduction (c. 5%), and Sound Exchange pays both parties *directly*. It made its first payment in 2001 and last year (2005) it collected and disbursed close to $36 million. Learn more at: http://soundexchange.com.

Synch Rights

In the music business, the term *synchronization* means combining recorded music with visual images. Copyright owners have the right to grant synchronization licenses for uses of their compositions in movies, television, and video. Here are some some pricing and criteria guidelines for each area to give you a basic grasp of how this kind of licensing works.

❐ Movies

A synchronization fee for the use of a song in a movie is negotiable and can total between $5,000 and over $50,000. The amount depends on: the movie production budget, how well known the song is, whether the song is sung on screen or used as background, the duration of the use (in minutes and seconds), the term of use, the territory of use, and whether the movie company guarantees inclusion of the song on a soundtrack album. (If the song will be used on a soundtrack album there will be separate mechanical royalties for the song owner, which is why owners sometimes agree to reduce the sync licensing fee if a soundtrack album will be issued.)

❐ Television

Synchronization fees for the use of compositions in television series, special programs, or made-for-TV movies can range from several hundred dollars to many thousands of dollars per composition. The amount will depend on many of the same variables cited in the preceding section about movies. Some other variables include whether the program will be released on home video, broadcast in additional media, or released in foreign movie theaters. Typically, the *licensee* (the person wanting to use the music, as opposed to to the *licensor)* will initially pay for a specified set of conditions and request an option to buy more as needed.

THE TELEVISION MUSIC BUDGET

Out of an overall budget of $750,000 to $1 million for the show, $20,000. – $25,000 per hour is allocated for all music-related costs. This is pays for:

- Composer's creative fee
- Studio rental time
- Tape
- Engineers
- Musicians
- Instrument cartage and rentals
- Music licensing fees
- Misc. costs

❒ **Video/DVD**

A synchronization fee for the use of a composition in a home video is paid in one of the following ways: a per-unit royalty (usually from 8 cents to 12 cents per song); a single buyout fee covering all quantities sold; or a advance covering a set number of copies, with additional amounts payable for additional specified quantities sold.

Commercial Advertising Licensing Fees. Licensing fees payable for the use of a composition in commercial advertising can range from a few thousand dollars to upward of half a million dollars. The amount will depend on such variables as how well known the song is; the advertising budget; the kind of media used (free television, basic cable, pay cable, radio, print); the geographic territory of use (local, regional, national, international); the term of use (usually one year, with an option to extend the license); the number of commercials produced in various formats (such as one 30-second TV ad and one 60-second radio ad); and whether the advertiser wants exclusivity.

By the way: Television commercial licenses are synchronization licenses. Radio licenses, on the other hand, are not synch licenses, because radio doesn't contain visuals. Radio involves *transcription licenses.*

Now that you have a grasp of how music publishing is set up to work, and assuming you have songs you're trying to market, you should take the next step and set up your own publishing company.

Starting Your Own Music Publishing Company

Besides the obvious profit potential, which is attractive to anyone seeking a good business to start, there are several situations that make setting up a publishing company a natural move:

❒ Songwriters may want greater control over their own copyrights, as well as earn more money from their use.

❒ New songwriters may want to short-circuit frustrations of trying to get publishers to accept their work.

❒ Writers with a co-writer who does well as his own publisher and where you can negotiate a portion of the rights for your own company. (NOTE: If your co-writer is a staff writer with a major company, you may find this very difficult unless you also have great contacts and are aggressive about pitching your songs).

❒ Record producers and recording artists may want to own some of the copyrights that they record.

❒ Artists' managers, music business attorneys, or accountants may want to handle clients' songs.

❒ Record labels should want to publish songs they release that aren't already signed to publishers.

❒ People who have a great casting sense that lets them present the right song to the right artist at the right time.

Another, more general, reason has to do with the shift in the industry from music as product, to music as *service.* As physical distribution atrophies, *access* to music becomes paramount, which in turn means greater emphasis on licensing the rights in music to those seeking access to it.

))) ILLUMINATING TRIVIA (((

In the early days of pop music, successful artists like Sam Cooke and Ray Charles used their own money to start independent labels and publishing companies. A shrewed move in an exploitative era.

The Nuts & Bolts Of Setting Up Your Own Publishing Company

1. You are eligible to have BMI, ASCAP, or SESAC process your application as a publisher if : (a) a record is being released containing a performance of the song; (b) a motion picture is being released that includes the song; (c) a television program will be or has been broadcast using the song; or (d) a radio program has been broadcast that played the song.

2. Come up with a name for your company (with three alternates) and clear the name with BMI, ASCAP or SESAC. You may use your own name but you should try to come up with something catchy that will make people want to open your envelopes with your demos inside. Unless you intend to publish the songs of other writers who may belong to other performing rights organizations, you need only set up a company with the one you're affiliated with as a writer.

There is a $50 annual fee for being a publisher-member of ASCAP. There is a one-time application fee to be a BMI publisher (with costs varying from $150-250, depending on your business structure), and no annual fee. There is no fee for SESAC publishers.

3. Once the name(s) have been cleared, go to your local city or town hall and obtain the forms to register a ficticious name certificate, also known as a d/b/a (doing business as...). Then go to your bank and open an account under your new business name. If you have any questions about the required business forms call the Secretary of State's office in your state.

Oh yes, *you* will also need a name, more accurately, a title. You can be President, Head Hauncho, License Broker, Song Plugger, Mr. Mogul, whatever you want. But I'd suggest "Creative Director". That's the most acceptable title for the person overseeing and marketing a song catalog.

4. Copyright all the songs you wish to have in your company on a PA form assigned to your company. If you have already obtained copyright registrations on your unpublished songs, you will now register them again as published works.

If the songs are already recorded, then file a SR (sound recording) form instead. Forms are available from the Library of Congress Copyright Office (www.loc.gov).

5. For songs being released on records, or for songs that will be or have been performed in a motion picture, television program or radio program (regardless of whether the song is included on any record), fill out both the writer's and publisher's clearance forms from the performing rights organization involved (BMI, ASCAP or SESAC). These forms notify the organization that a specific song is being released on a specific album so that, when it's performed on the radio, TV, or elsewhere, the organization will know who to pay, what percentage to pay the writer and the publisher, and where to send the checks. Directions are included on the forms and in the publisher's manuals provided by the organizations. Keep a copy of everything you send out for your files.

6. Organize yourself to be able to keep track of your "song shopping." Check out the software from Working Solutionz, "SongTracker" and "SongTracker Pro 3.0", an award-winning set of integrated templates that turns FileMaker Pro 3.0 into a full-featured publishing/song shopping system for professional songwriters and active music publishers. Or, you can adapt FileMaker Pro yourself to your own publishing needs.

Writer/Publisher Shares

First, be clear on what "writer's share" and "publisher's share" mean. Look at it as a 200% pie. One hundred percent of the writer's share is (usually) 50% of the copyright revenue generated; one hundred percent of the publisher's share is (usually) 50% of the copyright revenue gererated. It can be illustrated like this:

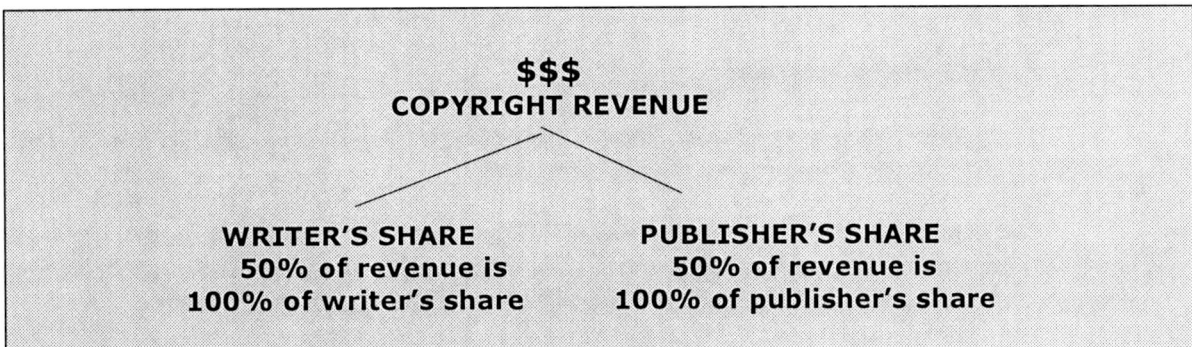

$$$
COPYRIGHT REVENUE

WRITER'S SHARE
50% of revenue is
100% of writer's share

PUBLISHER'S SHARE
50% of revenue is
100% of publisher's share

Typical splits between writer and publisher break down as follows:

❒ **Mechanical Income**
Publisher collects all mechanical income and pays 50% to composer.

❒ **Performance Income**
Publisher collects and retains all of "publisher's share" of performance income. Writer is paid income directly by his or her PRO and retains all such "writer's share" of performance income.

❒ **Print Income**
Publisher collects all revenue and pays writer 10 cents per printed edition.

❒ **Synchronization Income**
Publisher collects income and splits 50/50 with composer.

❒ **Foreign Income**
Net receipts (that amount received by or credited to publisher from subpublisher) are split 50/50 with composer.

Keeping Things Organized: Administrating Your Copyrights

Studies have shown that the average executive spends 90 minutes a day trying to find stuff. Double that for most songwriters and musicians. Perhaps it's that deep aversion to "systems" many "artistic personalities" have.

But in order to run your publishing operation as smoothly and effectively as possible you'll need to put some systems in place. A good deal of what you'll be doing as a publisher is *managing information,* so organization is key!

There is no need to re-invent the wheel here so the following is adapted from Eric Beall's fantastic book, *Making Music Make Money: An Insider's Guide to Becoming Your Own Music Publisher* (2004, Berklee Press).

Begin by setting up a file for each copyright. Eventually, this file will contain all the information and paperwork relevant to that particular song.

Each file should contain:

❒ **Lyrics**: Every song should have a lyric sheet (if relevant), stored both in the administration file or somewhere on the computer.

❒ **Copyright Administration Form.** This (see next page) is a crucial document that acts as a sort of checklist, ensuring you've taken care of all the necessary business around that song. The checklist should include reminders about the following:

• **Split Letters**: This is a simple document that outlines the basic agreement between the writers regarding the ownership of the composition.

• **BMI/ASCAP/SESAC Registration**: Once you've registered the song with your performing rights organization, you'll receive a copy of the registration form for your records. It should go into the file.

• **Harry Fox**: Again, once registering the song with the HFA, you'll receive a copy of this form for your records.

• **Copyright Registration**: Many writers (and publishers) register their songs immediately upon completion. Others wait until there is some sort of income-generating situation for the song. I recommend you take care of this earlier rather later. Follow the guidelines in the first part of this chapter and it won't be such a financial burden to register your songs with the Library of Congress.

Copyright Administration Form

Forms	Completed (x)	Date Completed
Split Letter		
Lyrics		
Performance Society Registration		
Mechanical License Registration		
Copyright Registration		

NOTES:

REVERSIONS: ________________________________

LIMITATIONS: ________________________________

APPROVALS REQUIRED FOR:

TELEVISION/FILMS ____________________

ADVERTISING ____________________

TRANSLATIONS ____________________

Translations

Language	% to Translator	Fee	Approved (x)	Territories

❒ **Notes**: The Notes section of this form should include any information that may be relevant to the copyright or its use. If you are the only writer for your publishing company, then there will likely be very few notes—and those will be the same for almost every song. But if you have several writers signed to your company or if there are outside co-writers that are part of the copyright, be sure that you have all the information you need. A few things to consider:

• **Reversions**: For how long do you own the copyright? Do the rights to the song revert back to the writer at some point in time? Under what conditions?

• **Limited Rights**: Do you have the right to exploit the copyright in any medium without restriction?

• **Approvals**: Do you need the writer's approval to place the song in certain situations? Writers often have approval over certain uses, as well as advertising (particularly as connected to certain products), movies (anything rated R or X), or parodies.

• **Translations**: Has there been a translation of the song for a foreign market? If so, how was the translator compensated — did he or she receive a percentage of the song or flat fee? Are there any other versions of the song in which the splits may be different than is outlined in the split letter?

These are just a few of the issues that can be addressed in the Notes section. Whatever you think you might need to know when shopping or collecting money on this song, put it in here...

Of course, the above is a fairly low-tech system of organizing your copyrights. But as Beall writes, "hundreds of publishing companies before the dawn of the computer era can attest, it will work. And it's cheap. As long as you don't run out of files or filing space, you're in business".

Song Marketing

Everything written in previous chapters of this book concerning marketing (especially chapters 2 & 4) applies here. Perhaps the most important principle earlier discussed to guide your song marketing is the priniciple of *focus*.

There are literally hundreds of potential markets for songs but it's virtually impossible to exploit them all. Each market has its own values, procedures, influencers (or tastemakers), dynamics, and culture. If the key to successful marketing is effective communication, then it's imperative for you to pick one or two markets and work *them.*

This means studying all the mainstream (and often marginal) information sources for each market.

INLETS / OUTLETS FOR MUSIC

- ad agencies
- animation companies
- audio books
- CD-roms
- corporate presentations
- documentary producers
- educational productions
- games
- Hollywood films
- independent films
- library music suppliers
- local cable companies
- music houses
- music supervisors
- news features
- production companies
- radio commercials
- record labels
- sample libraries
- software developers
- sound design companies
- theater & dance
- TV commercials
- TV programs
- webcasts

- Others include: karaoke, sequences, on-hold, ringtones, multimedia developers

How Music Publishing Works in the Marketplace

❒ Music publishers market songs *indirectly* to consumers. The publisher's *direct* market is music users: record companies, recording artists, record producers, broadcasters, film producers, advertising agencies, etc.

❒ Each music user/market has a *gatekeeper* (e.g., A&R rep., music supervisor, artist manager, etc.), the person the publisher must appeal to in order to get through the door.

❒ Keeping up with the changes: publishers must be aware of new signings, address changes, new companies, new deals, new production assignments, etc. All relationships must be nurtured for the long haul.

❒ **Gathering intelligence:** who's recording what, who's looking for material, etc.

❒ **Song Casting:** one of the most critical functions of a publisher is to attempt to match songs with performers (this was the traditional role of A&R). People who know how to do this well are scarce, in high demand and well paid. Eventually, as publishers build up a solid reputation, they become the target of active producers seeking songs for artists they're working with. That's a position you want to be in.

❒ **Cover Records:** Whatever the size of a publisher's catalog, the long-range income of the firm largely depends upon the number of "covers" generated over the years – that is, inducing other artists to record the song. The successful launch of such career artists as Celine Dion, Toni Braxton, and Joan Osborne was built on outside songs.

GREAT ADVICE!
Using the Music Trades
to Scope Out Song Needs

While the major trade magazines will not necessarily publish precise information about who's looking for songs, they will provide you with a comprehensive overview of what's happening in the industry. The main trades are *Billboard, New on the Charts, Hits,* and *Hollywood Reporter.* Since commercials have also become very lucrative outlets for songs, you'll also want to keep a finger on the pulse of the advertising industry by reading its trades, *Ad Age* and *Ad Week.*

This knowledge, combined with a little reading between the lines, should yield you a fair amount of names to add to your target list of customers. Here's what you're looking for:

- Any mention of new signings, new projects in development, or artists switching record labels.
- Information about newly created labels, production companies, or management firms.
- Notices of executives moving into new positions or new companies.
- Chart listings of artists who have a first single currently released, but no album out. If the single is doing well, you can be sure that the label is working on an album.
- Reference to movies or television shows currently in development.
- Information about new trends or upcoming companies in music-related businesses such as video games, advertising, or youth marketing.

Source: Eric Beall, *Making Music Make Money, p. 145*

"CO-PUBLISHING" =
WHEN TWO OR MORE PUBLISHERS SHARE OWNERSHIP OF A COPYRIGHT

Typically comes about when:

- two or more writers signed to diffferent publishers collaborate on a song;
- a record company, producer or artist acquires a copyright interest in return for recording a song;
- a film or television production company acquires interest in a copyright in return for using a song;
- a small publisher splits copyrights with a full-service publisher in return for an advance or other financial consideration;
- a small publisher splits copyrights with a full-service publisher who can handle promotion, administration and licensing.

Prospecting for Song Placements

According to music publisher Eric Beall, here's how the conversation should go:

1. Identify yourself as the Creative Director of the publishing company. *Do not* indicate in any way that you are also a songwriter. This will set off a four-alarm weasel alert, and will probably end your phone call abruptly. You are from a publishing company, nothing more.

2. If there's an inquiry, or if you feel it is truly necessary (and only if), offer some description of your company, mentioning any noteworthy activity, success, or business partners. This is the time to drop that name if you've got one on you.

3. Explain that your company is in the process of updating their list of projects currently seeking material, and ask if you can speak to the A&R person, manager, or music supervisor who is the object of your call. If the call is put through, then proceed again from Step 1. If the receptionist or assistant offers to provide the information, then proceed by inquiring as to what the company is working on at the moment.

4. Make sure you get the following information:
    - Name of artist or band
    - Type of material being sought
    - The appropriate A&R contact person
    - The current status of the project, and any deadline information

    If possible, try to find out:
    - What producers or other writers are involved in the project?
    - If the artist is involved in the writing, is he or she open to collaborations?
    - Is the company looking for finished songs or just tracks for others to write to?
    - Who's managing the act?

5. If, in your previous research, you've learned about the projects that haven't been mentioned in the conversation, inquire about those. You'll extra points for having done your homework.

Stories abound of publishers refusing to give up on a song after initial rejections, and having their faith rewarded after persistent songplugging efforts, and there are cases where label's persistence paid off after months of working and nursing albums to hit status.

Assuming you would never sign an artist or songwriter you didn't believe in wholeheartedly or market anything you consider substandard, each and every song or release is something you and your company should be thoroughly committed to fight for. With faith comes persistence. You won't always be right, but you must be prepared to fully test each release until the marketplace gives you a resounding no.

CH 13

Marketing Music thru Media Publicity

"It's not the size of the ship; it's the size of the waves." - Little Richard

Intro & Context

Market visibility for an artist tends to be a cumulative, rather than "overnight", experience. It is generally not one big event somewhere that creates a strong, national following for an act but instead:

- a number of stories in smaller, regional publications,
- pockets of heavy rotation airplay, usually on reporting college stations,
- several high-profile performances and hundreds of local or regional gigs,
- and perhaps a few TV interviews.

This is the "boot camp" phase of an artist's rise to national prominence. Hootie & the Blowfish are a great example of "cumulative" publicity. This eight year "overnight success story" was formed way back in 1986. Hootie toured incessantly, garnering reviews and write-up in the music press, and selling enough CDs at shows to get the attention of Atlantic Records. The band was signed in 1994 based on Soundscan reports of these sales. But even though 'Cracked Rearview Mirror' was released by Atlantic in July '94, it didn't even chart at Billboard's #1 until May of '95. The "dues" must be paid first.

Media is the collective term for the agencies of mass communication. Its individual participants - editors, reporters, critics, columnists, and commentators - are often described as the "tastemakers" of public opinion. Their job is to monitor the constant worldwide flood of new data and report only the information deemed most appropriate for targeted readers, viewers, and listeners.

One thing all artists have in their favor as far as publicity goes is this: *The media has space to fill and depends on us to provide the filler.* Did you know that 75% of what you read in magazines and newspapers is "planted?" This means it came to the media vehicle from *outside,* from people like you and me. Publicity, therefore, provides an open door for music promotion.

Dollar for dollar, hour for hour, publicity may very well be the best investment you can make for you marketing program. For example, if you were to purchase space for a "6 x 8" display ad in *The Boston Globe* newspaper, you would pay about $2000 for it (*on top of* the costs to design the ad). But say you get a story written about you and your music in the same publication, and it takes up the same amount of space. You're now $2000 ahead of the game!

Plus, publicity is more credible than a paid advertisements. You can make any product claim you want when you place an ad, and consumers know this. A journalist or reporter, however, doesn't have to feature you in their publication and, by doing so, lends more credibility to what you're about. Of course, the downside is you don't control the message when you don't pay for it.

The key to successful publicity is having a *strategic plan* that leaves no stone unturned in your efforts to get your signal through all the media noise out there. In this chapter we'll lay out the ingredients for a successful media plan.

Publicity: Pros & Cons

Pros

- Editorial coverage is more highly regarded than advertising.
- Editorial coverage is more credible than advertising.
- Maintaining a high profile within a specialty increases credibility
- PR can bring you in contact with peers throughout the business community.
- PR activates open doors to mentors and gatekeepers.
- PR coverage is free.
- Whatever you do for your community usually comes back to you tenfold.

Cons

- PR can take a considerable investment of time to create.
- PR takes time to produce results.
- You must develop and commit to a long-range plan.
- Because PR is unpaid, it is also out of your control.
- Media will print and broadcast their impression of you, not necessarily the one you want.
- Postage, media kits, and materials require financial investment.
- Getting media attention requires skill, knowledge, and creativity.

Where Publicity Fits In the Marketing Spectrum

It's sometimes difficult to understand the difference between publicity, public relations and other marketing methods.

The following story has circulated the marketing world for decades and offers some good answers for what's what in the field of marketing communications:

- If the circus is coming to town and you paint a sign saying "Circus Coming to the Fairground Saturday," that's *advertising*.
- If you put the sign on the back of an elephant and walk it into town, that's *promotion.*
- If the elephant walks through the mayor's flowerbed, that's *publicity*.
- And if you get the mayor to laugh about it, that's *public relations*.
- If the town's citizens go to the circus, and you show them the many entertainment booths, explain how much fun they'll have spending money there, and answer questions, ultimately, if they spend a lot of money at the circus, that's *sales*.

"PUBLIC RELATIONS" AND "PUBLICITY"

The Institute of Public Relations defines public relations (PR) as the "the planned and sustained effort to establish and maintain goodwill and mutual understanding between an organization and its publics." It's the framework in which publicity is strategized.

For publics, read *target audience* - the people whose attention the organization is trying to attract, be that potential funders, customers or volunteers.

Public relations involves ongoing activities that try to enhance an organization's public image as well as keeping it in the public eye. It involves helping the public to understand the organization and what it offers.

A good public relations exercise, such as a successful fundraising event, will hopefully result in publicity for the organization in the media.

Agencies specialising in public relations are often hired to plan, control and monitor an organization's public image.

Know Thy Audience

The first ingredient for a successful publicity plan is **a clear idea of your market audience**: *who* they are, *what* they read and listen to, *where* they go. Each style of music is a subcultural world with its own outlook, values, organizations and media. Your job is to understand this world inside and out.

For example, a jazz musician should be aware of the publications *Downbeat, Jazziz* and *All About Jazz,* organizations like the Jazz World Database and various cable TV and radio shows specializing in jazz performance, as well as the hundreds of generalist outlets for jazz music. Likewise a reggae band will be acquainted with *The Beat, Rhythm Vibes Magazine* and *Rootz Reggae & Kulcha,* record labels like VP, Heartbeat and Shanachie, and organizations like Reggae Ambassadors Worldwide. The same thing applies to folk, metal, alternative, blues, classical, country, latin, world, experimental and all other music styles.

Through learning about the who, what and where of your music's audience you also learn about the best ways to reach that audience. This is the foundation for an effective publicity plan.

How do you find out about your audience's preferences? Observe. Ask questions. Another good way is to go through one of the better industry directories (*The Recording Industry Sourcebook* and *The Yellow Pages of Rock* are excellent) and look for listings of organizations relevant to your style of music. These groups often serve as general information clearinghouses that can make your job easier. Also, don't overlook *local* sources relevant to your style-audience.

PUBLICITY OPPORTUNITIES

BE QUOTED OR FEATURED IN:

- Professional and trade papers
- Local newspapers
- National news-papers
- Books in your field
- Local and national magazines

BE INTERVIEWED ON:

- Network television news shows
- Local and national radio, news, or talk shows
- Cable television shows
- Public-access tele-vision programs
- Webcasts & Podcasts

BE FEATURED AS:

- Guest presenter at a special ceremony
- Sponsor for civic activities
- Contributor to a charitable event
- Recipient of a professional or civic award

Know Thy Media. What kinds of media should you target when trying to get publicity? That will depend on the kind of audience you are trying to reach. Each media entity has an intended audience, whether it be a mass audience or a small group interested in a specific topic.

As you're doing this research, take notes. This leads to the second component of a successful publicity plan: *developing your media contact list.* By "media" I mean print, radio and television primarily. The chart on the following page compares the advantages and disadvantages of these media choices and others.

Here is where a computer comes in *real* handy. Contact management programs like *Act!* (Symantec), *Touchbase Pro* (Aldus Corporation) and, more specifically for artists, *Indie Band Manager* help keep all your publicity information organized. I highly recommend you become acquainted with one of these programs for your own publicity efforts. Short of this, get yourself a Rolodex for phone numbers and addresses; separate file folders for newspapers, magazines, radio and television; and a big year-at-a-glance wall calendar. Staying organized is essential! A media list will forever grow and change based on your coverage needs.

The best approach is to start locally and then branch out from there. You'll be surprised at the wealth of publicity opportunities lying right at your doorstep.

When checking out local **print media** watch for names of music editors, writers, and record reviewers relevant to your particular area. Pay special attention to those writers who help break ground for new acts. Go to your local library to reference city newspapers, alternative weeklies, suburban publications and other regional papers you may not be familiar with. While there check out the various media directories in the reference section. Two good ones are *Bacon's Publicity Checker* listing over l8,000 newspapers and magazines, and *Gale's Directory of Publications and Broadcast Media* which additionally covers radio, TV and cable outlets in the U.S. and Canada. See chapter 17 for information on these and more media resources.

GREAT RESOURCE
Media Relations Glossary
http://www.jaffeassociates.com/Jaffe/GlossaryMR.php

Always call first before sending in your material to verify contact information. When you call, find out the names (with correct spellings!) and direct phone numbers of all editors and writers in the areas of music, entertainment and the performing arts. Also request a copy of their editorial calendar for upcoming months. This will alert you to what themes and topics it is planning so you can scope out possible story tie-ins with your band or act well in advance.

Radio also requires some research. Learn about the different formats of the various stations in your area and the types of programs they air. Consider who their target audiences are. Listen to the stations. Consult program guides (a station will send you one upon request). Check media reference books like the ones above for station contact information. Talk with program and/or music directors, producers and DJs. Always ask if they feature local and new artists in any special programming section. Write it all down.

MEDIA CHOICES

Media	*Advantages*	*Disadvantages*
Television	Wide reach Sight and sound Attention getting Prestigious High info content Pick audience (cable)	Short life High cost Clutter of ads Button (remote) pusher
Magazines	High quality ads High info content Long Life Choose audience	Long lead time Position uncertain
Newspapers	Good local coverage Good for price info Can place quickly Group ads by product Good demographic Cost effective	Poor quality presentation Short life Poor attention getting
Radio	Music, reinforce airplay Fair cost Can place quickly Can get high frequency Audience selectivity	Audio only Short attention span "Button pushers" Annoys young audience
Billboards	High exposure frequency Low cost	Message may not be read Shortness of message Environmental blight
Direct Mail	Best selectivity Large info content No interference from other ads Gets noticed	High cost per contact Associated with junk mail
Internet / WWW	High interactivity Multi-media High, targeted exposure International Low entry cost 24 hour/day access Large info content	Demo/psychographic constraints Technical constraints Difficulty of being found Insecure online transactions Some government anxiety

Information about commercial and college radio stations and the types of music they play can be found in ***The M Street Radio Directory*** and ***The Musician's Atlas***. There are also fairly complete lists of college stations online. See chapter 17 for contact information on these. When you discover which radio stations play music from independents (usually called "open" or "varied" formats) phone to inquire about the configuration they use. Some will play only CDs. Others will also vinyl, and very few will accept cassettes. Record all this information into your database. See more on marketing to radio in Chapter 10 of this book.

When it comes to **television** forget about MTV (at least for now). It has the tightest play list on the planet, catering exclusively to major label and high-charting artists. Focus instead on your own best bets: public television, local cable stations and community programs. If your research shows that there are specialized programs devoted to issues that appeal to your target audience (environmental, women's issues, etc.) add the names of the producers to your lists. If your project is "newsworthy" the person to contact is the Assignment Editor. Her job is to weed through the news and prioritize it for news programming. You can find out who these people are by phoning the station and requesting their names.

Types of Publicity to Seek for Artists & Their Music

- Calendar listings (performance dates)
- Reviews of Recordings
- Live Performance Reviews
- Interviews with the artist: in print, radio and TV
- Stories about the Artist: music or consumer press, or other related niche.
- "Associational" publicity: partnering with another artist or with a cause your support.

If you're involved with a non-profit cause, organization, or event, you can get your event or program listed in broadcast public service announcements ("PSAs") for free. Check radio and TV (network affiliates and local cable) station deadlines and requirements. Submit all pertinent information to Public Affairs or the PSA Director. Work with the benefit coordinator to make sure he has your band's information.

The geographical region covered by a media program, its frequency of publication, its ability to reach specialized markets, and its ability to provide color, sound, or movement are all factors that need to be factored in to your decision-making process.

Know Thy Publicity Tools

With a clear understanding of your audience and the media around it you are now ready for the third component of your publicity plan: **assembling your publicity tools**. While some of this was covered in previous chapters, it bears repeating. These tools will include promotional materials, photos, tape/CD, press kit and press releases. Each of these could fill a separate chapter. For now I will simply list them with their most relevant features.

1. Promotional materials. These include your band name, logo, letterhead, envelopes, business cards, labels, flyers, buttons, monthly calendars, posters, T-shirts, etc. Remember: You never get a second chance to make a first impression, so go for the highest quality affordable. These are "graphic ambassadors" sent before you to represent you to a select audience. If neither you nor your band mates are designers, then hire one. When creating your materials think unity: of color, tone, line and texture. Use your logo prominently on all your pieces. This enhances your image and instills top-of-the-mind awareness.

2. Photos. You can get a lot of publicity out of a good photograph. The 8xl0 black and white glossy is the standard. Have some 5x7 color shots available too. This will maximize your exposure possibilities.

The 8xl0s should have your band logo/name at the bottom along with current contact information. Soloists should have both head shots and full body shots.
When doing a photo shoot count on going through at least three rolls of film. If you get one useable picture from each roll you're doing fine. It's also a good idea to have a number of "action" shots of you performing at a high-profile event, receiving an award, or any other scene that's worthy of notice.

Use a professional photographer if at all possible. If the budget won't allow for a pro look elsewhere for less expensive talent. Check local art schools for students who want to earn a few extra dollars (and enhance their own portfolios).

As with all your marketing tools today, you will also need digital versions of your photos (most commonly, jpegs), both for your web site and for media reps who prefer this option.

3. Recording. For demo purposes a CD with three or four good songs is all you need. For more general marketing of your act, or when you're intent is to impress, a full-length CD is the best choice.

In all cases the music should be of the highest production quality affordable and the packaging (color, tone, line, etc.) consonant with all the other publicity materials. Be sure to include your name and contact number on all items! You'd be surprised how often promotional materials become separated.

As with the photo, you'll want your music available also in digital formats whenever possible, either for streaming audio or as MP3 downloads.

4. Press Kit. A press kit contains most of the materials listed above. Journalists and DJ's use your press kit to obtain the background information they need to write an article or interview your band. A press kit is a just a promo kit until you have actual press. So this is your first task. Get reviewed. Court journalists for interviews. Find your publicity angle. What's special about your band or band mates, your record, or your performance? To get mentions, you'll need to provide *newsworthy* information. "Dog bites man" isn't news; "Man bites dog" is. What's the hook or human interest pitch of your story? Give the media an angle that's fresh and informative and have your press kit reflect it.

EPKs (aka, electronic press kits) are increasingly becoming standard for today's music marketers. This is simply an "enhanced" electronic version of your physical press kit and is used both at promotional web sites (like Sonicbids.com and CDBaby.com) and to send via email to those who request this option. "Enhancements" would include things like extra music tracks, photos, animations and whatever else you can put in digital format. Just be careful to not overdo it. Most of the people you'll be sending this to are very busy and do not want to be overwhelmed with more information than they require.

5. Press Releases. How do you get the media interested in you and your projects? You send a press release, also called "news release." It's a standard tool that works better than letters and phone calls. It's universally used to publicize people and events. The release is essentially a pared-down news story that presents the outline of your event in a way that will *grab* an editor's attention.

Anything newsworthy should be publicized. You should define newsworthy as creatively as possible. Special upcoming shows; formation of a new band; record release parties; production of a video; signing a management, agent, distribution, publishing or recording deal; recitals; formation of your new indie label; involvement in a benefit; winning a band contest. These are just a few of the events worthy of mention.

Always type and double-space the band's information preferably on the band's own letterhead. Include all the pertinent details (who, what, when, where, and why). Use a bold and creative headline that magnetizes attention (check out some samples in the box below). Be sure to include the date, your contact information, and the city where your act or news is based. At the top write, "FOR IMMEDIATE RELEASE" and then send it off to everyone on your media list.

Today, a number of editors and journalists prefer either faxed or electronic press releases. When you call for current contact information, be sure to also inquire about preferred submission formats and obtain fax numbers and email addresses as needed.

PRESS RELEASE HEADLINES THAT GRAB ATTENTION

Here are a few headlines I pulled from Musicdish.com's news service over the past year or so. Note what makes them stand out and put the same tactic to work for your music.

THE GREAT BLUES SEA GOES DIGITAL;
Brook And Chimpkabob Use Weed Share
To Distribute "The Great Blues Sea" Digitally

INDIE ARTIST DEBBIE HENNESSEY
NOMINATED IN AC CATEGORY FOR UPCOMING
NEW MUSIC WEEKLY AWARDS; LA-based
Independent Artist Debbie Hennessey
(SqueakyCat Music) Is Nominated In The
"AC40 Female Artist" Category

LILIANA ROKITA LATIN POP
SINGER/SONGWRITER HELPS RAISE
$40,000 FOR CHARITIES; With The Donation
Of Her Debut Single 'Caminos Confusos' And
Live Concert Performance

C. JANE RUN RELEASES NEW EP; SLATES RELEASE PARTY TO HELP U.S. SOLDIERS OVERSEAS PHONE HOME; The Band Will Do A Jan. 24 Benefit For The USO's Phone Home America Program

DAY OF INFAMY BRINGS HOLIDAY CHEER TO HOSPITALIZED KIDS; Rock Band Day Of Infamy Visit Hospitalized Children; Prepare To Release Single, "Red Autumn"

RAVEN MOON SIGNS LEGENDARY SONGWRITERS TO EXCLUSIVE 3 YEAR CONTRACT; Signed Legendary Songwriters Artie Singer And Roy Strigis To An Exclusive Three Year Songwriters Contract

READERS VOTE ZAKK WYLDE #1 MVP AND "THE BLESSED HELLRIDE" #1 BEST METAL ALBUM; Zakk Wylde Takes Top Honors In Guitar World Magazine 2004 Readers Poll

CHERRY LANE MUSIC AND ANATOMICAL TRAVELOGUE RELEASE MUSICAL JOURNEY OF PREGNANCY; There Is An Extraordinary New CD On The Market Targeted At An Overlooked Demographic: Pregnant Women

7-STATES IN 7-DAYS?? NO PROBLEM; John Taglieri Hitting The Road Again...This Time A New State Each Day!

TREE SEEDS WITHIN MUSIC CD PACKAGING ENCOURAGE ENVIRONMENTAL STEWARDSHIP; Pianoscapes For The Trails Of North America Is A New Release Of Contemporary Instrumental Music

ALBUM OF SONGS INSPIRED BY "THE PASSION OF THE CHRIST" TO BE RELEASED ON APRIL 6TH; Special Compilation CD To Serve As A Companion Piece To Record-Breaking Film

...AND A FEW (yawn) NOT SO GOOD ONES...

METALEDGE RECORDS ANNOUNCES POSSIBLE LICENSING DEAL WITH FORMER GRIM REAPER FRONTMAN STEVE GRIMMETT AND LIONSHEART

ATMOSPHERIC GROOVE BAND NECTARPHONIC RELEASES NEW MUSIC; Atmospheric Groove Band Nectarphonic Releases New Music

EILEEN CAREY RELEASES "THAT TOWN"; Eileen Carey's Music (Rolleycstr Music) Is Reflective Of Her Life

Online PR

Regular public relations professionals – while they may be savvy about publicity in the real world – often reach their limits when the virtual world of the Web requires more than just contacting the media and arranging trade shows. Online publicity campaigns encompasses programming, graphic design, innovative promotion, creating strategic alliances, and developing and maintaining a schedule for revamping the Web site to keep the message fresh and inviting – all nontraditional PR duties.

As a result, specialists in online publicity are beginning to emerge, offering a tremendous variety of Net-specific services that use the technology to forward the visibility of a brand name.

What can you do to improve your Web image and increase exposure for your site? Here's what the experts recommend:

1. Keep the content of your Web site fresh.

2. Link your Web site to other allied sites. This may require frequent browsing of related sites and a continual correspondence campaign, with other Web site managers.

3. Post messages about your site in newsgroups and mailing lists of prospective Web site visitors.

4. Register your site with the appropriate Web search engines.

5. Contribute information to newsgroup discussions, but avoid the temptation to hype your Web site. Instead, contribute to the value of the discussions, make the occasional announcement, and put your Web site address in your signature file at the bottom of each post.

6. Synergize your online marketing with your conventional marketing, making sure the Web address is always included. The Web site should be congruent with the rest of the marketing initiative.

7. Use email to mass-mail press releases about your site to editors, writers, and new organizations. Do this carefully, always checking with individuals first to see if they accept material in this fashion.

Specialists in online publicity and promotion often go beyond the above list. Depending on the company, they will also:

- Coordinate web casts, chats and online interviews,
- Nurture awareness development at lifestyle sites,
- Implement linking strategies to official artist web site via URL marketing,
- Further fan club email list generation and data capture,
- Search top online retailers to verify they are stocking and selling artist's album,
- Confirm correct artwork, track listings and sound files are displayed. Update when necessary,
- Submit online album reviews,

- Set up promotional opportunities with online retailers such as giveaways, contests, downloads,
- Establish commercial digital distribution agreements,
- Service all significant Internet radio stations with single and/ or CD,
- Arrange interviews and guest appearances,
- Broker advertising opportunities such as banners, custom spots & email marketing,
- Service all significant online media outlets,
- Pursue features and music reviews,
- Distribute press releases to all relevant online music, technology, lifestyle and entertainment related publications.

Be sure to review chapter 5 ("Understanding Your Online Marketing Tools") for more guidance on these matters.

30 WAYS TO CREATE NEWS FOR YOUR COMPANY

1. Tie in with news events of the day
2. Work with another publicity person on cross-promotional opportunities
3. Tie in with a newspaper or other medium on a mutual project
4. Take a poll or conduct a survey
5. Issue a special report in your field, genre, etc.
6. Arrange an interview with a celebrity
7. Take part in a controversy
8. Report unusual or human-interest stories
9. Announce novel observations and discoveries
10. Make an analysis or prediction
11. Start a networking group
12. Hold a demo derby
13. Announce an appointment for new staff member
14. Celebrate an anniversary
15. Issue a summary of facts
16. Tie in with a holiday
17. Link up with a social organization or burning social issue
18. Sponsor an award
19. Hold a contest
20. Give a valuable but unusual donation
21. Secure a high-visibility performance opportunity
22. Stage a special event
23. Write a controversial letter to an editor
24. Establish a Seal of Approval or Best/Worst list
25. Adapt national reports and surveys for local use
26. Stage a debate or discussion
27. Tie into a well-known week or day
28. Honor an institution
29. Organize a tour
30. Compile a list of hot tips or fascination facts

So far we've looked at the basic ingredients of a successful music publicity plan. They are: *researching your niche audience* and the media preferences of this audience, *developing your media contact database* based on this research, and *assembling your publicity tools*, including photos, tapes, promo kits and press releases.

Now let's look at some guidelines for organizing your publicity efforts and then look at two ways these guidelines can be fleshed out in the marketplace.

Out of the Ordinary

"Wait for a slow news day".
The holidays are the slowest "news times" of the year. When government offices are closed so are most of the media's sources. Take advantage of it. – Jeff Crilley, author, *Free Publicity*

Scheduling Your Publicity Campaigns

Before sending anything out, get yourself one of those "year-at-a-glance" wall calendars. They can be obtained at any well-stocked office supply house like Staples or Office Depot. This will serve as your publicity map for the whole year.

Let me ask you a question. Can you remember what the lead feature was on the evening news three nights ago? All self-promoting bands take heed! John and Mary Public have an attention span of miniscule duration and a memory which is even shorter.

This is why your publicity objectives can only be realized through successive "waves" of media exposure. Each wave "coats" your market, raising the consciousness of your audience. These waves must come at regular, considered intervals so that your offerings are perceived as inevitabilities.

How many waves should you launch and how often? Each wave needs a promotional spearhead. For musicians this spearhead can take many forms: a high-profile performance, record release party, important contract signing, endorsement, contest award, etc. The more of these you have the more waves you can organize. One every three months, or four a year, should be effective.

Of course all of this assumes a good amount of *planning* . This is where your wall calendar comes in. Set some goals for yourself for the coming year and mark their realization dates on your calendar: "I want to set up a small tour for my act; "I will record a full-length CD"; "I will organize a show to benefit the environment." Whatever it is, you'll want to incorporate it into your publicity wave. Four or five strategic, well-organized waves per year will reap exposure aplenty for your act or business.

Check out the Sample Publicity Campaign for a regional band at the end of this chapter.

Timing a Music Publicity Campaign for an Upcoming Performance

Say you've booked a high-profile gig and it's a month away. Here's a sample publicity schedule you may follow to maximize the media exposure of this performance.

3-4 Weeks Prior to Performance

• Mail out a press release and bio to everyone on your media and blue-ribbon list. Follow this mailing with a phone call, two to three days after you think your materials have been received.

• Put up posters and flyers.

• If you have a record, send it along with a press release and bio to radio stations that your research has indicated might play it. Include a personal invitation to the gig. When you make your follow up phone call, ask if the station might be interested in interviewing a key person in your band.

2-3 Weeks Prior to Performance

• Send out the same release (or a longer one with more information) and a photograph, captioned with time, place, date and price), and other graphic materials. Include a personal letter of invitation. The personal letter might also contain a sentence or two of blatant hype pleading for attention and saying why it is important for the person to show up. Keep it short. This is also the time to request an interview of longer feature story.

• Send postcards or email messages to your fans.

• To other than media people (i.e. club owners, record company executives), send a personal letter inviting them to the performance, together with the press release and other publicity materials.

• Follow up with phone calls.

• Check the places where you placed flyers and posters to make sure that they are still there. Repeat if necessary.

Day of Performance

• Make sure that people who are invited are on the "guest list" (at the entrance to the bar or club or at the gate or ticket booth). I've seen quite a few embarrassing situations where key people showed up only to find that band had forgotten to place their names on the list. No good!

• When you get reviews, reprint them on your letterhead stationery. Include them in mailings. Hype breeds hype. When the media sees favorable reviews and articles on your band, it stimulates them to join the bandwagon.

• Two other nice ways to use reviews: make up a page of favorable quotes; blow up a review so that words are more easily read. Use favorable quotes in posters, flyers and on recording materials.

• Do these steps for every gig until you get results. Perseverance and repetition works.

• The eighth time a club owner or record company executive sees a press release about a band, they will realize that you are consistently performing. The fifth time a critic is invited to a gig, they may actually show up. The tenth time you send a press release and photograph announcing a gig, you may surprised to open up the newspaper an see it printed word for word.

The Importance of Media Follow-up

Follow-up allows you to monitor your coverage, maximize the benefits of good reviews, and maintain good relations with the press even after less-than-favorable reviews.

There will be a number of opportunities for follow up when you:

• ***Acknowledge good reviews*** with a thank you note. Have a stack of these stamped and ready to go on your desk. Good manners go far in the world of business.

• ***Politely correct errors in reviews.*** All publications work under tight deadlines and many don't spend the time to check every fact in the article with the sources. That's a sad fact, but true.

• ***Respond to bad reviews.*** Look as objectively as possible at what's being said in the review. Learn from it and thank the writer for the feedback.

• ***Build on positive reviews.*** The real value in a review, release announcement, or news story is not merely its immediate impact on the publication's readers. It's the impact you create by subsequently sending reprints of that article to anyone you choose: labels, distributors, retailers, new leads, outside contacts, etc. To stay on the right side of the law be sure to contact the publication to obtain the rights to reprint the article.

• ***Keep in touch.*** Help media people remember who you are by calling them periodically. You won't develop rapport overnight – it takes time. Until you feel you've established rapport, call only when you have news. Always have a goal in mind and a legitimate purpose for your call.

Another good planning tip is to obtain the ***editorial calendar*** from the publication you're planning to contact. This document will tell you what articles the publication is planning to print, the deadlines, and in some cases, the editor in charge. By obtaining the editorial calendar you'll learn what the publication is planning to write, when, and who their audience is. Use this knowledge to submit appropriate information about your product or event well in advance of the publication's deadlines.

Maximizing Interview Opportunities

While some artists may be "naturals" at creating strong, positive images for themselves through the media, many others must be coached by publicists and put through a "media school" where they are taught the basic skills of effective interviews, including how to answer awkward or touchy questions, how to always present their best side to the media and make the necessary points regardless of what the interviewer asks.

Once you've got the media's attention, you're going to want to make sure your message comes across effectively. You need to make sure you get your main points across loud and clear, whether you're being interviewed in the newspapers or on the internet, TV or radio.

Here are some pointers for making sure that interview sparkles:

• *Prepare.* Write out the key points or message you want to convey to the audience.

• *Keep the audience in mind.* Find out as much as you can about who will be reading, watching, or listening to your interview.

• *Don't try to sell yourself or your business.* Guest appearances and other interviews are not commercials, and the media is very sensitive to this distinction. Your job in an interview is to be informative and to do so in an entertaining way.

• *Arrange in advance for the audience to be able to contact you.* If appropriate, ask before the interview whether the interviewer would be willing to let people know how they can contact you for more information. Such a plug will be far more valuable to you than self-promotion.

• *Restate the question in beginning your answer*. For example:
Q: "Which song is most requested when you play out?"
A: "The most requested song when I play out is..."
This helps the audience stay with you and gives you a chance to focus your thoughts.

• *Keep your answers brief and to the point.* Radio and television interviews are a conversation, not a monologue, so if your response to a question lasts longer than 30 to 60 seconds you are probably over-answering. Print allows a bit more room for stretching out on answers.

• *Talk personally, concretely, and colorfully*. Avoid academic, theoretical, abstract, and clinical language.

• *Be positive and speak with enthusiasm and conviction.* Don't dwell on the negative aspects of your message. Provide info that inspires hope, encouragement, and confidence, and end each segment on an upbeat note.

HANDLING THE MEDIA SUCCESSFULLY

For lots of great info on developing the skills you need for working the media intelligently and with grace check out:

http://www.citizensconnection.net/xsp/xsc.asp?uri=/home/skills/media-skills/handle

The Professional Publicist: When to Seek Publicity Help

There is only one correct time to seek a publicist: When you yourself have become thoroughly familiar with the self-promotional universe, but because of manifold commitments and the lack of time, you fail to access all the publicity opportunities available to you. It's crucial for the do-it-yourselfer to have at least introductory experience working with the media. That way you're in a better position to evaluate a publicist's record and, once having done so, realistically evaluate just what is being done on your behalf.

Where do you find a publicist? Start by asking for local recommendations. Also notice which bands and musicians are getting a lot of quality press coverage. Call the publication and ask who the artist's publicist is. Publicists specializing in music will often advertise in music magazines. Shop around. Never take the first person who's available. You have nothing with which to compare his or her skills. Prices vary as does creativity.

Once you've found several possibilities use the following guidelines to be sure you get exactly what you need. Consider:

- Is the individual or firm inventive? Can they create distinction and dimension?
- Is the individual or firm interested in what you're doing?
- Is the individual or firm so overwhelmed by current clients that their ability to take on new work is limited?
- Does the individual or firm now serve clients with whom you compete?
- What will it cost?

It's completely reasonable to request samples of their work and client references (BTW, the same applies to *all* service providers you are considering spending your hard-earned cash on). After all, it's the musicians they've worked with who can give you the most relevant feedback about that publicist's work.

Understanding how the media works is not merely a matter of idle curiosity. Whether you're a band, a soloist, a personal manager, booking agent or other music professional, having access to the media on a continuing, positive basis is a decided advantage. A positive media relationship can be measured in enhanced prestige, greater recognition and larger profits.

Publicity can get you noticed, convince customers to buy from you, encourage other media to cover you, and expand your business. All in all, it's one of the best uses of your marketing time.

SAMPLE PUBLICITY PLAN FOR THE BAND: JACK THE KNIFE

Objectives

Jack the Knife is a four piece alternative funk band from Boston, Massachusetts. Their sound is reminiscent of Pavement, with a healthy dose of funky rhythms thrown in for good measure. Their simple, yet beat-based songs have attracted an enthusiastic audience to date. Together since 2001, Rich O'Brien (lead vocals), Alex Stams, (lead and rhythm guitar), Malcolm Simms (bass), and Delaney Roberts (Drums) have released 2 45's, and 2 EPs on their own, before signing to CHOCK-A-ROCK RECORDS in January of 2004. Their debut CD release "Bring It On" will be released on June 19th, 2004. The first single off the CD will be the song "Shoot Straight", which will be aimed at college radio at first, with an independently produced video available on a limited basis.

The publicity campaign's objective is to build upon the strong alternative print support the band received from their previous releases, with added concentration on expanding into some national music trades, and consumer magazines. We will position Jack the Knife as intelligent and politically concerned generation Xer's. Their unique propensity for meshing funky rhythms with driving melodies around social and political issues will make writers and editors in newspapers, magazines, and fanzines stand up a take notice of this issue-oriented band. The songwriting team of Rich O'Brien and Alex Stams will be made available to the print media and select college/alternative stations for interviews, in conjunction with their touring schedule.

The publicity campaign will support any and all promotion and marketing plans from CHOCK-A-ROCK RECORDS, and monitor all activities in radio and retail, as well as closely track attendance at live shows, to take full advantage of any developing newsworthy events that may develop.

Summary of Radio, Sales, and Live Show Plans

Radio: The song "Shoot Straight" will be made available to college radio on June 10th. Promotional concentration will remain with non commercial college stations for the first month. Based on the successes achieved at this level, commercial alternative rock stations (WFNX, WCGY etc.) will be approached next. If all goes well with those stations, Active Rock and Hard Rock stations will be targeted for adds quickly. Note: the video of "Shoot Straight" is an independently produced video that will be sent only to select cable access stations in the northeast. There is a commitment from CHOCK-A-ROCK RECORDS to fund a more professional video, should successful airplay demand it.

Sales: Distribution for the CD will be through the independent network of The Orchard with concentration on select mom and pop alternative music stores, as well as the chains, and any crossover retailers that can be brought on board. Posters, and blank covers of the CD will be made available to the stores. Promotions such as in-store visits and, in-store concerts will be set up through arrangements by the Artist Development department of CHOCK-A-ROCK RECORDS, and the band's management, coordinated through their touring schedule.

Live Shows: A northeast tour will kick off on June 24th in Boston (opening for The Dropkick Murphys), with stops along the New England leg of the tour in Providence, Hartford and Northhampton. Other stops on the tour will include college campus venues throughout the Northeast, including New York and New Jersey. As developments break the band is prepared to continue touring across the country as inroads are made in radio airplay, and through the publicity generated from the following plan.

Publicity Plan

The press kit for Jack the Knife will consist of a promo copy of the "Bring It On" CD, a bio, fact sheet, photo, and press clippings highlighting the positive feedback from the band's previous 45's and tapes, as well as live concert reviews. The campaign will build on the successes the band has already had, taking full advantage of their favorable reviews in such northeast publications as *Northeast Performer*, *Instant Magazine*, *Lollipop*, *The Boston Phoenix*, and the *Improper Bostonian.* Commitments for reviews from these publications have already been secured, and will be a priority in launching the Publicity campaign. Advance CD's will be sent to these publications on May 29.

Level One Targets: Upon Release

• Album reviews and features in regional publications to appear upon release:

Northeast Performer, Instant Magazine, Lollipop, The Boston Phoenix, and the *Improper Bostonian* (and all online expressions of each)

• Album reviews and features in national alternative magazines to break upon release:

Alternative Press, RayGun, Magnet, Seconds, etc. (and all online expressions of each)

• Album reviews and features in national and regional fanzines:

Flipside, Village Noize, Puncture, Cake, Fizz (and all online expressions of each)

• Album reviews in daily newspapers, weeklies, influential regionals, plus College Radio interviews in Boston (WUMB), and Providence (WBRU), and specialized Internet and satellite radio shows.

- Trade reviews and features:

CMJ, Virtually Alternative, Next, Hits (and all online expressions of each)

- Album reviews and features in national consumer press:

Spin, Pulse, Huh?, CD Review, Addicted the Noise (and all online expressions of each)

- Stir interest in band via MySpace.com, Friendster.com and other online communities and message boards.

Level Two Targets: Upon Touring

- Get press to live shows in every city and town they play.

- Tour coverage in daily newspapers, weeklies, regionals and college press

- Album reviews in consumer press: *Spin, Rolling Stone, Entertainment Weekly*, etc.

- Additional Radio interviews on college and commercial alternative stations, and larger specialized Internet and satellite radio shows.

Preliminary Publicity Timeline

Day	Date	Event
Fri	5/29	Advance promo copies at *Instant, Northeast Performer, Lollipop,* and others
Mon	6/1	Arrange interviews on WUMB, Boston and WBRU, Providence
Fri	6/5	Deadline for completing database of print/broadcast mailing list
Fri	6/12	Single sent to College radio
Fri	6/19	Bring It On CD release day
Mon	6/22	Album mention in *UW Daily/ Boston Globe*
Tues	6/23	Album mention in *Boston Phoenix*
Thur	6/25	Tour begins in Boston
Thur	6/25	Album mention in *CMJ/Hits*
Tue	6/30	Album mention in the *Northeast Performer* and *Lollipop*
Tue	6/30	Album mention in Boston and providence papers
Mon	7/6	Album mention in *Cake* and *Fizz*
Fri	7/10	Album mention in *Flipside* and *Village Noize*
Wed	7/8	Album mention in *Spin*
Wed	7/8	Album mention in *Virtually Alternative*
Fri	7/10	Album mention in *Next*
Fri	7/10	Album mention in *Magnet*

Mon	7/13	Interview on WBRU in Providence
Mon	7/13	Interview on WUMB in Boston
Tue	7/14	Feature story in *Instant*

Public Relations

Due to the fact that Jack the Knife's lyrical content is concerned with political and social issues of our times, it is imperative that their image of concerned "political rockers" be maintained at all times. Emphasis should be placed on their involvement with anti-censorship issues in particular. Backgrounders [one-sheets about the band] will be available to all broadcast and print media contacts highlighting the key issues that current legislation in Massachusetts and in Washington DC are concerned with. Any and all opportunities to discuss in print, or on the radio the anti-censorship stand that the band has taken should be explored thoroughly.

A concerted effort will be made to present the band in all "Rock The Vote" campaigns to help get their fans registered to vote in November.

Additional queries will be made to politically-oriented arts and entertainment publications and writers in order to secure interviews and stories written about the band.

After 4 years of laying down a foundation of independent, political thinking through their music, Jack the Knife is poised to seize the moment with their new CD "Bring It On".

The Publicity Department of CHOCK-A-ROCK RECORDS is ready to meet the challenge of breaking the band through a detailed and organized print and broadcast publicity campaign geared at working their existing fan base into a national audience for their music.

CH 14
Marketing Music in Foreign Territories

"The function of culture is to teach you new ways of dealing with the world."
– Brian Eno, British musician/producer

As international markets expand, they are, collectively, becoming larger players in the potential profits for an artist and label. Even the more remote regions of Latin America and Eastern Europe are developing at record paces. The sleeping giant China is poised to bring over a billion potential consumers to the music market. Although the U.S. is still the largest market in the world, its share in global business is clearly decreasing.

More and more media opportunities are being created in the foreign markets as well. The more opportunities to expose an artist to the public, the greater potential there is for sales (and income). As technology grows, the world continues to move towards one global culture. A label and an artist who work together to commit effort to development outside of the artist's own borders, will have the opportunity to become part of this global culture.

Marshall McLuhan coined the phrase "global village" to describe a world created by the homogenizing effects of the universal availability of electronic media. Since his time the world has shrunk even further and our horizons have grown wider through the new media technologies of computers, satellite broadcasting, cable tv, celluar technology and the Internet.

The evolution of these communication technologies have had many effects, not the least of which is the fact that the "stars" of the contemporary entertainment industry are increasingly catering to an international audience that is constantly growing.

It's probably fair to say that popular music is now the *lingua franca* for a large segment of the world's youth population. Music seems to be the most universal means of communication we now have, instantly traversing language and other cultural barriers in a way few of U.S. really understand. ***In fact, one could argue that music is perhaps the essential component linking the different sectors of the global entertainment industry.***

Recorded music sales are just one part of the picture. Licensing tracks and concert tours by both superstars and indie upstarts continue to make their mark in the global music village. For example, I know a blues harp player from Lynn, Massachusetts who's been in Southeast Asia for the past five years playing blues six nights a week with a Thai back

up band! He's just one of *many*.
But let's not get ahead of ourselves. First, some context.

The Ongoing Globalization of the Music Industry

Ever since the inception of Armed Forces Radio during WWII, American popular music has been penetrating every nook and cranny on the planet. The United States may be considered a global trendsetter as far as popular music is concerned. This holds true as well, though to a lesser extent, for the United Kingdom. The UK market is only one third the size of the American. However, the *role* of British popular music within the world's overall "sound" today is comparable to that of the U.S..

Before WWII, the U.S. recording industry was very insulated from the rest of the world, and it derived over 85% of its income from domestic sales. *International* sales were an afterthought at best.

A basic characteristic of the international music industry has been its domination by American interests - not only in terms on product and flow, but also in its legal, political, and economic practices.

This is because, first, the recording industry was initially formed in North America and, secondly, since its earliest days the recording industry had been dominated by a few American corporations. But the current picture couldn't be further from the truth.

One of the most interesting aspects of the new global music market is that it is not dominated by American-based corporations any longer. CBS and Epic are now part of the Japanese Sony empire; RCA has been absorbed by Bertlesman Group (BMG), a German-based company whose central interests are publishing and distributing books and magazines. Sony and BMG (Germany) merged their music interests in 2004. Of the other three "majors" EMI and Warner are based in the UK and Canada respectively, and Universal is owned by the French company Vivendi. Not a single major record label is owned by an American company any longer.

Some Music Industry Stats From Around the Planet

Top Ten Music Markets and % share (2004)

1. U.S..	**29%**
2. Japan	**16%**
3. Germany	**9%**
4. United Kingdom	**6%**
5. France	**6%**
6. Canada	**3%**
7. Netherlands	**2%**
8. Mexico	**2%**
9. Australia	**2%**
10. Spain	**1%**

Source: IFPI, International Federation of Phonogram and Videogram Industries (http://www.ifpi.org/).

Shares of the World Music Market

	1984	1989	1997	2004
Western Europe	31%	41%	33.3%	30%
United States	45%	34%	29%	25%
Japan	13%	16%	16.5%	18.5%
Rest of the world	11%	9%	21.2%	26.5%

Source: IFPI, International Federation of Phonogram and Videogram Industries (http://www.ifpi.org/); NOTE: this is only for music recordings and does not include revenues generated through the exploitation of rights (that is, publishing).

Characteristics of Top Ten markets 2004

Country	Piracy	Domestic repertoire	CD player penetration	Market share of Indies
U.S.	<10%	93%	262%	16.1%
Japan	<10%	72%	122%	55.3%
U.K.	<10%	47%	163%	20.6%
France	<10%	60%	128%	16.6%
Germany	<10%	48%	124%	20.9%
Canada	<10%	22%*	112%	14.5%
Australia	<10%	26%*	93%	20.7%
Italy	25-50%	48%	65%	N/A
Spain	10-25%	46%	111%	35.8%
Netherlands	10-25%	19%*	138%	23.8%

Source: IFPI

KEY RESOURCE:
SURFING THE INTERNATIONAL MUSIC INDUSTRY

Music organizations that act as repositories of information and resources for the represented country's music industry. See chapter 17 for a country-by-country list of these musical "grand central stations".

THE IFPI FACT SHEET 2005
Source: ifpi.org

Well over 100,000 album titles - both new and re-issues - were released in 2004

❐ Per capita album sales are higher in the UK than anywhere else in the world - with an average 2.9 albums bought by every man, woman and child in the country every year. Norway is second at 2.7, with the U.S..A third at 2.6

❐ The average age of music consumers is increasing. In 1999 music consumers over 30 accounted for less than half of all music sales. Now 55% of music is bought by the over 30s. The world's "oldest consumers" (% of over 30s) are in: Hungary (73%), Netherlands (73%), Austria (71%) and Germany (69%). "Youngest consumers": Brazil (37%), Mexico (26%) and Japan (30%)

❐ Singapore has the highest number of CD players per household in the world - at almost four (390%). The U.S..A is next (257%) followed by Hong Kong (212%) and the UK (166%)

❐ At 94%, U.S.. households have more DVD players than anywhere else in the world. The top ten markets for music DVD sales are U.S..A, Japan, Germany, France, UK, Brazil, Netherlands, Canada, Australia and Spain

❐ Canada has the highest broadband uptake in North America (46%). Denmark has the highest broadband penetration in Europe (44%) and Chile has the highest broadband penetration in Latin America (8%)

❐ Taiwan has the biggest number of mobile phones per household (110%) - at least one for every person in the country. Mobile penetration reached 100% in three other markets in 2004 - Czech Republic, Portugal and Sweden

The Dynamics of the Global Music Making

The breaking down of time/place barriers is not taking place evenly across the globe – there's also a re-affirmnation of local identity happening.

The domination of the "West over the Rest" in the distribution of popular music has, understandably, created a concern about the largely unidirectional flow of musical product around the world, fearing it will adversely affect cultural diversity.

This has often taken the form of a reaction against the perceived threat of a homogenous, undifferentiated "mass" culture being imposed from the outside. With this there is often a tendency to idealize and romanticize the "local" as an authentic expression of folk culture, and to condemn the "global" as artificial and unauthentic.

Fastest-Growing (emerging) Music Markets

1. China
2. Nigeria
3. Philippines
4. India
5. Thailand
6. Russia
7. Venezula
8. Indonesia
9. Poland
10. Malaysia

While the globalization of communications and, subsequently, the music industry appears at first glance to portend the possibility for world cultural homogenization, the reality shows a different picture.

What we actually see in almost every country are local musicians who are producing new combinations of musical elements and who are adding to global cultural diversity. They are not all sounding alike. In fact, within and among countries, there is an amazing diversity of music as creative musicians experiment with new forms and sounds. From Bulgaria to Boston, Zaire to Martinque and New York to Paris, pop is going global. As never before, exotic imports and weird new hybrids are flourishing: Polish reggae, Moroccan flamenco, even Cambodian heavy metal are on the rise.

Additionally, peripheral musicians are becoming indirectly acquainted with each other's music through new small, self-production recording and distribution processes that do not depend upon the mediation of the core music industry. The result of these interactions is a new eclectic approach to musicmaking. In observation of this new eclecticism, the core industry itself has begun to look to all cultures for potential raw materials and consequently its former rock and roll center has splintered into many sub-category fragments. Music has become increasingly experimental and fragmented while at the same time its once diverse and exotic elements are becoming more widely familiar, more accepted, and more predictable. The richness of world-cultural musics and their arrival on these shores is perhaps one of the most refreshing trends in the music industry today (at least in my opinion); and the movement will continue.

Notwithstanding, there continues to be a hunger overseas for American product, and there are plenty of opportunities for *you* to provide it.

Exporting Music:
Tips for Dealing with Overseas Labels & Distributors

Amalgam Entertainment president, Jay Andreozzi took a niche interest in hip hop and turned it into a growing $200,000+/year music distribution service, covering all of Europe, Japan, and the U.S. as well.

I asked Jay to share what he considers to be the essential things all would-be music exporters (whether labels or distributors) should understand before embarking on their venture. Here are his suggestions:

❒ **Target Specific Territories/Countries**

Consider using a different affiliated company (labels/wholesalers/distributors) exclusively in each territory as an alternative to dealing with one overseas distributor for all territories. Get to know that market and its customers' needs as they relate to your product. You will want to compare where similar artist/genre/formats are being sold. This can be done by using Internet search engines such as Google. Simply type in: artist or genre or format + the word "order" + the targeted territory/country. Example Google search: Jazz CD order Japan.

Going Global? –
Country Risk Assessment

Dun & Bradstreet's analysis of risk is a composite index of the following categories: socio-political, economic, external debt, and commercial. Variables within each group are assessed, scored, weighted and ranked globally to give an assessment of the risk of doing business in a country. Risk assessment should cover such issues as the ability of a country to generate sufficient foreign exchange to service its payment obligations; the willingness of the country to create an enabling environment for trade and foreign investment; and the resilience of an economy to withstand domestic and external shocks.

Riskiest Countries With Which To Do Business:

- Democratic Republic of the Congo
- Albania
- Myanmar (Burma)
- Yugoslavia
- Belarus.
- Tajikistan
- Ukraine
- Nigeria
- Sierra Leone
- Nicaragua

Least Risky Countries With Which To Do Business:

- United States
- Denmark
- Luxembourg
- France
- Germany
- United Kingdoms
- Japan
- Netherlands
- Austria
- Switzerland

Source: International Risk and Payment Review, Dun & Bradstreet UK Ltd. (2004)

❒ **Assess All Freight Options**

Shipping physical product is expensive. Regardless of who has agreed to pay freight costs, you will want to search out the most effective and cost-efficient method of shipping your product to foreign territories. Alternative freight options, such as using an international freight forwarder can save time and money vs. using the more traditional commercial services such as UPS, FED EX, and the U.S.P.S. You should also consider teaming up with another label in the U.S. who shares the same international customers in order to consolidate shipments together. See note on teaming up at the annual MIDEM confab below.

❒ Do The Math

Know the *most current* currency conversions of the U.S. dollar and it's worth compared to the currency of the territory/country you are dealing with. If you are set on a particular profit margin, you may want to adjust the price level of your product according to each country's value of the U.S. dollar. It's a good idea to solicit and price your product with a U.S. dollar amount as the rates in each country are always changing. There are many currency converting tools online such as: http://finance.yahoo.com/currency

❒ Know The Time

Be aware of the time zone differences around the globe and how it can affect your communication with international customers. This applies especially to time-sensitive issues. Example: You're sending an e-mail to a customer in Tokyo, Japan from an east coast U.S. city. There's an 11 hour time difference. Consider that you may not receive a response until your following workday. Another example would be e-mailing or calling Europe before noon in the U.S. if you are looking for a same day response.

There are many time zone converting tools online such as: http://www.timeanddate.com/worldclock/converter.html

❒ Break The Language Barrier

Don't short-circuit distribution and sales opportunities. When sending e-mails to a foreign territory you may want to try using a language conversion tool. Build a bridge. Try: http://world.altavista.com/

❒ Be Aware of Timing and Exclusives

You may want to solicit your international accounts with your product a reasonable amount of time in advance before soliciting other U.S. distributors or one-stops that export product outside the U.S. Also consider selling international accounts at a lower price level. This will help to avoid your product being imported into a territory that you deal with creating problems for your exclusive affiliated partner in that territory.

❒ Attend MIDEM

If at all possible, attend MIDEM (every January in Cannes, France) because it offers that all-important 'face time' with potential international partners, and also try making the trips more cost effective by teaming up with another small label from the States looking to do the same. Check it at: http://www.midem.com

❒ **Add Value**

Find ways to position your entity as your country's ideal go-to source for the brand of product you are offering. Examples would be to specialize in a particular genre or offer exclusive titles that are not available by any other means.

❒ **Remember The Risk!**

Always keep in mind that you are dealing with a company overseas. It's a good idea to find out what other U.S.. companies already do business with your potential international prospect and get references from other labels/distributors before making a decision.

For some great
"Practical Tips on Foreign Licensing Agreements"

check: http://wallacecollins.com/8.html

Overseas Gigging 101

Gigging overseas presents exciting opportunities for North American bands and artists, ***if*** your are ready for it *and if it is ready for you.*

In general, European and Japanese venues are more professionally run than those in the U.S. People have more experience arranging tours, sound systems are better quality, and bands are often provided food and drink (and even sleeping accomodations!) routinely. There is also a more organized DIY network, especially for punk and metal bands. For jazz, classical and world music acts there are other kinds of support infrastructures that allow international acts to set up performances fairly easily as you will see.

The first and biggest concern is knowing *when* you are ready to tour overseas. Currently Europe is full of U.S. and Canadian touring acts, both small, grassroots efforts as well as larger, "reunion" bands that are all the rage. This doesn't mean there isn't room for *your* act; it just means you need to be more resourceful and have personal contacts in the places you wish to tour.

It's recommended that a band wait until they have several releases in the overseas music market they're targeting before attempting to tour there. Too many acts take advantage of the ease of European travel before they really have an audience in those regions, and the result is less than satisfying both for your morale and your bank account.

Strange Experiences on the Road:

While in Jakarta, I also experienced a very strange New Year's Eve. We were playing the Blue Note and afterwards the entire staff of the club came up to us and sniffed us. At first, it seemed like they were trying to kiss us European-style, but they were actually smelling us! Not having been forewarned of this apparent custom, I was dumbfounded and wondered if the polite thing to do was to sniff them back. I opted not to.

– Lauren Kinhan, *New York Voices* (jazz vocal group)

If at all possible, team up with a label in the country you're going to tour. Ideally, you want to have a licensing or distribution deal with a company that knows the scene and is plugged into the channels that will help the tour go smoothly. This could be an exclusive release or a European pressing of a U.S. record.

Sometimes a "trade partnership" can be set up between the touring band and a label: they'll help sell your records in exchange for you taking some of their releases back to the States to sell. However, the DIY labels in the U.S. who are trading often find that there is a limit to the amount of European stuff they can reasonably get sell in the U.S.

I would recommend finding a European label you like and trust, and work closely with them to do a European release in advance of the tour, help you with booking, van, and backline and also to do a new release for the tour.

One caveat: European distributors are shameless when it comes to selling your records at *your shows*. Not too cool when you're also trying to sell your records and only making wholesale off of their sales, but this is "standard industry practice" over there.

As far as *where* to tour, conventional wisdom says you should center your tour around Germany, Switzerland, Austria and Scandinavia as these are the most profitable areas with the most developed scenes. However, since every other band is also touring in these areas you might find yourself playing a lot of gigs to sparse crowds.

A few bands have tried to be more adventurous, playing in more out of the way parts of Europe like Spain and Portugal, Eastern Europe and the Balkans.

Here's the "common wisdom": if you want to make money play in Germany; if you want fun shows go to Eastern Europe. The kids in Iberia, the Balkans, and Eastern Europe see less touring bands coming through and are, therefore, more likely to be excited when one does come through.

Depending on your music style, it is strongly recommend making contact with an Eastern European label to do a cassette release of your material before you tour there. Very few of the kids in Eastern Europe can afford imported records, but like in Southeast Asia, locally produced cassettes are very affordable and the best means to spread your music. CD-Rs are beginning to become more widespread in Eastern Europe, but the tape release still seems like your best bet.

!!! SECURITY ALERT !!!

I have heard some bizarre tales of shady promoters making arrangements with local mafia to steal bands' gear and bands having to pay the local mafia to get their stolen van and gear back. In Eastern and Southern Europe you should probably keep security conscious at all times, keep a person with your van, and think proactively.

A few more practical guidelines for touring Europe and elsewhere:

❐ Before traveling in Europe, be sure to purchase **a travel guide** in America before you leave. This travel guide will provide info on inexpensive hotels, restaurants, American Express Locations, and foreign-language phrases.

❐ When **checking in** at European Airlines, to minimize the potential for being charged baggage fees, collect all of the tickets and check in the band as group. This way the airline will consider the total amount of weight or number of bags allowed for the group as opposed to the individual amount allotted per person.

❐ When **traveling from country to country** in Europe travel by train. It's less expensive, more efficient and more comfortable than American train travel.

❐ Foreign **van rental** rates are similar to U.S. rates. You should probably hire a driver who also acts as a roadie.

❐ **Shows tend to start very late** by U.S. standards and set times approach, and often break, the one hour mark. So plan accordingly.

❐ **Your cell phone** doesn't work in Europe unless you get one that you can change the chip in when you get to Europe. Some people buy cheap phones just to use in Europe or maybe if you hire a driver they might have a phone. There is always pay phones which are more common in Europe that in the U.S..

❐ Europe uses **220 volt current** as opposed to our 110 volt and they have a different plug on the end of the cord. Simply putting an adapter on the plug isn't going to work. Marshall and other European made amps have a switch on the back to go from 110 to 220 and you just get a power cord with the European plug. You can use U.S. amps with a "step down" voltage converter, about the size of a small toaster, which plugs in between the amp and wall.

❐ **Driving on the highway** in Europe is so much nicer than in the U.S. People are more courteous and actually travel only in the right lane and use the left lane to pass. If you are in the left lane and come on a car going slower, they simply move into the right lane and let you pass. City driving, however, is *crazy* since the cities are old with tiny narrow streets many of which are one way and parking is an expensive nightmare.

❐ It's quite common in Europe for the bands to all share a **backline**. And, frustratingly, they all usually want to use the touring bands' backline. This is pretty rare in the U.S. but it happens on a regular basis in Europe. Bands show up with guitars, heads, cymbals and snare and expect to use someone else's gear. Most bands I know feel borrowing gear can lead to a lot of problems. I have both let people use gear that was broken and been in bands that broke other peoples gear and it's never fun or easy to deal with. Try to make sure that whomever sets up your tour gets a clear idea who is using what gear at the shows so you know in advance.

Entertaining Overseas Soldiers

The AFE has helped bands play abroad and find new fans at military bases around the world.

If you are looking to expand your fan base internationally and carry out a truly unique, memorable tour, the branch of the military known as Armed Forces Entertainment (AFE) may be looking for you. Charged by the Department of Defense to help entertain the troops overseas, the AFE is actively seeking talented U.S.. musicians to perform at military bases around the world.

Unlike the affiliate organization, the U.S..O. (think Bob Hope) who coordinate celebrity tours for the troops, the AFE focuses on booking up-and-coming talent and have helped hundreds of indie acts reach new and receptive audiences. The booking process may be a little more involved than the average stateside gig – this is the government after all – but the rewards are innumerable.

Info: Learn more about the AFE at http://afe.afsv.af.mil

❒ In general, the **coffee in Europe** is pretty lame. It's mostly instant Nescafe with grainy bits at the bottom of the cup served in a tiny little paper cup which is mostly foam and sugar on the top. In fact, most of what passes for coffee there is the same as that powdered stuff they call "cappuccino" you get at gas stations in America. Actual drip whole bean coffee is pretty rare, and if you do find some it's served in a paper cup.

❒ If your performances were paid in **local currency**, you'll save money on exchange rates by using that currency to pay hotel charges when you check out. Avoid paying the hotel bill with American currency. Or pay with credit card.

❒ The biggest challenges you'll face are trying to **maintain your body**. You have to be very vigilant about getting the proper rest and nutrition (hard to do on the road!) and knowing when to say 'no' to certain demands. However, road life teaches you - requires you - to know your limits and pace yourself.

INTERVIEW

with Steve Kercher, leader of the international touring group, Cartwheel Galaxy

1. Tell me a little about the performing act, Cartwheel Galaxy.

We are a five member Progressive Pop-Rock group featuring vocals, acoustic guitar, electric guitar, fiddle, bass and percussion.

2. Where have you toured overseas?

We have toured the country of Turkey and have been asked to do tours in other Asian countries as well as North Africa. The last few scheduled tours where cancelled due to the war in Iraq and travel warnings.

3. What occasioned your first tour overseas?

I had a friend living in Turkey and he put me in touch with a promoter there looking for American-based bands.

4. How did you prepare for this tour?

The promoter took care of most of the bookings. We had to arrange flights to Turkey and prepare passports. Our visas were issued upon our arrival in Istanbul. We rehearsed in Boston for a week before heading out as the fiddle player we used was from Texas.

5. What did you have to do in terms of the contracts and money in order to make it secure and feasible for you to go?

The promoter took care of all contracts and money for all the venues and travel arrangements. He really acted as a tour manager for us as well as a promoter. This was a great arrangement. All we did was show up and play. Everything was taken care of.

6. What was your biggest surprise during your first tour?

How wonderful the audiences were. They were very excited to have a band from the U.S. play for them. They treated us like royalty. We even received an honor from the mayor of a town in central Turkey. It was a big deal for them to have us.

7. What were the top 3 lessons you learned touring overseas?

a. Take Pepto-Bismol tablets before you eat (it coats your stomach where food might not be cleansed well).
b. Learn to squat over a toilet (Asia only).
c. Always receive hospitality gladly and with gratefulness.

8. How did you arrange for merchandise sales at shows overseas?

The promoter took care of it.

9. What advice would you give musicians considering touring overseas?

Go where there is a need for live music. You will get huge audiences. Learn a bit of the language, particularly how to say "thank you" and "hello". Be very respectful of the culture. Be a nice person.

10. Any resources you can recommend for those considering touring overseas?

Look on the internet for companies sponsoring concert tours. Sonicbids.com is a great resource to start with. Build your international network. Do you have a friend who has a friend in Tokyo that could get you connected to the local music scene? All of our overseas connections have been through someone we know who happens to have a connection we could use. Your network does not need to begin with industry connections. Connect with people who love your music and want to help expand your possibilities.

11. Where next for Cartwheel Galaxy?

We are scheduled to return to Turkey shortly. There is a lot of interest in North Africa as well as other Asian countries. I am also working on licensing opportunities.

Thanks Steve!

European State-Funded Art Spaces

According to American-born Kate Michaels, a ten-year veteran on the European music scene, "*many* places are open to touring artists, and not just from the United States, but from other lands too. People in Europe are generally *very* open to all kinds of 'foreign' influences in music. They love it! There is always some Russian choir, Spanish or Italian Bolero music, or a gospel singer, you name it"!

Michaels, a musical theater and jazz singer, suggests traveling artists should try targeting the following kinds of venues in Europe. Being a bit more formal than "clubs", these rooms are best suited for jazz, classical, world music, or "art music" acts:

1. **Gemeinde houses.** These are the equivalent of America's "grange" halls. The difference is that almost *every* community has one and they all have entertainment budgets established for the year. The room/theater size can range from a room with stage (or not), seats, few lights and no sound to a fully-staffed 2,000-3,000 seat theater. These places have their own mailing lists, connections with the press, etc and will do 90% of the PR for you.

2. **Stadt Theaters and Internationaltheaters.** Stadt (city) theaters are great rooms. Internationaltheaters are larger and more valued in a cultural sense. Fees can be great or terrible, depending on where you are and who you know, and though they provide a PR service, it's best to add your own promo content to whatever they plan on using. One great extra is they furnish all necessary sound and lights. Because of budget cuts to the state theater system, these venues are increasingly hiring outside acts for part of their season – great news for overseas artists.

3. **Kulturscheune** (Culture houses). These are similar to the Gemeinde houses. They are usually smaller, and might be physically attached to a local museum. They do their own advertising and usually have small budgets. Their clientele is usually pretty devoted and enthusiastic.

4. There are hundreds of **other small-to-mid size theaters,** each with 100-500 seats, that have various names but are all locally supported in some way. You have to be in the local area to hear of them and to find them.

5. Churches also host a diverse roster of concerts, often not the normal "churchy stuff" you might expect. They also schedule concert "series" which will often bring in a completely different type of act.

6. School concert events. Similar to the States, public and private schools routinely host concerts. The difference, however, is the local grammar school is likely to have a great theater, and the concert will be held in the evening for the parents. The schools will do all or most of the advertising.

Michaels continues: "What all of these places have that we don't seem to have the States anymore (at least from observing over here) is what the clubs used to have: a regular public and an advertising infrastructure. They don't really expect the artists to do anything except be gracious, show up and perform well. The audience members are usually GREAT listeners for any musician doing an interesting niche market. If you're doing pop, R&B, or rock, these are not really your places. These are places for people like me, or some avant-garde jazz player, or a percussion group, or someone doing Irish or specialized musical group or harpists, guitar soloists, a capella groups, Scottish music from the Hebrides, Bach motets that have been forgotten....stuff like that".

She suggests finding a booking agent or concert presenter in the U.S. that has connections with the specific places in Europe you're interested in touring. "Musicians from the States might also take a page out of the U.S. classical singers' efforts at getting jobs in Europe and book an 'audition tour'. Come over for a certain period, get appointments and book yourself or sing for agents over here". Of course, it's easier if you know the language or have a personal connection there. In the end, it's the music itself that rules in these settings: "If you are a brilliant musician, you will be very appreciated". But, she warns, just as with public schools in the U.S., there have been budget cuts throughout Europe that have affected music performance opportunities. The best strategy is still to know someone before embarking on such a journey.

Communication Lessons from International Marketing

• Coors put its slogan, "Turn it loose," into Spanish, where it was read as "Suffer from diarrhea."

• Scandinavian vacuum manufacturer Electrolux U.S..ed the following in an American campaign: Nothing sucks like an Electrolux.

• The American slogan for Salem cigarettes, "Salem-Feeling Free", was translated into the Japanese market as "When smoking Salem, you will feel so refreshed that your mind seems to be free and empty."

• When Gerber started selling baby food in Africa, they used the same packaging as in the U.S., with the beautiful baby on the label. Later they learned that in Africa, companies routinely put pictures on the label of what's inside, since most people can't read English.

• General Motors introduced the Chevy Nova in South America, apparently unaware that "no va" meant "it does not go" in Spanish. After someone pointed out the mistake, GM renamed the car "Caribe" in Hispanic markets.

• A food company named its giant burrito a "burrada," not knowing the colloquial meaning of that word is "big mistake".

• Cosmetic giant Estee Lauder was about to export its Country Mist makeup line when German managers pointed out that in German "mist" is slang for "manure."

• A large Japanese tourist office was baffled when it entered English-speaking markets and received requests for unusual sex tours.
The Kinki Nippon Tourist Co. opted for a name change.

Live and learn (the language)!

CH 15
MARKETING THROUGH SPONSORSHIPS

"Advertising can't sell any product; it can only help to sell a product the people want to buy."
– Jeremy Tunstall, British writer

When it comes to creative sponsorships, Brian Murphy is fearless. As president of marketing/event production firm Fearless Entertainment, Murphy oversees such events as Nokia Presents Hard Rock Live, a 20-date concert series filmed at Hard Rock Live Orlando (FL). Fearless also produced the Ford Cruisin' Legends Charity concert, part of a week-long event celebrating music and Ford automotive milestones in Birmingham, Michigan.

Then and now, Murphy has focused on marrying the artistic and corporate communities through dynamic events like Hard Rock Rock Fest. *"Our slogan is 'bands, brands and fans', and bringing them all together,"* he says.

"The music industry has gone through tremendous changes, as have the advertising and marketing industries," Murphy says. "We've gone from a simpler time to a very complex era in terms of marketing to individuals."

Murphy says that when he was at Warner Music, "event marketing was a non-core function because they considered their core business to be producing and marketing records. Now I don't think there is anyone in the music business that doesn't factor in bringing in corporate partners to help promote and market artists." (Source: *Billboard*, fall 04).

CONTEXT:

A Growing Trend

The headlines don't lie:

"Coca-cola Presents the 2004 Essence Music Festival"

"Seagram Dubs Music Sponsorships Royal and Regal"

"UBS Steps Up Its Commitment to Orchestral Music in the U.S."

"Cool Blasts Hitches to Warner Music for Mobile Sweeps"

"Music Marketing and Sponsorships Help Corporate Partners Get Hyperlocal"

Have an idea for a community event but need corporate sponsors? Want to set up a tour for your artist and need companies with deep pockets to foot the bill? Want to organize concerts and fundraisers in your town? Have a non-profit that could use the financial support of a local corporation? All of these are occasions for exploring how sponsorships can benefit your cause.

What is Sponsorship?

Sponsorship is a cash and/or in-kind fee paid to a property (typically in sports, arts, entertainment or causes) in return for access to the exploitable commercial potential associated with that property. This strategy of improving the fortunes of a company or brand by building a link in the target's mind between the sponsor and a highly valued organization or event can be used to win consumers and/or key accounts.

Although the recipient of sponsorship may be nonprofit, sponsorship should not be confused with philanthropy. Philanthropy is support of a cause without any commercial incentive. Fellowships and grants fall into this category. Sponsorship, on the other hand, is undertaken for the purpose of achieving *commercial* objectives.

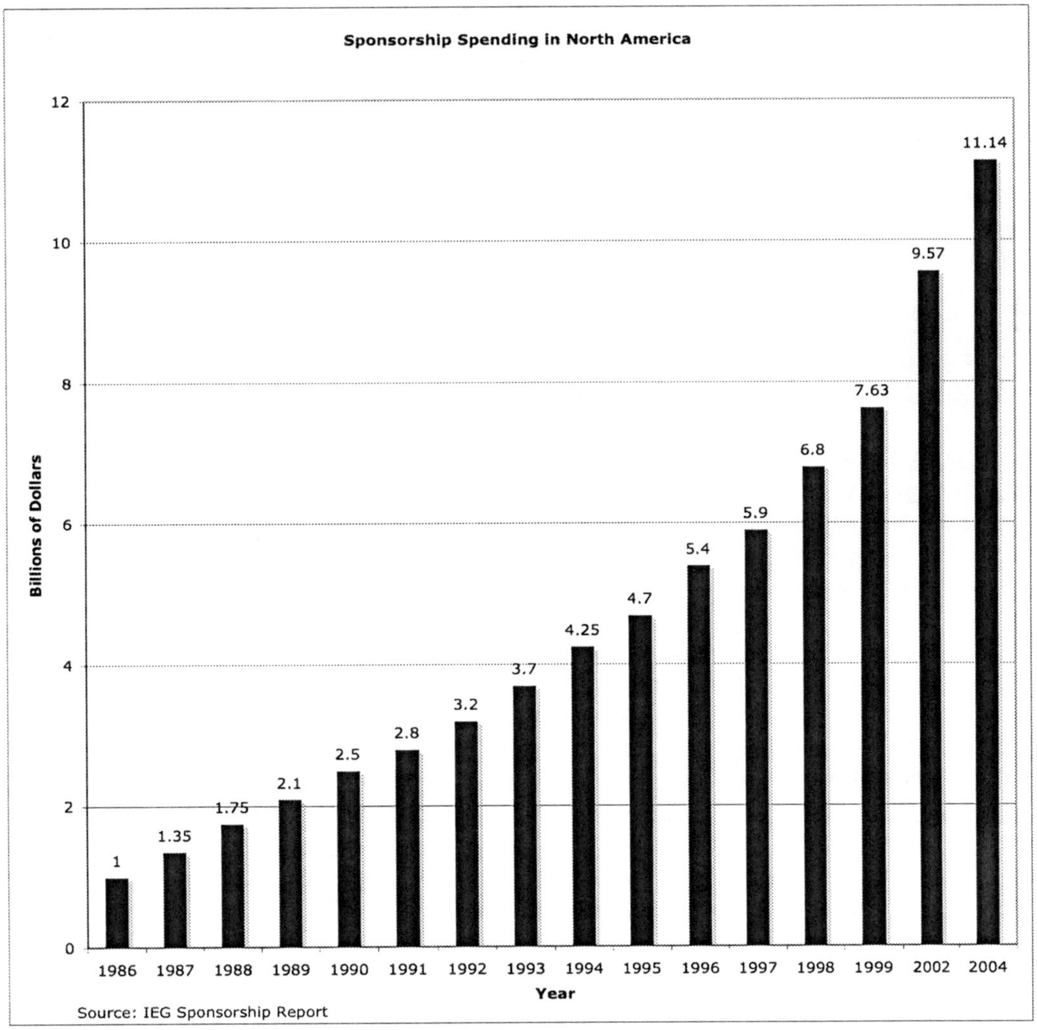

Music and Sponsorship

Music and Sponsorships are a no-brainer. A recent IEG Sponsorship Report projects music sponsorship spending alone rose 21% to $695 million in 2004, and is on track to increase again in '05 and '06. Check out the preceding chart for the amount of sponsorship money being spent across the board in North America alone.

After years of singing backup for the wide world of sports, music is finally staging two sets and an encore as marketers wake up to the simple fact that the world of tunes "is the rhythm of life. "It impacts fashion, politics, the economy - every aspect of the consumer's life," says Cory Isaacson, VP Business Development with Chicago-based Entertainment Marketing, Inc. "It's the essence of emotional branding. Everyone has a song that takes them back to a certain place in time."

Music is the here-and-now medium, tone-setter, attitude former, and the ultimate catalyst for marketing relevance. What other property changes daily?

Here are some music and sponsorship trends *from the sponsoring company's perspective* to consider when mapping out your own sponsorship strategy.

1. Material Exclusivity. A growing list of brands is demanding first dibs on new musical material, literally leaking songs before they hit shelves.

Pepsi spent the summer of 2004 dropping ditties via "Pepsi First Taste" radio spots (Agency: The Arnell Group, New York City). The first program out of the soda company's new multi-year pact with Sony Music, nailing exclusives on unreleased material "keeps the brand looked at as forward-looking and in-the-know," says Pepsi marketing manager Scott Parker.

2. Alternative Media. Others are finding ways to integrate music into actual products or services.

T-Mobile USA staged an All Access event initiative with five concerts in five cities—Dallas, Chicago, Los Angeles, New York, and Philadelphia—all on one day. Consumers in the five markets text-messaged to win tickets. The events were held at non-traditional venues: The Philadelphia concert at the Pier 1 Cruise terminal, the Dallas show at the Gypsy Tea Room, etc.

Motorola, meanwhile, is leveraging music inside wireless phones with MOTOMixer, a feature on handsets customers use to modify tunes from current and emerging bands into customized ring tones. Fans also submit remixed rings to win tickets or chat with sponsored acts. "We want to offer an opportunity for consumers to celebrate their individuality through music," says Monica Rohleder, a marketing communications staffer at Motorola. The company is also "keeping an eye out" for touring opportunities that allow products to be featured as experiential devices, such as providing them to crews charged with producing the tours and ensuring the properties run smoothly. "It's not just about sponsoring a tour—it's about being a part of it."

3. Up and Comers. Brands are being choosier about which acts to sponsor, with many latching onto *next* big things rather than *now* big things. Hooking up with bands on the rise—in addition to usually being more affordable—boosts street cred, and street cred is what face-to-face marketing is all about.

Miller Brewing Co. scours industry trades such as *Radio & Records* and leans on agencies to tap radio play lists. "There's a big difference between relevance and popularity," says Peter Laatz, the brewer's manager of entertainment marketing.

Laatz checks bulletin boards and sizzle sheets online. AOL teen chat rooms are fertile ground for research, as well. "Keep an eye on incubator labels, who develop artists before they end up with a major record company," says Kevin Adler, VP Sponsorships and events at Relay Sports & Event Marketing, Chicago.

4. Go Intimate. Mainstream sponsorships drive awareness, but intimate engagements make the connection. Miller took a gamble and won when it unleashed the Rellim campaign that proved intimate, exclusive, and memorable. The 19-market program turned around more than the company's name, giving attendees a backstage experience by literally flipping tiny venues inside out to provide a view from the inside of up-and-coming acts (Agency: ClearChannel Entertainment, New York City). "Arena shows are more of a circus," says Laatz. "One of the things that really resonated with people was the ability to get close to the bands and hang out with them."

5. Get Proprietary. Many sponsors aren't waiting for the labels; they're creating their own tours. The payoff is three-fold. One, you're in control of the event. Two, you can subsidize investments to co-marketing partners. Three, ticket prices are generally lower on proprietary tours, which means there's more of a chance people will show up.

"We weren't doing any custom tours a few years ago, says Bruce Eskowitz, president-national sales and marketing with ClearChannel. "We've done ten major ones in the last year."

Proprietary tours usually offer a more personal setting for connecting with customers. Tip: Creating a private-label tour that brings together several musicians in a particular music genre may be a better draw and a safer investment. Companies that stick with one act stand to get hurt if the group goes out of style—or takes a controversial stand. Lipton took more than a few licks when Dixie Chick Natalie Maines told a live audience she was "ashamed" of the President.

With a multi-artist private tour, if one act falls out of favor, there are others to lean on or recruit. "The question is, do you define the music or does the music define you?" asks John Zamoiski, president of GEM Entertainment, New York City.

Nintendo of America uncorked its first music marketing initiative over the summer of '03, a *Nintendo Fusion Tour* meshing entertainment, music, and gaming in 25 cities. The tour launched in August with Evanescence as lead act and other up-and-comers chiming in. In addition to the tunes, each concert boasted an event footprint with activities and Nintendo GameCubes and Game Boy Advance systems. Other entities traveling with the program included retail partner Circuit City, as well as Yahoo and *Blender* magazine (Agency: US Concepts, New York City).

"Any time you create an umbrella where you bring different music together—and become a destination for customers to find the music—over the long run you're going to be more successful," says Zamoiski.

A Music Sponsorship Success Story -
Persistence Pays

Meet Aden Holt from Dallas, founder of Buzz-Oven. Holt is sort of a public figure in the local music scene. He started a record label his senior year at college and soon turned his avocation into a career as a music promoter, putting out 27 CDs in the decade that followed.

In 2000, as Internet access spread, Holt cooked up Buzz-Oven as a new way to market concerts. His business plan was simple. First, he would produce sample CDs local bands. Dedicated followers would do the volunteer marketing, giving out CDs for free, chatting up the concert online, and slapping up posters and stickers in school bathrooms, local music stores, and on telephone poles. Then Holt would get the bands to put on a live concert, charging them $10 for every fan he turned out. But to make the idea work, Holt needed capital to produce the free CDs. One of his bands had recently done a show sponsored by Coke, and after asking around, he found the marketer's company's Dallas sales office. He called for an appointment. And then he called again. And again.

Coke's people didn't get back to him for weeks, and then he was offered only a brief appointment. With plenty of time to practice his sales pitch, Holt spit out his idea in one breath: Marketing through social networks was still an experiment, but it was worth a small investment to try reaching teens through virtual word of mouth. Coke rep Julie Bowyer thought the idea had promise. Besides, Holt's request was tiny compared with the millions Coke regularly sinks into campaigns. So she wrote him a check on the spot.

By the time Ben Lawson became head of Coke's Dallas sales office in 2001, Buzz-Oven had mushroomed into a nexus that allowed hundreds of Dallas-area teens to talk to one another and socialize, online and off. What Lawson really likes about Buzz-Oven is how deeply it weaves into teens' lives. Sure, the network reaches only a small niche. But Buzzers have crated an authentic community, and Coke has been welcomed as part of the group.

Coke pays Buzz-Oven less than $70,000 a year. In October '05, Holt signed a new contract with Coke to help him launch Buzz-Oven Austin. The amount is confidential, but he says it's enough for 10,000 CDs, three to four months of street promotions, and 50,000 fliers, plus some radio and print ads and a Web site promotion.

Source: Businessweek (12/12/05)

Finding a Potential Sponsor and Selling Your Project

Finding a potential sponsor and then selling your project is one of the most difficult marketing jobs imaginable and can be the cause of tremendous frustration.

First of all, as mentioned already, it is definitely *a buyers market*. The number of individuals and organizations all trying to do the same thing as you is huge. They're all after a share of a finite sponsorship cake and they are all approaching much the same companies and small businesses as you will be.

Seekers of sponsorship come in many different forms. First are the professional agencies, agents and managers who make regular presentations to many companies, who get to know the types of projects different companies are interested in, and are known to the people whom they are selling.

Then come the sports, arts, or to a lesser degree, those who run events. Some of these organizations are extremely professional and experienced at marketing their activity or events. They will be used to dealing with sponsors and can be approached with new projects. Many of this type of organization don't need to use agencies to sell for them since they have their own in-house marketing team devoted to sponsorship. Other organizations are inexperienced in this area, may just be starting to exploit the sponsorship opportunities of their activity, and have little experience in the use of marketing skills.

Finally come the individuals or small groups of enthusiasts trying to raise money for some particular project or event they wish to undertake.

Potential sponsors select sponsorships based on established requirements for communication. Sponsorships will be evaluated by the special events department for their effectiveness in meeting these criteria. No specific restrictions will be placed on the types of sponsorship that may be considered but it is expected that no sponsorship will be undertaken that involves the abuse of alcohol or which may provide ammunition for auction groups opposed to the potential sponsors industry.

HOW SPONSORSHIPS CAN ACHIEVE BRAND NAME AND CORPORATE OBJECTIVES

- Building or reinforcing corporate awareness
- Building or reinforcing brand awareness
- Reinforcing or adjusting corporate image
- Reinforcing or adjusting brand values
- Positioning a brand in a new market sector
- Targeting specific brand or corporate audiences
- Building sales or distribution opportunities
- Supporting brand advertising campaigns

APPROACH:

As a sponsored competitor you must be able to demonstrate your ability and resources to run the event as described, whether it's a concert, a tour or a time-limited project. Most potential sponsors will want independent verification of these claims before commitment to expenditure is made. Most potential sponsors require a high level of control over the development of the project and should also offer the opportunity of a long term relationship. Sponsors prefer to make payments in stages against specific performance objectives to ensure the program is executed as planned.

THE TOP 60 U.S. SPONSORS - 2005

1.	Anheuser-Busch Cos.	**31.**	The Home Depot, Inc.
2.	Philip Morris Cos.	**32.**	Texaco Inc.
3.	General Motors Corp.	**33.**	Kmart
4.	The Coca Cola Co.	**34.**	Xerox
5.	Pepsi Cola, Inc.	**35.**	Shell Oil Co.
6.	Nike, Inc.	**36.**	Reebok Int'l Ltd.
7.	DaimlerChrysler	**37.**	Bell South Corp.
8.	Eastman Kodak Co.	**38.**	Coors Brewing Co.
9.	Ford Motors	**39.**	United Parcels Services
10.	McDonald's Corp.	**40.**	Qwest Communications Int'l
11.	AT&T	**41.**	United Airlines Inc.
12.	IBM	**42.**	Sony Corp. of America
13.	Master Card	**43.**	Exxon Mobil Corp.
14.	Visa Int'l	**44.**	The Gillette Co.
15.	Quaker Oats Co.	**45.**	Sears, Roebuck and Co.
16.	Motorola	**46.**	Lucent Technologies
17.	P.J. Reynolds Tobacco Holdings	**47.**	Dayton-Hudson Corp.
18.	Worldcom, Inc.	**48.**	Hewlett-Packard Corp.
19.	Dupont Co.	**49.**	Mars, Inc.
20.	Bank of America	**50.**	American Express Co.
21.	American Airlines, Inc.	**51.**	Nestle USA, Inc.
22.	Federal Express Corp.	**52.**	Toyota Motor Sales, USA
23.	John Hancock Services	**53.**	Charles Schwab & Co.
24.	Delta Airlines, Inc.	**54.**	General Mills, Inc.
25.	The Procter & Gambles Co.	**55.**	Yahoo! Inc.
26.	Sprint Corp.	**56.**	American Honda Motor Corp.
27.	Verizon Communications	**57.**	Time Warner Inc.
28.	Sara Lee Corp.	**58.**	MBNA Corp.
29.	Pennzoil-Quaker State	**59.**	Valvoline Corp.
30.	SBC Communications	**60.**	Microsoft Corp.

❒ **Be Informed & Persuasive**

The fact is that many people who approach possible sponsors know, roughly, what they want money for but have not put sufficient thought into *the reasons why the sponsor might find the proposition worthy of investment.* Indeed, many are surprised to be asked for a detailed financial breakdown and then find it difficult to produce the figures and to justify them in the light of hard commercial questioning.

The key fact is that unless you know your planned project inside and out, and then understand its potential benefits from a sponsor's commercial viewpoint, you are unlikely to be able to sell the idea to a hard nosed marketing director.

Although sponsorship is the fastest growing communications medium and is becoming more respectable and understood by the day, it is certain that the number of individuals and projects requiring sponsorship is far greater than the number of companies prepared or able to consider the use of the medium in their communications mix.

This means that the individual or organization seeking sponsorship has to face tough competition and must be prepared for a long, and sometimes dispiriting, marketing exercise. In order to achieve success in this competitive marketplace a sponsorship proposal must be actively marketed rather than treated as a fund-raising exercise. To be able to market your proposal effectively you must first understand your product, know it inside and out, and be crystal clear on its associational benefits (review chapters 2-4).

❒ Put Your Money Where Your Mouth Is

You are more likely to receive a favorable response if the sponsor recognizes that you are spending your own money as well as wanting to spend his! This is often a test of commitment that companies who take the risk of sponsoring individuals want to see. Talk to your bank manager and check out loan agreements, perhaps conditional on support being found. Involve as many friends as possible in what you want to do, organize local fund raising events, talk to representatives of your hometown or city council.

Check out charitable funds for the activity you are involved in and keep an eye on the papers for any local patrons who appear to be active. Starting by invoking your local community is often the best way to begin a fund raising campaign. A surprising amount of support can often be raised in this way and if you can raise the level of local awareness enough to interest the media you will find this support can rapidly snowball.

❒ Identify the Marketable Aspects of Your Project

Before setting out to write a proposal you must identify the marketable assets that can be used to sell the deal. The first stage is to write down your plans in a simple and straightforward way. You should begin your listing of the assets of the project by describing it as fully as possible. You can expect to be questioned closely on all aspects of your plans, and the more homework you do now, the easier you will find things when you have to give a presentation to interested parties.

Of primary importance to most sponsors will be the type of size of the expected audience for the project. Who can be made aware of the undertaking and the sponsor? And who can be influenced by the sponsorship? One of the most common reasons given by companies making use of sponsorship is to increase public awareness of the company or a product. Another sponsorship reason associated with audience type and size is the need to reinforce or alter public perception of a company or a brand. In this case it is the image of the company or product that is being changed.

❐ How to prepare and organize a marketing campaign for your sponsorship

Before you are ready to begin selling you need to do a bit of preparation and organize a marketing campaign. Now is the time to get the organization and support activities in place. The first thing you need is time, because the whole business takes plenty of time, and because companies tend to make their sponsorship plans well ahead, often in the autumn for the following year. If you have a very short deadline you restrict your chances of finding sponsorship enormously.

The next thing you have to ensure is the ownership of all the rights you wish to sell. These can include the act's name, the company name under which the act performs, the ownership of the songs the act performs, etc. The last thing you need is for squabbles over rights ownership developing when you are negotiating with a sponsor or after he has signed the deal. You also have to ensure that your own organization is equipped to handle the marketing campaign. An individual may have to work alone or rely on volunteers for help but an organization, especially one responsible for an activity like a national tour, needs competent individuals to handle the marketing of the project. This may involved having specialist staff to manage sponsorship and to handle publicity and public relations for the activity.

❐ How to organize a proposal for a potential sponsor

Proposals vary from a simple typed letter to full color printed brochures and promotional DVDs. The type to go for depends very much on the size and type of your own event – using a full color brochure to sell a $10K sponsorship would be as inappropriate as trying to sell an Olympic sponsorship with a xeroxed circular. Obtain as many proposals from other seekers of funds as possible and study their approaches.

The most common advice for approaching a sponsor is to present him with a single sheet of paper. This is based on the fact that all company managers and executives do not have the time to waste reading a lengthy letter and proposal. This is quite true but it also has to be borne in mind that it is very difficult to pack important selling points into a single typed page. Prepare all the information you want to include in each stage and, unless you have experience and talent in these areas, consider using a specialist writer and designer to prepare the package. The finished product should then be of a standard that can impress company executives and owners with your professionalism.

PACKAGING YOUR PROPERTY FOR SPONSORS

Examples of Assets and related Benefits

Asset	Related Benefit
• Marks & Logos	• Promotional rights
• Audience – Members – Volunteers – Donors – On-site Attendees – Event Participants – Exhibitors – TV Viewers	• Access for Sales, Sampling and Surveying
• Publications & Collateral Materials – Newsletter – Program Book – Posters – Ticket Brochures – Merchandise Catalogs – Invitations – Maps – Schedules – Tickets – Annual Report	• Guaranteed Visibility
• Sites – Stages – Ticket Booths – Information Booths – Perimeter Signage – Scoreboards – Directional Signage – Exhibits – Booths – Tents	• On-Site signage, Sampling, Display

❒ **Alternative methods to acquiring sponsorship funding**

There are more ways of approaching companies than simply telephoning or writing to them. If you are prepared to invest some funds to do so, you could consider advertising your activity and or project in marketing magazines, the newspaper, or local journals. If yours is an activity that companies have not thought of sponsoring before, some attention getting advertising should at least help to make them aware of you before you contact them directly. You may also decide to advertise the specific project for which you need funds and may receive direct approaches from interested parties.

❒ How to prepare for a meeting with a potential sponsor

When you are invited to a meeting with a potential sponsor increase your efforts to obtain marketing information on the company. Find out how experienced they are in the use of sponsorship, whether they have been involved in your activity before, who will have to take the final decision and what the hierarchy and in-house politics are within the marketing department.

You should have approached a decision-maker with your first call or letter, but you may be passed down to more junior staff for a first meeting. Try to find out in advance who you will be meeting, what their position and status are, and their known views on sponsorship in general and your activity in particular. It is surprising how much you can find out just by asking and explaining why you want to know. Don't be afraid to ask. If you can find out which organizations the company has sponsored before you could approach them for information on how good the company is to work with on sponsored projects. But don't base assumptions on criticisms that may be caused by jealousies or other personality conflicts. These sometimes arise in sponsorship and can generate a great deal of bad feeling.

❒ Develop Tiered Sponsorship

Arrange several sponsorship "packages" or tiers so that potential sponsors can choose among different levels of involvement in exchange for different levels of advertising and promotion. For example, you can set up the options like the following:

Gold, Silver, Bronze, and Associate Sponsorship Plan

- **Gold - $10,000** plus per year
- **Silver - $5,000** plus per year
- **Bronze - $2,500** plus per year
- **Associate - $1,500** as negotiated

❒ Getting your sponsors to renew

As the end of the sponsorship approaches you must consider the options open to you for renewing the contract. If all has gone well for the sponsor and yourself with this event you have a good chance of renewing the sponsorship for the next event or for another expanded involvement. Wherever possible try to conduct your own research into whether you have achieved the sponsor's objectives. Compile as much supporting information as you can for presentation at the end of the sponsorship and make your plans for future events in enough time to be able to offer firm proposals for future activities.

Grants for Music-Related Projects

Another form of sponsorship is the receiving of grant support.

While it is beyond the scope of this book to delve into the arcane world of grantsmanship (yes, it is a specialized skill set), there are some brief guidelines that can help move you in the right directions if you're interested in pursuing them.

❒ First, **clarify exactly what your project is** and what kinds of benefits it holds for social and cultural enrichment (often a key qualifier for grant support). Are you looking to tour?, start a music educational series?, develop a recording lab for inner city kids? Each one of these requires a clear statement about purpose and outcomes.

❒ Second, **investigate all available grants**. I'm told that millions of dollars in grant money is left unclaimed each year either because no one applied for the grant, or because no one *qualified* applied. There are the highly visible grants (for example, the National Endowment for the Arts) and then there are the less visible, more idiosyncratic grants.

To find out what kinds of grants are available, go to a well-stocked pubic or university library and find these two books:

The Grants Register and *The Annual Register of Grant Support.*

Begin with grants for *anyone* and then, using the terrific indexes of these books, zero in on grants specifically for what you're doing. You may find some grants available to only people who live in the town or city you reside in, or with your ethnic background, or who went to a particular high school. You'll be surprised how specific they can get!

Don't overlook non-traditional funding options too, like housing funds, community re-development projects and human service outreach projects.

❒ Third, **get some training** in how to write a grant proposal. Either speak to someone you know who has written one, or read a book on how it's done. Some cities, like Boston, have branches of the public library that specialize in providing grant resources and expertise to citizens (btw, it's called, The Associated Grantmakers of Massachusetts; 617-426-2606). Check with your own local library for similar organizations in your area.

There's plenty of great information online as well. Check the resources in chapter 17 for more on finding and applying for grants, and developing sponsorship proposals.

CH 16

Mapping Out Your Marketing Plan(s)

"It's never too late - in fiction or in life - to revise." - Nancy Thayer

This final chapter is your opportunity to braid together all the different strands of this book. After reading through *Indie Marketing Power*, you are now in the enviable position of understanding the key foundations of successfully marketing your music products and services.

You now:

- understand the essence of marketing;
- discern the important trends affecting your industry;
- have taken stock of your skills, values and priorities;
- clarified, set and wrote down goals for yourself and your products;
- figured out your compelling desires, your inner and outer resources, and the opportunities currently presenting themselves to you;
- explored and evaluated possible niches for your product or service;
- identified and articulated your own unique market niche;
- developed a preliminary budget for reaching your market;
- explored the various inlets and outlets for what you're marketing; and
- inventoried the best possible routes for reaching your niche market.

If you haven't yet read through the previous chapters and just skipped to this one, some of what follows may not make much sense. So review what has come before. You'll be glad you did.

Marketing Mind Check

Before launching into the market plan, and just in case the above list doesn't fully resonate with where you are curently, here are some key questions to ask yourself at this important juncture:

___ Have you analyzed the total market for your product or service (that is, your primary, secondary and referral markets)? Do you know which features of your product or service will appeal to different market segments?

___ In forming your marketing message, have you fully described how your product or service will benefit your customers?

___ Have you prepared a pricing schedule? What kinds of discounts do you offer, and to whom do you offer them?

___ Have you decided which media you will use in your marketing campaign?

___ What will the role of the internet be in your marketing?

___ Have you planned any special sales promotions?

___ Do your marketing materials mention any optional accessories or added services that consumers might want to purchase?

___ What type of customer service or support do you offer after the sale?

___ Have you obtained all necessary paperwork and metadata (if applicable) you need?

___ Is your packaging likely to appeal to your target market? Have you created different packaging for different markets?

___ If your product is one you can patent, have you done so?

___ How will you distribute your product?

___ Can your product or service be digitized, and what kinds of new challenges does this present?

___ Have you prepared job descriptions and operaton plans for all of the employees, contractors and interns needed to carry out your marketing plans?

Once you've answered the above to your satisfaction, you can feel free to move on to writing your plan.

First, some cautions about plans:

• *Plans are provisional documents* and not the final word – they are always in "draft" form. Plans are maps to help get you to your destination in the most cost-effective way possible. Maps, however, are *not* the territory; therefore,

• *Plans should be flexible* so they can adapt to shifting circumstances – ongoing plan review is normal and crucial to undertake at least once every two weeks normally, and every day during a campaign.

Materializing Your Goals

A person or a business without a plan is like a ship without a rudder; whichever way the wind blows is the way you'll go. You'll end up somewhere, but it may not be where you want to be. A written strategic marketing plan will help you reach the goals you've set.

Why write it down? Well, check this out.

An illuminating study on goal setting sponsored by the Ford Foundation found that,

• 23% of the population has no idea what they want from life and as a result they don't have much;

• 67% of the population has a general idea of what they want but they don't have any plans for how to get it;

• Only 10% of the population has specific, well-defined goals, but even then, 7 out of the 10 of those people reach their goals only half the time;

• The top 3%, however, achieved their goals 89% of the time – *an .890 batting average!*

What accounts for the dramatic difference between that top 3% and the others? Are you ready?: the top 3% *wrote down their goals*. Hold it! It can't be that simple. Or can it? Dreams and wishes are not goals until they are written as specific end results on paper. In some very real sense, writing them down materializes them and brings them to life.

Goals have been described as "dreams with a deadline". Written, specific goals provide direction and focus to our activities. They become a road map to follow. And the mind tends to follow what's in front of it.

Establishing Goals

Goals are established to capitalize on strengths and minimize (or eliminate) weaknesses. They are the road maps to a more effective business. For example, if customer service is a weakness then one of your goals may be, "Develop a customer service program to reduce complaints 50% by next June."

So what about you?

Considering your company's strengths, weaknesses, opportunities, threats, marketable assets and mission, list the goals that relate to your company for the next year.

Goal # 1 ____

Goal #2 ____

Goal #3 ____

Goals are nice, but...

Goals provide focus, but the keys to success are the action steps to reach the goals you have set. Good objectives tell how a goal will be addressed. They are specific and measurable. Based on your goals, what are some of the action steps you'll take?

Goal 1: ____

Action Step 1 ____

Action Step 2 ____

Action Step 3 ____

Goal 2: ____

Action Step 1 ____

Action Step 2 ____

Action Step 3 ____

Goal 3: ____

Action Step 1 ____

Action Step 2 ____

Action Step 3 ____

The Marketing Plan: Your Blueprint for Success

The following is the step-by-step process I go through when developing a marketing plan with my clients and one you can use to develop your own profitable marketing strategy too.

Marketing is a process and, as such, it never ends. Once the information is compiled and the plan designed, it has to be refined and revamped to accommodate changes in the marketplace, in your budget and in your offerings.

The following steps are to be completed by you and/or your marketing staff. Make copies and use it as a worksheet. Make sure anyone affected by the plan is included in its development.

OK, here we go.

❐ My Business/Market Niche

The best-run companies have mission statements which are really reflections of their market niche. They are used to establish a direction and focus and are extremely important. Mission statements help you, your associates and customers know exactly what you do. They also provide direction for routine activities and innovation. For example, Music Business Solutions' mission statement and reason for being is, "Helping musicians, songwriters and industry careerists start and grow successful music businesses through vital information and creative management strategies." Review chapter 2 for more on this.

• The most compelling features and benefits of my product are:

–

–

–

• My most significant resources from my experience I can draw on for marketing this product or service are:

–

–

–

–

–

–

• My best opportunities (most promising markets) are:

–

–

–

–

• Putting this all together, my music business/marketing niche is:

• My other music business/marketing niches might include:

• My mission statement therefore is:

❒ **My Audience / Customers / Clients**
Reflect on your marketable assets and goals. Then ask who is or might be most interested. For a marketing plan to be effective, the targets must be clearly identified. These are the people to whom you will direct your communication efforts. Of all the people served by your company which ones will be the primary targets?

• I would describe my primary audience/customers/clients as:

• I would describe my secondary audience/customers/clients as:

• These audiences are *geographically* located at:

• The *demographic* (income, age, gender, occupation, marital status, etc.) profile of my audience can be described as:

• The *psychographic* (lifestyle, interests, opinions, etc.) profile of my audience can be described as:

• My possible other audiences, client pools and customer bases may include:

❒ **Trends and Movements**

Trends and opportunities are things that you can't control. For example, an opportunity may be a new hunger in the marketplace for roots reggae music. This may be an opening for your business to shift to an alternative strategy. On the other hand, a threat could be that certain new government regulations may require online retailers to begin taxing their customers. By knowing and anticipating various trends, opportunities and threats we can determine multiple ways to handle them. Be sure to review chapter 3 for how the music marketplace is changing.

• General social, economic and cultural trends affecting my audience include:

–

–

–

• Music-specific trends afffecting my audience include:

–

–

–

• How I plan on dealing with each of these trends as I market myself to the music industry:

❒ **The Competition**

It is essential to know who your competition is, to understand their strengths and weaknesses, and how you plan to differentiate yourself. Factors to consider include: your competitor's experience, staying power, market position, and strength. Look for gaps you can fill.

• Competitor #1:

• How I will differentiate myself:

• Competitor #2:

• How I will differentiate myself:

• Competitor #3:

• How I will differentiate myself:

❒ **Marketing Tools and Methods** (list and tell why you chose each one)

- My *primary offline* marketing tools will include:

  Tool:

  Reason to use:

  Tool:

  Reason to use:

  Tool:

  Reason to use:..etc...

- My *secondary offline* marketing tools will include:

  Tool:

  Reason to use:

  Tool:

  Reason to use:

  Tool:

  Reason to use:..etc...

- My *primary online* marketing tools will include:

  Tool:

  Reason to use:

  Tool:

  Reason to use:

Tool:

Reason to use:..etc...

- My *secondary online* marketing tools will include:

Tool:

Reason to use:

Tool:

Reason to use:

Tool:

Reason to use:

❐ **Budget:** Two Scenarios (you fill in the amounts)

- Conditions: $__________ allocated

My preliminary budget will be allocated as follows:

• Conditions: $__________ allocated
My preliminary budget will be allocated follows:

❒ **Milestone Timetable** (Deadlines, due dates and time frames should all be listed here)

Milestone	*Start date*	*End Date*
1.		
2.		
3.		
4.		
5.		
6.		
7.		

❒ **Goals Revisited:**

- My marketing goals for he **next five** years are:

1.

2.

3.

4.

- My marketing goals for the **next year** are:

1.

2.

3.

4.

- My marketing goals for the next **three months** are:

1.

2.

3.

4.

As mentioned earlier, its advisable to make copies of this plan template so you can re-use it for any additional service or product you may wish to develop later.

Coda

I hope you feel better prepared now than before you read this book. As you digest and distill the guidance and resources this book offers, seek to develop a marketing mindset that says: ***I am offering continuous and creative value to my market***. That is the mantra to go forth with.

Gather your resources and your plans, because the music-related opportunities are multiplying daily.

Here's to an ever-increasing music appetite and an ever-evolving army of smart music marketers to satisfy it.

And lest we forget the depths and heights of what we are involved in:

> *"It (the theory of relativity) occurred to me by intuition, and MUSIC was the driving force behind that intuition.*
> *My discovery was the result of my musical perception."*
>
> – Albert Einstein (when asked about his theory of relativity)

Music !

FURTHER RESOURCES TO FUEL YOUR MUSIC MARKETING

GENERAL INDUSTRY NEWS & REFERENCE

All Music Guide
http://www.allmusic.com
The online "grand central" of all things musical

Arts Journal
http://artsjournal.com
Filters arts-related articles into an easy-to-use directory (classical & pop music mainly).

The Daily Chord
http://sxsw.com/music/daily_chord/

Music Biz
http://www.musicbiz.com
Entertainment news with a slant towards media-related events.

Music Biz Insight and ***Music Career Juice***
http://www.mbsolutions.com
Free monthly newsletters by Peter Spellman filtering niche-oriented music business- and career-building information and news.

MusicDish
http://musicdish.com
Music-related news and other content categories. Indie music-oriented.

The Music Business Registry
http://www.musicregistry.com
Great informational resources for the music entertainment industry.

Recording Industry Sourcebook
Artist Pro Publishing
http://www.recordingindustrysourcebook.com
Excellent resource with an emphasis on recording, mixing and mastering services

Wired & Wired News
http://wired.com
News from the tech corners of the entertainment world.

http://www.billboard.com
Core industry news

And please...
...get acquainted with your own public library, particularly its online databases (e.g., *InfoTrac*, Lexis-Nexus, *Music Periodicals Index, etc.). You'll be surprised how helpful this can be when doing market research and just for idea stimulation.*

GENERAL BUSINESS MARKETING RESOURCES

• *Books*

Small Business Marketing for Dummies, *Second Edition*
by Barbara Findlay Schenck (2005, For Dummies).

Marketing Outrageously by Jon Spoelstra (2001, Bard Press).

Confessions of Shameless Self-Promoters : Great Marketing Gurus Share Their Innovative, Proven, and Low-Cost Marketing Strategies to Maximize Your Success! by Debbie Allen (2005, McGraw-Hill).

The Ten Demandments: Rules to Live By in the Age of the Demanding Customer by Kelly Mooney & Laura Bergheim (2003, McGraw-Hill).

Marketing Demystified by Dale Falcinelli (2005, McGraw-Hill).

The Pursuit of WOW by Tom Peters (1994, Vintage).

The Tipping Point: How Little Things Can Make a Big Difference by Malcolm Gladwell (2002, Little, Brown, and Co.).

• *General Business & Marketing Sites*

Entrepreneur.com
http://entrepreneur.com
The online home of Entrepreneur magazine is an invaluable resource for growing a business. It contains how-to guides and articles - such as, "Best Banks for Small Business" - and links to experts who'll answer a wide range of questions on everything from financing and employee relations to marketing.

Small Business Now
http://SmallBusinessNow.com
Small biz expert Kim Gordon created this site four years ago, and it's the largest on the Web devoted exclusively to marketing a small business. You'll find about 100 how-to articles on everything from creating a marketing program, writing great letters, branding, brochures, public relations, direct mail, television and radio spots to handling cold calls. You can ask Gordon a marketing question or read hundreds of previous answers, and get one-on-one coaching.

The Marketing Resource Center
http://www.marketingsource.com/articles/
Great library of marketing-related articles and guides.

American Marketing Association
http://www.marketingpower.com/
Official site of the American Marketing Association which supplies marketing professionals with the information, products and services required to succeed in their jobs and careers.

Direct Marketing Association
(http://www.the-dma.org/)
Provides information, articles, resources, and service to direct marketing professionals. The Direct Marketing Association (The DMA) is the oldest and largest trade association for users and suppliers in the direct, database and interactive marketing fields.

Business Marketing Association
http://www.marketing.org/
Association for business-to-business marketers and communicators. Offers broad information and education resources, in addition to networking opportunities through local chapters, conferences and seminars.

Promotion Marketing Association
http://www.pmalink.org/
Association representing the promotion marketing industry and is the official voice for companies and professionals involved in promotion marketing.

Small Business Marketing Resource Center
http://www.sbanetwork.org/smallbusinessmarketingmanagement/
Step by Step instructions on thinking through and writing a marketing plan.

MarketingProfs
http://www.marketingprofs.com/
Marketing Know-How from professors and professionals. Marketing articles and tutorials from professors and marketing professionals

• *Associations & Trade Groups*

Directory of Associations
http://www.marketingsource.com/associations

Trade Shows Directory
http://www.tsnn.com/

Also, refer to the following hard-copy books:

Trade Shows and Professional Exhibits Directory, published by Gale Research.

Trade Show Week Data Book published by Trade Show Week.

• *Key Marketing Magazines*

Advertising Age's Business Marketing
http://www.businessmarketing.com/

American Demographics
http://www.adage.com/section.cms?sectionId=195

BrandWeek
http://brandweek.com

Creative, The Magazine of Promotion & Marketing
http://www.creativemag.com/

Direct
http://www.directmag.com/

Direct Marketing Magazine
http://www.directmarketingmag.com/

Display & Design Ideas
http://www.ddimagazine.com

DM News (Direct Marketing Magazine)
http://www.dmnews.com

Incentive
http://www.incentivemag.com

Inside Direct Mail
http://www.insidedirectmail.com/

Journal of Marketing
http://www.marketingpower.com/content1053.php

License!
http://www.licensemag.com/licensemag/

The Licensing Book
http://www.LicensingBook.com/licensingbook.html

Market Smart
http://www.marketing.org/Publication.asp

MediaWeek
http://www.mediaweek.com

PROMO
http://promomagazine.com/

Target Marketing
http://www.targetonline.com/

The Trends Journal
http://www.trendsresearch.com/journal06.html

Web Marketing Today
http://www.wilsonweb.com/

• *Top Marketing Blogs*

Seth Godin's Blog
http://www.sethgodin.com/sg/blog.html

Adrants
http://www.adrants.com

MarketingVOX
http://www.marketingvox.com

Marketing Genius
http://marketinggenius.blogspot.com

Media Guerrilla
http://mmanuel.typepad.com/mediaguerrilla

Guerrilla Consulting
http://guerrillaconsulting.typepad.com

Duct Tape Marketing
http://www.DuctTapeMarketing.com/weblog.php

Small Business Trends
http://www.smallbusinesses.blogspot.com

Chris Baggott's Best Practices in Email
http://exacttarget.typepad.com/chrisbaggott

Charlotte Li's Blog
http://blogs.forrester.com/charleneli/

Ypulse - Media for the Next Generation
http://www.ypulse.com/

GENERAL MUSIC MARKETING

This Business of Music Marketing & Promotion, 2nd ed. by Tad Lathrop & Jim Pettigrew, Jr. (2003, Billboard Books).

Guerrilla Music Marketing Handbook by Bob Baker (2005, Spotlight Publications). Also, the ***Encore Edition*** (2006).

Guide to Releasing Independent Records by Tim Sweeney & Mark Geller (1996, TSA Books).

How to Make and Sell Your Own Record,5th ed. by Diane Rappaport (2000, Jerome Hedlands Press).

I Don't Need a Record Deal!: Your Survival Guide for the Indie Revolution by Daylle Deanna Schwartz (2005, Billboard Books).

Making and Marketing Your Music by Jodi Summers (2004, Allworth Press)

Making & Selling Your Own CDs by Jana Stanfield (1997, Writer's Digest).

Marketing in the Music Industry by Charles W. Hall & Frederick J. Taylor, 3rd ed. (2000, Simon & Schuster Custom Publishing).

Record Label Marketing by Tom Hutchison, et. al. (2005, Focal Press). *Major label marketing; not indie.*

The DJ Sales and Marketing Handbook: How to Achieve Success, Grow Your Business, and Get Paid to Party! by Stacy Zemon (2005, Focal Press).

The Self-Promoting Musician: Strategies for Independent Success by Peter Spellman (2000, Berklee Press).

CH 1 CONTEXT: HOW MUSIC GETS TO OUR EARS

An International History of the Recording Industry by Pekka Grownow and Ilpo Saunio (1998, Cassell).

Any Sound You Can Imagine: Making Music/Consuming Technology by Paul Theberge (1997, Wesleyan University Press).

The Global Jukebox: The International Music Industry by Robert Burnett (1996, Routledge).

Hit Men: Power Brokers and Fast Money Inside the Music Business by Fredric Dannen (1991, Vintage).

Little Labels, Big Sound by Rick Kennedy, et. al. (1999, Indiana University Press).

Music At the Margins: Popular Music and Global Cultural Diversity by Deanna Robinson, et. al. (1991, Sage Publications).

Off the Charts: Ruthless Days & Reckless Nights Inside the Music Industry by Bruce Haring (1996, Birch Lane Press).

Pennies From Heaven: The American Popular Music Business in the Twentieth Century by Russell Sanjek & David Sanjek (1996, Da Capo).

Playback: From the Victrola to MP3s by Mark Coleman (2003, Da Capo Press).

Rockonomics: The Money Behind the Music by Mark Eliot (1989, Franklin Watts).

Rock & Roll is Here to Pay: The History and Politics of the Music Industry by Steve Chapple and Reebe Garofalo (1987, Nelson-Hall).

Stage to Studio: Musicians and the Sound Revolution, 1890-1950 by James Kraft (1996, Johns Hopkins University Press).

CH 2
FINDING & DEFINING YOUR MARKET NICHE

The Artist's Way At Work by M Bryan and J. Cameron (1998 William Morrow and Company).

The Career Guide For Creators and Unconventional People by Carol Eikleberry (1995 Ten Speed Press).

Career Opportunities in the Music Industry by S. Fields (1995 Facts on File).

Career Renewal by Stephan Rosen and Celia Paul (1998 Academic Press).

Career Solutions for Creative People by Dr. Ronda Ormont (2001, Allworth Press).

The Complete Idiots Guide to Starting Your Own Business by Ed Paulson with Marcia Layton (1998 Alpha Books).

The E-Myth Revisited: Why Most Small Businesses Don't Work and What To Do About It by Michael E. Gerber (1995 Harper Business).

Finding Your Niche by Laurence Pino (1994, Berkley Pub. Group).

Finding Your Perfect Work by Paul and Sarah Edwards (1996 G.P. Putnam's Sons).

Going to Plan B by N.K. Schlossberg and S.P. Robinson (1996 Simon and Schuster).

Staying Sane in the Arts by E. Maisel (1992 G.P. Putnam's Sons).

Working in Show Business: Behind the Scenes in Theater, Film, and Television By L. Rogers (1997 Back Stage Books).

Zen and the Art of Making a Living by Laurence Boldt (1998, Penguin Press).

CH 3
HOW THE MUSIC MARKET IS CHANGING & WHAT THIS MEANS FOR YOU

Clicking: 16 Trends to Future Fit Your Life, Your Work, and Your Business by Faith Popcorn, Lys Marigold, Gerti Bierenbroodspot (1996, HarperCollins).

The Entertainment Economy: How Mega-Media Forces are Transforming Our Lives by Michael J. Wolf (1999, Times Books).

Entertainment Industry Economics: A Guide for Financial Analysis, 5th ed. by Harold Vogel (2001, Cambridge University Press).

The Future Ain't What it Used to Be: 40 Cultural Trends Transforming Hour Job, Your Life, Your World by Mary Meehan, Larry Samuel, Vickie Abrahmson (1998,Riverhead Books).

The Future of Music *by David Kusek & Gerd Leonhard (2004, Berklee Press).*

The Future of the Music Business by Steve Gordon (2005, Backbeat Press).

Global Paradox: The Larger the World Economy, the More Powerful its Smallest Players by John Naisbitt (1994, Wm. Morrow & Co.).

The Invisible Touch: The Four Keys to Modern Marketing by Harry Beckwith (2000, Warner Books).

Madison & Vine: Why the Entertainment & Advertising Industries Must Converge to Survive by Scott Donaton (2004, McGraw Hill).

Marketing Encyclopedia: Issues & Trends Shaping the Future, ed. by Jeffrey Heilbrunn (1995, American Marketing Assoc.).

Megatrends 2000 by John Naisbitt & Patricia Aburdene (1990, Wm. Morrow & Co.).

***Next: Trends for the Near* Future** by Ira Matathia & Marian Salzman (1999, Overlook Press).

Smart Mobs: The Next Social Revolution *by Howard Rheingold (2005,*

Technotrends: 24 Trends That Will Revolutionize our Lives by Daniel Burrus (1993, HarperBusiness).

The One-To-One Future: Building Relationships One Customer at a Time by Don Peppers and Dr. Martha Rogers (1993, DoubleDay).

Street Trends: How Today's Alternative Youth Cultures are Creating Tomorrow's Mainstream Markets by Janine Lopiano-Misdom and Joanne De Luca (1998, Harper-Business).

The Third Wave by Alvin Toffler (1980, Wm. Morrow & Co.).
Remarkably prescient.

▼
CH 4
MARKETING BASICS

❒ General Marketing Resources

• *Books*

Big Ideas for Small Service Businesses by Marilyn & Tom Ross (1993, Communication Creativity).

Best Small Budget Self Promotions by Carol Buchanan (1996, North Light Books).

Guerilla Marketing Excellence by Jay Conrad Levinson (1993, Houghton Mifflin).

Marketing Without Advertising by Michael Phillips and Salli Rasverry (1993, Nolo Press).

Money Making Marketing *and* ***The Unabashed Self-Promoter's Guide***, 2nd eds. by Jeffrey Lant (1997, JLA Publications, 617/547-6372).

Power Marketing for Small Businesses by Jody Horner (1993, The Oasis Press).

The 22 Immutable Laws of Marketing by Al Ries & Jack Trout (1994, Harper Business).

The Tipping Point by Malcolm Gladwell (2000, Little, Brown & Company).

❒ SPECIAL SECTION: Market Research Resources

Federal Government Data

A great deal of demographic data is either free or inexpensive because it is collected and published by the federal government. Your tax dollars fund it. The following publications are from the Commerce Department and Census Bureau.

Every ten years, the United States Census Bureau, in its attempts to count the number of people in the U.S., gathers in the process a vast array of data about its citizens. The 1990 Census is available in print format in many libraries. The Census is also available for the first time in CD-ROM format. In addition, the Census Bureau monitors the population through its regular surveys, including monthly Current Population Survey (CPS). The March issue of CPS contains household and income data. Contact the Government Printing Office at (202)703-3238 to obtain the annual publication THE CENSUS PUBLICATION AND GUIDE which explains publications available from the Census Bureau and how to order them. The customer service department of the Census Bureau can be reached at (301)763-4100.

Data For American States:
The simplest way to collect state and local data is to make a telephone call to the appropriate source. The phone numbers for other state data centers can be obtained from the Bureau of the Census at (301)763-1580. City or county planning departments often compile demographic data. Additional sources for local information are chambers of commerce, local business associations, regional economic development groups, Realtors and school boards. Local experts may also be able to help you with detailed data. Sources listed under "Federal Government Data" and "On-line Demographic Information" also contain state data.

Online Demographic Information
On-line databases and their companion CD-ROM products have made it possible to sift through the mountains of information created by the Census Bureau and other sources quickly and easily. For a complete listing of demographic and other databases, consult the Quandra Directory of On-line Databases (available at most large libraries). The following databases are available online:

United States Data

American FactFinder (FREE)
http://factfinder.census.gov/home/saff/main.html
Provides users with the capacity to browse, search, and map data from many Census Bureau sources.

County and City Data Book (FREE)
http://www.census.gov/statab/www/ccdb.html
Contains statistical tables for 220 data items at the US, census region & division, state, and county levels. Also contains statistical tables for 194 data items for cities, and population and income data for smaller places. Updated every six months.

State & Metropolitan Area Data Book (FREE)
http://www.census.gov/statab/www/smadb.html
Contains a collection of statistics on social and economic conditions in the United States at the state and metropolitan area levels.

Statistical Abstract of the United States (FREE)
http://www.census.gov/statab/www/
A collection of stats on social and economic conditions in the U.S.

Official City Sites (FREE)
http://officialcitysites.org
Just what it says – local, hometown directories of Chambers of Commerce, businesses, happenings and news from all over the country.

International Data

International Database (FREE)
http://www.census.gov/ipc/www/idbnew.html
A data bank containing statistical tables of demographic, and socio-economic data for 227 countries and areas of the world.

Statistics Portal (FREE)
http://www.oecd.org/statsportal/0,2639,en_2825_293564_1_1_1_1_1,00.html
The OECD [Organization for Economic Co-operation and Development] collects stats needed for the analysis of economic and social developments by its in-house analysts, committees, working parties, and member country governments from statistical agencies and other institutions of its member countries.

United Nations Statistics Division (FREE)
http://unstats.un.org/unsd
The Statistics Division compiles statistics from many international sources and produces global updates.

Dun & Bradstreet's Donnelly Demographics
Updated annually, Donnelly Demographics

provides access to the 1980 and 2004 Censuses, as well as estimated and projections development by the Donnelly Marketing Information Services. The database provides census information in an easy to use and comprehensive manner. Information can be searched by a variety of fields, including age, sex, race, industry, occupations and geographic areas. Current year estimates and five-year projections are also available for certain data.

Economic Development Information Network (EDIN)
Available free of charge from the Pennsylvania State Data Center, EDIN contains an on-line interactive database with information for each of the 50 states, Pennsylvania counties and Pennsylvania municipalities. Information is constantly being added, EDIN also contains bulletins and news releases related to demographics, procurement opportunities (including federal and state contract information), small business assistance program information, directories of experts, local county planning offices, chambers of commerce, and other demographic files. Call (717)948-6336 for further information or fax (717)948-6306.

• *Books*

Breaking Up America by Joseph Turow (1997, University of Chicago Press).

The Future Consumer by Frank Feather (1998, Warwick Publishing).

The New Mainstream : How the Multicultural Consumer Is Transforming American Business
by Guy Garcia (2005, Rayo).

Hispanic Marketing & Public Relations: Understanding And Targeting America's Largest Minority
by Elena Del Valle (2005, Poyeen Publications).

• *Marketing Basics Online*

Ad Bumb
http://www.adbumb.com
Shares tons of pertinent information on online advertising.

CH 5 ONLINE MUSIC MARKETING TOOLS

• *Books*

How to Build a Music Web Site That Sells by Mihkel Raud (eBook: 2003, Raud Meedia OY).

The Musician's Internet: Online Strategies for Success in the Music Industry by Peter Spellman (2002, Berklee Press).

The Ultimate Guide to Electronic Marketing for Small Business : Low-Cost/High Return Tools and Techniques that Really Work by Tom Antion (2005, John Wiley).

Search Engine Marketing, Inc.: Driving Search Traffic to Your Company's Web Site by Mike Moran, Bill Hunt (2005, Prentice Hall).

• *Music News and Internet Developments*

Digital Music Weekly
http://www.digitalmusicweekly.com
The best daily distillation of digital music news. Subscribe for free.

Fez Guys: Internet Audio Enlightenment
http://www.fezguys.com

MusicDish
http://musicdish.com

Music-related news and other content categories. Indie music-oriented.

The Virtual Chronicle of the Digital Music Revolution
http://www.virtualrecordings.com/mp3_2.htm

• *Internet Stats and Surveys*

CyberDialogue
http://www.cyberdialogue.com

CyberStats
(http://cyberatlas.internet.com)

Living Internet
http://livinginternet.com/

Nua Surveys
http://www.nua.ie/surveys/
International in scope.

• *Web Site Development Tools*

NIMBIT
http://www.nimbit.com
Website management tools and hosting services designed for the entertainment industry.

Great Website Design Tips
http://www.unplug.com/great/
Ideas for effective and quick Web site design

Webdeveloper.com
http://www.webdeveloper.com
The one-stop shop for advice and tools for building better web sites.

Web Diner
http://www.webdiner.com/
Tips and tutorials for beginners and intermediate Web page builders

Webmonkey: The Web Developer's Resource
http://hotwired.lycos.com/webmonkey/index.html
Intermediate-level resource for web designers

• *Web Site Resources*

Web Host Providers (Top 25 Web Host Providers
http://webhostlist.com
Where to find the best host for your web site.

Hostbaby.net
http://www.hostbaby.net

Artist Server
http://www.artistserver.com/

Network Solutions
http://www.networksolutions.com

Register.com
http://register.com
Domain Name Registration

• *Sound Utilities for the Web*

Goldwave
http://www.goldwave.com

Cool Edit Pro
http://www.syntrillium.com

Harmony Central
http://www.harmonycentral.com

Shareware Machine
http://hitssquad.com/smm

• *Online Business Development*

E-Commerce Advisor
http://www.sotkin.com

Idea Site for Business
http://www.ideasiteforbusiness.com

Webentrepreneurs.com
http://www.webentrepreneurs.com

• *Advanced Internet Promotion & Marketing*

Clickz.com
http://www.clickz.com

eMarketing Digest
http://www.webbers.com/emark/

Internet Marketing Center
http://www.marketingtips.com

Virtual Promote
http://www.virtualpromote.com

Web Marketing Info Center
http://www.wilsonweb.com/webmarket

• *Internet Radio*

Broadcast.com
http://www.broadcast.com
A portal to thousands of traditional and Web-only stations.

Net Radio
http://www.netradio.com

Spinner.com
http://www.spinner.com

Rolling Stone Radio Network
http://www.rollingstone.com

List of Radio Stations on the Internet
http://wmbr.mit.edu/stations/list.html

• *The Legalities of Online Music*

Kohn on Music Licensing
http://www.kohnmusic.com
Find extensive legal information about copyright law and music licensing specifically relating to music delivery on the Internet.

Legal Information Institute
http://www4.law.cornell.edu/uscode/17/index.text.tml

CopyrightGuru
http://www.copyrightguru.com

Recording Industry Association of America
http://www.riaa.com
Be sure to go these pages on the RIAA site: Copyright Basics, Music and the Internet, audio Technologies, and Licensing and Royalties.

United States Copyright Office
http://www.loc.gov/copyright
Get all the copyright law you can handle from these new pages: Webcasting, the Digital Millennium Copyright Act, Napster, and Digital Tranmissions.

• *Online Independent Music Stores*

Amazon Advantage Program
http://www.amazon.com/advantage

CD Baby
http://www.cdbaby.com

CD Now
http://www.cdnow.com

CD Street
http://www.cdstreet.com

COMA-The Canadian On-Line Musician's Association
http://www.coolname.com/coma

Emusic
http://www.emusic.com

CD Universe
http://www.cduniverse.com

CH 6 MARKETING DIRECT TO FANS & CUSTOMERS

• *Books*

The Conference And Event Management Handbook: Understanding The Creativity, Methodology And Money by Howard Evans (2005, Kogan Page).

Creating Customer Evangelists: How Loyal Customers Become a Volunteer Sales Force by *Ben McConnell (2002, Dearborne Trade).*

Endless Referrals: Network Your Everyday Contacts Into Sales Money by Bob Burg (1993, McGraw Hill).

Networking in the Music Business by Dan Kimpel, 2nd ed. (1998, Writer's Digest Books).

Networking in the Music Industry by Jim Clevo and Eric Olsen (1993, Rockpress).

Never Eat Alone: And Other Secrets to Success One Relationship at a Time by Keith Ferrazzi (2005, Currency/ Doubleday).

Permission Marketing : Turning Strangers Into Friends And Friends Into Customers by Seth Godin (1999, Simon & Schuster)

The Secrets of Word-of-Mouth Marketing: How to Trigger Exponential Sales Through Runaway Word of Mouth by George Silverman (2001, American Management Assoc.)

Word-Of-Mouth Marketing by Jerry Wilson (1991, John Wiley & Sons).

• *Street Teams*

On.omotion.net
A "grand central station" of street teams across the country.

Streetteampromotion.com
Service offering event promotion, mobile marketing, wallscapes and other guerrilla marketing solutions. Observe their approach and learn from what they're doing.

Word13.com
Highly targeted street and buzz marketing strategies.

• *Catalog Marketing/Direct Mail Marketing*

Catalog Copy That Sizzles, 2nd ed. by H. G. Lewis (1999, McGraw Hill).

Creating a Profitable Catalog: Everything You Need to Know to Create a Catalog That Sells by Jack Schmidt (2000, McGraw-Hill).

Desktop Direct Marketing: How to Use Up-to-the-Minute Technologies to Find and Reach New Customers by Kim and Sunny Baker (1994, McGraw Hill).

How to Start a Home-Based Mail Order Business, 3rd ed. by Georganne Flumara (2005, Globe Pequot).

National Directory of Mailing Lists (annual, Oxbridge Communications, 800-955-0231, x200)

Start Your Own Mail Order Business by Entrepreneur Press (Entrepreneur Magazine).

• *Mailing Lists*

GreatLists.com
An excellent site to learn about and find mailing lists. GreatLists.com is an independent broker of both domestic and international business-to-business and professional marketing lists, offering high-quality list information. Since 1979, the firm has been collecting, verifying and maintaining detailed information on thousands of lists — both those that work and those that don't. Call (800) 296-0888.

InfoUSA, Inc.
http://www.infoUSA.com

A huge source of sales leads and business or consumer mailing lists. InfoUSA offers numerous business directories on CD-ROM, including state business directories for all 50 states, American big business (193,000 companies), US businesses of all sizes (11 million), manufacturers (645,000), doctors (575,000) and entrepreneurs (4.5 million). The site offers search functions to help you find exactly what you need. Call (800) 321-0869.
Mailing-Solution.com is dedicated to providing professional direct mail, e-mail and broadcast fax services to small and mid-sized companies.

Hugo Dunhill Mailing Lists
http://www.hdml.com
A leading source for business, consumer and e-mail lists, as well as telemarketing leads.

Caldwell List Company
http://www.caldwell-list.com
Offers mailing, telemarketing, e-mail and fax lists plus other helpful direct mail and marketing information.

Mailers Software
http://www.mailerssoftware.com
A leading source of direct marketing software, services, sales leads and databases.

The Direct Marketing Association
http://www.the-dma.org
The top trade association for the direct marketing industry. Get seminar dates and info, or read about issues affecting the industry.

• *Trade Show Marketing*

Guerrilla Trade Show Selling by Jay Conrad Levinson, et. al. (1997, Wiley).

How to Get the Most Out of Trade Shows by Steve Miller (1996, NTC Business Books).

Trade Show and Event Marketing : Plan, Promote & Profit by Ruth Stevens (2005, South-Western Educational Pub.).

Trade Shows and Professional Exhibits Directory (annual, Gale Research Inc. 313-961-2242).

• *Advertising Rates*

Standard Rate and Data Service, Inc., 3004 Glenview Road, Wilmette, IL 60091. *Provides advertising rates in magazines and newspapers.*

• *Resource List*
for the Advanced
Internet Music Marketer

NOTE: *Web tools & resources for Net marketing, advertising and promotion are plenteous, though some of the best aren't that well known. Here are several great services & tools to help take your Net marketing to new levels.*

Direct Marketing

Direct Marketing Insights
http://www.dminsights.com
Catalog marketer Jim Padgitt has been in the business for more years than many of you have been alive. His invaluable site tackles the art of catalog marketing online, also known as e-commerce. Learn from his experience with his Catalog Business Efficiency Evaluator tool... according to Jim, "In less than 10 minutes, this handy tool shows you how your business measures up to the best run, most profitable catalogs in the industry."

Optimost
http://www.optimost.com
Imagine testing 10, 20 or more versions of your critical conversion or landing page – before you put it out there in a full-blown campaign. With Optimost you can do exactly that. Their service enables you to test all components of your page from graphics, buttons and bulleted lists to colors, copy length, placement and more. After all, your vision of the perfect direct marketing campaign may be quite different than the reality that motivates visitors to act This technology helps you isolate and test all the motivating factors, learn from

your results and fine tune your Web pages efficiently, all in the service of improving conversion rates. Optimost offers several different pricing options based upon your short-term or long-term needs; contact the company for details.

Vertster
http://www.vertster.com
Vertster specializes in the split run testing of online landing pages such as newsletter signups, lead generation forms, e-commerce product pages and other online direct marketing vehicles. Vertster's servers divide your site's traffic between multiple versions of your test pages, which are rotated through your audience to determine which page gives you the most return on your investment. If you just want to explore the concept a little further, check out their blog entries for valuable tips on creating effective landing pages. If you want to give the technology a spin, there is a Small Business Pro pricing plan that will get your feet wet -- a monthly fee of $17.99(US) entitles you to test 10 creatives/20,000 pageviews.

Email Delivery

EmailReach
http://www.emailreach.com
In the old days of direct marketing, a leaky mailing list represented untold amounts of lost revenue, frustration and angst. Email has its own set of problems – after all, the first rule of direct marketing is that your message must reach the recipient. There's nothing worse than having your legitimate email disappear into the black hole of sp@m filters, and it's a real problem that is only getting worse. EmailReach attacks this problem head on by running your message through a gamut of ISPs and sp@m filters to find all the problems before you actually send it out to the masses. They then try to retrieve your email from every major ISP and flag those that dump your email into a bulk folder. You get a report on why your email was flagged and suggestions on what you can do to change it (including technical changes), and then it's retested until you "test clean". The company claims that it can improve the performance of your email file by over 30% with its services. Subscriptions start at $49.95(US) per month. There's a trial that costs zippo so you can see how it works.

Direct Marketing Gurus

Bly.com Blog
http://www.bly.com/blog/index.php
All-round marketing guru Bob Bly's blog. Regular postings on Internet marketing, written in a style that simply demands commentary. The result is an active Internet marketing forum where you can learn tips and techniques from one of the industry's best. This guy's blog has this editor/marketer's attention – it's really good.

GuruDAQ
http://www.gurudaq.com
In an attempt to create a one-stop-shop *where you can discover and learn from online marketing gurus, marketer John Sikora created the GuruDAQ site. Here you will find a compilation of the top Internet marketing experts and their resources. In the spirit of NASDAQ, each guru's ranking is associated with a value or "stock price" based on site traffic, online longevity, number of site links and the clickthrough rate on each guru's profile. To keep things competitive, he posts a Winners and Losers list based on daily stock price guidelines.*

Datacard Databases

Direct Marketing A-Z
http://www.dma-z.com
DataCard Network manages a datacard database with over 44,700 active titles of mailing lists, card decks, package insert programs and other direct response programs and opportunities. For instance, if you search for Internet marketing newsletters, you'll get a list of matching publications that are likely candidates for your advertising dollars. Explore further if you like -- each publication has a summary overview that includes a description, the number of subscribers and the price of the full list as well as pricing for selected buys. Yes, Web Digest For Marketers was listed in this database, complete with current pricing. This site is a tentacle springing forth from marketing INFORMATION network (mIn®), which is a widely used network for DM list managers and brokers.

In addition to the ability to conduct datacard research, the site's DataCard Dispatch delivers list releases, hotline counts and other direct marketing news to your email IN box. No-cost registration will give you access to all the site offers.

Data Drilling

FlexPoint
http://www.marketimprove.com
FlexPoint helps marketers acquire and/or develop customers who are more profitable at a lower cost per sale. Their technology consists of a database tool that looks at a client's direct marketing campaign and divides their customer base into identifiable segments. It then identifies where the audience drops from profitable to loss-making segments for that campaign. The client can then eliminate the loss segments from their campaign, thus improving ROI (return on investment). The company estimates that you will see improvement in your direct marketing campaign results within four weeks with this service.

Direct Marketing Resources

The Institute of Direct Marketing
http://www.theidm.com
The Institute of Direct Marketing is Europe's leading professional development body for direct, data and digital marketing. It offers numerous direct marketing training courses taught by industry practitioners (the IDM has created more than 700 in-company training programs for companies such as IBM and Vodafone). You can benefit from all of this knowledge -- their Knowledge Center has hundreds of online documents that are available for download, plus hundreds of checklists, examples, tables and case studies. Some are gratis and some are fee-based, and they represent a wealth of information for the direct marketer.

▼ CH 7 MARKETING THROUGH LIVE PERFORMANCES

• *Gigging Directories*

The Musician's Atlas
http://musiciansatlas.com/
Contact directory supplying more comprehensive information than any other music industry resource - details such as company focus, submission policy, booking advance, stage size, in-house equipment, broadcast coverage, distribution, circulation, styles of music sought and other specifics professionals use to build and sustain their careers.

Musician's Guide to Touring and Promotion (*Billboard* magazine). This city-by-city booking guide is also available on CD-Rom. Call 212/536-5248.

• *Books*

Be Your Own Booking Agent, 2nd ed. by Jeri Goldstein (2004, The New Music Times).

Book Your Own Tour: The Independent Musician's Guide to Cost-Effective Touring and Promotion by Liz Garo (1997, 2nd ed., Rockpress).

Booking & Tour Management for the Performing Arts, 2nd. ed. by Rena Shagan (1996, Allworth Press).

The Self-Promoting Musician: Strategies for Independent Music Success by Peter Spellman (2000, Berklee Press).

Standing Room Only: Strategies for Marketing the Performing Arts by Joanne Scheff & Philip Kotler (1997, Harvard Business School Press). Good for organizing larger shows and concerts.

Playing for Pay: How to Be a Working Musician by Janes Gibson (1990, Writers Digest Books).

How to Make a Living as a Musician So You Never Have to Have a Job Again! by Marty Buttwinick (1993, Sonata Publishing).

Note By Note:
A Guide to Concert Promotion
Folk Alliance
962 Wayne Ave., Suite 902
Silver Spring, MD 20910-4480
E-mail: fa@folk.org
Web: http://www.folk.org

The Touring Musician: A Small Business Approach to Booking Your Band on the Road by Hal Galper (2000, Watson-Guptil Publications).

• *Specialized Gigging Resources*

Encyclopedia of Associations (Gale Research).

The Best Public Golf Courses in the United States, Canada, the Caribbean and Mexico by Robert McCord, 2nd ed. (1996, Random House).

Golf Courses : The Complete Guide to over 14,000 Courses Nationwide (Lanier Guide); Arthur Jack Snyder, J. C. Wright (1996, Ten Speed Press).

The Municipal Executive Directory (check your local library).

How to Get a Job with a Cruise Line by Mary Fallon Miller, 2nd ed. (Ticket to Adventure, Inc., PO box 41005, St. Petersburg FL 33743-1005).

Parks Directory of the United States : A Guide to More Than 4,700 National and State Parks, Recreation Areas, Historic Sites, Battlefields, Monuments by Darren L. Smith (1994, Omnigraphics).

How to Make Money Performing in Public Schools by David Heflick (Silcox Productions, PO Box 1407, Orient, WA 99160).

• *Online Touring Resources*

Musi-Cal Performer Index
http://www.musi-cal.com/cgi-bin/list-perf
Provides an international concert calendar for folk, bluegrass, blues, and world music performers, organized alphabetically by artist. Also, add your own concerts.

Pollstar
http://www.pollstar.com
Concert tour information database including all genres of music and other events.

Sonicbids
http://sonicbids.com
580 Harrison Avenue, Fourth Floor
Boston, MA 02118
P: (617) 275-7222
An electronic alternative to the traditional press kit and LOTS more.

• *Chain Store Venues*

Barnes & Noble
http://www.barnesandnoble.com
List of stores nationwide.
Contact community relations coordinator at each store.

Borders Books and Music
http://www.borders.com/stores/index.html
List of stores nationwide by state, contact, phone, address, directions.
Contact the community relations coordinator at each store.

Starbucks/Hear Music
http://www.starbucks.com/hearmusic
Call local store in each town. May have booking coordinator for a number of stores.

• *Festivals and Venues Online*

Festival Finder
http://www.festivalfinder.com

Folk Venues
http://www.folkmusic.org/shows.html

Musi-Cal
http://www.musi-cal.com

Music Links
http://www.yahoo.com/entertainment/music

Opera America
http://www.operaam.org

• *Tour Directories*

AustralAsia Music Industry Directory
GPO Box 2977
Sydney, N.S.W.
Australia 2000
P: +61-02-9557-7766
F: +61-02-9557-7788
E: directories@immedia.com.au
W: http://www.immedia.com.au
Purchase $50 US or free at international trade fairs like MIDEM
Online Directory: $40—6 months; $80—12 months.

Facilities Directory
650 First Avenue
New York, NY 10016
P: (212) 532-4150
F: (212) 213-6382
Conventions, expositions, event management, and large production.
Annual directory: Call for current directory price.

The North American Folk Business Directory
Folk Alliance
962 Wayne Ave., Suite 902
Silver Spring, MD 20910-4480
P: (301) 588-8185
F: (301) 588-8186
W: http://www.folk.org
Listing U.S. and foreign folk venues, folk press, radio stations, newsletters, publications, record companies, agents, managers, performers, publicists.

Musical America
10 Lake Drive
Highstown, NJ 08520-5397
Phone: (800) 221-5488, ext. 7783
W: http://www.musicalamerica.com
Listing of presenters and festivals for ethnic, folk, children's dance, Jazz, theater, classical, opera.

Music Directory of Canada
23 Hanover Drive #7
St. Catherine's Ontario L2W 1A3
Phone: (905) 641-3471
Fax: (905) 641-1648
W: http://musicdirectorycanada.com

Theatre Communications Group, Inc.
520 Eighth Ave.
New York, NY 10018-4156
P: (212) 609-5960
F: (212) 609-5901
E: tcg@tcg.org
W: http://www.tcg.org
Theatre Directory—Lists regional theatre companies and organizations around the U.S.

CH 8 MARKETING TO PRODUCERS & RECORD LABELS

• *Books*

A & R: A Novel by Bill Flanagan (2000, Random House).

Bad Boy: The Influence of Sean Puffy Combs on the Music Industry by Ronin Ro (2002, Pocket Books).

Behind the Glass: top record Producers Tell How They Craft the Hits by Howard Massey (2000, Backbeat Books).

Exploding: The Highs, Hits, Hype, Heroes, and Hustlers of the Warner Music by Stan Cornyn, Paul Scanlon (Contributor) (2002, Harper Entertainment).

Getting Signed! An Insider's Guide to the Record Industry by George Howard (2003, Berklee Press).

Little Labels – Big Sound: Small Record Companies and the Rise of American Music by Rick Kennedy, et al. (1999, Indiana University Press).

The Men Behind Def Jam: The Radical Rise of Russell Simmons and Rick Rubin by Alex Ogg (2002, Omnibus Press).

Motown: Money, Power, Sex, and Music by Gerald L. Posner (2002, Random House).

Music Genres and Corporate Cultures by Keith Negus (1999, Routledge).

Rhythm & Business: The Political Economy of Black Music, ed. by Norman Kelly (2002, Akashic Books).

Secrets of Negotiating a Recording Contract by Moses Avalon (2001, Backbeat).

So You Wanna Be a Rock & Roll Star by Jacob Slichter (2004, Broadway Books).

The Operator: David Geffen Builds, Buys, and Sells the New Hollywood by Tom King (2000, Random House).

The Real Deal by Daylle Schwartz (2002, Billboard Books).

• *Directories*

ProductionHUB, Inc.
(www.productionhub.com)
An online resource and industry directory for film, television, video and digital media production.

Producer & Engineer Directory
http://www.rpmdirect.com
A good annual print directory, co-published by The Music Business registry and RPM direct, is the. Check it out.

Record Company Roster
Pollstar
http://www.pollstar.com
4697 W. Jacquelyn Avenue
Fresno, CA 93722
P: 1-800-344-7383
F: (559) 271-7979
Record companies with A&R contacts/artist rosters. Also music publishers and distribution groups.

A&R Registry (annual directory)
http://www.musicregistry.com.

CH 9 MARKETING TO DISTRIBUTORS & RETAILERS

• *Books*

1,001 Ideas to Create Retail Excitement by Edgar A. Falk (1994, Prentice Hall Trade).

Billboard Record Retailing Directory
http://www.billboard.com/store/directories

How to Develop and Manage Successful Distributor Channels in World Markets by William Fath (1996, Amacom Book Division).

• *Trade Organizations*

Almighty Institute of Music Retail
(http://www.almightyretail.com/)

CIMS (Coalition of Independent Music Stores)
http://www.cimsmusic.com/

NARM (National Association of Recording Merchandisers)
http://www.narm.com

• *Top U.S. Indie Music Distributors*

Action Music Sales
6541 Eastland Rd.
Brookpark, OH 44142
Phone: (440) 243-0300

Allegro Corporation
14134 N.E. Airport Way
Portland, OR 97230-3443
Phone: (503) 257-8480
Web: http://www.allegro-music.com

Alternative Distribution Alliance
72 Spring Street 12th Floor
New York, NY 10012
Phone: (212) 343-2485
Web: http://www.ada-muisc.com

Bayside Distribution
885 Riverside Pkwy.
West Sacramento, CA 95605
Phone: (916) 371-2800
Web: http://www.baysidedist.com

Big Daddy Music Distribution
162 North 8th Street
Kenilworth, NJ 07033-1127
Phone: (908) 653-9110
Web: http://www.bigdaddymusic.com

Burnside Distribution Corp.
3647 S.E. 21st Ave.
Portland, OR 97202
Phone: (503) 231-0876
Web: http://www.bdcdistribution.com

Butterfly International Distribution
230 Franklin Road Bldg. 2 2nd Fl.
Franklin, TN 37064
Phone: (615) 468-2060
Web: http://www.butterflygroup.net

Caroline Distribution
104 W. 29th Street 4th Fl.
New York, NY 10001
Phone: (212) 886-7500
Web: http://www.carolinedist.com

Distribution Fusion III
5455 Pare #101
Montreal, QC H4P 1P7
Canada
Phone: (514) 738-4600
Web: http://www.fusion3.com

KOCH Entertainment Distribution LLC
22 Harbor Park Drive
Port Washington, NY 11050
Phone: (516) 484-1000
Web: http://www.kotchint.com

Mordam
731R North Market Blvd.
Sacramento, CA 95834
Phone: (916) 641-8900
Web: http://www.mordamrecords.com

Music Design, Inc.
4650 North Port Washington Road
Milwaukee, WI 53212
Phone: 1-800-862-7232
Web: http://www.musicdesign.com

NAIL Distribution
A Division of Allegro Corp.
14134 N.E. Airport Way
Portland, OR 97230-3443
Phone: (503) 257-8480
Web: http://www.naildistribution.com

Navarre Corporation
7400 49th Ave. North
New Hope, MN 55428
Phone: (763) 535-8333
Web: http://www.navarre.com

RED Distribution
79 Fifth Ave
New York, NY 10003
Phone: (212) 404-0600
Web: http://www.redmusic.com

Redeye Distribution
1130 Cherry Lane
Graham, NC 27253
Phone: (877) 733-3931
Web: http://www.redeyeusa.com

Rev Distribution
P.O. Box 5232
Huntington Beach, CA 92615
Phone: (714) 375-4264
Web: http://www.revhq.com

Ryko Distribution
30 Irving Place
New York, NY 10003
Phone: (212) 287-6100
Web: http://www.rykodistribution.net

Select-O-Hits
1981 Fletcher Creek Dr.
Memphis, TN 38133
Phone: (901) 388-1190
Web: http://www.selectohits.com

Sumthing Distribution
9 E. 45th Street
New York, NY 10017
Phone: (212) 818-0047
Web: http://www.sumthing.com

Synergy Distribution
3650 Osage Street
Denver, CO 80211
Phone: (888) 355-9387
Web: http://www.synergydistribution.com

Viastar Distribution
2451 W. Birchwood Ste. 105
Mesa, AZ 85202
Phone: (480) 894-0311
Web: http://www.viastarcorp.com

VITAL
338a Ladbroke Grove
London, England W10 5AH
United Kingdom
Phone: (44) 20-8324-2400
Web: http://www.vitaluk.com

• *One Stops*

Directory of One Stops
http://mergerecords.com/faq.php?content_id=6&cat_id=5&

CH 10 MARKETING YOUR MUSIC TO RADIO

• *Books & Articles*

Getting Radio Airplay by Gary Hustwit (1996, Rockpress).

Radio Success Stories
Published by the Interep Radio Store
100 Park Ave.
New York, NY 10017
(212) 916-0524

"Getting Radio Airplay" Series by Bryan Farrish (http://musicdish.com).

• *Radio Directories*

College Radio Station Directory
http://www.therecordingindustry.com/collegeradio-ak.htm
Indie recording industry resources. U.S., Canada, Europe, Asia.

Folk DJ-L
http://www.folkradio.org
Lists folk stations, shows, DJs, playlists and charts.

Internet Radio Index.com
http://www.internetradioindex.com
Links to over 1800 Internet radio stations.

International Radio Station List
http://www.radio-locator.com
Lists U.S., Canadian, European and other international stations.

SPECIAL: The Live 365 Lowdown
Live365.com makes it easy for independent artists to get their tracks into broadcasters' hands and listeners' ears. The ever-expanding library http://www.live365.com/cgi-bin/library.cgi is a virtual record pool, (a secure service that lets all Live365 DJs preview and add your tracks directly into their stations' playlists.) You can also allow broadcasters and listeners to download your entire track, if you prefer. Live365 is licensed and pays royalties to ASCAP, BMI and SESAC. Each week, Live365 reports its DJs' playlists to Radio and Records, College Music Journal, Billboard Online, New Age Reporter, and other web properties.

With the help of Radiowave.com, Live365 also compiles and reports a run-of-site weekly airplay chart. As the largest Internet radio network, with thousands of active broadcasters and over 2 million unique listeners a month, Live365 provides independent artists with an unprecedented opportunity for large-scale radio exposure. You can also submit your album or track to Live365's editorial department for consideration to be listed, free of charge.
(http://www.live365.com/labelservices)

• *Public Radio*

National Public Radio
http://www.pri.org
National Public Radio
635 Massachusetts Avenue, NW
Washington, DC 20001
P: (202) 513-2000
F: (202) 513-3329

• *Cable Radio*

MTV Radio Network
http://www.mtv.com/music/mtvonradio

VH1 Radio
http://www.vh1.com/radio

• *Radio Monitoring*

BDS (Broadcast Data Systems)
http://www.bdsonline.com

MediaGuide
http://mediaguide.com

• *Radio Trades*

Album Network
http://www.musicbiz.com
120 N. Victory Blvd., 3rd floor, Burbank, CA 91502
P: 818-955-4000

CMJ New Music Report,
http://www.cmjmusic.com
11 Middleneck Rd. #400, Great Neck, NY 11021; 516-466-6000

Friday Morning Quarterback (FMQB)
http://www.fmqb.com
Executive Mews, Bldg, F-36
1930 East Marleton Pike
Cherry Hill, NJ 08003
P: (856) 424-9114
F: (856) 424-6943
Send recordings to appropriate department: AC, Triple A, CHR, Modern Rock, Rock. Rhythm crossover, metal.

Hits
http://www.buzznetonline.com
14958 Ventura Blvd., Sherman Oaks, CA 91403
P: 818-501-7900

Radio & Records, 10100 Santa Monica Bl. 5th floor, Los Angeles, CA 90067; 310-553-4330;
http://www.radioandrecords.com
P: (310) 553-4330
F: (310) 203-9763
Industry news, radio news, reviews. Radio charts: AC, Active Rock, Adult Alternative, Alternative, CHR/Pop, CHR/Rhythm, Country, Hot AC, NAC/Smooth Jazz, Rock, Urban, Urban AC.

• *Radio Syndicates*

Syndicates are networks that re-distribute broadcasts to a variety of radio stations around the country. One spin on a syndicate means you're music is heard on every station in that syndicate, making them a cost-effective marketing tactic.

A Prairie Home Companion
Carried on 356 Stational!
Two Million Listerenal!
45 E. 7th St., St. Paul, MN 55101
Artists/Labels Contact: Stevie Beck
Radio Stations Contatct: Katy Reckdahl
http://www.prairiehome.publicradio.org

E-Town
Broomfield, CO
Carried by Over 100 Stations Nationwide!
Anne McConnell, Marketing Dir
F: 303 443-4489
http://www.Etown.org/

Echoes
Chester Springs
Syndicated to 135 Public Radio Stations
Jonh Diliberto, Music Director
P: 610 458-0780
E: Echoes@Well.Com
http://www.echoes.org

The Midnight Special
WFMT - Fm, Chicago, IL
Rich Warren, Producer
2nd Longest Running Folk Show in U.S. - 44 years.
Carried by 60 Stations & 150 cable channels
P: 773 279-2000
E: Special@Shout.Net

Mountain Stage
Charleston, WV
Andy Ridenour, Producer
Carried by over 90 Stations nationwide
http://www.mountainstage.org

River City Folk
KVNO - FM 90.7
Omaha, NE
Tom May & Steve O'gorman
P: 402 559-5866
F: 402 554-2440
http://www.tommayfolk.com/rivercityfolk/index.htm

World Café
Philadelphia, PA
Daily two-hour show on 111 affiliate Stations
Bruce Warren, MD
P: 215 989-6677
F: 215 898-0707
http://www.npr.org ("Programs & Schedules")

Sheridan Gospel Network- The Light
4025 Pleasantdale Radio
Suite 240
(770) 416-2220
(888) 467 7754
http://www.sgnthelight.com

▼ CH 11 BUSINESS-TO-BUSINESS MUSIC MARKETING

• *Directories*

The Hollywood Music Industry Directory (Hollywood Creative Directories) http://www.hcdonline.com

The Shoot Directory (annual Directory). http://shootonline.com
Provides plenty of great contact info from the post-production world – ad agencies, multimedia houses, sound design studios, etc.

Adweek Agency Directory
Published by *Adweek* Magazine
Circulation Dept.
P.O. Box 2006
Lakewood, NJ 08701

B to B: The Magazine for Marketing Strategists
http://www.btobonline.com/index.cms

• *Books*

Kohn on Music Licensing by Al & Bob Kohn (1996, Aspen Law & Business).

Business To Business Direct Marketing by Robert W. Bly, 2nd ed. (1998, McGraw Hill).

Music, Money & Success by Jeffrey and Todd Brabec (1994, Schirmer).

Negotiating for Dummies
Michael C. Donaldson, Mimi Donaldson (IDG Books Worldwide).

25 Role Plays For Negotiation Skills
Sandy Aherman and Ira G. Asherman (Human Resources Development Publishers).

Win-Win Negotiating
Fred Edmund Jandt w/ Paul Gillette (John Wiley & Sons, Inc.).

EPM Communications, 488 East 18th St., Brooklyn NY 11226-6702; (718) 469-9330. Publishes *Entertainment Marketing Letter*, *The Licensing Letter* & others. Excellent leads! Also hosts annual Entertainment Marketing Conference.

• *B-2-B Directories*

World Chambers of Commerce Directory
http://www.worldchambers.com

❐ Commercial Jingle Markets

Adtunes
http://www.adtunes.com
Site that reveals the music behind commercials.

Film/TV Music Guide (annual) published by SRS Publishing (800-377-7411). *Full contact information on Music Supervisors, Music Publishers specializing in film and TV placement, and record label personnel involved in the same.*

Who Killed the Jingle?: How a Unique American Art Form Disappeared by Steve Karmen (2005, Hal Leonard).

How to Make Money: Scoring Soundtracks and Jingles by Jeffrey P. Fisher (1997, Emeryville, CA: MIX Books).

Profiting From Your Project Studio *by Jeffrey Fisher* (2001, Allworth Press).

❐ TV/Film Music Markets

Film/TV Music Guide (annual) published by SRS Publishing (800-377-7411). *Full contact information on Music Supervisors, Music Publishers specializing in film and TV placement, and record label personnel involved in the same.*

Film Music Channel
http://www.filmmusicchannel.com

Film Music Resources
http://www.filmmusicsociety.org

Film Music World
http://www.filmmusicworld.com
The Industry's Source for Information, Education and Communication. Jump site for Film Music Magazine, Film Music Network, Film Music Store, Film Music Institute, and Film Music Online.

The Hollywood Reporter
http://www.hollywoodreporter.com

Internet Movie Database
http://www.imdb.com
A wealth of information about past film productions.

Mandy
http://www.mandy.com
Directory of creative talent and companies.

MovieTunes.com
http://sites.hollywood.com/movietunesThe premier source of information about film soundtracks, composers and movie music news.

Popular Music Libraries
http://www.bmi.com/licensing/commercials.asp

ProductionHUB, Inc.
http://www.productionhub.com
An online resource and industry directory for film, television, video and digital media production.

TuneData
http://www.tunedata.com.
Subscription-based service that allows you to query their database for what music various productions are seeking and how your music might be appropriate.

• *Magazines*

Film Score Monthly, Monthly Edited by Lukas Kendall. Information and suscriptions: 5967 Chula Vista Way #7 - Los Angeles, CA 90068.

❒ Business Music Services

DMX Music Services
http://www.DMXMusic.com

Muzak
http://www.muzak.com

❒ Game Music Market

• *Books*

Audio for Games: Planning , Process & Production by Alexander Brandon (2004, New Riders Games).

Game Development Business and Legal Guide (Game Development) by Ashley Salisbury (2003, Muska & Lipman).

Game Plan: The Insiders Guide to Breaking In and Succeeding in the Computer and Video Game Business by Alan Gershenfelf, et. al. (2004, St. Martins).

Indie Game Development Survival Guide by David Michael (2004, Charles River Media).

• *Online Resources*

Game Audio Network Guild
http://audiogang.org/
A non-profit organization established to educate the masses in regards to interactive audio by providing information, instruction, resources, guidance and enlightenment not only to its members, but to content providers and listeners throughout the world.

Gamasutra
http://www.gamasutra.com
The leading employment site serving the interactive entertainment industry.

Game Developers Network
http://www.gamedev.net

Great Links to Game Music
http://iwritethemusic.com/gamemusic.html

Happy Puppy
http://www.happypuppy.com

Video Game Yellow Pages
http://vgyellowpages.com/
Online directory servicing every market segment of the electronic gaming industry, from ad agencies and PR firms to developers, retailers and distributors.

Game Jobs
http://www.gamejobs.com/
Another employment site serving the interactive entertainment industry.

Music 4 Games
http://music4games.net

Gamespot
http://www.gamespot.com

• *Conferences*

Electronic Entertainment Expo
(E3)http://www.e3expo.com

Game Developer's Conference (GDC)
http://www.gdconf.com

SIGGRAPH
http://www.siggraph.org

❒ Incentives & Premiums Markets

Articles About the Gift & Incentives Industry
http://www.cardex.com/articles/incentives.html

Premium, Incentives & Travel Buyers Directory (annual, Douglas Publications).
Over 21,000 decision-makers that plan or purchase ad specialties, corporate gifts and awards, sales incentives and safety incentives from more than 12,500 firms.

PROMO Magazine
http://www.promomagazine.com
This well-organized, easy-to-read and informative trade publication is updated daily online with the latest incentive news stories, articles on promotional campaigns and updates on developments in the regulatory world. The "Key Tactics" section, which is divided into categories such as event marketing, entertainment marketing, games/ contests/ sweepstakes, etc., is a good resource worth exploration. There you will also find the category of interactive marketing, which features articles of interest to the online marketer. It covers the latest online incentive marketing techniques, offering insights that you won't find anywhere else online. For instance, at the time of writing Doritos was running an integrated campaign that included a text messaging sweepstakes used to drive visitors to the Doritos website for prizes, video and audio clips and games. Check in often to discover the newest applications of technology in the online incentive marketing space.

Incentive Central
http://www.incentivecentral.org
Incentivecentral.org is a not-for-profit alliance of incentive product manufacturers and associations. The organization was created to provide "objective and thorough information on all aspects of incentive programs and to list all available resources without favoring one commercial entity over another." A wonderful resource, the site has information on industry surveys, interviews with key executives, a library of white papers and extensive case studies and articles on how incentives motivate customers, sales teams, employees and channel partners. You will also find articles on how to measure the success of incentive programs.

A subset of the group, the Online Incentive Council, is comprised of companies that have extensive expertise in the online incentive industry. According to their research, online incentive programs generate greater participation and are more cost-effective than traditional direct marketing programs. Good to know.

The Incentive Show
http://www.piexpo.com/incentiveshow/index.jsp

Founded in 1935, The Incentive Show is an annual tradeshow held currently at New York City's Jacob Javits Convention Center. The show is the go-to for "the hottest new merchandise, travel destinations, rewards, gift certificates, debit cards and new products in the incentives marketplace." Can't make it to the show? Use the site to explore vendor lists and the latest trends in incentive marketing.

CorporateRewards.com
http://www.corporaterewards.com
CorporateRewards.com is an incentive provider that specializes in employee incentives, corporate rewards and employee recognition programs. Rewards are issued in the form of GiveAnything.com gift certificates, which can be redeemed for products on their network of e-commerce sites or for gift cards from even more national retailers.

The company has managed incentive programs with as many as 500,000 participants. If you have a small program to manage, try their "Do It Yourself" model. Fund the program with a credit card, use their incentive modules and point participants to the "Spend Your Award" website that you've customized with your branding. A unique feature of this program is that participants can combine their rewards for larger purchases. They are able to check current balances online to see how quickly they are building points for those more expensive desires - quite an incentive.

❒ Ringtones

Digital Rights Agency
http://www.digitalrightsagency.com

The Orchard: Mobile Partnerships
http://www.theorchard.com/marketing/orchard_mobile_partners.htm

Xingtone
http://www.xingtone.com

IRIS
http://www.irisdistribution.com

Bandaidonline.com
http://www.bandonline.com

Primetones.com
http://www.primetones.com

CH 12 MARKETING YOUR MUSIC TO MUSIC PUBLISHERS

• *Key Organizations*

United States Copyright Office
Register of Copyrights
Library of Congress
http://www.loc.gov/copyright
101 Independence Ave., S.E
Washington, DC 20559
(202) 707-3000 (Information)
All copyright forms are online.

National Music Publishers Association (NMPA)
http://nmpa.org

Association of Independent Music Publishers (AIMP)
http://www.aimp.org

Harry Fox Agency
http://harryfox.com

Sound Exchange
http://soundexchange.com/

World Intellectual Property Organization (WIPO)
http://www.wipo.org

• *Performing Rights Organizations*

Each PRO has offices in New York, Los Angels and Nashville.

American Society of Composers, Authors and Publishers (ASCAP)
http://www.ascap.com

Broadcast Music Incorporated (BMI)
http://www.bmi.com

SESAC, Inc.
http://www.sesac.com

• *Contact Directories*

Music Publishers Directory
By the Music Business Registry
http://www.musicregistry.com

The Songwriter's Market (annual, Writer's Digest Books).
Provides profiles of companies open to listening to new songs, including contact names, what they're looking for, and how to submit songs.

The Muse's Muse
http://www.musesmuse.com

The Songwriter's Directory
http://www.songwritersdirectory.com /index.htm

• *Music Publishing & Songwriting*

All You Need to Know About the Music Business by Donald Passman (2004, Simon & Schuster).

Get It In Writing: A Musician's Guide To The Music Business
By Brian McPherson (Hal Leonard Publishing).

How to Pitch & Promote Your Songs by Fred Koller (2001, Allworth Press).

Kohn on Music Licensing by Al & Bob Kohn (1996, Aspen Law & Business).

Legal Aspects of the Music Industry: An Insider's View of the Legal and Practical Aspects of the Music Business by Richard Schulenberg (2005, Watson-Guptil).

Making Music Make Money: An Insider's guide to Becoming Your Own Music Publisher by Eric Beall (2004, Berklee Press).

Music Publishing: The Real Road to Music Business Riches by Tim Whitsett (1999, MIX Books).

Music, Money & Success by Jeffrey and Todd Brabec, 2nd ed. (1999, Schirmer).

Songwriters on Songwriting by Paul Zollo (1997, De Capo).

Songwriter's Guide to Nashville by Sherry Bond (2000, Allworth Press).

The Craft & Business Songwriting by John Braheny, 2nd ed. (2004, Writer's Digest Books).

The Musician's Business & Legal Guide ed. by Mark Halloran, et. al. (2001, Jermore Hedlands/Prentice-Hall).

The Songwriter's Guide to Collaboration by Walter Carter (1997, Hal Leonard).

Tunesmith by Jimmy Webb (1998, Hyperion).

• *Tip Sheets*

New On the Charts
http://www.notc.com

Songlink International
http://www.songlink.com

Row Fax
http://www.musicrow.com
Country music mainly.

Bandit A&R Newsletter
http://www.banditnewsletter.com

CH 13
MUSIC PUBLICITY

Media Directories:

Burrelle's Media Directories
Burrelle's Information Services
75 East Northfield Road
Livingston, NJ 07039
P: 1-800-876-3342
E: directory@burrelles.com
W: http://www.burrelles.com
Information available for U.S., Canada, and Mexico.
Newspaper and Related Media—Daily Newspaper
Newspaper and Related Media—Non-Daily Newspapers
Magazines and Newsletters
Broadcast Media—Television and Cable
Broadcast Media—Radio
Available in print, CD-ROM, Internet, costs for the set, print and disks.

Gale Directory of Publication and Broadcast Media
Gale Research
27500 Drake Road
Farmington Hills, MI 48331
P: 1-8---877-4253
W: http://www.gale.com
Annual Guide listing newspapers, magazines, journals, radio stations, television stations and cable systems. - Sold in 3 volume set, cost $460.00.
Newsletters in Print—lists 11,000 newsletters.
Encyclopedia of Associations—USA 3-parts, 23,000 associations.
International Associations—2-volume set.
Regional, State and Local Associations—one volume.
Available in libraries.

Editor & Publisher
770 Broadway
New York, NY 10003-9595
P: 1-800-336-4380
F: (646) 654-5370
W: http://www.editorandpublisher.com
Editor & Publisher International Year Book—
U.S. Daillies, U.S. Weeklies and Special Newspapers, Canadian Newspapers, Foreign Newspapers, News, Picture and Syndicated Services. Annual Editor & Publisher/Free Paper Publisher, Community, Specialty & Free Publications Year Book Community Weeklies, Shoppers/TMC, Specialty and Niche Publications, Non-Daily Newspaper Groups Database available on disk or labels, call for prices.
Editor & Publisher Syndicate Directory—list of syndicates, authors, byline features.

Newspapers Worldwide
http://www.newspapers.com

Online Newspapers
http://www.onlinenewspapers.com
Lists of the world's newspapers
Media Manager
http://www.mediamanager.com/
Searchable database that provides fairly complete contact info for every publication in the areas of lifestyle & entertainment.

United Entertainment Media
http://www.uemedia.com/divisions/musicplayer.shtml
UEA is a "grand central" of music and digital entertainment media outlets.

The Musician's Atlas
http://musiciansatlas.com/
Contact directory supplying more comprehensive information than any other music industry resource - details such as company focus, submission policy, booking advance, stage size, in-house equipment, broadcast coverage, distribution, circulation, styles of music sought and other specifics professionals use to build and sustain their careers.

Indie Contact Bible
http://indiebible.com/
Similar to The Musician's Atlas, but divides resources along genre lines and includes a lot more online promotional inlets and outlets.

- *Books on Publicity Strategies*

Getting Publicity: A Do-It-Yourself Guide for Small Business and Non-

Profit Groups by Tana Fletcher & Julia Rockler (1991, Self Counsel Press).

Organizing Special Events and Conferences: A Practical Guide for Busy Volunteers and Staff by Darcy Campion Devney (1993, Pineapple Press).

Publicity & Media Relations Checklists: 59 Proven Checklists to Save Time, Win Attention, & Maximize Exposure With Every Public Relations & Publicity by David Yale (1995, NTC Business Books).

Six Steps to Free Publicity by Marcia Yudkin (1994, Plume/Penguin).

Targeted Public Relations: How to Get Thousands of Dollars of Free Publicity for Your Product, Service, Organization, or Idea by Robert W. Bly (1994, Owlet Press).

The Unabashed Self-Promoter's Guide: What Every Man, Woman, Child and Organization in America Needs to Know About Getting Ahead by Exploiting the Media by Jeffrey Lant (JLA Publications, 50 Follen St., Suite 507, Cambridge MA 02138; 617/547-6372).

The Zen of Hype by Raleigh Pinskey (1991, Citadel Press).

• *Web sites*

Creative Publicity Solutions
http://yudkin.com/publicityideas.htm

Internet Publicity Resources
http://www.wilsonweb.com/

Publicity Insider
http://www.PublicityInsider.com/freepub.asp

CH 14 MARKETING MUSIC OVERSEAS

• *General Resources for Doing Business Overseas*

How to Develop and Manage Successful Distributor Channels in World Markets by William Fath (1996, Amacom Book Div.).

ExecutivePlanet.com
Has detailed information about 45 countries. Learn about appropriate business attire, gift-giving, entertaining, public behavior, and negotiations.

LonelyPlanet.com
Provides maps, pictures, and essential facts for many countries around the world.

ColumbusGuides.com
Includes general and statistical information, business profiles and business etiquette, and detailed travel guidelines.

• *Overseas Gigging*

Passports. 3 Months before you leave make sure all band members have a current passport. If a band member needs to obtain or renew his/her passport application and renewal forms can be downloaded from the Internet at http://travel.state.gov/passport_services.html or mailed from your passport office.

Visas. Make sure you have passport size photos on file for all band members in case they need a visa. Visas are not required for Canada, Mexico, the Caribbean Islands and most Western European countries. For those European countries where visas are required you can contact the embassy of that country for a visa application form, and apply at least two months before the gig. The U.S> government publishes a pamphlet that is updated yearly entitled

"Foreign Entry Requirements" which is available for .50 from the consumer information center department 363F, Pueblo, Colorado 81009. OR you can call 1-719 948-3334.

Eurail. Traveling by train in Europe is cost efficient and extremely comfortable. The Eurailpass is the least expensive way to travel by train in Europe. For information, contact Rail Europe, B mail at 2100 Central Avenue, Suite 200, Boulder, Colorado 80301, by phone @ 1-800-438-7245 or on the internet @ www.raileurope.com

• *International Music Organizations*

First, tap the resources of the target country's grand central music organizations. Here is a non-exhaustive list to get you started:

AIM (Association of Independent Music)
http://www.musicindie.org/

F.I.P.I. - International Federation of Independent Phonographic Producers
http://www.ifipp.org/

IFPI - International Federation of the Phonographic Industry
http://www.ifpi.org/

IAMIC, The International Association of Music Information Centres
http://www.iamic.ie

Austria
AKM - Autoren, Komponisten, Musikverleger Gen.mbH
http://www.akm.co.at

Denmark
Danish Music Information Centre
http://www.mic.dk

Finland
Finnish Music Information Centre
http://www.fimic.fi

IFPI Finland
http://www.ifpi.fi

Germany
Bundesverband der phonographischen Wirtschaft e.V.
http://www.ifpi.de

Sweden
Swedish Music Publishers Association
http://www.smff.se/

Switzerland
HUGO
http://www.hugo.ch/
A virtual community of independent, free floating, non-profit cultural centers and music clubs in Switzerland.

The Netherlands
Conamus Foundation
http://www.conamus.nl

The Dutch Rock & Pop Institute (NPI)
http://www.popinstituut.nl/

UK
BPI (British Phonographic Industry)
http://www.bpi.co.uk

British Music Information Centre
http://www.bmic.co.uk/

Music Publishers Association
http://www.mpaonline.org.uk

• *Tour Directories*

AustralAsia Music Industry Directory
GPO Box 2977
Sydney, N.S.W.
Australia 2000
P: +61-02-9557-7766
F: +61-02-9557-7788
E: directories@immedia.com.au
http://www.immedia.com.au
Purchase $50 US or free at international trade fairs like MIDEM
Online Directory: $40—6 months; $80—12 months.

Facilities Directory
650 First Avenue
New York, NY 10016
P: (212) 532-4150
F: (212) 213-6382
Conventions, expositions, event management, and large production.

Annual directory: Call for current directory price.

The North American Folk Business Directory
Folk Alliance
962 Wayne Ave., Suite 902
Silver Spring, MD 20910-4480
P: (301) 588-8185
F: (301) 588-8186
http://www.folk.org
Listing U.S. and foreign folk venues, folk press, radio stations, newsletters, publications, record companies, agents, managers, performers, publicists.

Musical America
10 Lake Drive
Highstown, NJ 08520-5397
P: (800) 221-5488, ext. 7783
http://www.musicalamerica.com
Listing of presenters and festivals for ethnic, folk, children's dance, Jazz, theater, classical, opera.

Music Directory of Canada
23 Hanover Drive #7
St. Catherine's Ontario L2W 1A3
P: (905) 641-3471
F: (905) 641-1648
http://www.musicdirectoryofcanada.com
Website cannot be found
Listings of artists, agents, managers, labels, festivals, presenters, and other music related resources.

Theatre Communications Group, Inc.
520 Eighth Ave.
New York, NY 10018-4156
P: (212) 609-5960
F: (212) 609-5901
E: tcg@tcg.org
http://www.tcg.org
Theatre Directory—Lists regional theatre companies and organizations around the U.S.

• *Websites for Touring and Career Assistance*

Folkmusic.org
http://www.folkmusic.org
Folk music venues, shows, house concerts, business databases, folk radio list, and more.

Gig Swap
http://www.gigswap.com
Gig swapping has existed for decades and is constantly pursued on an informal basis throughout the United States and beyond. GigSwap.com was invented to streamline and support this empowering method of artist development.

Musician's Gig Link
http://www.musiciansgiglink.com

• *Internet Currency Exchange Rate Sites*

Xenon Laboratories Universal Currency Converter
http://www.xe.net/currency/

Currency Converter by Oanda, Inc.
http://www.oanda.com/cgi-bin/ncc

Currency Converter by Yahoo
http://finance.yahoo.com/m3?u

Exchange Rate.com
http://www.exchangerate.com

▼

CH 15 MARKETING MUSIC THROUGH SPONSORSHIPS

• *Foundation Centers And Resource Organizations*

Foundation Center
1627 K Street, NW
Washington, DC 20006
Phone: (202) 331-1400
Web: http://www.fdncenter.org
Foundation Center
79 5th Avenue, 8th Floor
New York, NY 10003
P: (212) 620-4230
F: (212) 691-1828
W: http://www.fdcenter.org

National Assembly of State Arts Agencies
1029 Vermont Avenue, NW 2nd Floor
Washington, DC 20005
P: (202) 347-6352
F: (737-0526
E: nasaa@nasaa-arts.org
W: http://www.nasaa-arts.org

• *Sponsorship Directories*

IEG Sponsorship Report
IEG Sponsorship Sourcebook
IEG Legal Guide to Sponsorship
IEG Sponsordex
IEG Event Marketing Conference Series
IEG Consulting
IEG SR Briefing - Media, Supermarkets, Music & Entertainment Tours, Telecommunications, Beer, Financial Services
640 North LaSalle Street, Suite 600
Chicago. IL 60610-3777
P: (312) 944-1727
F: (312) 458-7111
W: http://www.sponsorship.com

• *Sources on the Web:*

Arts Grants Opportunities:
Http://www.booksatoz.com

Arts International:
http://www.ArtsInternational.org

Government Agencies:
http://galaxy.einet.net/galaxy/government.html

National Endowment for the Arts:
http://www.arts.endow.gov

National Endowment for the Humanities: http://www.neh.gov

New York Foundation for the Arts:
http://www.nyfa.org

See also, ***IEG/Billboard Tour Sponsorship Roundup*** (published monthly in *Billboard* Magazine, detailing 4 or 5 music tours, along with illuminating notes on expected sponsorship outcomes)

• *Grants Directories & Books on Grant Writing/Sponsorships*

The Annual Register of Grant Support (annual, Information Today). Check your local library.

The Grants Register (annual, Palgrave Macmillan). Check your local library.

Grant Writing for Dummies *by Bev Browning (2001, Hungry Minds, Inc.).*

Made Possible By: Succeeding With Sponsorship by Patricia Martin (2003, Jossey-Bass).

The Sponsorship Seeker's Toolkit by Anne-Marie Grey et. al.(2002, McGraw-Hill Book Company).

• *Angel Investing*

Circle Lending
http://www.circlelending.com
Can act as an intermediary between business owners and their family or friends, who have loaned them money

CH 16 WRITING YOUR MARKETING PLAN

• *Books*

A Marketing Plan for Life : 12 Essential Business Principles to Create Meaning, Happiness, and True Success by Michael Fried (2005, Perigee Trade Paperback).

Marketing Plans for Service Businesses: A Complete Guide by Malcolm McDonald, Adrian Payne (2005, Butterworth-Heinemann).

The Marketing Plan Workbook (The Sunday Times Business Enterprise Guide Series) by John Westwood (2004, Kogan).

Powerhouse Marketing Plans: 14 Outstanding Real-Life Plans and What You Can Learn from Them to Supercharge Your Own Campaigns by Winslow Johnson (2004, AMACOM).

Streetwise Marketing Plan by Don Debelak (2000, Adams Media).

The Ultimate Marketing Plan: Find Your Hook. Communicate Your Message. Make Your Mark by Dan S. Kennedy (2006, Adams Media).

• *Sample Marketing Plans Online*

http://www.mplans.com/spm/

http://www.bplans.com/sp/Marketingplans.cfm

GLOSSARIES

- **Gen Music Biz Terms**
- **Gen Mktg. Terms**
- **Internet Mktg. Terms**

General Music Business

A&R (Artists and Repertoire) - The department of the record company that is in charge of discovering new talent.

Accounting, an - The periodic (usually semiannual or quarterly) financial reports given by record companies or publishing companies to artists. It details sales and royalties earned. It shows how much the artist has earned against their advance. If the advance is recouped, a check usually accompanies the statement.

Administration Fee - The fee charged by a music publisher for managing and exploiting an artist's songs. Fees vary widely, usually a percentage between 5%-25%.

Administration Rights - The rights granted to a music publisher to manage or exploit a catalogue of songs.

Advance - A pre-payment of royalties. A sum of money paid to an artist or songwriter in anticipation of, and chargeable against, the artist's or songwriter's future royalties. An advance is usually paid on the signing of a contract, the exercise of an option, or some other event. Advances, though recoupable out of future earnings, are not traditionally returnable if not earned.

AF of M (American Federation of Musicians) - The musician's union.

AFTRA (American Federation of Television and Radio Artists).

AGAC (American Guild of Authors and Composers) - A national songwriter's association, which performs various administrative, educational and political functions for its members.

Agent - A person or organization that procures employment for clients for a fee.

ASCAP (American Society of Composers, Authors and Publishers) - A performing rights organization whose sole function is the issuance and enforcement of licenses for the public performance of the nondramatic songs of its publisher and songwriter members and the distribution of the revenues derived from such licenses.

BMI (Broadcast Music, Inc.) – Another performing rights organizations (PRO), similar to ASCAP (above).

Bottom Line - Either the maximum one party give or the minimum the other party will take.

Bullet - The black dot or star appearing adjacent to the titles of records on the charts of music trade publications which connotes unusual activity or the growth of a record's popularity. The loss of a bullet signifies the record has peaked and is on the way down.

Bump - Bumps are contractual increases that take effect on the happening of some event. For example, a record contract might provide that artist royalties are calculated at 15% until 500,000 units are sold and then jump to 16%.

© - The international symbol for the word "copyright." It usually appears with the year date of the copyright and the copyright owner. It is not mandatory on works first published after March 1, 1989, the date the U.S. adopted the Berne Convention.

Catalogue - A group of songs characterized by something in common such as common ownership and/or authorship.

Controlled Composition - The phrase appears in record contracts meaning a composition owned or controlled by the artist and recorded under the contract. The record company seeks a reduced mechanical royalty on these controlled compositions. It is a negotiable term. Young artists almost always have to agree to a reduced rate of approximately 75%/limit of 10 songs. As the artist's track record and negotiating power improve, the percentage goes up.

Co-Publishing - When more than one publisher has acquired publishing rights to the same song. It also refers to a publishing deal in which the publisher gets sole administration rights but takes less than 50% of the total publishing income.

Copyright © - A limited monopoly granted by Congress as an incentive to creators of certain literary and artistic works so that they can control the destiny of the work and enjoy the fruits of their creativity. It protects the <u>expression</u> of an idea. It lasts for the life of the artist plus 50 years. Copyright exists at the moment the "idea" is put in a tangible form.

Copyright Registration - Although copyright protection begins when the idea is put in tangible form, the copyright can be registered with the U.S. Copyright Office (fill out the forms) and more rights accrue to the copyright holder.

Cross-Collateralization - The application by a record or publishing company of an artist's royalties from one source against unrecouped recording costs or advances from another. This usually happens when the record company and publisher are the same or related entity.

Cut in - The practice of ascribing to a person (usually the performing artist) writer credit for a song not written by that person, meaning they get a cut of the royalties. A cut in is usually extracted from the songwriter as a condition for the artist to record the song.

Cutout - A record that has been deleted from a record company's active catalogue. Cutouts are sold at much reduced prices and the record contract usually provides that the artist royalties are reduced.

Distribution - The process by which a record finds its way from the studio to the consumer. Most major record companies have their own distribution systems which distribute their own product and that of other record companies. Distribution is a key factor for the majors but especially the smaller record companies.

Employee for Hire - The Copyright Act of 1976 provides that if you write a song as an employee for hire of a publisher, the publisher, not the writer, is considered the author for purposes of the Copyright Act and "owns all the rights comprised in the copyright." But because of a Supreme Court case, its pretty difficult for the publisher to deem any songwriter an employee for hire.

Execution (of a contract) - Legal jargon for the formal completion of a contract by the parties signing it.

Folio - A bound collection of printed songs usually with a theme (The best of the '70s). "Matching folios" match the contents of a particular record and usually have the same cover art. "Personality folios" contain songs, biographical material and pictures of a particular artist.

Free Goods - The record company gives away records free to either customers or distributors or record stores to encourage them to buy more records. The record contract provides that they don't pay the artist royalties on these "promotional" free goods. Because artists aren't especially fond of this and have kicked and screamed, some record contracts will not refer to "free goods" but say that royalties are paid on 85% of all records sold.

Front Money - same as Advance.

Gold Record - A gold record is one certified by RIAA as having a minimum sale of 500,000 units.

Grand Performing Rights - Usually distinguished from "nondramatic" rights. The difference between the rights in a play like "Funny Girl" which includes song, music, dance and costumes (G.P.R.), and the rights to an individual song written outside the context of a theatrical play (nondramatic).

Gross Income - The total income before deductions of expenses or other costs. Gross income minus expenses and costs is "net income."

Harry Fox (The Harry Fox Agency, Inc.) - The Harry Fox Agency issues licenses on behalf of its music publisher clients for the use of their songs on phonograph records (mechanical licenses) and in connection with motion pictures, commercials, television films, and videotapes (synchronization licenses). It also collects and distributes to its clients the income from such licenses.

Independent Producer - An independent producer or production company is like a mini record company. They discover and sign talent, and usually produce a demo. They then try to sell the demo to a larger record company who provides the costs to record, manufacture, distribute and promote the record. The artist is signed to the producer, not to the larger record company. The record company "pays" the producer, who "pays" the artist.

Independent Promotion - The practice by record companies of engaging third parties to "promote" their records. Fees can range from $1,000 to $250,000.

Individual Producer - The person who manages and oversees the studio recording of the artist, including the selection of material and the communication with the engineer. Generally responsible for the "sound" of the product. Producers usually receive a fee up front (an advance) and a percentage of royalties from the record.

Infringement of Copyright - Anyone who violates any of the exclusive rights of a copyright owner under the Copyright Act is an infringer of the copyright.

Joint Work - According to the Copyright Act, a joint work "is a work prepared by two or more authors with the intention that their contributions be merged into inseparable and interdependent parts of a unitary whole." If you, a composer, write a song with a collaborator who is the lyricist, you both jointly own the resulting song. You own an undivided half-interest in his/her lyric, and they own an undivided half-interest in your music.

Key-Man Clause - If one person in a company is essential to the artist's career (a manager in a management company, a particular executive in a record company), they may ask for a key man clause, meaning that if that person leaves, the contract ends. Tough to get in contracts with major companies.

Label Deal - A multi-artist production deal (see Production Deal).

Litigation - a lawsuit, and everything that goes on between filing a suit (suing) and it ending either by a trial or settlement.

Loanout - More popularly used in the 1980s for tax purposes, an artist or songwriter would enter into a personal services contract with a corporation she owned or controlled, which then entered into a contract with a record company or publisher in which the corporation would "loanout" the artist's services.

Manager, Business - When the artist gets to the point in his/her career that they have more money coming in than you can intelligently handle, they hire someone with (usually) an accounting background to make sure they don't blow it all. The business manager (of course) works on a percentage basis.

Manager, Personal - The person hired to help mold and oversee all aspects of the artist's career.

Mechanical Royalties - Usually referred to as "mechanicals," its the royalty payable to a copyright owner for the use of a song on a record. The payment of mechanicals are required by the Copyright Act. The "statutory rate" is currently 6.95 cents per song. The record company will try to negotiate this rate down, usually to 75% of statutory rate, and limit it to 10 songs.

Merchandising - The use of an artist's name, fame, and likeness in connection with the exploitation of products and services (T shirts and beer ads).

Name and Likeness - The term used to describe the exclusive right of an artist to grant to others the right to use his/her name and picture in connection with the commercial exploitation or marketing of products and services.

Net Income - Total income (gross) minus expenses and costs is "net income."

Option - Usually contained in record or publishing deals, an option gives the company the right to extend a contract for a period of time, for example another year or another album.

P - The symbol for copyright notice appearing on records and CDs. It connotes the "Publication" of the work. It will usually read P ABC Record Co., 1995. Although the copyright to the underlying song belongs to the songwriter/publisher, the copyright in the sound recording <u>usually</u> belongs to the record company.

P&D (Pressing and Distribution) - This is a deal in which an independent record label enters into an agreement with a distributor. The distributor, for a fee or a percentage of income, distributes the record through its channels.

Packaging Costs - The record company deducts a percentage of the retail or wholesale price of the record for (supposedly) the costs of packaging the product. The artist royalty is based on the price after deduction of the packaging (and countless other deductions).

Pass - When you shop your tape to record or publishing companies, and they aren't interested in you at this time, they "pass" on you.

Pass Through - A clause most often used in independent producer deals. The independent producer contracts for an artist's services, and then attempts to make a deal with a record company. The "pass through" clause provides that whatever the producer gets from the record company, she/he will "pass through" (a percentage) to the artist.

Performing Rights Societies - (ASCAP, BMI and SESAC) license for songwriters and publishers the right to perform (use) songs publicly, and collect public performance royalties from such users. Users include radio stations, nightclubs, karaoke bars, anyone who uses music as entertainment.

Platinum Record - A platinum record is one certified by RIAA as having a minimum sale of 1.000,000 units.

Points - Royalty percentage points. An artist may say, I just signed a record deal, I got 16 points," meaning artist royalties are 16%.

Power of Attorney - When you give "power of attorney" you authorize and empower that person or entity to enter into binding contracts for you.

Premium Records - These are records given away with a product to sell the product. ("Buy a tank of gas and get a SPITTONS CD Free!") A "standard" record contract will provide that the record company can do this and give you a much reduced royalty rate.

Print Rights - Printed copies of music; sheet music. Not a major source of publishing income.

Product - The demo, record, or CD. The "hard copy" of the songs and the artist.

Production Deal - An artist signs a recording agreement with a production entity (usually owned by a producer), who in turn signs a deal with a major label to deliver the artist and the artist's recordings to the major. Artist - Production Entity - Major Label (three players). (Also see Independent Producer.)

Promotional Records - Giveaways to DJs, radio and television stations, publications, etc. to promote interest in and sales of the record. No royalties are paid to artists on these.

Public Domain (PD) Works - These are works that for a variety of reasons, nobody owns the copyright to. One reason is that the copyright period has passed, for instance, songs written early in this century. Another reason might be that there were no copyright laws at the time, Mozart's tunes. Or songs that you can't point to an "author", old Blues songs (but there can be copyright in arrangements of these).

Public Performance Rights - The Copyright Act grants to the copyright owners of certain works the exclusive right to perform the copyrighted work publicly. Perform a work publicly means playing a song (usually by playing the record) where a substantial number of people are. (The DJ plays a 2 Live Crew record at a dance club: 2 Live Crew get paid for that "performance," their record company doesn't.) The definition also includes transmission of a performance by any means or device to a place or the public (The radio or in a GAP store.). ASCAP, BMI and SESAC collect these royalties. These performance rights applied to the underlying musical works, but until 1995, did not apply to sound recordings of the work. The 1995 Performance Right in Sound Recordings Act grants the copyright owner of the SR the right to authorize digital transmissions of their works, and receive compensation. Note: this applies only to digital transmissions, not analog.

Publishing - The person or entity that takes partial ownership and management of a song in exchange for their promise to sell or exploit the song.

Publisher's Share - The portion of the song income kept by the publisher after paying the writer her/his share. A traditional deal was 50/50 but there are more deals recently that give 25% to the Publisher, and 75% to the Writer.

Recording Budget - After the record contract is signed, a recording budget must be submitted to the company by the band, or more usually the producer, putting in black and white what the project will cost.

Recording Costs - The costs of making a recording. All costs are chargeable against the artist's royalties excluding the manufacturing costs. This usually includes the studio costs, the mastering costs, the food and drink, and the limos the company so graciously send.

Recoupable - When the record company or publisher gives the Artist an "advance," they almost always get this money back from the Artist's percentage of profits; they recoup the advance.

Release Commitment - The "standard" record contract usually doesn't provide a commitment to commercially release a recording. Not releasing the recording does not necessarily end the recording contract.

Reserve Against Returns - When paying royalties pursuant to a recording contract, the record company wants to hold back royalties as a "reserve against returns." You don't want to pay you royalties on 350,000 units and find out in six months that only 310,000 units were sold, and 40,000 were returned. So you hold a good chunk of royalties back. The contract provides when the reserve is "liquidated." How much is held back depends on the parties bargaining strength.

Reversionary Rights - Rights that come back to the author upon certain events. For example, an artist signs a publishing deal and the lawyer successfully negotiates a clause that if the publishing company does not exploit the songs within four years, the copyright ownership will "revert" to the songwriter, and the publisher will have no further rights in the song. This is tough to get with the major publishers but can be negotiated with a smaller publishing company.

RIAA – Acronym for the Recording Industry Association of America. Founded in 1952, the RIAA represents more than 500 companies engaged in t he creation, manufacturing and distribution of music. Their members represent approximately 85% of all legitimate sound recordings produced and sold in the United States. They include EMI-Recorded Music; Sony/BMG Music Entertainment, Inc; Universal/Interscope Music Group; and smaller labels such as Rhino, Tommy

Boy, HOLA Records, La Face and Zero House.

Royalties - The proportional share of income the songwriter or artist receives as compensation for their song or performance, subject to the terms of the deal.

Showcase - The big gig where the record company A&R people are going to come and check the artist out. They might like the songs, but before offering a deal they want to see what kind of performing chops the artist has.

Sound Recordings - You will hear and read this term because this is the term the Copyright Act uses. Sound recordings are defined as works that result from the fixation of a series of sounds (excluding those accompanying motion pictures or other audio-visual works) regardless of the nature of the materials in which they are embodied. "Phonorecords" are the material objects, including CDs and cassettes, from which sounds can be perceived.

Source, at the - Publishing contracts usually provide that the writer receive 50% of the publishing income from territories outside the U.S. and Canada. This has in the past provided ample opportunity for the publishing companies to skim 50% several times before its 50% reaches the States. For example, if a song earned one dollar in Sweden, the Swedish publisher would keep 50% and send 50 cents to the U.K publisher, who would then keep 50% of the 50 cents and send 25 cents to the U.S. publisher, who would keep its 50% and send you 12.5 cents. What makes it even better is that most of these companies were owned by the same people (Sony Sweden, Sony U.K., Sony of America) After writers finally figured this scam out, their lawyers started insisting that the royalty be computed "at the source," which has cut down but not eliminated this practice.

Staff Writer - A songwriter who is employed by a music publisher and is given a salary. This is an "employee for hire" and the publisher becomes the "author" of the copyright of anything the writer composes during her employment. There aren't many of these gigs anymore.

Standard Contract - If anyone hands you a contract and says this is their standard contract, BEWARE! They are probably trying to make you believe that this is what everyone signs and you needn't seek legal or other professional advice before signing. Signing "standard contracts" can hang you up for long periods of time, be counterproductive to your career, and cost you a ton of dough paying a lawyer to try to get you out of a bad contract.

Synchronization License - To use a song in connection with a motion picture, video, or a TV commercial, a license must be acquired from the copyright owner(s). The term comes from copyright law language which referred to the "synchronization of music in timed relationships with a visual image." Thus, a synchronization, or "synch" license.

Term - The duration of a contract.

Trades - The magazines devoted to the music business, *Billboard, Cash Box, Pollstar*. Gives the ins and outs, charts the sales of records, or concert grosses, gives the comings and goings of people in the industry, both artists and business people.

Universal Product Code (UPC)
An American and Canadian coordinated system of product identification by which a ten-digit number is assigned to products. The UPC is designed so that at the

checkout counter an electronic scanner will read the symbol on the product and automatically transmit the information to a computer that controls the sales register.

Wholesale Price - The price at which the record company sells records to its record store customers, usually half of the suggested retail price. Artist royalties in record contracts can be keyed to wholesale or retail prices; so the numerical royalty given by a company that pays on wholesale will be twice that of a company that pays on retail.

Writer's Share - The portion of the income from a song that the publisher pays to the writer; the writer's royalties.

General Marketing Terms

Advertising
The paid-for promotion of goods and services through the mass media. For example, the radio, newspapers, TV or the internet.

Brand
The particular characteristic of a product or service that makes it recognisable to an audience and the message or attributes people associate with it.

Channels of distribution
The various methods of distributing and delivering products ultimately to the consumer

Competitors
Businesses or organisations that sell products or services to the same target audience as another organization.

Competition-based pricing
Attempts to set prices based on those charged by the company's competitors.

Consumer-based pricing
Using the buyer's perceptions of value to determine the retail price, a reversal from the cost-plus approach.

Cost-based pricing
Determining retail price based on the cost of product development and manufacturing, marketing and distribution, and company overhead and then adding the desired profit.

Demand
The number of people who want the service or product.

Direct mail
Personalised promotional literature such as a letter or greeting card sent through the post to the customer.

Direct marketing
Methods of getting your marketing message direct to the customer without an intermediary. For example door-to door or telemarketing.

EAN
The European Article Numbering system. Foreign interest in UPC led to the adoption of the EAN code format, similar to UPC but allows extra digits for a country identification, in December 1976.

E-marketing
Marketing over the internet.

Focus groups
A group of people brought together by an organisation in order to gather their views on a particular issue or product.

Four P's
The four p' s are product, price, promotion and place. They are the factors that you should try to control in order to successfully market your product or service.

Guerrilla marketing
Using unconventional marketing methods, often associated with protesters, to reach your target audience.

Internal marketing
Making sure that your marketing message is understood and championed by those inside the orgnisation, for example, staff or volunteers.

Logo
A graphic,illustration or symbol that identifies a particular organisation or product.

Loss leader pricing
The featuring of items priced below cost or at relatively low prices to attract customers to the retail store.

Market
A group of people or organisations that share a need for a particular product, and have the willingness and ability to use/pay for it.

Market research
Collecting and analysing research relating to the target market, such as customer needs, competitors, future demand.

Marketing Mix
The combination of tools and tactics you use to carry out your marketing program.

Market segmentation
Process of dividing the market into smaller groups that share one or more characteristics.

Market share
The proportion of the total market that is using a particular organisation's product.

Mission Statement
A brief statement summarising an organisation's beliefs and goals.

Personal selling
Method which involves one-to-one contact with the customer, such as telemarketing.

Place
The way in which a product or service is distributed, or where it is located (eg, are searches delivered to people's mailboxes, or do users have to fetch them).

Positioning
Deciding where your product fits in, and how it should be perceived, in relation to its competitors.

Price fixing
The practice of two or more sellers agreeing on the price to charge for similar products.

Process
The process by which the client obtains the product (e.g. what they have to do to register as a borrower, or order a search).

Product
In marketing jargon, means both products and services.

Product differentiation
What makes your product different from those of your competitors (e.g. you supply better quality, or more timely, searches).

Product life cycle
The course that a product's sales and profits take over what is referred to as the lifetime of the product.

Product positioning
The customer's perception of a product in comparison with the competition.

Promotion
Any activities and methods used to create demand for a product or service and keep it in the public eye.

Public relations
Activities undertaken to strengthen an organization's image within the target audience. For example a fun day for children in a local park.

Pull strategy
The company directs its marketing activities toward the final consumer, creating a demand for the product that will ultimately be fulfilled as requests for product are made from the consumer.

Push strategy
Pushing the product through the distribution channel to its final destination through incentives aimed at retail and distribution.

Segment
Sub-group within an overall target audience that falls into a distinct category with its own tastes and needs,

for example, 'teenagers'.

Supply
The extent of the product or service that is available to customers.

SWOT analysis
An examination of both the internal factors (to identify strengths and weaknesses) and external factors (to identify opportunities and threats).

Target market
A group of people for whom you create and maintain a specific marketing mix.

Internet Marketing

Amazoned: When a traditional retail company suddenly finds part of its business going to a totally on-line competitor, it's been "Amazoned" (from amazon.com).

Anchor: A place in an html document that you jump to when following an internal link.

Anonymous FTP: An anonymous FTP site allows Internet users to log in and download files from the computer without having a private user id and password. To login, you typically enter "anonymous" as the user id and your email address as the password.

Applet: A program that can be downloaded over a network and launched on the user's computer.

ASCII: American Standard Code for Information Interchange. ASCII is a standard computer character set used by most computer systems worldwide. An ASCII file is a text-only file.

Bandwidth: The amount of digital data that can be sent through the phone lines or other connections.

Banners: Banners have become ubiquitous as a form of advertising on the Web. These are usually narrow graphics, sometimes logos, sometimes signboards, about an inch and a half high and about 4 inches long.

Baud: Term generally used in rating the older modems, sometimes mistakenly used in place of bps.

BBS: Bulletin Board System. Most BBS's are run by hobbyists and companies, trying to get a certain type of user (fans of a genre, education, "adult," brand x product users, writers, etc.), and are accessed directly by modem. Many private BBS's charge for accessing (except to look around) and most either have time limits or charge for the time. Many of the larger BBS's are going onto the Internet, at least for e-mail. Corporate bbs's are generally free to use, except for long-distance charges.

Beta: "Beta testing" or "in beta" means that a program isn't ready for sale because there are still some bugs in it. Because of the fast development of the web, most of the browsers, applets, etc., i.e. the programs you use to access what you want, almost always seem to be "in beta."

"Alpha testing" therefore means a v. rough program; "Gamma" would be when everything is finished, except perhaps for the technical writing (manuals etc)

Bitmap File: A common image format (.bmp) defined by a rectangular pattern of pixels.

Bookmark: A way that you can mark your favorite places on the Internet with your Web browser.

bps: Bits per second. This is how modem speed is measured (e.g. 14,400 bps).

browser: A program used to view sites on the World Wide Web, send e-mail and read Newsgroups.

Burn, Burning: Recording music to a CD using home equipment.

Cache: Cache (pronounced *cash*) actually has several different technical meanings. But the most important one in regard to the Web has to do with trying to speed things up. Remember--every request you send over the Internet for a picture or text takes time. The Cache is a file on your reader's computer where their system stores a copy of things they've asked for recently. Then, if the reader asks for the same thing again, instead of issuing another Internet request, the reader's computer can simply use the copy from the Cache, sometimes saving as much as 10 or 20 seconds.

cc: Back in the old days of typewriters, carbon copy -- use of an ancient product called "carbon paper" allowed multiple copies to be typed at once. It would be better thought of now as "computer copy", and on-line refers to copies of a post sent to more than the main receiver. Also a verb: "I'll cc you a copy of that memo."

CD-R: Compact Disc-Recordable. A compact disc that can be recorded using a computer. CD-Rs are inexpensive but cannot be rewritten.

CGI: CGI=Common Gateway Interface; a special type of UNIX program which allows a web server to access an application and transfer the information to your display. If you access a homepage and are told you are visitor #____, that information is usually provided & updated by programs via CGI.

Chat: Communicating with someone in real time over the Internet.

Click-and-Mortar
A store that has an online presence as well as an actual building.

Clickstream
The record of a user's Internet activity including Web sites visited, length of the visit, and what pages were viewed.

Client: A program (like a Web browser) that connects to and requests information from a server.

compression: Decreasing a file's size so that it can be more easily transferred over the Internet. Stuffit is a popular compression program.

Clickthrough: The process by which a visitor navigates through websites by clicking on links.

Client-Server Protocol: A communication protocol between networked computers in which the services of one computer (the server) are requested by the other (the client).

Codec: As the name implies, codecs are used to encode and decode (or compress and decompress) various types of data - particularly those that would otherwise use up inordinate amounts of disk space, such as sound and video files. See, for example, MP3.

Compressed: Data files available for download from the Internet are typically compacted in order to save server space and reduce transfer times. Typical file extensions for compressed files include zip (DOS/Windows) and tar (UNIX).

Cookies: Software tools designed to save passwords and other data on someone's computer. The data can be called up automatically when the user shops online or visits Web sites on which they've surfed before, thus saving the user time by not having to re-key required data.

Cracker: One who breaks security on a computer system with malicious intent. Coined by hackers in defense against journalistic misuse of the term "hacker".

CU-SeeMe: Software that allows you to hook up a video camera to your computer and see video of other people you're communicating with on the Internet.

Cybercafe: Establishment with both coffee and internet access. Trendy in some places, unknown or failures in others.

Dial-up Connection: A connection to the Internet via phone and modem. Connection types include PPP and SLIP.

Direct Connection: A connection made directly to the Internet - much faster than a dial-up connection.

Discussion Group: A particular section within the USENET system typically, though not always, dedicated to a particular subject of interest. Also known as a newsgroup.

domains: The different parts of a World Wide Web URL. The Top Level Domain designates whether the host computer is a business (.com), a school (.edu), a non-profit organization (.org), a branch of the government (.gov), etc.

download: To transfer a file from another computer to your computer via the Internet.

Downloading vs. Streaming: Rather than downloading a whole MP3 and then listening to it, streaming an MP3 allows the user to listen to the MP3 as it is being downloaded.

Emoticon: A combination of characters that form a facial expression. For example, if you turn your head sideways, the characters :) make a smiley face, and the characters 8) make a four-eyed smiley. Frequently used in email messages to convey a particular tone.

encryption: A way to scramble a file or e-mail message so that only the intended recipient (who has the correct decoding software, or "key") can read it.

FAQ: Frequently Asked Questions - a collection of common questions and answers on a particular subject.

Firewall: A Firewall is a security barrier set up between a company's internal systems and outside systems. Firewalls can be designed to keep hostile visitors out, as a way of protecting the company's internal information--or they can be designed to keep company employees in, usually as a means of discouraging people from playing games or visiting recreational sites on company time.

Flame, Flamewar: Flame is a nasty note, or hostile letter, either written to a public forum or sent privately. Flamers usually think they're justified, and are particularly fierce in attacking what they see as misuses of the Internet.

Flash: Animation Technology

frames: An HTML construction which allows two Web pages to be viewed as one page divided into distinct areas or frames. Usually one frame will remain static while the other changes. Often used as a navigational devise.

freeware: Free software available on the Internet.

FTP: File Transfer Protocol. The Internet method of transferring files from one computer to another.

GIF: Graphics Interchange Format - a common image format. Most images seen on web pages are GIF files.

GUI: = Graphic Users Interface, all those pretty icons, etc. which make macs, windows, x-windows, etc. look the way they do.

Hacker: 1) A person who enjoys exploring the details of programmable systems and how to stretch their capabilities; 2) One who programs enthusiastically; 3) A person who is good at programming quickly; 4) An expert in a particular language, as in "a Unix hacker."

Home Page: The first page of a Web Site. Also, the Web site that automatically loads each time you launch your browser.

host: A computer linked to the Internet, that "hosts" Web sites or other resources.

Hot Java: A Web browser developed by Sun Microsystems that takes full advantage of applets written in the Java programming language.

HTML: Hypertext Markup Language. The language that is used to write web pages. Browser programs read HTML and translate it for your computer.

Hyperlink: A connection between two anchors. Clicking on one anchor will take you to the linked anchor. Can be within the same document/page or two totally different documents.

hypertext: Text that contains links to other documents.

Intranet: When a company uses Internet technology to deliver information to a closed group of its own employees – and possibly stockholders and customers – it is called an Intranet.

IP Address: Internet Protocol Address - every computer on the Internet has a unique identifying number, like 191.1.24.2.

IRC: Internet Relay Chat. A protocol and program that lets you chat with people in real time on the Internet.

ISDN: Integrated Services Digital Network - a system of all digital, high bandwidth telephone lines allowing for the simultaneous delivery of audio, video and data. Data travels at 128K bps.

ISP: Internet Service Provider. A company that offers access to the Internet, but that usually does not provide its own content.

Java: A programming language that allows you to use special programs inside the browser window of Java-savvy Web browsers.

JPEG: Joint Photograhic Experts Group - a common image format. Most of the images you see embedded into Web pages are GIFs, but sometimes, especially in art or photographic Web sites, you can click on the image to bring up a higher resolution (larger) JPEG version of the same image.

kps: A measurement of modem speed, in kilobits per second (e.g. 14.4kps).

LAN: Local Area Network - a network of computers confined within a small area, such as an office building.

Listserv: An electronic mailing list typically used by a broad range of discussion groups. When you subscribe to a listserv, you will receive periodic email messages about the topic you have requested.

Lurking: The act of reading through maillists and newsgroups without posting any messages. Considered good

netiquette to get the feel of the topic before adding your own two cents.
Mailing List: A list of email addresses to which messages are sent. You can subscribe to a mailing lists typically by sending an email to the contact address with the following in the body of the message: the word subscribe, the name of the list, and your email address.

Majordomo: The other major e-mail discussion computer program. See Listserv.

MIDI: Musical Instrument Digital Interface - a high quality (underused) audio file format.

MIME: Multipurpose Internet Mail Extensions, a protocol for allowing email messages to contain various types of media (text, audio, video, images, etc.).

Mirror Site: An Internet site setup as an alternate to a busy site; contains copies of all the files stored at the primary location.

modem: A device that connects your computer to the phone line, and to the Internet or another computer.

MPEG: A compressed file format for video and sound. MPEG file names have the extension .mpg.

MP3: An acronym for the Motion Picture Experts Group, Audio Layer 3. It refers to an algorithm for file compression originally developed for broadcast use. The algorithm was invented by a German research firm, the Fraunhofer Institute, in 1991.

MUD: "Multi-User Domain" or "MultiUser Dungeon." A text-only computer role playing game environment, played over the net.

Multimedia: A combination of media types on a single document, including: text, graphics, animation, audio and video.

Nameserver: A computer running a program that converts domain names into appropriate IP addresses and vice versa.

Netiquette: Emily Post meets the Internet. Short for Internet etiquette.

Network: A system of connected computers exchanging information with each other. A LAN is a relatively smaller form of a network in comparison to the Internet, a world wide network of computers.

Newbie: A new Internet user. If you are reading this definition, you probably are one (or at least were one before you read this).

Newsgroup: A particular section within the USENET system typically, though not always, dedicated to a particular subject of interest. Also known as discussion groups.

Newsreader: A program designed for organizing the threads received from a mailing list or newsgroup.

Online Service: Services such as America Online, CompuServe, Prodigy and the Microsoft Network which provide content to subscribers and usually connections to the Internet, though sometimes limited.

Packet: A chunk of data. The TCP/IP protocol breaks large data files into smaller "packets" for transmission. When the data reaches its destination, the protocol makes sure that all packets have arrived without error.

.pdf: Portable Document File, a document which, with the proper acrobat reader, is displayed the same way on all systems. Many cd's of documents, and many documents and forms on government internet sites, are in pdf.

PGP: Pretty Good Privacy - an encryption scheme which uses the "public key" approach - messages are encrypted using the publicly available key, but can only be deciphered by the intended recipient via the private key.

Pixel: Short for picture element - the smallest unit of resolution on a monitor. Commonly used as a unit of measurement.

Plug-In: A small application which extends the built in capabilities of your Web browser. Examples include Macromedia's Shockwave, providing animation, and RealAudio, offering streamed sound files over the Internet. Compared to helpers, the multimedia files do not need to be downloaded before shown or played.

POP: Post Office Protocol - a method of storing and returning email.

Pop-Unders: A window that appears under the browser window..

Pop-Ups: A window that pops-up over the browser window.

Post: To send a message to a mailing list or newsgroup.

PPP: Point-to-Point Protocol - a protocol for converting a dial-up connection to a point-to-point connection over the Internet. Frequently used for accessing the World Wide Web over phone lines. Considered more stable than a SLIP connection.

Protocol: An agreed upon set of rules by which computers exchange information.

Provider: An Internet Service Provider, or ISP.

Push: Internet services that automatically update info on your computer when you log onto the internet.

QuickTime: A common video file format created by Apple Computer. Video files found on the Internet are often stored in the QuickTime format - they require
a special viewer program for playback.

Real Audio: A streaming audio format, which allows you to listen to a sound file while it's being downloaded to your computer, instead of having to download the entire file first.

Rip, Ripping: Digitally extracting audio tracks from a CD (usually at high speeds) to a file on your computer.

Ripper: If you want to move a song, or WAV file, from a CD to your hard drive, this program works with the encoder to help the process along. A ripper can be downloaded separately or as part of an all-in-one player or software package.

SDMI: Acronym for the Secure Digital Music Initiative. This initiative is organizing the efforts of a consortium of worldwide recording industry and technology companies to develop an interoperable architecture and specification for digital music security.

Search Engine: A tool for searching information on the Internet by topic. Popular engines include InfoSeek, Alta Vista and Web Crawler.

Secure Servers: A Secure Server uses a special code to make sensitive information difficult to read for anyone not authorized to access it. They're not perfect, but they're far better than unsecured servers. Most companies that accept credit cards over the Web do so through a secured server.

Server: The application on a host computer that allows Internet users to access it. Also used to refer to the actual host computer.

shareware: Software available on the Internet that you can download and test drive. If you like it and use it, you must register it, with the person or company that produced it, and pay for it.

Shell: Another name for a dial-up account, especially in UNIX.

Shopping Cart: Software that allows the user to hold merchandise selected for purchase until shopping is complete and the user is ready to check out.

Signature (.sig): A personal tag automatically appended to an email message. May be short, such as the author's name, or quite long, such as a favorite quote.

SGML: Standard General Markup Language - a standard for markup languages. HTML is one version of HTML.

Skins: Formats for decorating or changing the appearance of an MP3 player.
Stickiness: A measure of the degree of attractiveness of a website, measured by how long people spend within or at the site.

SLIP: Serial Line Internet Protocol. Similar to PPP, it's a way to connect to the Internet via modem.

SMTP: Simple Mail Transfer Protocol - a protocol dictating how email messages are exchanged over the Internet.

Snail Mail: Plain old paper mail. United States Post Office.

SPAM: Non-Internet: Delicious "meat" in a can! Internet: Sending multiple, sometimes thousands, of unwelcome messages to a newsgroup or mailing list to promote a commercial product or Web site.

Spider Robot: Spiders and Robots (or "bots") are simply automated programs that explore the Web, looking for information. The most common kinds of Spiders are the ones that collect Web addresses for the Search Engines to catalogue.

Subscribe: To become of a member of. One can subscribe to a mailing list, a newsgroup, an online service or an Internet Service.

Sysop: Systems Operator -- an owner or manager of a bbs, site, forum, service, etc..

T1: A category of leased telephone line service, allowing transfer rates of 1.5 Mbps (megabytes per second) over the Internet. Too expensive for home users (around $2000 per month), but commonly found in business environments.

TCP/IP: Transmission Control Protocol/Internet Protocol - this protocol is the foundation of the Internet, an agreed upon set of rules directing computers on how to exchange information with each other. Other Internet protocols, such as FTP, Gopher and HTTP sit on top of TCP/IP.

Thread: An ongoing message based conversation on a single subject.

Thumbnail: A small graphic image which gives you enough information to decide if you want to see it full-sized. Many galleries of images on web-sites have the images in thumbnail, rather than making you download each large image one at a time. Many usenet posters, who post collections of images, will also post an index of thumbnailed images, which then allows you to choose which of the other images to download.

TIFF: Tag Image File Format - a popular graphic image file format.

UNIX: A powerful operating system used on the backbone machines of the Internet. World Wide Web servers frequently run on UNIX.

Upload: 1) To transfer programs or data over a digital communications link from a smaller or peripheral client system to a larger or central host one. A transfer in the other directions is, of course, called a download. 2) [jargon] To send data (especially large relatively standalone pieces of data like files and images) over the wire to a remote location.

URL: Uniform Resource Locator. The address of a WEB page or site.

USENET: Short for User's Network. The collection of the thousands of bulletin boards residing on the Internet. Each bulletin board contains discussion groups, or newsgroups, dedicated to a myriad of topics. Messages are posted and responded to by readers either as public or private emails.

Visit: Synonymous with viewing a World Wide Web site.

WAIS: Wide Area Information Servers - a system of searchable text databases.

WAN: Wide Area Network - a system of connected computers spanning a large geographical area.

WAV: Waveform Audio (.wav) - a common audio file format for DOS/Windows computers.

World Wide Web: A system of Internet servers comprised of HTML documents and graphics that can link to one another. Not all Internet servers are part of the World Wide Web.

WYSIWYG: What You See Is What You Get;
1) software that's supposed to be so easy you don't need a manual. Yeah, right.
2) any word processor or editor that claims that what you see on the screen is exactly how it'll look on the printed page.

zip file: A type of compressed file used on PCs.

INDEX

MORE BUSINESS-BUILDING BOOKS BY PETER SPELLMAN

❒ **INDIE POWER: A BUSINESS-BUILDING GUIDE FOR RECORD LABELS, MUSIC PRODUCTION HOUSES & MERCHANT MUSICIANS**, 3-ring binder, 350 pages. ***Contains:*** *Unique strategies for starting a label today • Checklist for going into business • Sample contact management system • Record label personnel flow-chart with task assignments • Budget projection sheets for new releases • Real examples of: income/expense balance sheets, quarterly payment report from distributor, retail vendor agreement, distribution sell-sheets, radio bounce-back cards and MORE • Sample artist contracts • Examples of music licensing agreements • Music-related tax deductions sheet • Current list of reputable record distributors & manufacturers AND MUCH, MUCH MORE!* ***$39.95 (print) / $24.95 (eBook)***

❒ **THE SELF-PROMOTING MUSICIAN**, 252 pages, pb. *Written primarily for performing / recording musicians looking to create a buzz on a budget, this book addresses the entrepreneurial needs of musicians and offers tried-and-true guidelines on writing a business plan, securing radio airplay, obtaining publicity, finding out-of-way gigs, booking shows and penetrating the lucrative multimedia market.* ***$21. (print only)***

❒ **SAMPLE CD MARKETING PLAN,** *36-page full-spectrum marketing plan for a Massachusetts-based rock band. This CD Marketing Plan will help make your music more visible in today's crowded music market. Why reinvent the wheel? Learn from those who've gone before you!* ***$17.95*** **(eBook only).**

❒ **THE MUSICIAN'S INTERNET**, 142 pages, pb. *An easy-to-follow handbook for building site traffic, raising your visibility, expanding your music career, creatively marketing your music, and spark a global fan base! " 'The Musician's Internet' is the best how-to book I've ever read on how to get your music to the world." – Derek Sivers, CDBaby.com. "Nothing short of the 'key' to the internet for musicians and performers". – Mark Northam, Film Music Network. What are you waiting for?* ***$21. (print only)***

❒ **RECORD COMPANY BUSINESS PLAN,** *36-page stapled document. Complete with mission statement, executive summary, company description, industry analysis, marketing & promotion plans, management description, complete financials, and bonus tips for hunting down financing. Designed for a multi-genre label that puts out a broad spectrum of music, from jazz to rock, the plan is easily adaptable and relevant for any label venture. This plan will help whip your own business plan into shape and multiply your chances for securing financing.* ***$24.95 (print) / $19.95 (eBook)***

Ordering info at:

http://www.mbsolutions.com

Author
Peter Spellman

Peter Spellman is Director of Career Development at Berklee College of Music, Boston and the author of several handbooks on the music business, including The ***Self-Promoting Musician: Strategies for Independent Music Success*** (2000, Berklee Press), ***The Musician's Internet: Online Strategies for Success in the Music Industry*** (2002, Berklee Press), and his latest, ***Indie Power: A Business-Building Guide for Record Labels, Music Production Houses and Merchant Musicians*** (2004, MBS Business Media). He also wrote the chapter on Internet promotion for the 2nd and 3rd editions of ***The Musician's Business and Legal Guide*** (1996, 2001, Prentice-Hall/ Jerome Hedlands), the most used music business textbook in U.S. colleges and universities.

A recognized expert on music industry trends, the impact of the Internet on music, and music career issues, Peter is a popular speaker at colleges, universities, and music conferences around the country.

Peter has over thirty years' experience as a performing and recording musician and is also President of Music Business Solutions (**www.mbsolutions.com**), a business and marketing consultancy for independent musicians, songwriters and music businesses. He has worked as a booking agent, label director, music editor, artist manager and producer.

In addition, Peter teaches courses on entrepreneurship, music publishing, and music marketing at the University of Massachusetts-Lowell.

Peter performs and records as percussionist with world music ensemble Friend Planet.

Printed in the United States
87206LV00001B/39-52/A